Migration Theory

Migration Theory

Talking across Disciplines

Second edition

Edited by
Caroline B. Brettell
and James F. Hollifield

Routledge
Taylor & Francis Group

New York   London

Routledge
Taylor & Francis Group
270 Madison Avenue
New York, NY 10016

Routledge
Taylor & Francis Group
2 Park Square
Milton Park, Abingdon
Oxon OX14 4RN

© 2008 by Taylor & Francis Group, LLC
Routledge is an imprint of Taylor & Francis Group, an Informa business

Printed in the United States of America on acid-free paper
10 9 8 7 6 5 4 3 2

International Standard Book Number-13: 978-0-415-95427-3 (Softcover) 978-0-415-95426-6 (Hardcover)

Library of Congress Cataloging-in-Publication Data

Migration theory : talking across disciplines / edited by Caroline B. Brettell and James F. Hollifield. -- 2nd ed.
    p. cm.
    Includes index.
    ISBN 978-0-415-95426-6 (hardcover : alk. paper) -- ISBN 978-0-415-95427-3 (pbk. : alk. paper) -- ISBN 978-0-203-95044-9 (e-book)
    1. Emigration and immigration. I. Brettell, Caroline. II. Hollifield, James Frank, 1954-

JV6035.M545 2007
304.8--dc22
                                               2007004167

Visit the Taylor & Francis Web site at
http://www.taylorandfrancis.com

and the Routledge Web site at
http://www.routledge.com

Contents

Preface

As scholars and teachers, we are constantly engaged in writing and speaking. But in our haste to produce that next article or lecture, we do not always take the time to listen, especially to those working in sister disciplines. It is in the spirit of dialogue and in the hopes of gaining greater insight into the phenomenon of international migration that we began this project. It is also the reason that we have decided to publish a second edition, since during the last decade the issue of migration has become even more important globally and has raised heated debates within particular receiving countries around the world. The readers must judge whether or not we have succeeded in creating a dialogue and shedding light on why individuals move across national boundaries, how they are incorporated into host societies, and why some migrants may return to, or at least continue to be engaged with, their countries of origin.

Migration is a subject that cries out for an interdisciplinary approach. Each discipline brings something to the table, theoretically and empirically. Anthropologists have taught us to look at networks and transnational communities, while sociologists and economists draw our attention to the importance of social and human capital and the difficulties of immigrant settlement and incorporation. Geographers are interested in the spatial dimensions of migration and settlement. Political scientists help us to understand the play of organized interests in the making of public policy; together with legal scholars, they show us the impact migration can have on the institutions of sovereignty and citizenship. Historians portray the migrant experience in all of its complexity, giving us a much greater empathetic understanding of the hopes and ambitions of migrants. Demographers have perhaps the best empirical grasp on the movement of people across boundaries, and they have the theoretical and methodological tools to show us how such movements affect population dynamics in both sending and receiving societies.

In bringing together this particular group of scholars, our ambition is to take a step in the direction of creating a more unified field of study by making migration scholars, no matter what their disciplinary training, more aware of what is happening in other fields. The first edition of this volume included revisions of several papers that were initially presented at a meeting of the Social Science History Association and several other solicited contributions by leading scholars in their respective fields. For the second edition, several authors (Brettell, Chiswick, Diner, Hollifield, Heisler, and Schuck) have updated their essays. We have also added three new chapters, one by demographer Michael Teitelbaum, a second by geographer Susan Hardwick (a field not covered in the first edition), and a third by sociologist Adrian Favell that addresses quite directly the question of a unified field of study.

We wish to thank those who had a direct hand in the production of the second edition. The editors at Routledge, Robert Tempio and Michael Kerns, have enthusiastically and patiently supported the idea of issuing another edition, and have shepherded the book from review to production. The contributors themselves have been both conscientious and patient. Finally, Southern Methodist University has provided us with the resources and the environment in which to do such a productive scholarly work.

Migration Theory
Talking across Disciplines

Caroline B. Brettell and James F. Hollifield

Interest in international migration in the social sciences has tended to ebb and flow with various waves of emigration and immigration. The United States is now well into the fourth great wave of immigration. At the beginning of the twenty-first century, the immigrant population stands at a historic high of 36 million, representing 12.5 percent of the total population. As the foreign-born share of the U.S. population continues to rise, the number of second-generation Americans, the children of immigrants, also will increase. In 1995, first- and second-generation Americans accounted for 20 percent of the U.S. population, and this figure is projected to rise to one-third of the population by 2025. Europe has experienced a similar influx of foreigners that began, in some countries, as early as the 1940s. In 2005 the foreign-born population of Europe, including nationals of European Union (EU) member states and third-country nationals, stood at 8.8 percent of the population. The foreign born constitute 12.3 percent of the German population, 10.7 percent of the French population, 14.1 percent of the Irish population, and 22.9 percent of the Swiss population, to take but a few examples. In Canada, the establishment in 1967 of a point system for entry based on skills and the reunion of families has not only increased the volume of immigrants but also diversified their places of origin. The same is true for Australia where 40 percent of population growth in the post–World War II period has been the result of immigration. With the abandonment in the 1960s of the White Australia Policy barring non-European settlers, Australia has become a multicultural nation (Castles and Vasta 2004), just as the United States became a more multicultural society in the wake of the 1965 Hart-Celler Act, which radically altered the composition of immigration, opening the door to Asians, Latin Americans, and immigrants from the four corners of the globe. Even Japan, a country that has long had a restrictionist immigration policy, began admitting foreign workers in the 1980s (Cornelius and Tsuda 2004). Finally, the movement of large populations throughout the developing world, such as refugees in Africa or "guest workers" in Asia and the Persian Gulf states, led some analysts to speak of a global migration crisis (Weiner 1995).

Whether and where there might be a migration crisis remains an open question. But clearly we are living in an age of migration (Castles and Miller 2003). Scholars in all of the social sciences have turned their attention to the study of this extraordinarily complex phenomenon.[1] Yet, despite the volume of research interest in a host of academic fields, when members of the various disciplines meet, it is, as Silvia Pedraza (1990:44) cleverly remarked, in much the same fashion as when "one sometimes arrives at a party and is . . . surprised to find out who else is there." It seems that only rarely do we talk across the disciplines.[2] Douglas Massey and his colleagues (1994:700–1) state the problem in succinct terms: "Social scientists do not approach the study of immigration from a shared paradigm, but from a variety of competing theoretical viewpoints fragmented across disciplines, regions, and ideologies. As a result, research on the subject tends to be narrow, often inefficient, and characterized by duplication, miscommunication, reinvention, and bickering about fundamentals and terminology. Only when researchers accept common theories, concepts, tools, and standards will knowledge begin to accumulate." Jan and Leo Lucassen (1997) argue that the deepest disciplinary canyon is between historians on the one hand, and social scientists on the other. A canyon almost as deep separates those social scientists who take a top-down "macro" approach, focusing on immigration policy or market forces, from those whose approach is bottom-up, emphasizing the experiences of the individual migrant or the immigrant family. It may be too much to hope for a unified theory of migration—one that encompasses all possible motives for moving or all possible results of that movement—but unless we begin the process of dialogue across the disciplines, social scientists will be doomed to their narrow fields of inquiry and the dangers of constantly reinventing wheels will increase.

This book therefore represents an effort to bridge these canyons, particularly with respect to theorizing about international migration. Here, we have brought together in a single volume essays by a historian, a demographer, an economist, two sociologists, an anthropologist, a geographer, a political scientist, and a legal scholar. Each was asked to assess and analyze the central concepts, questions, and theoretical perspectives pertaining to the study of migration in his or her respective discipline and in the intersection between disciplines.

Most of the authors adopt a broad "survey of the literature" approach, but a few have chosen to situate their discussion in relation to a more focused research question. Rather than reaching for a unifying theory, as Massey et al. (1993, 1998) attempt to do,[3] in this introduction we examine the essays in this volume as a whole, noting convergence and divergence in how questions are framed, how research is conducted and at what levels and with what units of analysis, how hypothesis testing proceeds, and ultimately how theoretical models are constructed. In the concluding chapter, the sociologist Adrian Favell gives an assessment of the book as a whole, seeking to determine whether we have successfully "rebooted" migration theory, and arguing for "interdisciplinarity, globality, and postdisciplinarity in migration studies." Our goal is dialogue and cross-disciplinary conversation about the epistemological, paradigmatic, and explanatory aspects of writing about and theorizing about migration in history, law, and the social sciences. If this book moves the conversation in the direction of what Castles (1993:30) has called for—"the study of migration as a social science in its own right . . . strongly multidisciplinary in its theory and methodology," it will have achieved its objective.

FRAMING THE QUESTION

In the social sciences, students are taught that they must start any inquiry with a puzzle or a question, whatever the topic of study may be. Of course, the way in which that question is formulated or framed is dependent upon the discipline, and the construction of hypotheses is also driven by disciplinary consider-ations. Intense disagreements and debates about the meaning and interpreta-tion of the same body of data exist within single disciplines. Sometimes there can be agreement across the disciplines on the nature of the problem, or even on the methodology. However, agreement on a single explanation or model is less likely; it is even rarer to find hypotheses that are truly multidisciplinary, drawing upon concepts and insights from several disciplines simultaneously. Each discipline has its preferred or acceptable list of questions, hypotheses, and variables.

In the Table I.1, we have constructed a matrix that summarizes princi-pal research questions and methodologies, as well as dominant theories and hypotheses for each of the disciplines represented in this volume. The matrix is necessarily schematic and cannot include every question or theory, but it provides a framework for establishing a dialogue across disciplines.

For historians, who nowadays straddle the divide between the humanities and the social sciences, principal research questions are related to particular places and times. As Diner points out in her contribution to this volume, histo-rians of migration tend to eschew theory and hypothesis testing, although their questions are similar to those of other social scientists—what are the determi-nants and consequences of population movement? In more precise terms, they

TABLE I.I: MIGRATION THEORIES ACROSS DISCIPLINES

Discipline	Research Question(s)	Levels/Units of Analysis	Dominant Theories	Sample Hypothesis
Anthropology	How does migration effect cultural change and affect ethnic identity?	Micro/individuals, households, groups	Relational or structuralist and transnational	Social networks help maintain cultural difference.
Demography	How does migration affect population change?	Macro/populations	Rationalist (borrows heavily from economics)	Migration has a major impact on size, but a small impact on age structure.
Economics	What explains the propensity to migrate and its effects?	Micro/individuals	Rationalist: cost–benefit and utility-maximizing behavior	Incorporation varies with the level of human capital of immigrants.
Geography	What explains the spatial patterns of migration?	Macro, meso, and micro/individuals, households, and groups	Relational, structural, and transnational	Incorporation depends on ethnic networks and residential patterns.
History	How do we understand the immigrant experience?	Micro/individuals and groups	Eschews theory and hypothesis testing	Not applicable
Law	How does the law influence migration?	Macro and micro/ the political and legal system	Institutionalist and rationalist (borrows from all the social sciences)	Rights create incentive structures for migration and incorporation.
Political Science	Why do states have difficulty controlling migration?	More macro/ political and international systems	Institutionalist and rationalist	States are often captured by pro-immigrant interests.
Sociology	What explains incorporation and exclusion?	Macro/ethnic groups and social class	Structuralist or institutionalist	Incorporation varies with social and human capital.

ask who moves, when do they move, why do they move? Why do some people stay put? How do those who move experience departure, migration, and settlement? These questions are generally applied to single groups (or even individuals), rather than to a comparison across groups, an effort that would require, as Diner suggests, vast linguistic competence.[4] In history, it is the narrative of how various groups settled, shaped their communities, and constructed their identities that has taken precedence over the analysis of the migration process. On the issue of structure and agency, historians tend to focus more on individual migrants as agents. They are less concerned with explaining how social structures influence and constrain behavior.

Anthropologists tend to be context specific in their ethnographic endeavor, and much of their theorizing is idiographic. But their ultimate goal is to engage in cross-cultural comparisons that make possible generalizations across space and time, and hence nomothetic theory building. Although Bjeren (1997) has argued that anthropologists never formulate theories divorced from context, this is not necessarily the case. While context is generally very important to anthropologists, some theorizing moves away from it. Anthropologists who study migration are interested in more than the who, when, and why; they want to capture through their ethnography the experience of being an immigrant and the meaning, to the migrants themselves, of the social and cultural changes that result from leaving one context and entering another. Brettell (in this volume, Chapter 5) notes that this has led anthropologists to explore the impact of emigration and immigration on the social relations between men and women, among kin, and among people from the same cultural or ethnic background. Questions in the anthropological study of migration are framed by the assumption that outcomes for people who move are shaped by their social, cultural, and gendered locations and that migrants themselves are agents in their behavior, interpreting and constructing within the constraints of structure.

Geographers are primarily interested in spatial relationships. In migration research their attention is therefore directed, as Hardwick (this volume) points out, to studying the relationship between employment patterns and residential patterns, the formation and development of ethnic enclaves, and the changing segregation patterns of various ethnic and racial groups. Geographers, like anthropologists, explore the transnational and diasporic dimensions of migration, as well as the role of social networks in connecting populations and individuals across space, but as Hardwick observes, geographers put space–time relationships at the center of their theorizing about transnationalism, diasporas, and networks. Space and place are also central to the geographical recasting of assimilation theory. Finally, even in the study of race and whiteness, geographers ask how time and place influence the way in which race is constructed.

For sociology, as Heisler (this volume, Chapter 4) emphasizes, the central questions are: Why does migration occur, and how is it sustained over time? Sociologists share a common theoretical framework with anthropologists. Both are grounded in the classic works of social theory (Marx, Durkheim, and Weber), and each tends to emphasize social relations as central to understanding the processes of migration and immigrant incorporation. However, sociologists have worked primarily in the receiving society with a few notable exceptions (see the works of Douglas Massey on Mexico, for example), while anthropologists have often worked at the sending, receiving, or at both ends. The difference is a result of the historical origins of these two disciplines— sociology in the study of Western institutions and society, anthropology in the study of "the other." Anthropology "came lately" to the study of migration and immigration, but in sociology it has been a topic of long-standing interest. Sociological questions are generally also outcomes questions. Although many sociologists are interested in the causes of migration, the discipline places great emphasis on the process of immigrant incorporation.

Sociological theory has moved from postulating a single outcome (assimilation) to manifold outcomes that depend on such factors as social capital, labor markets, and a range of institutional structures. Heisler points to the significance of sociological research on the ethnic enclave economy and ethnic entrepreneurship. While anthropologists have emphasized the cultural construction and symbolic markers of ethnic identity, sociologists have emphasized the institutional manifestations of ethnic difference (Light 2006). Both are equally important, but they reflect a difference in disciplinary epistemologies, and hence in how questions are framed. However, there is also a good deal of interchange and cross-reading between these two disciplines. One area where scholars in both fields come together is in their study of the social relations of immigration—specifically an assumption about the importance of social networks as both a causal and sustaining factor influencing the migration process.

The central question for demographers is the nature of population change. Births, deaths, and migration are the major components of population change. Drawing largely on aggregate data, they document the pattern and direction of migration flows and the characteristics of migrants (age, sex, occupation, education, and so forth). Teitelbaum in this volume (Chapter 2) makes a key distinction between formal demography, which is highly mathematical and theoretical, and social demography, which borrows freely from other social science disciplines and is more eclectic. Teitelbaum stresses that demographers do not shun theory and explanation; however, migration is only one factor in population change—fertility and mortality are the other two, and they have received far more attention from formal demographers than migration because migration, as Teitelbaum points out, is "rather messy." It is difficult, he suggests, to capture in a parsimonious way the "realities and complexities inherent in the patterns of international migration." Thus, demographers by necessity have bridged the canyons between the disciplines, and Teitelbaum, echoing Hollifield's analysis of the politics of migration, draws our attention to the key role of the state in shaping migration flows. Demographers are as interested as historians, anthropologists, and sociologists in the questions of who moves and when, but to answer these questions, they engage in the construction of predictive models. Demographers can and do project the future. Historians, anthropologists, and sociologists, by contrast, focus on actual behavior of individuals and groups in the past or in the present.

Economists also build predictive models. Chiswick's chapter in this volume offers an excellent example of the methodology of economics. Using the utility maximizing framework of microeconomics, he addresses the question of "who migrates." He focuses specifically on a central debate within economics: under what conditions will the most favorable (in human capital terms and for labor market success) individuals migrate? Chiswick develops models that predict more or less positive selectivity under various conditions. This is a *supply-side theory*, rather than an *outcomes theory*, and it reflects the broader assumption that frames much of the research on migration within the discipline of economics—that individuals act rationally to maximize their utility (Sjaastad 1962; Straubhaar 1988). Economists call this the *microeconomic model of individual choice*.

Anthropologists and historians argue that economic factors cannot and do not fully predict population movement when they are divorced from social and cultural context. Anthropologists in particular reject a universal rationality. Furthermore, anthropologists and historians are reluctant, if not averse, to framing questions in relation to evaluations of positive and negative inputs or outcomes. But economists (and economic demographers) are often called upon (by those who formulate policy) to assess the fiscal and human capital costs and benefits of immigration in precisely these evaluative terms. It therefore shapes many of the theoretical debates in their discipline (Borjas 1999; Huber and Espenshade 1997; Rothman and Espenshade 1992), not to mention broader debates about immigration policy. For example, in earlier work using data from the 1970 census, Chiswick (1978) addressed the economic assimilation rate of immigrants. He demonstrated that although immigrants start with earnings that are approximately 17 percent below those of natives, after 10 to 15 years of employment in the United States, they tend to surpass the average wage level and subsequently rise above it. This conclusion was challenged on the basis of 1980 census data by George Borjas (1985), but Borjas's work in turn has been challenged by Chiswick (1986) and others (Duleep and Regets 1997a, 1997b) using data from multiple censuses. Economists and demographers have also explored the educational, welfare, and social security costs of immigrants (Passel 1994; Simon 1984), thereby responding to national debates that erupt periodically in the political arena. Americans in particular are concerned about the costs and benefits of immigration and want to harness the social sciences, especially economics, to shape and inform policy debates (National Research Council 1997; Hanson 2005). Europeans are also concerned about the macroeconomic impact of immigration, but most European states and governments are preoccupied with perceived crises of integration and with the effects of immigration on the welfare state (Favell 1998; Bommes and Geddes 2000).

Chiswick's chapter in this volume ends with a discussion of the way that immigration laws and regulations (the *demand side* for immigrants) shape selectivity factors. A country that emphasizes skills as the primary criterion upon which to issue visas will experience a different pattern in the growth and composition of its immigrant population from that of a country that constructs a policy based on family reunification or refugee status. It is with attention to these questions that political scientists and legal scholars have entered as relative newcomers the arena of migration research.

As Hollifield emphasizes in his chapter, the questions for scholars of immigration within political science follow three themes. One is the role of the nation–state in controlling migration flows and hence its borders; a second is the impact of migration on the institutions of sovereignty and citizenship, and the relationship between migration on the one hand, and foreign policy and national security on the other; a third is the question of incorporation, which raises a host of ethical, normative, and legal issues. Political science has paid attention to what sociologists and economists have written about social and economic incorporation and added to it the dimension of political incorporation—specifically questions of citizenship and rights, familiar themes for legal scholars as well (Schuck in this volume, Chapter 8). It is worth noting, however, that Diner discusses a particular historical monograph, Salyer's *Law Harsh as Tigers*, which addresses similar issues for the Chinese who immigrated to the United States in the late nineteenth century. Salyer shows how these Chinese "sojourners" exercised their rights to challenge discriminatory laws. A more recent historical example is Gardner's (2005) fascinating analysis of the impact of U.S. citizenship laws on immigrant women in particular.

Like sociologists, political scientists work largely at the receiving end, although one can find a few examples of those whose research has addressed emigration policy (rules of exit), rather than immigration policy (rules of entry), according to similar themes of control, but with a greater focus on development issues (Leeds 1984; Russell 1986; Weiner 1987, 1995). Whether they are looking at the sending or receiving societies, political scientists tend to be split theoretically. Some lean heavily toward a more interest-based, microeconomic (rational choice) approach to the study of migration (Freeman 1995, 1998; Kessler 1998), while others favor institutional, cultural, and ideational explanations for increases in immigration in the advanced industrial democracies (Hollifield 1992; Zolberg 1981). All agree, however, that it is important to understand how the state and public policy affect migration flows, or as Zolberg (2006) puts it, how nations are designed and shaped by immigration policy.

Both traditions of inquiry can be found in the study of law as well, with one group of scholars taking a more rationalist, microeconomic approach to understanding migration, and another group (for example, Schuck in this volume, Chapter 8; Legomsky 1987) focusing on institutions, process, and rights as the key variables for explaining outcomes. As Schuck points out, most legal scholars are skeptical of the possibility for developing a "science of law"; and they devote most of their efforts to the analysis and assessment of case law. But in his work, Schuck breaks with this atheoretical tradition as he attempts to explain how the law shapes the phenomenon of international migration, and how immigration in particular affects American political development. Schuck points to the difficulties of establishing a coherent regulatory regime for immigration and attempts to explain why there are such large gaps between immigration policy (the law on the books) and the implementation of policy (the law in action or in people's minds). His analysis is reminiscent of similar work in political science (Cornelius, Martin, and Hollifield 1994; Freeman 1995; Hollifield 1986; Zolberg 2006), which seeks to explain the difficulties of immigration control in liberal democracies. The emphasis that Schuck places on the institution of rights as a key determinant of policy outcomes echoes work by political scientists and sociologists (Hollifield 1992; Jacobson 1996; Soysal 1994). Following the ideas of the sociologist Robert Merton, Schuck suggests that the failure of immigration law may actually serve some latent social function: it helps to finesse or cover up the profoundly ambiguous attitudes of the American public toward illegal immigration, which Schuck describes provocatively as a "victimless crime," drawing on the work of lawyer-sociologist Robert Kagan (2001). In effect, Schuck argues that the law is extremely limited in what it can do to regulate international migration, and particularly illegal immigration, even though law plays a crucial role in constructing the "complex array of incentives that individuals and groups take into account in deciding whether, when, and where to migrate." On the one hand, legal admissions largely determine the types of naturalized citizens; on the other, the enforcement of immigration law is often constrained by cost or by liberal and human rights ideologies. In the work of Schuck, we can see how the jurist's approach to the study of migration differs from that of many social scientists and historians. Legal scholars are less concerned with theory building and hypothesis testing, and more inclined to use the eclectic techniques of analysis in social science to argue for specific types of policy reform. Equally, they draw on detailed understandings of institutional and practical realities (mostly costs) to debunk general theories.

LEVELS AND UNITS OF ANALYSIS

Objects of inquiry and theory building are closely related to the levels and units of analysis. In migration research, these vary both within and between disciplines. An initial contrast is between those who approach the problem at a macrolevel, examining the structural conditions (largely political, legal, and economic) that shape migration flows, and those who engage in microlevel research, examining how these larger forces shape the decisions and actions of individuals and families, or how they effect changes in communities. *World systems theory* is one manifestation of the macro approach. Historians, Diner notes, know about world systems theory, but have tended to avoid it.[5] By contrast, in a range of social sciences, particularly sociology and anthropology, it has been influential (Portes 1997; Sassen 1996). However, as Hollifield points out, political scientists have tended to be critical of world systems theory and the types of globalization arguments that often flow from it. The logic of world systems theory is heavily sociological and structural, and it discounts the role of politics and the state in social and economic change. Mainstream scholars of international relations continue to place the state, as a unitary and rational actor, at the center of their analyses of any type of transnational phenomenon, whether it is trade, foreign direct investment, or international migration (Hollifield 1998).

Despite the importance of world systems theory to both sociology and anthropology, Heisler and Brettell suggest that more theorizing in these fields takes place at the microlevel, or at what Thomas Faist (1997) has labeled a "meso-level," which focuses on social ties.[6] By contrast, political science, with its central concern with the role of the state, operates more comfortably at the macrolevel. This is also true of the law, especially when law intersects with politics and economics. However, legal scholars equally focus on individual cases and on patterns of case law and hence operate at a microlevel of analysis as well. Economics also operates at both levels, depending on the research questions. Economists have not only theorized about how wage or employment opportunity differentials between sending and receiving societies affect general flows of populations, but also about how such differentials influence individual or household cost–benefit and utilitarian decision making about migration. Demography is perhaps a special case because the primary unit of analysis for the demographer is the population. Hill (1997:244) has argued that the "easy definition of a population has blinded [demographers] to more complex thoughts about what holds people together and what divides them." In other words, the meso-level at which sociologists and anthropologists frequently operate to theorize about the maintenance or construction of kinship, ethnic, or community ties among immigrants is not of primary concern to demographers.

Some geographers also work at a meso-level, while others work at the macrolevel to trace and map broad patterns of movement across space. Still others work at the microlevel of communities, households, and individuals. Geographers are attentive to varied units of analysis because the concept of scale is at the core of their research. *Scale,* in geography, refers primarily to space, but temporal scale, which addresses the size of time units, and thematic scale, which addresses "the groupings of entities or attributes such as people or weather variables" (Montello 2001:13501), are also important. Montello (2001:13502) also describes analysis scale, "the size of the units in which phenomena are measured and the size of the units into which measurements are aggregated for data analysis and mapping." Clearly all these elements of scale have framed the ways in which geographers have theorized about migration.

For sociologists, anthropologists, and some economists it is the individual or household that is the primary unit of analysis. The sociologist Alejandro Portes (1997:817) has argued strongly in favor of something other than the individual as the unit of analysis. "Reducing everything to the individual plane would unduly constrain the enterprise by preventing the utilization of more complex units of analysis—families, households, and communities, as the basis for explanation and prediction." Brettell in fact traces a shift in anthropology from the individual to the household that accompanied the realization that individual migrants rarely make decisions in a vacuum about whether to leave and where to go, and that immigrant earnings or emigrant remittances are often pooled into a household economy. Similarly it is in the distinction between individual decision making, on the one hand, and household or family decision making, on the other, that Massey et al. (1993) locate the difference between neoclassical microeconomic migration theory and the new economics of migration. New economics theorists argue that households send workers abroad "not only to improve income in absolute terms, but also to increase income relative to other households, and, hence, to reduce their relative deprivation compared with some reference group" (Massey et al. 1993:438; see also earlier works by Mincer 1978; Stark 1991). This is an economic theory that, with a different unit of analysis, must take sociological and anthropological questions into consideration.

Economists asking a different set of research questions that are shared with sociologists often focus on other units of analysis—the labor market in the receiving society or the economy of a sending society. These generate different bodies of theory about dual and segmented labor markets, about aggregate income and income distribution, about the impact of capitalist development, about the political implications of emigrant remittances, or about global cities (Sassen 1991). In all cases, the needs and interests of entities other than the individual are of interest here.

Political scientists and legal scholars have generally entered into the debate at this point, taking as their primary unit of analysis the state. Bringing the state in as the unit of analysis focuses attention on regulation of population movements, whether domestic (as in the old Soviet Union or China today) or international. As Zolberg (1981) has noted, micro-analytic theories often do not distinguish between domestic and international flows, nor do meso-level theories. The politics of the state (or states) are often behind refugee and illegal flows (Hollifield 1998; Zolberg, Suhrke, and Aguayo 1986). Rules of entry and exit formulated by the state regulate migration flows. State sovereignty and control are at issue in debates about citizenship, and since citizenship and sovereignty are cornerstones of the international legal system, migration always has the potential to affect international relations. In this case, the level of analysis may move (from the individual or the state) to the international system itself, and normative issues of morality and justice come into play (Carens 2000).

Contrasts between the perspectives of political science and those of anthropology are stark on the issue of the relationship between immigration and citizenship. Anthropologists are more concerned with the meaning of citizenship for the individual migrant—whether and how it is incorporated into a new identity—than are their colleagues in political science, who may be focused on the international systemic or national security implications of population movements (Hollifield 2004; Rudolph 2006). Sociologists, with their interest in institutions, have, it appears, aligned themselves more with political scientists and lawyers than with anthropologists on this particular question (Brubaker 1992). As Heisler points out, the theoretical focus in the citizenship literature, particularly in the European context, is primarily on the transformation of host societies and only secondarily on the immigrants. It is here that some intriguing interdisciplinary interchange could occur by combining different units of analysis (the state and the individual) and different questions (sovereignty and identity) (Kastoryano 1997). The utilitarian aspects of citizenship might also be a dimension of such interdisciplinary exploration. In their work on citizenship, for example, Peter Schuck (Schuck and Smith 1985; Schuck 1998) and Rogers Smith (1997) explore the way in which naturalization law and policy (a state-level variable) affect the rate of political incorporation of newcomers.

DATA AND METHODOLOGY

The units of analysis in migration research are closely linked to matters of data and methodology. When the unit of analysis is the population, research is conducted at an aggregate level, using primarily census data, but sometimes also data from large surveys. Demographic data are abundant, discrete, and accessible, and theorizing is driven by the data (Hill 1997). Demographers are perhaps most preoccupied with the accuracy of the data and with esoteric matters of method.[7] Because they use secondary data, they must be concerned with how migration and immigration were defined by those who collected the data. Sociologists and economists of migration, particularly if they are also trained as demographers, often use the same secondary data and engage in similar kinds of statistical methods of analysis. Yet when they do this, it is with an awareness of the limitations of census data. "They undernumerate undocumented migrants, they provide no information on legal status, and they are ill-suited to the study of immigration as a process rather than an event," write Massey and colleagues (1994:700). They realize that data sets vary in their suitability for addressing various questions and the task of social scientists is to identify the most appropriate data for a given problem or question.

Sociologists and some economists also generate their own individual- or household-level data, generally using surveys of samples that can range from two hundred to two thousand. This is equally true of much geographical and anthropological research on migration, but anthropologists also generate primary individual- and household-level data through extended and sometimes arduous periods of ethnographic fieldwork and participant observation. While it may not be the basis for extensive theory construction, the life history method has been employed to some effect by anthropologists to access the rich texture of the lived experience of being a migrant and the cultural context of decision making.[8] Benmayor and Skotnes (1994b:15) are most articulate in outlining the way personal testimony "speaks . . . to how im/migrant subjects constantly build, reinvent, synthesize, or even collage identities from multiple sources and resources, often lacing them with deep ambivalence. Knowing something of the utter uniqueness of particular individual migrant experiences certainly enhances our generalizations about the group experience, but it also elicits humility about the adequacy of these generalizations and a realization that few actual individual lives fully conform to the master narratives."

In political science and the law, common methods often involve interviews with key politicians and lawmakers. They also involve a careful reading of texts, as well as statistical analysis of aggregate or individual-level data, depending on the types of questions that are asked. Policy analysis and political economy are often focused on aggregate data (Hollifield 1992), whereas studies of political and voting behavior, as well as public opinion, involve the use of individual-level survey data (DeSipio 1996). Legal scholars are less likely than economists or political scientists to use formal models or statistical analysis, relying instead on interpretation of case law, institutional analysis, and political history (Schuck 1998). But, with the theoretical and methodological borrowing that goes on between law and economics or political science, legal scholars have come increasingly to draw on more formal methods of data analysis.

Clearly, historical methods, which rely on archival sources, are quite distinct and well developed within that discipline. In recent years, of course, historians and historical anthropologists have turned increasingly to quantitative methods of data analysis, which has in turn expanded and enriched the range of sources drawn upon to study migration and immigration. These include manuscript census data and ownership and housing records (Gabaccia 1984), population registers (Kertzer and Hogan 1989), official statistics containing aggregate data on emigration and immigration (Hochstadt 1981), passport registers (Baganha 1990), ships' manifests (Swierenga 1981), and even local parish records (Brettell 1986; Moch and Tilly 1985). However, historians also use the kinds of documents to study migration that they have used for other historical projects—letters, autobiographies, newspapers and magazines, urban citizenship registers, sacred and secular court documents, tax and land records, settlement house and hospital admission records, organization booklets, and oral histories (Baily and Ramella 1990; Diner 1983; Gjerde 1985; Mageean 1991; Miller 1985; Yans-McLaughlin 1990).

The diverse methods of history and the social sciences, and the various bodies of data that are used, yield different knowledge about migration. They access different voices and leave others out. They provide for different types of generalizations and hence different levels of theorizing. Bjeren (1997:222) outlines the implications of different methods for migration research. She writes:

Large-scale social surveys are certainly necessary in migration research since it is only through such studies that the relative (quantitative) importance of different phenomena, the distribution of characteristics and their relationship between variables can be ascertained. However, the limitations imposed by the method of investigation must be respected for the results to be valid. The same holds true for detailed studies of social contexts, where the fascination of the complexity of life may make it difficult for the researcher to step back and free herself from the idiosyncrasies of an individual setting or situation.

If survey data miss some of the intersubjective meanings characteristic of social situations revealed in participant observation (Kertzer and Fricke 1997:18), research based on an intense examination of a limited number of cases (such as occurs in history and anthropology) can in turn limit generalization.

While method also involves comparison, in the study of migration, there are differences of approach within each discipline. As mentioned above, historians have tended to avoid comparisons mostly because they pose methodological challenges in terms of time and the skills necessary to command archival sources in different countries and distinct languages. The concept of "my group"—the Irish, the Italians, the Germans—described by Diner is also characteristic of anthropology, although the roots of anthropology as a discipline are in the comparative method. The anthropologist feels equally compelled to have command of the language of the immigrant population among whom he or she is conducting ethnographic fieldwork (participant observation), be it the Portuguese in Paris, the Hmong in Minneapolis, or the Koreans in New York. When an anthropologist engages in comparison, it is often based on data gathered by another ethnographer and tends to be more impressionistic than systematic. There are, however, some examples of anthropologists who have studied the same national immigrant population in two different receiving societies, and hence engaged in a process of controlled comparative analysis of quite specific questions that provide the foundation for the construction of middle-range theories of processes of migration and settlement (Brettell 1981; Foner 1985, 1998, 2005). Olwig (1998:63) notes, with reference to Caribbean migration, that comparative studies can generate quite distinct conclusions depending on the framework of analysis adopted.

A framework which singles out for comparison the disparate experiences of migrating from a variety of Caribbean places of origin to their different respective (neo-) colonial metropoles leads to quite different conclusions than one which takes its point of departure in the multifaceted experiences of people who move from a single island society to a multiplicity of metropoles. The former form of comparison can have the effect of privileging the perspective of the metropoles . . . however, if one takes as one's point of departure a particular island society, or even a particular family, one will see that there is a long heritage of moving to different migration destinations.

Foner (1998:48) suggests that the comparative approach to migration reveals "a number of factors that determine the outcome of the migration experience. . . . Cross-national comparisons allow us to begin to assess the relative weight of cultural baggage, on the one hand, and social and economic factors, on the other."

Some social scientists use historical analysis to frame their comparisons (Foner 2000; Freeman 1979; Hollifield 1992; Perlman and Waldinger 1997). An excellent example is Robert Smith's (1997) comparison of the transnational practices of Italians who came to New York in the late nineteenth and early twentieth centuries with Mexican and other immigrants who have entered that city more recently. In particular, he notes differences in the longevity of community/ethnic organizations of the present by contrast with those of the past, the greater extent of participation in the development of sending communities, and an international political context and weaker anti-immigrant tenor that fosters continued ties with the homeland. But the comparison also allows him to argue that the "global nation is not a new idea" (Smith 1997:123).

When historians of migration have themselves engaged in comparison, it is largely based on secondary sources used to complement primary research (Campbell 1995). Thus, Gjerde (1996) has drawn on a range of works to write his masterful and ambitious analysis of the Midwestern immigrant experience in the nineteenth and early twentieth centuries. Similarly, Gabaccia (1994) uses a wealth of both primary and secondary sources to explore similarities and differences in the experiences of migratory women who came to the United States between 1820 and 1990. Historian Nancy Green (1997:59ff) rightly argues that only through comparison can we understand what is specific and what is general in migration, and that "by changing the unit of analysis to compare immigrant groups to each other in their cities of settlement, we can focus on the intermediary—'mezzo'—level of analysis more pertinent to understanding the social construction of ethnic identities" (61). Historical comparisons that are "explicit, systematic, and methodologically rigorous" would, as Samuel Baily (1990:243) observes, "provide a corrective to the misleading assumption of U.S. exceptionalism," a problem raised in this volume by both Diner and Heisler. Indeed, Heisler calls most strongly for the development of cross-national comparative research. For her, the ocean that divides the study of immigration in Europe from that in the United States is perhaps as wide as the canyon that separates scholarship of the different disciplines—she calls for a bridge between Americanists and comparatists/globalists. Only through such comparison can the "national models" of migration be tested for cross-cultural validity. Portes (1997:819) has made a similar plea by suggesting that there are many questions that have flourished in the North American immigration literature that lack a comparative dimension.[9] The research of some European scholars of immigrant communities on ethnic enclaves and ethnic entrepreneurs in cities such as Amsterdam, Paris, and Berlin begins to address this problem (Rath 2002).

While the case study is commonly used in all of the social sciences, much of the most important and path-breaking work on migration has taken the form of systematic comparison, often with very sophisticated research designs using the comparative method as a way of testing hypotheses and building theories. Some of the earliest work on immigration in political science and sociology involved systematic comparisons of politics and policy (Castles and Kosack 1973; Freeman 1979; Hammar 1985; Miller 1981; Schmitter 1979). These studies, which followed a most-similar-systems design, gave rise to a new literature in the comparative politics and sociology of immigration and citizenship (Bade and Weiner 1997; Brubaker 1992; Hollifield 1992; Horowitz and Noiriel 1992; Ireland 1994; Sowell 1996; Soysal 1994; Weiner and Hanami 1998; Joppke 1999; Rudolph 2006). Such systematic, cross-national research has helped to illuminate similarities and differences in immigration and citizenship policy and to explain different outcomes. It is safe to say that the comparative method has been a mainstay of migration research across the social science disciplines, and it has resulted in some of the most innovative scholarship in the field.

IMMIGRATION, INTEGRATION, AND CITIZENSHIP

For history, economics, sociology, anthropology, and geography one of the dominant paradigms in migration theory is the assimilation model. As mentioned above, Heisler argues that this model, which predicts a single outcome, has given way to new models that predict a range of outcomes. This is best encapsulated in Portes and Rumbaut's (1990) complex model of incorporation. This model, formulated in relation to the United States, postulates outcomes for different groups according to contexts of reception that vary with reference to (1) U.S. government policy that passively accepts or actively supports; (2) labor market reception that is neutral, positive, or discriminatory; and (3) an ethnic community that is nonexistent, working class, or entrepreneurial/professional. Heisler reviews the literature in sociology that deals quite specifically with the ethnic enclave economy and its role in either facilitating or delaying the process of incorporation. Sociologists who emphasize social capital (the social networks and social relationships of immigrants) tend to argue the former, while economists, like Chiswick in this volume, place greater emphasis on human capital criteria (schooling, professional qualifications, language proficiency, and the like) in facilitating incorporation.

Chiswick argues, in contrast to George Borjas, that higher levels of inequality in the country of origin do not necessarily lead to negative selectivity of immigrants, but rather to less favorable positive selectivity. In effect, according to Chiswick, even though immigrants may come from very poor countries, they are still favorably selected compared to those who stay behind, and are likely to add to the human capital stock of the receiving country and to assimilate fairly quickly. In this framework, immigrants' earnings are still likely to increase at a higher rate than the earnings of natives. Hence, economists and sociologists are focused on many of the same questions concerning the incorporation or assimilation of immigrants, even though their theories and methods are quite different (see Table I.1).

A range of outcomes is equally manifested in the model of transnationalism that was first formulated by anthropologists, but which has had an impact on migration research in several other disciplines including sociology, geography, and political science. The roots of transnationalism within anthropology can be found in earlier work on return migration that emphasized links with the homeland and the notion that emigration did not necessarily mean definitive departure in the minds of migrants themselves. But equally transnationalism implies that return is not definitive return. Furthermore, and as Heisler observes, for political sociologists the maintenance of home ties among European immigrants (a transnational perspective) was hardly surprising given policy that did not encourage permanent settlement. Even sending countries have developed transnational policies, encouraging, as in the case of Portugal and more recently Mexico, dual nationality to maintain a presence abroad as well as attachment to home. Although Diner does not address it in her chapter, there is also a body of historical work that has documented return movement in an era prior to global communication and cheap and easy mass transportation (Wyman 1993). Social scientists have yet to take advantage of this historical dimension to refine their understanding of contemporary flows. What precisely is different? Is transnationalism simply a characteristic of the first generation of contemporary migrants, or will it endure and hence mean something different in the twenty-first century from the return migration flows of the late nineteenth and early twentieth centuries? Are scholars of immigration talking about something totally new when they use the term *transnational space* (Faist 1997; Gutiérrez 1998)? Robert Smith (1997:111) argues that although the practices are not new, they are "quantitatively and qualitatively different . . . because, in part, of differences in technology as well as in the domestic and international politics of both sending and receiving countries." He also suggests that simultaneous membership in two societies does not mean coequal membership and that "local and national American identity [for the second generation] are most likely to be primary and the diasporic identity, secondary" (Smith 1997:112). Others would argue that there is something qualitatively different about the new culture that exists across borders and that powerfully shapes migrant decisions. Massey et al. (1994:737–38) link this new culture to the spread of consumerism and immigrant success that itself generates more emigration. Migration becomes an expectation and a normal part of the life course, particularly for young men and increasingly for young women. What emerges in today's world of rapid, inexpensive communication and transportation is a culture of migration and ethnic enclaves, which allow one to migrate but remain within one's culture.

Finally, one could argue that the growth of work on the second generation, particularly within the discipline of sociology, is a result of the rejection of the assumptions of assimilation theory (Perlman and Waldinger 1997; Portes and Zhou 1993; Portes 1996). Essentially, given postindustrial economies and the diversity of places of origin of today's immigrant populations, the path to upward mobility (and hence incorporation) will be much less favorable for the contemporary second generation than it was for the second generation of the past. Clearly, this is a topic of intense debate and another area of research and theory building dominated by research on U.S. immigrants that cries out for cross-national comparison and interdisciplinary perspectives that accurately assess the past as well as the present. Perlman and Waldinger (1997:894), for example, argue, "the interpretive stance toward the past, and toward certain features of the present situation as well, puts the contemporary situation in an especially unfavorable light." Later they point to the problem and implications of the absence of conversation across the disciplines on this topic: "Economists read Borjas, sociologists read their colleagues, and historians do not regularly read the literature produced by either discipline. Since Borjas's writings are also widely read and cited by policy analysts in connection with immigration restriction issues, this divergence of emphasis regarding the 'common knowledge' about long-term character of immigrant absorption should not be ignored" (Perlman and Waldinger 1997:898–99). In fact, their close analysis of the historical evidence to illuminate contemporary trends is exemplary. They reveal continuities between the difficulties experienced by earlier immigrant groups and those of today that suggest "that the time frame for immigrant accommodation was extended and that we should not expect different today" (915).

Perhaps the controversial nature of the debate about the contemporary second generation, and the power of the transnational model, have placed the assimilation model back on the table. Alba and Nee (2003), for example, suggest that assimilation theory should be resurrected without the prescriptive baggage formulated by the dominant majority, which calls for immigrants to become like everyone else. They argue that assimilation still exists as a spontaneous process in intergroup interactions. Certainly the current preoccupation in several fields with the transnational model may be a reflection of research that is largely focused on the first generation and that lacks a historical perspective. Herbert Gans (1997) has suggested that rejection of straight-line assimilation may be premature, given not only the different generations of immigrants studied by those who originally formulated the theory and by those carrying out contemporary research, but also differences in the background (outsiders versus insiders) of researchers themselves. This latter observation brings reflexivity, powerfully formulated within anthropology, to bear on sociological theory.[10]

BRIDGE BUILDING AMONG THE DISCIPLINES

Our discussion reveals that despite some strong statements to the contrary, there is already a good deal of interchange among the disciplines. Historians draw on many of the theories formulated by sociologists; demographers are attentive to both sociological and economic theory, and increasingly to those emerging from political science; law has close affinity with all the social sciences and with history, while political science borrows heavily from economics and to a lesser extent from sociology and law; and anthropology shares much with history, sociology, and geography. Although economists also borrow and work with other disciplines—demography, sociology, and history, for example—they maintain a focus on their own methodology and models, especially the rational choice model. Proponents of rational choice might argue that this is an indication of how much more advanced economic modeling is, as a science, when compared with other social science disciplines. Detractors would say that economists are so wedded to the rationalist paradigm that they cannot admit that any other theoretical approach might be as powerful as a straightforward, interest-based, microeconomic model. An economist might respond with the metaphor of Occam's Razor—simple and parsimonious models are more powerful than the complex models offered by other social science disciplines, and that economics is a more advanced "science" because there is agreement on a unified (rationalist) theory and a common methodology.

Our discussion also demonstrates clear divergences in which questions are asked and how they are framed, in units of analysis, and in research methods. Bridge building, in our view, might best proceed through the development of interdisciplinary research projects on a series of common questions to which scholars in different disciplines and with different regional interests could bring distinct insights drawn from their particular epistemological frameworks. How, for example, might anthropologists and legal scholars collaborate in the study of so-called cultural defenses (Coleman 1996; Magnarella 1991; Volpp 1994), which often involve new immigrants, and how might the results of this work lead to refinements in theories about migration and change?

Bridge building would also entail identifying a common set of dependent and independent variables, so that it is clear what we are trying to explain and what factors we stress in building models to explain some segment of migrant behavior or the reaction of states and societies to migration. In this vein, we propose the following (suggestive) list of dependent and independent variables, broken down by discipline (see Table I.2).

Clearly, we endorse the call for more cross-national interdisciplinary research projects (Castles 1993; Massey et al. 1998), whether at a micro- or a

TABLE I.2: MODELING MIGRANT BEHAVIOR AND ITS EFFECTS

Discipline	Dependent Variables	Independent Variables
Anthropology	Migrant behavior (emigration, integration)	Social and cultural context (transnational networks)
Demography	Migrant behaviors	Distributions of geographical residence or educational attainment
Economics	Migrant flows and adjustment and macroeconomic impact	Wage/income differentials, demand-pull/ supply-push, human capital, factor proportions, structure of the economy and transfer systems
Geography	Migrant decision making	Spatial, environmental, political, cultural, and socioeconomic contexts
History	Migrant experience	Social/historical context
Law	Legal, political, social, and economic treatment of migrants	Law or policy
Political Science	Policy (admissionist or restrictionist) Outcomes (control and integration)	Institutions, rights, interests
Sociology	Migrant behavior (immigration and incorporation)	Networks, enclaves, social capital

macrolevel of analysis. How, for example, are first-generation immigrants differentially incorporated (economically, politically, and socially) in Germany as opposed to the United States, in Britain by comparison with France, in Australia by contrast with Canada, or in Singapore by comparison with Riyadh? Similarly, how and to what extent are immigrants, their children, and subsequent generations differentially incorporated in a cross-national context?

A second topic crying out for interdisciplinary and cross-national examination is the impact (political, economic, social, and cultural) of emigration and transnationalism on sending societies (Massey 1999). As noted above, primarily anthropologists and to a lesser extent historians have conducted the most work in the countries of emigration, but the questions asked must be expanded through the participation of those in other disciplines, particularly political science and economics. For example, some scholars have already noted how crucial migrants have become for national economies. Writing about the Dominican Republic, Guarnizo (1997:282–83) observes that "migrant's monetary transfers (excluding their business investments) now constitute the second, and according to some the first, most important source of foreign exchange for the national economy, and they are a *sine qua non* for Dominican macro economic stability, including monetary exchange rates, balance of trade, international monetary reserves, and the national balance of payments."

In countries of immigration, we foresee exciting collaboration on the question of citizenship between the political scientists and political sociologists who frame the question in relation to the nation–state and the rights of a democratic society, and the anthropologists who frame the questions in relation to ethnicity, the construction of identity, and a sense of belonging. One of the central debates, emerging largely from within the field of economics but with resonance in law and political science, is between those who see a positive impact of immigration and hence propose an admissionist policy, and those who highlight the negative impact and advocate more restrictionist policy.[11] Economic models alone do not offer a complete explanation. Getting to the roots of anti-immigrant sentiments and their connection to the way nationals of the receiving society construct their own identities in relation to immigrants should be a prime research agenda for scholars of international migration. This would require the input of sociologists and anthropologists. Again it is a question that would be better served by cross-national and comparative research on the question of reception.

The broader implications of multidisciplinary and comparative approaches for theory are exciting to contemplate, particularly if bridges can be built between causal explanations and interpretive understandings, between statistical regularities and unique occurrences, and between the economic and structural forces that shape migrant behavior and the individual agency that operates both harmoniously and disharmoniously in relation to those forces. In his concluding essay, Adrian Favell challenges migration scholars to think globally and to avoid the tendency to focus narrowly on a single-country case. Like Heisler, he laments the dominance of the U.S. case and of American social scientists in the study of migration. He also explains how the organization of migration research in university departments is a constraining factor on truly interdisciplinary work. He strives mightily to square some very difficult social scientific circles, between what he calls naïve positivism and constructivism, arguing instead for what he calls "constructive realism," which "might enable a rethinking of migration theory . . . and help us rebuild a more politically autonomous and scientific form of studying [migration]." He wants to move away from an approach to the study of migration that is wedded to "time- and place-specific narratives." In this, he is closer to Brettell and Heisler in rejecting a nation–state-centered approach and takes issue with Hollifield, who wants to give primacy to the state and policy in explaining international migration. He takes the counterintuitive view that mobility is natural and normal in human history, and that "what is abnormal . . . is the idea that human societies need to construct political borders . . . that constrain . . . spatial mobility." Not surprisingly, he points to the European Union with its open borders as the wave of the future.

NOTES

1. Normally, a conceptual distinction is drawn between migration and immigration, the former referring to movement that occurs within national borders (internal migration) and the latter to movement across national borders

(emigration or immigration). We use the term *migration* somewhat loosely here to refer to international migration, generally the emphasis of all the essays in this volume. However, from a theoretical perspective it is worth noting that economic theories of migration can often apply to either internal flows or international flows (Stark 1991; Martin, Abella, and Kuptsch 2006), and some sociologist and human geographers may prefer the more general term "mobility" to migration (Smith and Favell 2006).

2. Hammar and Tamas (1997:13) observe that research is "frequently undertaken without consideration or consultation of related work in other disciplines" and call for more multidisciplinary research endeavors. Similarly, in an edited volume on Mexican immigration to the United States, Suárez-Orozco (1998) calls for more "interdisciplinary dialogue." An early effort at interdisciplinary dialogue is Kritz, Keely, and Tomas (1981).

3. Portes (1997:10) argues that any attempt at an all-encompassing theory would be futile and that even the macro and the micro are not easily united into a single approach. Cf. also Portes and DeWind (2004).

4. However, historians such as Donna Gabaccia (1992, 1999, 2004) have for some time been calling on migration historians to engage in more comparative, cross-national, global, and interdisciplinary work.

5. One example of a monograph in the historical literature that invokes both world systems theory and transnationalism is Friedman-Kasaba (1996). Her conclusion includes an analysis of theoretical debates. See also Gabaccia 2004.

6. Faist (1997:188) has usefully reformulated these three levels of analysis as the structural (the political-economic and cultural factors in the sending and receiving countries), the relational (the social ties of movers and stayers), and the individual (the degrees of freedom of potential movers). He also views macro- and micromodels as causal, while meso-models are process related. Hoerder (1997) offers a slightly different trilevel model: analysis of world systems, analysis of behavior among individual migrants from the bottom up, and analysis of segmentation and individual actions in terms of networks and family economies.

7. Caldwell and Hill (1988) have noted a similar "obsession" in other areas of demographic research and have consequently called for more micro approaches. Massey et al. (1994:700) see the focus on methodological and measurement issues in the literature on North American immigration as limiting to the advancement of theoretical understanding of what shapes and controls flows of migration.

8. Some examples are Brettell (1995), Hart (1997), Kibria (1993), Gmelch (1992), Olwig (1998), Stack (1996), and several of the chapters in Benmayor and Skotnes (1994a). Yans-McLaughlin (1990) writes about the use of subjective documents in history for similar purposes. See also Brettell 2003.

9. Massey et al. (1998) make such an attempt in a volume that compares the migration systems in North America, Western Europe, the Gulf region, Asia and the Pacific, and the Southern Cone region of South America.

10. For a contrary view, see Rumbaut (1997).

11. There are those policy analysts, like Chiswick in this volume, who see the impact of immigration varying with the characteristics of the migrants and the nature of the host economy; hence visas should be rationed according to the "national interest" and a strict cost–benefit logic.

REFERENCES

Alba, Richard, and Victor Nee. 2003. *Remaking the American Mainstream: Assimilation and Contemporary Immigration.* Cambridge, MA: Harvard University Press.

Bade, Klaus, and Myron Weiner. 1997. *Migration Past, Migration Future: Germany and the United States.* Providence/Oxford: Berghan Books.

Baganha, Maria Ioannis. 1990. *Portuguese Emigration to the United States, 1820–1930.* New York: Garland.

Baily, Samuel L. 1990. "Cross-Cultural Comparison and the Writing of Migration History: Some Thoughts on How to Study Italians in the New World," in Virginia Yans-McLaughlin, ed., *Immigration Reconsidered: History, Sociology, and Politics,* pp. 241–53. New York: Oxford University Press.

Baily, Samuel L., and Franco Ramella, eds. 1990. *One Family, Two Worlds: An Italian Family's Correspondence across the Atlantic, 1901–1922.* New Brunswick, NJ: Rutgers University Press.

Benmayor, Rina, and Andor Skotnes. 1994a. *Migration and Identity.* Oxford: Oxford University Press.

———. 1994b. "On Migration and Identity," in Rina Benmayor and Andor Skotnes, eds., *Migration and Identity,* pp. 1–18. Oxford: Oxford University Press.

Bjeren, Gunilla. 1997. "Gender and Reproduction," in Tomas Hammar, Grete Brochmann, Kristof Tamas, and Thomas Faist, eds., *International Migration, Immobility and Development: Multidisciplinary Perspectives,* pp. 219–46. New York: Berg Publishers.

Bommes, Michael, and Andrew Geddes. 2000. *Immigration and Welfare: Challenging the Borders of the Welfare State.* London: Routledge.

Borjas, George J. 1985. "Assimilation, Changes in Cohort Quality and the Earnings of Immigrants," *Journal of Labor Economics* 3: 463–89.

———. 1999. *Heaven's Door: Immigration Policy and the American Economy.* Princeton, NJ: Princeton University Press.

Brettell, Caroline B. 1981. "Is the Ethnic Community Inevitable? A Comparison of the Settlement Patterns of Portuguese Immigrants in Toronto and Paris," *Journal of Ethnic Studies* 9: 1–17.

———. 1986. *Men Who Migrate, Women Who Wait: Population and History in a Portuguese Parish.* Princeton, NJ: Princeton University Press.

———. 1995. *We Have Already Cried Many Tears: The Stories of Three Portuguese Migrant Women.* Prospect Heights, IL: Waveland.

———. 2003. "Migration Stories: Agency and the Individual in the Study of Migration," in Caroline B. Brettell, *Anthropology and Migration: Essays on Transnationalism, Ethnicity, and Identity,* pp. 23–45. Walnut Creek, CA: Altamira Press.

Brubaker, Rogers. 1992. *Citizenship and Nationhood in France and Germany.* Cambridge, MA: Harvard University Press.

Caldwell, John C., and Allan G. Hill. 1988. "Recent Developments Using Micro-Approaches to Demographic Research," in John Caldwell, Allan Hill, and Valerie Hull, eds., *Micro-Approaches to Demographic Research,* pp. 1–9. London: Kegan Paul International.

Campbell, M. 1995. "The Other Immigrants: Comparing the Irish in Australia and the United States," *Journal of American Ethnic History* 14: 3–22.

Carens, Joseph. 2000. *Culture, Citizenship, and Community: A Contextual Exploration of Justice as Evenhandedness.* New York: Oxford University Press.

Castles, Stephen. 1993. "Migrations and Minorities in Europe. Perspectives for the 1990s: Eleven Hypotheses," in John Wrench and John Solomos, eds., *Racism and Migration in Western Europe*, pp. 17–34. Oxford: Berg Publishers.

Castles, Stephen, and G. Kosack. 1973. *Immigrant Workers and Class Structure in Western Europe*. London: Oxford University Press.

Castles, Stephen, and Mark Miller. 2003. *The Age of Migration: International Population Movements in the Modern World*. New York: Guilford Press.

Castles, Stephen, and Ellie Vasta. 2004. "New Conflicts around Old Dilemmas," in Wayne A. Cornelius et al., eds., *Controlling Immigration: A Global Perspective*. Stanford, CA: Stanford University Press.

Chiswick, Barry. 1978. "The Effect of Americanization on the Earnings of Foreign-Born Men," *Journal of Political Economy* 86: 897–921.

_____. 1986. "Is the New Immigration Less Skilled than the Old?" *Journal of Labor Economics* 4: 168–92.

Coleman, Doriane Lambelet. 1996. "Individualizing Justice through Multiculturalism: The Liberals' Dilemma," *Columbia Law Review* 96: 1093–1167.

Cornelius, Wayne A., Philip L. Martin, and James F. Hollifield, eds. 1994. *Controlling Immigration: A Global Perspective*. Stanford, CA: Stanford University Press.

Cornelius, Wayne A., and Takeyuki Tsuda. 2004. "Japan: Government Policy, Immigrant Reality," in Wayne A. Cornelius et al., eds., *Controlling Immigration: A Global Perspective*. Stanford, CA: Stanford University Press.

Cornelius, Wayne A., Takeyuki Tsuda, Philip L. Martin, and James F. Hollifield, eds. 2004. *Controlling Immigration: A Global Perspective*. Stanford, CA: Stanford University Press.

DeSipio, Louis. 1996. *Counting on the Latino Vote: Latinos as a New Electorate*. Charlottesville: University of Virginia Press.

Diner, Hasia. 1983. *Erin's Daughters in America: Irish Immigrant Women in the Nineteenth Century*. Baltimore, MD: Johns Hopkins University Press.

Duleep, Harriet O., and Mark C. Regets. 1997a. "Measuring Immigrant Wage Growth Using Matched CPS Files," *Demography* 34: 239–49.

_____. 1997b. "The Decline in Immigrant Entry Earnings: Less Transferable Skills or Lower Ability?" *Quarterly Review of Economics and Finance* 37 (Special Issue on Immigration): 89–208.

Faist, Thomas. 1997. "The Crucial Meso-Level," in Tomas Hammar, Grete Brochmann, Kristof Tamas, and Thomas Faist, eds., *International Migration, Immobility and Development: Multidisciplinary Perspectives*, pp. 187–217. New York: Berg Publishers.

Favell, Adrian. 1998. *Philosophies of Integration: Immigration and the Idea of Citizenship in France and Britain*. New York: St. Martin's Press.

Foner, Nancy. 1985. "Race and Color: Jamaican Migrants in London and New York City," *International Migration Review* 19: 706–27.

_____. 1998. "Towards a Comparative Perspective on Caribbean Migration," in Mary Chamberlain, ed., *Caribbean Migration: Globalised Identities*, pp. 47–60. New York: Routledge.

_____. 2000. *From Ellis Island to JFK: New York's Two Great Waves of Immigration*. New Haven and New York: Yale University Press and Russell Sage Foundation.

_____. 2005. *In a New Land: A Comparative View of Immigration*. New York: New York University Press.

Freeman, Gary P. 1979. *Immigrant Labor and Racial Conflict in Industrial Societies: The French and British Experiences*. Princeton, NJ: Princeton University Press.

————. 1995. "Modes of Immigration Politics in Liberal Democratic States," *International Migration Review* 19: 881–902.

————. 1998. *Toward a Theory of the Domestic Politics of International Migration in Western Nations.* South Bend, IN: The Nanovic Institute, University of Notre Dame.

Friedman-Kasaba, Kathie. 1996. *Memories of Migration: Gender, Ethnicity and Work in the Lives of Jewish and Italian Women in New York, 1870–1924.* Albany: SUNY Press.

Gabaccia, Donna. 1984. *From Sicily to Elizabeth Street: Housing and Social Change among Italian Immigrants, 1880–1930.* Albany: SUNY Press.

————. 1992. *Seeking Common Ground: Multidisciplinary Studies of Immigrant Women in the United States.* Westport, CT: Greenwood Press.

————. 1994. *From the Other Side: Women, Gender and Immigrant Life in the U.S. 1820–1990.* Bloomington: Indiana University Press.

————. 1999. "Is Everywhere Nowhere? Nomads, Nations, and the Immigrant Paradigm of United States History," *The Journal of American History* 86: 1115–34.

————. 2004. "A Long Atlantic in a Wider World," *Atlantic Studies* 1: 1–27.

Gans, Herbert J. 1997. "Toward a Reconciliation of 'Assimilation' and 'Pluralism': The Interplay of Acculturation and Ethnic Retention," *International Migration Review* 31: 875–92.

Gardner, Martha. 2005. *The Qualities of a Citizen: Women, Immigration and Citizenship, 1870–1965.* Princeton, NJ: Princeton University Press.

Gjerde, Jon. 1985. *From Peasants to Farmers: The Migration from Balestrand, Norway, to the Upper Middle West.* Cambridge: Cambridge University Press.

————. 1996. *The Minds of the West: Ethnocultural Evolution in the Rural Middle West, 1830–1917.* Chapel Hill: University of North Carolina.

Gmelch, George. 1992. *Double Passage: The Lives of Caribbean Migrants Abroad and Back Home.* Ann Arbor: University of Michigan Press.

Green, Nancy L. 1997. "The Comparative Method and Poststructural Structuralism: New Perspectives for Migration Studies," in Jan Lucassen and Leo Lucassen, eds., *Migration, Migration History, History: Old Paradigms and New Perspectives,* pp. 57–72. Bern: Peter Lang.

Guarnizo, Luis Eduardo. 1997. "The Emergence of a Transnational Social Formation and the Mirage of Return Migration among Dominican Transmigrants," *Identities* 4: 281–322.

Gutiérrez, David G. 1998. "Ethnic Mexicans and the Transformation of 'American' Social Space: Reflections on Recent History," in Marcelo M. Suárez-Orozco, ed., *Crossings: Mexican Immigration in Interdisciplinary Perspectives,* pp. 309–40. Cambridge, MA: Harvard University Press.

Hammar, Tomas, ed. 1985. *European Immigration Policy: A Comparative Study.* New York: Cambridge University Press.

Hammar, Tomas, and Kristof Tamas. 1997. "Why Do People Go or Stay?" in Tomas Hammar, Grete Brochmann, Kristof Tamas, and Thomas Faist, eds., *International Migration, Immobility and Development: Multidisciplinary Perspectives,* pp. 1–19. New York: Berg Publishers.

Hanson, Gordon H. 2005. *Why Does Immigration Divide America? Public Finance and Political Opposition to Open Borders.* Washington, D.C.: Institute for International Economics.

Hart, Dianne Walta. 1997. *Undocumented in L.A.: An Immigrant's Story.* Wilmington, DE: Scholarly Resources Inc.

Hill, Allan G. 1997. "'Truth Lies in the Eye of the Beholder': The Nature of Evidence in Demography and Anthropology," in David I. Kertzer and Tom Fricke, eds., *Anthropological Demography: Toward a New Synthesis*, pp. 223–47. Chicago: University of Chicago Press.

Hochstadt, Steve. 1981. "Migration and Industrialization in Germany, 1815–1977," *Social Science History* 5: 445–68.

Hoerder, Dirk. 1997. "Segmented Macrosystems and Networking Individuals: The Balancing Function of Migration Processes," in Jan Lucassen and Leo Lucassen, eds., *Migration, Migration History, History: Old Paradigms and New Perspectives*, pp. 73–84. Bern: Peter Lang.

Hollifield, James F. 1986. "Immigration Policy in France and Germany: Outputs versus Outcomes," *Annals of the American Academy of Political and Social Science* 485: 113–28.

———. 1992. *Immigrants, Markets, and States: The Political Economy of Postwar Europe.* Cambridge, MA: Harvard University Press.

———. 1998. "Migration, Trade, and the Nation–State: The Myth of Globalization," *UCLA Journal of International Law and Foreign Affairs* 3(2): 595–636.

———. 2004. "The Emerging Migration State," *International Migration Review* 38: 885–912.

Horowitz, Donald, and Gerard Noiriel. 1992. *Immigrants in Two Democracies: French and American Experience.* New York: New York University Press.

Huber, Gregory A., and Thomas J. Espenshade. 1997. "Neo-Isolationism, Balanced-Budget Conservatism, and the Fiscal Impacts of Immigrants," *International Migration Review* 31: 1031–54.

Ireland, Patrick. 1994. *The Policy Challenge of Ethnic Diversity: Immigrant Politics in France and Switzerland.* Cambridge, MA: Harvard University Press.

Jacobson, David. 1996. *Rights across Borders: Immigration and the Decline of Citizenship.* Baltimore, MD: Johns Hopkins University Press.

Joppke, Christian. 1999. *Immigration and the Nation–State: The United States, Germany, and Great Britain.* New York: Oxford University Press.

Kagan, Robert A. 2001. *Adversarial Legalism: the American Way of Law.* Cambridge, MA: Harvard University Press.

Kastoryano, Riva. 1997. *La France, l'Allemagne et leurs immigrés: négocier l'identité.* Paris: Armand Colin.

Kertzer, David, and Dennis Hogan. 1989. *Family, Political Economy, and Demographic Change: The Transformation of Life in Casalecchio, Italy, 1861–1921.* Madison: University of Wisconsin Press.

Kertzer, David I., and Tom Fricke. 1997. "Toward an Anthropological Demography," in David I. Kertzer and Tom Fricke, eds., *Anthropological Demography: Toward a New Synthesis*, pp. 1–35. Chicago: University of Chicago Press.

Kessler, Alan E. 1998. "Distributional Coalitions, Trade, and the Politics of Postwar American Immigration," paper presented at the Annual Meeting of the American Political Science Association, Boston, MA.

Kibria, Nazli. 1993. *Family Tightrope: The Changing Lives of Vietnamese Americans.* Princeton, NJ: Princeton University Press.

Kritz, Mary M., Charles B. Keely, and Silvano M. Tomasi, eds. 1981. *Global Trends in Migration: Theory and Research in International Population Movements.* New York: Center for Migration Studies.

Leeds, Elizabeth. 1984. "Salazar's 'Modelo Económico': The Consequences of Planned Constraint," in Thomas C. Bruneau, Victor M. P. da Rosa, and Alex Macleod, eds., *Portugal in Development: Emigration, Industrialization, the European Community,* pp. 13–51. Ottawa: University of Ottawa Press.

Legomsky, Stephen. 1987. *Immigration and the Judiciary: Law and Politics in Britain and America.* Oxford: Oxford University Press.

Light, Ivan. 2006. *Deflecting Immigration: Networks, Markets, and Regulation in Los Angeles.* New York: Russell Sage.

Lucassen, Jan, and Leo Lucassen, eds. 1997. *Migration, Migration History, History: Old Paradigms and New Perspectives.* Bern: Peter Lang.

Mageean, Deirdre M. 1991. "From Irish Countryside to American City; The Settlement and Mobility of Ulster Migrations in Philadelphia," in Colin G. Pooley and Ian D. Whyte, eds., *Migrants, Emigrants and Immigrants: A Social History of Migration,* pp. 42–61. London: Routledge.

Magnarella, Paul J. 1991. "Justice in a Culturally Pluralistic Society: The Cultural Defense on Trial," *Journal of Ethnic Studies* 19: 65–84.

Martin, Philip, Manolo Abella, and Christianne Kuptsch. 2006. *Managing Labor Migration in the Twenty-first Century.* New Haven, CT: Yale University Press.

Massey, Douglas S. 1999. "International Migration at the Dawn of the Twenty-First Century: The Role of the State," *Population and Development Review* 25: 303–22.

Massey, Douglas S., Joaquin Arango, Graeme Hugo, Ali Kovaouci, Adela Pellegrino, and J. Edward Taylor. 1993. "Theories of International Migration: A Review and Appraisal," *Population and Development Review* 19: 431–66.

————. 1994. "An Evaluation of International Migration Theory; The North American Case," *Population and Development Review* 20: 699–751.

————. 1998. *Worlds in Motion: Understanding International Migration at the End of the Millennium.* Oxford: Clarendon Press.

Miller, Kerby. 1985. *Emigrants and Exiles: Ireland and the Irish Exodus to North America.* New York: Oxford University Press.

Miller, Mark J. 1981. *Foreign Workers in Western Europe: An Emerging Political Force.* New York: Praeger.

Mincer, Jacob. 1978. "Family Migration Decisions," *Journal of Political Economy* 86: 749–73.

Moch, Leslie Page, and Louise A. Tilly. 1985. "Joining the Urban World: Occupation, Family and Migration in Three French Cities," *Comparative Studies in Society and History* 25: 33–56.

Montello, D.R. 2001. "Scale in Geography," in N. J. Smelser and P. B. Baltes, eds., *International Encyclopedia of the Social and Behavioral Sciences*, pp. 13501–504. Oxford: Pergamon Press.

National Research Council. 1997. *The New Americans: Economic, Demographic, and Fiscal Effects of Immigration.* Washington, D.C.: Commission on Immigration Reform and National Academy of Sciences.

Olwig, Karen Fog. 1998. "Constructing Lives: Migration Narratives and Life Stories among Nevisians," in Mary Chamberlain, ed., *Caribbean Migration: Globalised Identities,* pp. 63–80. New York: Routledge.

Passel, Jeffrey S. 1994. *Immigrants and Taxes: A Reappraisal of Huddle's 'The Costs of Immigration.'* Washington, D.C.: Urban Institute.

Pedraza, Silvia. 1990. "Immigration Research: A Conceptual Map," *Social Science History* 14: 43–67.

Perlmann, Joel, and Roger Waldinger. 1997. "Second Generation Decline? Children of Immigrants, Past and Present—A Reconsideration," *International Migration Review* 31: 893–922.

Portes, Alejandro. 1997. "Immigration Theory for a New Century: Some Problems and Opportunities," *International Migration Review* 31: 799–825.

———. ed. 1996. *The New Second Generation.* New York: Russell Sage.

Portes, Alejandro, and Josh DeWind, eds. 2004. "Conceptual and Methodological Developments in the Study of International Migration," *International Migration Review* 38: special issue.

Portes, Alejandro, and Rubén G. Rumbaut. 1990. *Immigrant America: A Portrait.* Berkeley and Los Angeles: University of California Press.

Portes, Alejandro, and Min Zhou. 1993. "The New Second Generation: Segmented Assimilation and Its Variants among Post-1965 Immigrant Youth," *Annals of the American Academy of Political and Social Sciences* 530: 74–96.

Rath, Jan, ed. 2002. *Unravelling the Rag Trade: Immigrant Entrepreneurship in Seven World Cities.* Oxford: Oxford University Press.

Rothman, E. S., and Thomas J. Espenshade. 1992. "Fiscal Impacts of Immigration to the United States," *Population Index* 58: 381–415.

Rudolph, Christopher. 2006. *National Security and Immigration: Policy Development in the United States and Western Europe since 1945.* Stanford, CA: Stanford University Press.

Rumbaut, Ruben G. 1997. "Assimilation and Its Discontents: Between Rhetoric and Reality," *International Migration Review* 31: 923–60.

Russell, Sharon Stanton. 1986. "Remittances from International Migration: A Review in Perspective," *World Development* 41: 677–96.

Sassen, Saskia. 1991. *The Global City.* Princeton, NJ: Princeton University Press.

———. 1996. *Losing Control? Sovereignty in an Age of Globalization.* New York: Columbia University Press.

Schmitter, Barbara E. 1979. *Immigration and Citizenship in West Germany and Switzerland,* unpublished Ph.D. dissertation, University of Chicago.

Schuck, Peter H. 1998. *Citizens, Strangers, and In-Betweens: Essays on Immigration and Citizenship.* Boulder, CO: Westview Press.

Schuck, Peter H., and Rogers Smith. 1985. *Citizenship without Consent.* New Haven, CT: Yale University Press.

Simon, Julian. 1984. "Immigrants, Taxes and Welfare in the United States," *Population and Development Review* (March): 55–69.

Sjaastad, Larry A. 1962. "The Costs and Returns of Human Migration," *Journal of Political Economy* 70 (Supplement): 80–93.

Smith, Michael Peter, and Adrian Favell. 2006. *The Human Face of Global Mobility: International Highly Skilled Migration in Europe, North America and the Asia-Pacific.* New Brunswick, NJ: Transaction Publishers.

Smith, Robert. 1997. "Transnational Migration, Assimilation, and Political Community," in Margaret E. Crahan and Alberto Vourvoulias-Bush, eds., *The City and the World: New York's Global Future,* pp. 110–32. New York: Council on Foreign Relations.

Smith, Rogers. 1997. *Civic Ideals: Conflicting Visions of Citizenship in U.S. History.* New Haven, CT: Yale University Press.

Sowell, Thomas. 1996. *Migration and Cultures: A World View.* New York: Basic Books.

Soysal, Yasemin N. 1994. *Limits of Citizenship: Migrants and Postnational Membership in Europe.* Chicago: University of Chicago Press.

Stack, Carol. 1996. *Call to Home: African Americans Reclaim the Rural South.* New York: Basic Books.

Stark, Oded. 1991. *The Migration of Labor.* Cambridge: Basil Blackwell.

Straubhaar, Thomas. 1988. *On the Economics of International Labor Migration.* Bern and Stuttgart: Verlag Paul Haupt.

Suárez-Orozco, Marcelo M. 1998. *Crossings: Mexican Immigration in Interdisciplinary Perspectives.* Cambridge, MA: Harvard University Press.

Swierenga, Robert. 1981. "Dutch International Migration Statistics, 1820–1880: An Analysis of Linked Multinational Nominal Files," *International Migration Review* 15: 445–70.

Volpp, Leti. 1994. "(Mis)Identifying Culture: Asian Women and the 'Cultural Defense,'" *Harvard Women's Law Journal* 17: 57–101.

Waldinger, Roger, and David Fitzgerald. 2004. "Transnationalism in Question," *American Journal of Sociology* 109/5: 1177–95.

Weiner, Myron. 1987. "International Emigration and the Third World," in William Alonso, ed., *Population in an Interacting World,* pp. 173–200. Cambridge, MA: Harvard University Press.

_____. 1995. *The Global Migration Crisis.* New York: HarperCollins.

Weiner, Myron, and Tadashi Hanami. 1998. *Temporary Workers or Future Citizens? Japanese and U.S. Migrations Policies.* New York: New York University Press.

Wyman, M. 1993. *Round Trip to America.* Ithaca, NY: Cornell University Press.

Yans-McLaughlin, Virginia. 1990. "Metaphors of Self in History: Subjectivity, Oral Narrative, and Immigration Studies," in Virginia Yans-McLaughlin, ed., *Immigration Reconsidered: History, Sociology, and Politics,* pp. 254–90. New York: Oxford University Press.

Zolberg, Aristide R. 1981. "International Migration in Political Perspective," in Mary M. Kritz, Charles B. Keely, and Silvano M. Tomasi, eds., *Global Trends in Migration: Theory and Research in International Population Movements.* New York: Center for Migration Studies.

_____. 2006. *A Nation by Design: Immigration Policy in the Fashioning of America.* New York: Russell Sage; and Cambridge, MA: Harvard University Press.

Zolberg, Aristide R., A. Suhrke, and S. Aguayo. 1986. "International Factors in the Formation of Refugee Movements," *International Migration Review* 20: 151–69.

CHAPTER I

History and the Study of Immigration
Narratives of the Particular

Hasia R. Diner

In 1990 Roger Daniels, an immigration historian well worthy of his distinguished reputation in the field, tried to do something never before attempted. In his synthetic book, *Coming to America: A History of Immigration and Ethnicity in American Life*, he acknowledged the existence of migration theory and the possibility that those who hoped to understand the experience of immigrants to America ought to do so through some kind of theoretical lens. His reference to the work of the British demographer E. G. Ravenstein early in the first chapter of *Coming to America*, in a section entitled "The Laws of Migration," seemed to herald a new era in the history of immigration history. Maldwyn Allen Jones's hardy *American Immigration*, first published in 1960 and then reissued with an update in 1992, Alan Kraut's *The Huddled Masses* (1982), and Thomas Archdeacon's *Becoming American* (1983) preceded Daniels's as books that sought to encapsulate in a single volume "how people have come from all over the world to North America and how they have formed the population and society of the United States" (Archdeacon 1983:xi). These earlier survey books unabashedly avoided referring to, contending with, or confronting the existence of a body of scholarship called *migration theory*.

So, too, the monumental and authoritative *Harvard Encyclopedia of American Ethnic Groups* of 1980 made no mention of migration theory in either a separate entry or in the general ones on "Immigration: Economic and Social Characteristics" and "Immigration: Settlement Patterns and Spatial Distribution." In a way, the *Harvard Encyclopedia* set the tone by which American historians of immigration to the United States snubbed their collective noses at theory. Immigration to America, the *Harvard Encyclopedia* noted, was of a "magnitude . . . unmatched in the history of mankind" (Thernstrom and Orlov 1980). The historical geographer David Ward, who wrote the entry on modes of settlement, declared that immigrants to America created "distinctive locational patterns," and as such dismissed the possibility of fashioning some overarching theories to explain the migration phenomenon (Ward 1980:496). Finally, the reference volume provided a useful and comprehensive bibliography, and did so, organized by group, with no theoretical books and articles included.

Daniels's inclusion of the phrase "migration theory," and his reference to Ravenstein therefore seemed to be going against the paradigm. He admitted, "One needs a kind of generalized conceptual framework within which the experiences of groups and individuals can be structured, compared and contrasted" (Daniels 1990:16). So, unlike other American historians who had tried their hand at the monumental task of writing in a single volume a history of overseas migrations to America, Daniels understood that the vast body of data about people, places, and time ought to be organized around some theoretical model or models.[1] He turned early on in his book to Ravenstein's essays written in 1885 and 1889 as "The Laws of Migration" and presented in the *Journal of the Royal Statistical Society.* "Remarkably," Daniels wrote, "most of Ravenstein's generalizations seem valid to contemporary scholars" (1990:16).

Oddly enough, however, Daniels never returned to Ravenstein, or to any other theory or theorist of migration as he went on to author this solid, four-hundred-page narrative about immigration devoid of a "generalized conceptual framework." He moved his book along the trajectory of time and group: "Pioneers of the Century of Immigration: Irish, Germans, and Scandinavians," "From the Mediterranean: Italians, Greeks, Arabs, and Armenians," "Eastern Europeans: Poles, Jews, and Hungarians," "Minorities from Other Regions: Chinese, Japanese, and French Canadians" represented some of the chapters within part II, "The Century of Immigration (1820–1924)," proving that for historians of American immigration "when" and "whence" remained the organizing questions.

Rather than ushering in a new era in immigration history, Daniels offered the scholarly community another, solid, densely packed, well written, information-laden book on the experiences of *all* of the American people, including the indigenous residents of North America, the forced African migrants who were brought as slaves, alongside the millions who left homes in Asia, Europe, South and Central America, the Caribbean, other parts of North America, the Middle East, from the late sixteenth century through the end of the twentieth. By implication it seems that Daniels wanted to break with tradition and use theory, but ultimately could not.

Daniels's dilemma grew out of the disjunction between history as an enterprise, immigration/ethnic history in particular, and the broad world of academic discourse of the 1990s. Emphasizing the need for interdisciplinarity, scholars in the humanities joined those in social sciences and invoked "theory" as they never had before. They sought expansive, but precise, language by which they could organize large bodies of data drawn from diverse sources and covering almost infinite situations. They engaged in the process of model building that undergirds the theoretical focus, and those models, once fashioned, can be applied to other fitting examples, other situations.

Daniels no doubt *wanted* to join the discursive moment of the 1980s and 1990s. But as a product, and producer, of the field of immigration history, he could not. American historians of immigration and ethnicity have by and large shied away from theory, even when they paid lip service to it. They confess to the intellectual benefits that would enrich their work if they would use it, and the academic cache that accompanies theoretical formulations. But they continue down a well-trodden road, avoiding theory even as they acknowledge its salience to their project.

American historians' fundamental disinterest in theory is notable. They have, since Marcus Hansen in the 1930s called for a study of immigration (Hansen 1938, 1940), and explored the same set of problems that sociologists, anthropologists, demographers, and economists have simultaneously studied. Like scholars in those "harder" fields, scholars whose right to call themselves "social scientists" has been unchallenged, historians have for seventy years been captivated by the almost universality of the migration experience and by a series of interlocking questions about it: Who moves? For how long? Why do some human beings get up and shift residence? Why do others stay put? Why do they migrate when they do? How do they decide where to go? How do they get there? How do they experience on a cultural level the act of leaving one place and relocating elsewhere?

But unlike the practitioners of those disciplines, historians have been disinterested in both creating "laws," to use Ravenstein's term, and in using existing ones to explain their data. Ironically, the rise of history as an enterprise coincided with the first studies of migration as a theoretical issue. Scholars in the newly formed history departments in the newly formed universities of the late nineteenth century in England, Germany, and the United States had ample opportunity from the start to learn from their colleagues in the other newly constituted departments of political economy, sociology, and a bit later anthropology. Those scholars, down the hall as it were, understood, like Ravenstein, the significance of the historic dimension. Ravenstein in his formative articles claimed to have surveyed human migrations of the past, and after that immersion in history, he posited his "laws" governing human movements across time and place.

In the century since Ravenstein, an enormous corpus of scholarship from multiple social science disciplines has been available for historians to dip into. Harry Jerome in 1926, in a research project sponsored by the National Bureau of Economic Research, studied immigration to the United States and linked the ebbs and flows in the numbers to the ups and downs of the business cycle. Jerome acknowledged that although he could not find a perfect fit, he did see enough "general similarities in the appearance of the curves" to warrant a theory of why people migrated when they did. Written for policymakers, Jerome's study would have been cogent for even those unfamiliar with economic terms and formulas, yet none of the historians who have been interested specifically in this question has cited or employed his theory (Jerome 1926:240).

Likewise, just as Maldwyn Allen Jones was in the process of preparing *American Immigration*, William Petersen (1958) published "A General Typology of Migration" in the *American Sociological Review*. In 1966, at the moment when immigration and ethnic history as subfields (or a single subfield) within American history emerged, Everett S. Lee published "A Theory of Migration."[2] Both pieces offered, in language not intended just for disciplinary specialists, ideas about the timing, nature, and structure of immigrating populations. Neither piece garnered any attention from American historians, who busily had embarked upon the enterprise of writing about Italian, Polish, Irish, Jewish, Swedish, Mexican, Greek, Chinese, Swiss, and other immigrants to America in general or to particular places therein.

Lee and Petersen constructed models that have been somewhat replaced by writings of a newer generation of migration scholars, and those theoretical innovations also lay in close reach of historians. Aristide Zolberg (1989), for example, wrote of the need to reconceptualize thinking about migration in light of the great human movements since the 1960s. His call to develop models based on analyses of global inequalities, the role of borders in limiting migrations, and the impact upon (potential) workers of "the dynamics of the transnational capitalist economy" could be applied to explaining the behavior of migrants not only in the contemporary world but also in centuries past. These forces, which could be included in the category of state theory and world systems theory, resonated to the experiences of many of the subjects that American immigration historians have studied, but they avoided these new theories as well as the more classic formulations.

What has developed could be seen as a huge chasm between the ways in which historians have worked as they tried to analyze the vast body of material that confronted them and the workings of social scientists interested in studying migration. In the same decade that American historians turned to the newly published *Harvard Encyclopedia of American Ethnic Groups* with its total absence of interest in the theory extant in the social scientific world, the *International Encyclopedia of Social Sciences* tackled migration and provided for historians a place to go to get a synopsis of current theory, should they want it. One of the authors of the social science reference work's entry on immigration (Peterson 1968) began his piece by defining migration, and characterized prevailing ideas about the timing, modes, and typologies of migration as well as how to measure migrations. Brinley Thomas (1968), author of a highly respected book of the 1950s (Thomas 1954), focused on the economic aspects of migration. Importantly, in distinction to the historical enterprise, Thomas and Peterson made only the rarest references to particular groups and in their extensive bibliographies; these two essays contained no entries on particular groups or places that either sent or received migrants.

Historians and social scientists obviously approach problems differently. The latter depend fundamentally on models. The former generally cringe at the idea. This disinterest may be endemic to the orientation of most historians, shaped by their focus on the particular; by their training, which requires them to stay close to empirical sources; and a basic orientation to *time* as a key factor. Historians search for the transformative moment that can divide the past into an analytic "before" and "after." Two Dutch historians who have worked on labor migrations within Europe used particularly dramatic imagery to describe how far apart historians and other social scientists stand when it comes to migration theory: "The migration landscape is full of canyons and fast running rivers. The deepest canyon separates social scientists from historians" (Lucassen and Lucassen 1997:10). The Lucassens rightly understood this distinction as existing between historians and social scientists.

But American historians, those who study the history of the United States, emerge as particularly theoretically challenged when compared to Europeanists. Beginning in 1960, when Frank Thistlethwaite delivered a paper at the 11th International Congress of Historical Sciences in Stockholm in which he challenged the prevailing idea that migrations ought to be thought of as unilinear, straight-shot movements from one place to another and as indicators of crisis, European historians have attempted, more than their American counterparts, to turn to theory to explain their data. Following Thistlethwaite's lead are such European historians as Charles Tilly (1978), Leslie Page Moch (1992), James H. Jackson and Leslie Page Moch (1989), New Zealander J. D. Gould (1989), William McNeil and Ruth Adams (1978), and Nancy Green (1991).

Two exceptions of scholars of American immigration need to be mentioned. Dirk Hoerder, a German scholar, has studied German immigration to the United States. His work grew out of European historical traditions with their greater sensitivity to theory, at the same time that it has taken its place among the literature of United States history. Hoerder (1993, 1994) has demonstrated a strong interest in creating analytic categories around his data, framed by an interest in social scientific theories of migration. As such, Hoerder functions as a liminal figure, a Europeanist and an Americanist, and an Americanist who is a European.

Walter Nugent, however, in his 1992 analysis of migrations in the Atlantic world, *Crossings*, stands in a class by himself. Nugent, a relative latecomer to immigration history, had made a distinguished career for himself as a scholar of populism and late-nineteenth-century American political history. In *Crossings* he jumped off from Frank Thistlethwaite's call to cast aside the conventional categories of "emigrant" and "immigrant" and focused instead on the interconnected processes of migration. He particularly wanted to use the data on migrations to interrogate prevailing social science theories about modernization and its impact on demography. Throughout the book he challenged notions of ethnic and national particularism, group distinctions, and the premise that functioned as the reigning assumption that underlay much of American immigration history. From a theoretical stance, however, Nugent had a greater interest in modernization theory than in migration theory, and he addressed the latter lightly, and only as it informed his project of dismantling the former.

With the exception of Walter Nugent's book, the literature that makes up the field of American immigration history, then, stands out as nontheoretical when compared to European scholarship as well as when compared to the social sciences. How can one measure the disinterest of American immigration historians in the enterprise of theory? What standards might be invoked to prove that the goals of historians of immigration history in America and the goals of migration theorists have heretofore remained quite separate? Negative evidence, an absence of theory in the work of a particular cadre of historians would go to some length to show the disinterest, or conversely, the presence of theory would indicate that theoretical concerns inform the field.

One method for arriving at either of these, or the balance between them might be to scan an array of books and articles produced in the field and examine issues such as: What other works did the authors cite? Which of those works fall into the category of theory? When and how often have authors incorporated theoretical models into their writings? Since our concern here is migration theory, as opposed to theories of ethnic group formation, ethnic identity, or cultural hybridization, we can also ask how much emphasis books in the field of immigration history give to the phenomenon of migration itself. Obviously, for an essay of this length it would be impossible to survey all of the books and articles in the field, or even to sample them systematically. Rather a few stellar works will suffice. The Immigration History Society (which I discuss later in more elaborate detail) has offered the Theodore Saloutos Book Award every year since 1983. Intended to honor the best book published in a given year dealing with some aspect of the history of immigration, a few winners of the prize might be reasonable to examine for American historians' embrace of, or disregard for, theory.

George Sanchez's *Becoming Mexican American* garnered the Immigration History Society's highest accolade in 1994. This study of Mexican immigrants to Los Angeles in the period from 1900 until the end of World War II focused on "the related questions of cultural adaptation and ethnic identity." He noted in his introduction that his study revolved around a particular "cultural adaptation," which occurred, "without substantial economic mobility." In those same prefatory remarks he commented on the state of the field. He, like others of his cohort, felt called upon to interrogate previously fixed categories, among them, the notion that the place which immigrants left could be understood as definite and finite. Rather, that entity called "Mexico" (or any other "back there") should be thought of as contested, fluid, and in the process of renegotiation. Sanchez further made the point that "'Mexico,' maybe even more . . . than other nations, was a national community that had to be 'imagined' to exist, particularly given its racial and regional diversity" (Sanchez 1993:9–14).

Becoming Mexican American squarely confronted the immigration issue in the context of what has in American historical studies come to be called "borderland studies."[3] In the borderland, an amorphous zone of multiple populations spanning "fictive" borders, people came and went, constantly in the process of juggling identities and places of residence. Sanchez's Mexican immigrants to Los Angeles come and go. Even though they bade "farewell homeland," and went "across the dividing line," they remained engaged in the world of their premigration homes. When the policies of the U.S. government, or the vagaries of the American economy, as well as the needs of kin back home, intervened, they went back for some duration of time, and as such constantly engaged themselves with the question, "Where is home?"

Law Harsh as Tigers won the Soloutos Prize for 1995. Its author, Lucy Salyer, would no doubt *not* define herself as an immigration historian. Indeed, in the introduction to her book she exposed herself as a composite social and legal historian. Studying the ways in which Chinese immigrants to the United States struggled in, and against, the administrative agencies and federal courts to counteract the harsh restrictions imposed upon their immigration, Salyer confessed that she had stumbled upon immigration as a scholarly issue. She noted:

> I could not have predicted a decade ago that my research interests would lead me into immigration history. My primary aim was to explore the roots of the American administrative state in the Progressive Era. . . . I planned to analyze Federal judicial response to expansion of administrative power [in the Northern District of California]. But as I studied the court docket books, I was struck by the number of cases brought by Chinese litigants. (Salyer 1995:xiii)

Meticulous and complicated, *Law Harsh as Tigers* challenged some fundamental assumptions in American immigration history. It dispelled the notion of the "passive" Chinese immigrants, depicted primarily as sojourners, who temporarily settled in America and made no cultural investment in learning the American system. Rather, her subjects as individuals and particularly through their Triad (or tongs) societies, ably mastered the judicial process for their own advantage and mounted sophisticated legal campaigns to mitigate discrimination. Likewise, Salyer demonstrated the willingness of the courts to hear their voices. The harsh law had loopholes, and one judge after another found in favor of the plaintiffs, who had more rights than commonly assumed.

Unlike Sanchez, Salyer had little interest in immigration per se, despite the accolades she won from among the ranks of immigration historians. Little in the book explained *who* those Chinese plaintiffs were, where they came from, why they chose to come to America, and why they waged such vigorous court battles to stay in a place they knew did not want them. Of the immigration process, which Sanchez explored in its legal and administrative complexity, Salyer offered little. Many of the Chinese immigrants fell into the "illegal" category. The California Chinese almost all came from one province, Kwangtung (Canton), and they lived in tightly drawn communities based around their surname or family societies. By implication Salyer built an argument around the idea of exceptionalism. The Chinese *were* exceptional immigrants. No other group of foreign nationals was the subject of such specific discriminatory legislation. Their need to learn how to manipulate the system grew out of their unique place in the American legal system.

The 1996 Saloutos Prize winner would have seemed the most likely to link the world of American immigration history to that of migration theory. Ewa Morawska won the award for her study, *Insecure Prosperity: Small-Town Jews in Industrial America, 1890–1914.* That expectation would have been based on two indicators about Morawska. First, a trained sociologist, Morawska revealed in an appendix, "(Self-)Reflection of a Fieldworker," that the most lasting impact upon her life as a scholar came from her doctoral work in Poland with Florian Znaniecki.[4] Znaniecki, she noted, taught her that "social life can and should be studied by rigorous scientific methods and explained by empirically testable theories." Likewise, she expressed an intellectual debt to Robert Merton, who called for social science based upon a "continuous dialogue between theory and data" (Morawska 1996:256).

Second, Morawska has been a major player in various efforts to bring about a marriage between history and social science. Fittingly, she lived in both worlds, nudging historians to think theoretically and sociologists to consider the implications of time- and group-specific circumstances. In a 1990 article, for example, she wrote of the yawning gap between the two:

> Although they ran parallel for considerable stretches, these two intellectual movements are not sufficiently aware of each other. Students in one discipline "discover" what has been acknowledged and treated in each other's research for quite some time. Not infrequently . . . I hear comments like that of an ethnic historian reacting to the latest "vogue" in immigration research. . . . "But we have known that for a decade!" And an immigration sociologist had a similar response to some new volume put out by ethnic historians: "Well, don't they ever read what we write?" (Morawska 1990:188)

Insecure Prosperity is a remarkable book. It compares the immigrant Jews of a small, culturally parochial Pennsylvania steel town in their skeletal community, with their sisters and brothers in the infinitely more complex big cities like Pittsburgh and New York. It compares the Jews of Johnstown with Johnstown's other "others," the Slavic industrial laborers, whom Morawaska (1985) had analyzed in her earlier book, *For Bread with Butter.* Within the Jewish enclave of Johnstown she compared the earlier German Jewish residents with her subjects, the newcomers from Eastern Europe, just as she juxtaposed the experiences of children with those of their parents, and probed issues of change over time, by positing generational comparisons.

Insecure Prosperity did operate around a theoretical framework, or as Morawska (1996:xvii–iii) put it, around a theoretical double "concentric circle." She explored the world of the Jews of Johnstown, compared around these many facets, through theories of "structuration," that is, the interplay of "human action" and "social environment." She unpacked the ways that Jews learned to "maneuver in their situation in the pursuit of the desired goals," employing ideas of Anthony Giddens (1976). Morawska's other theoretical circle focused on the theory of ethnicization, "a process of blending from inside the ethnic group of the old (country of origin) sociocultural patterns with the new—traditions and lifestyles of the dominant (host) society" (1996:xviii). Here, she admitted to being influenced by the well-established sociological model of the dichotomy between *Gemeinschaft* and *Gesellschaft.*

The theories that Morawska ignored, and the material that got short shrift, happened to be those involving the migration process. Surprisingly for the author of the words from *Immigration Reconsidered* (1990) about the almost hermetically sealed worlds occupied by immigration historians and immigration sociologists, little of the "stuff" of immigration made its way into the book. Her Jews lived on the edge of survival in Eastern Europe as part of the first chapter of the book. At the end of that chapter, in about four pages, they made their way to Johnstown. By the second chapter they were already recycling old economic relations with their Slavic neighbors and calling upon traditional commercial skills from back home and keeping alive a consciousness that life can always get worse. The migration process and theories that might be employed to explain it got lost.

Each one of these scholars could have either drawn from the available theoretical literature on migration or could have formulated their own models.[5] Sanchez, for example, would have been well equipped to look back to Ravenstein or Everett Lee, who specifically addressed issues of distance between the point of origin and the point of destination. Mexicans, like French Canadians, Jamaicans, and migrants from the Caribbean, differed from the Chinese immigrants Salyer studied or the Jews Morawska analyzed in that "back home" lay so close at hand. While Sanchez surely explored the back-and-forth phenomenon of the Mexicans in Los Angeles, he did not connect that possibility to either the experiences of others who migrated short distances or to the theoretical literature on precisely that subject. He could have turned to Zolberg, whose theories about the impact of state policies indeed directly touched upon the lives of the subjects of *Becoming Mexican American.* Likewise, Morawska could have drawn upon theoretical literature about the size of the immigrant population—her east European Jews in Johnstown—in light of Lee or Peterson. In Morawska's analysis of the fabric of Jewish communal life in Johnstown, size counted for much. Lee and Peterson also used size in their typologies, yet their theories of migration based on size did not show up at all in Morawska's work. Finally, Salyer studied a group of people so eager to live in America that, despite the blatant racism that cast them as inferiors and put them outside of the orbit of citizenship, they continued to come and fought the system so that they could stay. Inherent in much of migration theory is the issue of motivation: Why do some people at certain moments in the history of their particular homes choose to leave to resettle in certain particular, sought-after destinations? Again, Ravenstein, Lee, Peterson, and even more contemporary theorists like Zolberg presented much theoretical modeling Salyer could have employed—and possibly rejected—had she been interested in writing a book about immigration.

These three authors of Saloutos Prize-winning books share much in common with each other. They wrote outstanding books. Each challenged some long-held assumptions about an individual immigrant group, in particular American settings. All three also rushed through the migration experience (or, in the case of Salyer, avoided it completely) in order to get to the heart of their project: the negotiation within the group, and between the group and the larger society, over the nature of identity and community. That being the shared vision, all three authors had no need to glean from the theoretical literature about immigration.[6]

Bringing this discussion into the early twenty-first century confirms the lack of real interest in theory among historians of immigration and demonstrates their continued interest in the specifics of particular dramas of the past. Pleas for theory and theoretical thinking, such as called for by Roger Daniels, pervaded the world of academia in the 1990s. The ten years following the publication of his book might easily be thought of in retrospect as the "decade of theory," an era in which academics from many disciplines bandied that word about and passionately argued for it as a way of getting at social, political, and cultural experiences.

Did that decade inaugurate a new way of conceptualizing problems in the history of immigration as practiced by scholars in the United States? If employing, as a barometer of interest on the part of immigration historians in theory the same measure as used above (the books honored by the Immigration and Ethnic History Society with the Saloutos Prize), but this time looking at those honored in the opening years of the new century, we can see that the discipline remained firmly ensconced in its deep concern with the particulars, with its focus on ethnic group behavior in America, and on the continued lack of interest in model building or model testing.

The field surely changed. These award-winning works, Erika Lee's *At America's Gates: Chinese Immigration during the Exclusion Era* (2003),

Mae N. Ngai's, *Impossible Subjects: Illegal Aliens and the Making of Modern America* (2004), and Eiichiro Azuma's *Between Two Empires: Race, History, and Transnationalism in Japanese America* (2005) demonstrated the broadening of the geographic focus of immigration history scholarship and the emergence, particularly of Asia, as the continent of concern for research. These books, more than earlier ones, made the politics of the state a crucial aspect of the history. But when it comes to the matter of migration, they did not push the theoretical envelope any further than those who came before them.

Lee and Azuma focused on single groups, and both told dramatic stories that chronicled the ways in which immigrants negotiated in an American system that demonized them. Both works dealt with the process of community building and on the ways in which the stigmatized immigrants made their way around and through the legal and cultural obstacles with which they had to live. Keeping well within the established paradigm of the field, neither paid much attention to the process of migration or the demographic or economic character of the immigrants. Lee's book began with the Chinese in America, and put at the center of the narrative the actions of American immigration officials, popular American attitudes toward the Chinese, and the multiple ways in which the Chinese in the United States sought to subvert, manipulate, and live with the realities of a gated society. *At America's Gates* offered much about the Chinese *in* America but nearly nothing about migration itself, other than the fact that they wanted the gates to be more open so their family members could join them and they could move easily in and out and back in again. So, too, Azuma's study of the impact of Japan's emergence as a world power on the Japanese in the United States provided little to anyone interested in immigration per se. Azuma offered fewer than twenty pages on the Japanese as immigrants, while the rest of the book situated the Japanese in the many decades after immigration as people living "between two empires," between the two contestants for power around the Pacific rim—the United States (their new home) and Japan (the place they had left). Neither Lee nor Azuma in their single group studies offered new theories about migration, or challenged or validated any extant ones.

So, too, Mae Ngai's book analyzed the United States and not the immigration phenomenon itself. She took as her subject American policy and the ways in which the creation of the category of "illegal immigrant" transformed the nature of the state and its immigration policies, which consumed the attention of lawmakers and the public. Her book ended with chapters on the Filipinos, Mexicans, Chinese, and Japanese in the United States, with sections on legislation and the courts, making it clear that the focus of this fine work was the state's actions rather than immigration as a phenomenon to be studied and theorized about. Ngai's award-winning book, like those of Lee and Azuma, provided historians with new ways of thinking about the interplay between state policy and ethnic community formation, between the law and the lived life of immigrants who found themselves for some length of time in the United States, and finally on the emergence of an American-born generation that faced a variety of opportunities and challenges, in part shaped by the anomalous legal status of the group. None of these books however, the accolades of the Immigration and Ethnic History Society not withstanding, furthered a larger conceptual discussion about immigration as a global phenomenon that has shaped human history.

Why would the scholarly group awarding the prize, the Immigration and Ethnic History Society (IEHS), routinely choose to honor books that (their excellence notwithstanding) focus so little on the actual set of experiences surrounding immigration? The society was founded in 1965 as the Immigration History Society, and in its founding clearly announced its commitment to the study of migration. It described itself as dedicated to "promot[ing] the study of the history of immigration to the United States and Canada from all parts of the world, including studies of the background of emigration in the countries of origin."[7] The next phrase in the IHS's statement of purpose may provide the clue to the conundrum concerning its decisions and about the field as a whole: it went on to include among its goals and foci, "to promote the study of ethnic groups in the United States, including regional groups in the United States, Native-Americans, and forced immigrants."

American historians of immigration, more than their European peers or their colleagues in the social sciences, have actually been interested in ethnicity rather than migration. For those who define themselves as immigration historians, who belong to the Immigration History Society, who sit on its prize committee (myself included), and who have written the books that make up the body of scholarship in the field, the narrative of how various groups settled, shaped their communities, and constructed their identities has taken precedence over the analysis of the migration process. That process appeared in the books and articles as a necessary prelude to that which really informed their imagination, the negotiation between identities, the formation of ethnicity, and the molding of community life in the United States.[8]

This phenomenon itself can be unpacked and used to explain the general indifference of American immigration historians to migration theory and the manipulation of models. First, the interest in ethnicity often, although definitely not always, has grown out of the reality that most of the scholars writing have chosen their own group as the subject of their research. They benefit from insider knowledge, and that intimate understanding of the inner life of the group often closes off the imperative to place it into a model or type. While they have written in a broad humanistic framework, and not remotely as narrow chauvinists (an earlier brand of writing labeled *filiopietistic* has long been the model of what should be avoided at all costs), most immigration/ethnic historians in America have been convinced that the specific details of their group, or the group they have decided to study, are worthy of study in and of themselves. Concern with the particular has *far* outweighed the interest in creating typologies, categories, or models.

As such, the field has been characterized by a group-by-group approach. Books and articles, dissertations, and the very organization of courses on the undergraduate and graduate level are based on the categories Irish, Chinese, Norwegian, Jewish, Haitian, Italian, Polish, Mexican, and the like. Over time the number of groups standing under the umbrella of American immigration scholarship has grown, but the basic mode of analysis has not. In each case, groups of scholars working on particular groups have emphasized in one way or another that their group's story truly stands out as different, notable, and particularly worthy of being told.

Because of this, few scholars have set out to write comparative histories, which would seem to be fundamental to a scholarly format for both the incorporation of existing theories and the creation of new ones.[9] So long as immigration historians set out to study the Italians of Buffalo, the Chinese of New York, or the Czechs of Chicago by themselves, theories of migration serve no real purpose. The experience of each group stands for itself and in and of itself ought to be studied. If, by contrast, historians would try to compare these three groups, then the fundamental structures of their migrations arrayed side by side and analyzed in a comparative framework would call for theory to explain differences or similarities. This comparative approach calls for models, whereas the group approach cannot employ them.

But American scholars of immigration history have refrained from comparative history for both practical and cultural reasons. In the first category, the scholar wanting to compare Italian, Chinese, and Czech immigrants, for example, would need linguistic competence in three radically different languages. Without the ability to read the sources, to deal with primary documents in their own context, the analysis would be derivative and of dubious value. On another level, most ethnic historians believe that the group they are studying deserves to be studied in its own name, and that comparative studies often create invidious distinctions that have no place in scholarly discourse.

The avoidance of theory in the field of American immigration history can also be set against the backdrop of an ironic intellectual legacy on the matter of grand overarching theory. The first truly big and notable book in the field of immigration history, Oscar Handlin's Pulitzer Prize-winning *The Uprooted* (1951) projected a theory of sorts. This book, which might be said to have launched the scholarly enterprise of the history of immigration to the United States, claimed to describe the experiences of all immigrants to America and purported that all those millions had been drawn from the ranks of the peasants, all had been violently uprooted from their traditional homes, all had found themselves unprepared for life in industrial America, and all found themselves subjected to a deeply disruptive and anomic experience in a new place, which they would never consider to be their homes. Handlin's theory, while it might not have been called that, set the field in motion. For decades beyond the book's publication, scholars sought to chip away at it, finding fault with its universalizing of all immigrants to America into one archetypical uprooted individual and its lack of empirical evidence for any of its assertions, and showing that immigrants had in fact engaged in rational planning as they weighed and measured the advantages versus the liabilities of migration, and that they found multiple and creative strategies to create the kinds of communities they wanted once settled in America. Slovaks in Pittsburgh, Norwegians in Wisconsin, Italians in Buffalo, and Mexicans in Los Angeles had calculated the benefits of immigration before departure, had moved along family and community chains, and in their new homes picked and chose among a set of cultural options. Indeed, historians in the six decades since Handlin have taken on his theory to prove, in their individual and particularistic studies, that immigrants rather than having been uprooted ought in fact to be seen as being embodied in the title of John Bodnar's book, *The Transplanted* (1985). By building their intellectual enterprise against *a* theory and against *the* theory that created the field, immigration and ethnic historians have instead embraced a way of thinking that claims that every historical negotiation, the experience of every group, must be told in its own context and in terms of its specificities of time and place.

History itself, as a discipline has, by and large, not been a hospitable locus for theory. Historians have been trained to think about time and place as the key variables by which to explain behavior. While historians have long been concerned with the same kinds of issues struggled with by anthropologists, economists, sociologists, and political scientists—questions of how human beings have organized their lives and why they have done so in particular ways—historians work on the assumption that without knowing the particulars of where and when phenomena took place, no answers are possible. Historians fundamentally say, both directly and indirectly as reflected in the structure of the field, that context is everything and contexts differ from place to place and change over time. As such, models cannot deal with the variations that the passage of time and the specifics of place mark upon peoples' behaviors. Historians operate close to the sources, and those sources have been grounded in particular moments in time, anchored to particular spots on the globe, and embodied in the experiences of particular people even as they moved from one of those settings to other new ones.

Furthermore, history, as a field that straddles the social sciences and the humanities, considers the narrative format the basic way of presenting its findings. While historians have, since the middle of the 1960s and the rise of quantitative history, inspired by sociology, begun to embrace some of the modes of other disciplines, it remains a field committed to telling stories. Even the most notable products of the cliometric moment of the 1970s still presented to readers tales of particular people in particular places, Puritans in Dedham, steelworkers in Pittsburgh, slaves in their plantation communities, and very specific groups of immigrants that would become "ethnics" creating their enclaves in America.

American historians have one more powerful legacy that prevents them from embracing theory. However much they resist and write against it, they still operate within the idea of American exceptionalism. More so than their European counterparts, who seem much more comfortable seizing upon theory and juxtaposing the experiences of groups in widely divergent times and places, American historians remain loyally wedded to an American focus. Even when works invoke the importance of comparative thinking, they rarely do so in fact and do not do so in order to advance the building of theory. Not surprisingly, and with few exceptions,[10] scholars of American immigration devote one chapter at most to "back home," a few pages (or perhaps a short single chapter) to the physical process of migration, and then devote the rest of their books to the American narrative, which is indeed what they wanted to study.

They have almost completely ignored the fact that immigrants, leaving the same towns and regions in the places of origin, dispersed themselves all over the world. Their analytic lenses have been trained on America and that has occluded the possibility of seeing migration in a broad global context, a prerequisite for thinking theoretically. As Donna Gabaccia (1997:177) noted in one of the few articles to depart from this practice, "Historians rightly approach global studies with trepidation. . . . Our discipline requires us to respect culture, context, and chronology." Again, American historians do so more than scholars based in other countries.

Therefore, the nature of history as a field, the particular perspective of American history, and the inner dynamics of American immigration history as a field have militated against a conjoining of the study of immigration to the United States and migration theory. The two have gone their separate ways. While they both may be the poorer for it, there is no reason to predict that in the immediate future they will find common ground.

NOTES

1. In the bibliographic essay to *From the Other Side: Women, Gender and Immigrant Life in the U.S., 1820–1990*, Donna Gabaccia (1994:176) directed "Students interested in theories of migration," to "begin with E. G. Ravenstein." She then offered three examples of "more recent work" concerned with theory. Unlike Daniels, Gabaccia did not organize her book around the "group" framework. But she, too, despite references studded through the book about theory and theoretical questions, opted for themes in which group experiences would carry the narrative.

2. For an excellent compendium of representative articles dealing with migration theory, see Cohen (1996).

3. See Anzaldúa (1987).

4. Znaniecki himself played a pivotal role in American immigration scholarship. He coauthored with W. I. Thomas a monumental five-volume study of Polish immigrants in Chicago, published between 1918 and 1920 (Thomas and Znaniecki 1984).

5. This group-by-group approach to immigration history in the United States is reflected in the full list of Saloutos Book Award winners, and not just the three analyzed here. Of those winners, the only ones to deviate from the group approach were Bailyn (1985), Fuchs (1990), Kraut (1993), and Jon Gjerde (1996). The rest since 1983 have been studies of a particular group in America. See Butler (1982), Wyman (1993), Miller (1984), Mormino and Pozzetta (1986), Ostergren (1987), Fischer (1988), Helweg and Helweg (1990), Hall (1991) and Gjerde (1996).

6. This same kind of group-oriented, empirically based scholarship also describes projects that have won the Immigration History Society's George E. Pozzetta Dissertation Research Award: for 1996, Russell Kazal, "Becoming Old Stock: Religion and the Waning of German-American Identity in Philadelphia, 1900–1930"; for 1997, Nancy C. Carnevale, "Living in Translation: Language and Italian Immigrants in the U.S., 1900–1968"; and for 1998, Richard Suk-joo Kim, "The Dialectics of Nationalism and Ethnicity: Korean Immigration to the United States and Transnational Politics, 1882–1945." Likewise, the winners of the Qualey Prize for the Outstanding Article to appear in the *Journal of American Ethnic History* prove the lack of interest in theory and the group approach. See Barry Chiswick, "The Labor Market Status of Hispanic Men," 7 (fall 1987); Victor A. Walsh, "'Drowning the Shamrock': Drink, Teetotalism, and the Irish Catholics of Gilded-Age Pittsburgh," 10 (fall 1990–winter 1991); K. Scott Wong, "Lian Qichao and the Chinese of America: A Re-evaluation of his Selected Memoir of Travels in the New World," 11 (summer 1992); Bettye Collier-Thomas and James Turner, "Race, Class and Color: The African American Discourse on Identity," 14 (fall 1994); Cheryl Greenberg, "Black and Jewish Responses to Japanese Internment," 14 (winter 1995).

7. The statement of purpose of the Immigration History Society appears on the inside of the cover of the society's journal, *Journal of American Ethnic History*.

8. In 1998 the Immigration History Society voted to change its name to the Immigration and Ethnic Society.

9. Perlmann (1988) and Kessner (1977) are two examples, but the body of scholarship like this is rare.

10. See, for example, Gjerde (1984).

REFERENCES

Anzaldúa, Gloria. 1987. *Borderlands/La Frontera: The New Mestiza.* San Francisco: Spinster/Aunt Lute.

Archdeacon, Thomas. 1983. *Becoming America: An Ethnic History.* New York: Free Press.

Azuma, Eiichiro. 2005. *Between Two Empires: Race, History, and Transnationalism in Japanese America.* New York: Oxford University Press.

Bailyn, Bernard. 1985. *Voyagers to the West: A Passage in the Peopling of America on the Eve of the Revolution.* New York: Alfred A. Knopf.

Bodnar, John. 1985. *The Transplanted: A History of Immigrants in Urban America.* Bloomington: Indiana University Press.

Butler, Jon. 1982. *The Huguenots in America: A Refugee People in New World Society.* Cambridge: Harvard University Press.

Cohen, Robin. 1996. *Theories of Migration.* Cheltenham, U.K.: Edward Elgar.

Daniels, Roger. 1990. *Coming to America: A History of Immigration and Ethnicity in American Life.* New York: HarperCollins.

Fischer, David Hackett. 1988. *Albion's Seed: Four British Folkways in America.* New York: Oxford University Press.

Fuchs, Lawrence H. 1990. *The American Kaleidoscope: Race, Ethnicity and the Civic Culture.* Hanover, NH: University Press of New England.

Gabaccia, Donna. 1994. *From the Other Side: Women, Gender and Immigrant Life in the U.S., 1820–1990.* Bloomington: Indiana University Press.

———. 1997. "The 'Yellow Peril' and the 'Chinese of Europe': Global Perspectives on Race and Labor, 1815–1930," in Jan Lucassen and Leo Lucassen, eds., *Migration, Migration History, History*, pp. 177–96. Bern: Peter Lang.

Giddens, Anthony. 1976. *New Rules of Sociological Method: A Positive Critique of Interpretive Sociology.* London: Hutchinson.

Gjerde, Jon. 1984. *From Peasants to Farmers: The Migration from Balestrand, Norway to the Upper Midwest.* New York: Cambridge University Press.

———. 1996. *The Minds of the West: Ethnocultural Evolution in the Rural Middle West, 1830–1917.* Chapel Hill: University of North Carolina Press.

Gould, J. D. 1989. "European Inter-Continental Emigration, 1815–1914: Patterns and Causes," *Journal of European Economic History* 8 (3): 593–679.

Green, Nancy. 1991. "L'immigration en France et aux États-Unis, Historiographie comparée," *Vingtième Siècle* 20 (January–March): 67–82.

Hall, Gwendolyn Midlo. 1991. *Africans in Colonial Louisiana: The Development of Afro-Creole Culture in the Eighteenth Century.* Baton Rouge: Louisiana State University Press.

Handlin, Oscar. 1951. *The Uprooted.* Boston: Little Brown.

Hansen, Marcus Lee. 1938. *The Problem of the Third Generation Immigrant.* Rock Island, Ill.: Augustana Historical Society.

———. 1940. *The Immigrant in American History*, Arthur M. Schlesinger, ed. Cambridge, MA: Harvard University Press.

Helweg, Arthur M., and Usha M. Helweg. 1990. *An Immigrant Success Story: East Indians in America.* Philadelphia: University of Pennsylvania Press.

Hoerder, Dirk. 1993. *People on the Move: Migration, Acculturation, and Ethnic Interaction in Europe and North America.* Washington, D.C.: German Historical Institute.

———. 1994. "Changing Paradigms in Migration History from 'To America,' to World-Wide Systems," *Canadian Review of American Studies* 24 (2): 105–26.

Jackson, James H., and Leslie Page Moch. 1989. "Migration and the Social History of Modern Europe," *Historical Methods* 22 (1): 27–36.

Jerome, Harry. 1926. *Migration and Business Cycles.* New York: National Bureau of Economic Research.

Jones, Maldwyn Allen. 1992 [1960]. *American Immigration.* Chicago: University of Chicago Press.

Kessner, Thomas. 1977. *Beyond the Golden Door: Italian and Jewish Immigrant Mobility in New York City, 1880–1915.* New York: Columbia University Press.

Kraut, Alan M. 1982. *The Huddled Masses: The Immigrant in American Society, 1880–1921.* Arlington Heights, IL: Harlan Davidson.

———. 1993. *Silent Travelers: Germs, Genes, and the "Immigrant Menace."* New York: Basic Books.

Lee, Erika. 2003. *At America's Gates.* Chapel Hill: University of North Carolina Press.

Lee, Everett S. 1966. "A Theory of Migration," *Demography* 3 (1): 47–57.

Lucassen, Jan, and Leo Lucassen. 1997. "Migration, Migration History, History: Old Paradigms and New Perspectives," in Jan Lucassen and Leo Lucassen, eds., *Migration, Migration History, History*, pp. 9–38. Bern: Peter Lang.

McNeil, William, and Ruth Adams, eds. 1978. *Human Migrations: Patterns and Policies.* Bloomington: Indiana University Press.

Miller, Kerby A. 1984. *Emigrants and Exiles and Their Irish Exodus to North America.* New York: Oxford University Press.

Moch, Leslie Page. 1992. *Moving Europeans: Migration in Western Europe since 1650.* Bloomington: Indiana University Press.

Morawska, Ewa. 1985. *For Bread with Butter: Life-Worlds of East Central Europeans in Johnstown, Pennsylvania, 1890–1940.* Cambridge: Cambridge University Press.

———. 1990. "The Sociology and Historiography of Immigration," in Virginia Yans-McLaughlin, ed., *Immigration Reconsidered: History, Sociology and Politics*, pp. 187–240. New York: Oxford University Press.

———. 1996. *Insecure Prosperity: Small-Town Jews in Industrial America, 1890–1940.* Princeton, NJ: Princeton University Press.

Mormino, Gary R., and George Pozzetta. 1986. *The Immigrant World of Ybor City: Italians and Their Latin Neighbors in Tampa, 1885–1985.* Urbana: University of Illinois Press.

Ngai, Mae M. *Impossible Subjects: Illegal Aliens and the Making of Modern America.* Princeton, NJ: Princeton University Press.

Nugent, Walter. 1992. *Crossings: The Great Transatlantic Migrations, 1870–1914.* Bloomington: Indiana University Press.

Ostergren, Robert C. 1987. *A Community Transplanted: The Trans-Atlantic Experience of a Swedish Immigrant Settlement in the Upper Midwest, 1835–1915.* Madison: University of Wisconsin Press.

Perlmann, Joel. 1988. *Ethnic Differences: Schooling and Social Structure among the Irish, Italians, Jews, and Blacks in an American City, 1880–1935.* New York: Cambridge University Press.

Peterson, William. 1958. "A General Typology of Migration," *American Sociological Review* 23 (3): 256–66.

———. 1968. "Migration: Social Aspects," in David Sills, ed., *International Encyclopedia of Social Sciences*, vol. 10, pp. 286–92. New York: MacMillan.

Ravenstein, E. G. 1885. "The Laws of Migration," *Journal of the Royal Statistical Society* 48: 167–227.

———. 1889. "The Laws of Migration," *Journal of the Royal Statistical Society* 52: 214–301.

Salyer, Lucy. 1995. *Law Harsh as Tigers: Chinese Immigrants and the Shaping of Modern Immigration Law.* Chapel Hill: University of North Carolina Press.

Sanchez, George J. 1993. *Becoming Mexican American: Ethnicity, Culture and Identity in Chicano Los Angeles, 1900–1945.* New York: Oxford University Press.

Thernstrom, Stephan, and Ann Orlov. 1980. *Harvard Encyclopedia of American Ethnic Groups.* Cambridge, MA: Harvard University Press.

Thistlethwaite, Frank. 1960. "Migration from Europe Overseas in the Nineteenth and Twentieth Centuries," XIème Congrés International des Sciences Historique, Stockholm 1960, *Rapports, V: Historie Contemporaine*, pp. 32–60. Gothenberg: Almquist and Wiksell.

Thomas, Brinley. 1954. *Migration and Economic Growth: A Study of Great Britain and the Atlantic Economy.* Cambridge: Cambridge University Press.

_____. 1968. "Migration: Economic Aspects," in David Sills, ed., *International Encyclopedia of Social Sciences*, vol. 10, pp. 292–300. New York: MacMillan.

Thomas, William I., and Florian Znaniecki. 1984. *The Polish Peasant in Europe and America*, edited and abridged by Eli Zaretsky. Urbana: University of Illinois Press.

Tilly, Charles. 1978. "Migrations in Modern European History," in William McNeill and Ruth Adams, eds., *Human Migrations: Patterns and Policies*, pp. 48–68. Bloomington: Indiana University Press.

Ward, David. 1980. "Immigration: Settlement Patterns and Spatial Distributions," in Stephan Thernstrom and Ann Orlov, eds., *Harvard Encyclopedia of American Ethnic Groups*, pp. 496–508. Cambridge, MA: Harvard University Press.

Wyman, Mark, 1993. *Round-Trip to America: The Immigrants Return to Europe, 1880–1930*. Ithaca, NY: Cornell University Press.

Zolberg, Aristide R. 1989. "The Next Waves: Migration Theory for a Changing World," *International Migration Review* 23 (3): 403–30.

CHAPTER 2

Demographic Analyses of International Migration
Michael S. Teitelbaum

Demography is a distinct discipline that in many settings has been closely linked to economics, other social sciences, and some parts of biology and statistics. It traces its theoretical origins back to the ancient world, and its quantitative roots go back to the seventeenth century at least. In its modern form the focus of demography has been upon human populations in terms of their size, composition, and change, with three fundamental demographic drivers: fertility, mortality, and migration (both internal and international).

From the point of view of some social scientists, demography is a discipline largely lacking in "theory." They see it instead as heavily quantitative and empirical, a "number-crunchers'" field with little in the way of coherent and overarching theoretical concepts (Weiner and Teitelbaum 2001:12–13).

This perception is not really an accurate one. Indeed, one important and prestigious domain of demography, known as *formal demography*, is actually very highly theoretical, and theoretical in ways that would be more familiar to physicists and chemists than to political scientists or sociologists. The core of formal demography is based on quite abstract mathematical models of human populations. Like much of theory in the natural sciences, these formal demographic models are highly simplified abstractions from the real world that allow for powerful mathematical solutions of phenomena that would otherwise defy mathematical treatment.

With respect to international migration, however, formal demographic models typically simplify reality in extreme ways, by assuming that *zero* migration occurs across the physical, political, ethnic, or other boundaries by which the particular population is defined—the assumption of a "closed population." Embrace of this simplification makes the mathematics of such models tractable in several respects: a new member of the defined population can enter only at a precisely specified age (age zero, to be exact), whereas in a real (i.e., nonclosed) population new members can enter at any age. Moreover, in a closed population any individual can exit only by death, a phenomenon that, unlike international migration, has its own statistical regularities and mathematical characteristics. Finally, in a closed population each individual can enter or exit the population only once, whereas in a nonclosed population the same individual can enter and depart many times.

Hence, a correct statement about theory in demography would be that one of the most important domains of demographic analysis, formal demography, is very highly theoretical—more so than nearly all of the social sciences. Yet the simplifying assumptions that are essential to such theoretical treatment make formal demography rather unhelpful in addressing populations in which the phenomenon of migration is a substantial reality.

The other major domain of demography, often termed social demography, seeks to better understand the factors that affect the primary demographic forces of fertility, mortality, and migration. As such, this part of demographic research necessarily draws upon both theoretical and empirical research in other disciplines including, for example, economics, sociology, anthropology, history, geography, political science, ecology, and so on. In pursuit of such understanding, most demographers have long been both eclectic and cautious in embracing overarching theoretical explanations of demographic trends. Eclectic in recognition that collective rates of human fertility, mortality, and migration are obviously affected by a wide range of forces that cannot be the province of a single discipline, cautious in acknowledgment that past efforts at grand theories by earlier students of demographic patterns did not live up to their authors' ambitious explanatory claims.

It also needs to be said that until quite recently at least, the study of international migration was something of a backwater among demographers of all types. Of the three primary forces of demographic change—fertility, mortality, and migration—demographers of the twentieth century focused primarily upon the first, secondarily on the second, and often peripherally on the third.

Eclectic theories are rarely elegant or simple, but elegance and simplicity are not everything. Indeed, as is implicit in the cross-disciplinary structure of the present volume, the theoretical eclecticism of demographers bespeaks not intellectual weakness, but rather forthright skepticism about the explanatory power of any single perspective on such matters. The reality can be simply stated: no discipline has produced a coherent and convincing theory of international migration. Hence, when demographers address the phenomenon they tend to call upon the theoretical insights drawn from many perspectives.

As will be seen shortly, it is also quite incorrect to claim, as some have, that there is a dearth of theoretical perspectives and writings on international migration. To the contrary, there is a wealth—some might say an excess—of such theoretical views, each with its energetic adherents and enthusiasts. Meanwhile many demographers tend to be cautious in taking any theoretical propositions about international migration too seriously. They do so not only because no theoretical perspectives have proved to be highly convincing, but also out of awareness that past demographic projections incorporating international migration have turned out to be poor predictors of the futures to which they were being addressed.

As noted above, demography other than formal demography is fundamentally an empirical and quantitative discipline. The quantitative and often long-term projections routinely produced by demographic offices at the United Nations and in numerous governments typically incorporate elements of theories as a basis for their quantitative assumptions regarding fertility, mortality, and migration. Hence the credibility of such theoretical inputs can be tested empirically by comparing subsequent demographic patterns against the assumptions incorporated in such projections. The results of such comparisons offer cautionary guidance regarding the explanatory power of many theoretical views.

THEORETICAL PERSPECTIVES IN DEMOGRAPHY[1]

Over the past century, much demographic research has focused on gaining understanding of fertility behavior. The first impetus for such a focus was the very low fertility rates experienced in Europe and North America during the 1930s, a source of widespread concern, and often alarm, among political elites. In countries such as France and the United Kingdom, such concerns led to financial support for serious demographic research, either via creation of formal governmental institutions (such as the 1946 establishment of l'Institut National d'Etudes Demographique [INED] in France), official governmental commissions (such as the Royal Commission on Population established in 1944 in the United Kingdom), or university-based population studies centers (the Princeton Office of Population Research was established in 1936). When fertility rates rose noticeably in the years and decades after World War II, such concerns waned.

During the 1950s concerns about too-low fertility were often replaced by new understanding that due to rapid declines in mortality accompanied by sustained high levels of fertility, rates of demographic increase were accelerating to unprecedentedly high levels in the decolonizing third world of Asia, Africa, and Latin America. Again, empirical and theoretical understanding of fertility trends was the primary focus, if for quite different reasons.

Theorizing about international migration among demographers often reflected such emphases. Some demographers who focused upon the effects of rapid demographic increase, especially in countries already facing resource constraints, anticipated that one of its effects would be to stimulate emigration toward countries offering better prospects. A number of theoretical speculations were advanced, embodying a range of different perspectives. High fertility rates in the context of declining rates of infant and child mortality would eventuate, with a delay of perhaps two decades, in rapid growth in the numbers of young adults, a category known from empirical experience to have the highest propensities for migration. Similarly, because young adult males are known to have higher propensities toward violence and crime, large youth cohorts concentrating in urban areas with high unemployment rates might produce political and social instabilities (for example, higher crime rates), which in turn might be expected to stimulate substantial outward movement of people. Rapid demographic increase in rural areas of developing countries could be expected to increase the volume of rural-to-urban migration, and available evidence suggested that urban residents were more likely than rural migrants to move internationally. Others suggested that rising agrarian population densities in rural areas approaching ecological limits might result in overgrazing and related environmental damage that would also mobilize increasing numbers to depart.

Demographers who focused upon low fertility rates also saw implications for increasing international migration. Low fertility rates, following a lag of approximately two decades, would result in declines in the rate of increase, or even in the size, of age cohorts newly entering the labor force. This would produce, other things being equal, rising demand by employers and governments for imported workers. Such demands would relate to both ends of the adult age continuum. First, assuming continuing growth in demand for workers, small entry-level cohorts would lead to rising wages, and in some limited cases to bottlenecks in labor markets that would limit overall expansion. Second, again other things being equal, low fertility would predictably result in increases in the proportion of those beyond retirement age, and hence in rising tax burdens on employers and more generally on the working-age population to support public pension systems, which in most industrialized countries are financed on a pay-as-you-earn (PAYE) basis. Under such hypothesized circumstances, increased numbers of immigrant workers would allow employers to avoid increased wage costs, and governments to increase the number of workers contributing to their financially unstable PAYE pension systems.

Yet demography-driven explanations, while illuminating, have not succeeded in addressing the rather messy realities and complexities inherent in the patterns of international migration. In reality, much international migration takes place between source and destination countries that both report high or low fertility rates, such as from Eastern to Western Europe. In some cases the actual flows are in a direction opposite to that suggested by simple demographic explanations, for example, in many cases in which destination countries' fertility rates are higher than those of source countries.

Hence while many theoretical propositions based on purely demographic patterns seem highly plausible, they often have not been borne out by reality.

Nondemographic Theoretical Perspectives—Economics

In recognition of these weaknesses, demographers have often turned to economic theories for understanding of migration patterns. There are many such theoretical schools, though none is widely seen as coherent and convincing.[2] These schools include:

Neoclassical macroeconomic: International arbitrage among labor markets characterized by wide differences in labor supply and demand. Migration flows are initiated by such differentials, and should terminate when these differentials are eliminated.

Neoclassical microeconomic: Decisions to migrate made by rational individuals seeking to maximize their utility, in full recognition of both benefits and costs. Benefits and costs determined by supply and demand differentials across national labor markets that produce differences in both employment prospects and earnings.

New economics of migration (social group and family theories): Decisions to migrate made by the social group or family unit rather than the individual, again rationally calculating whether the interests of the group would be served by its members migrating internationally. Migration is seen not only as raising collective income, but also as means of diversification or insurance to minimize the group's exposure to risk from local conditions and to increase access to credit.

Dual labor market (recruitment) theories: Pull factors predominate over push. Employers and governments in industrialized countries benefit by recruiting low-wage workers, who limit wage increases by providing a contingent labor force that can be expanded or contracted in response to varying demand.

World systems theories: Pull also dominates push, but markets are global rather than national. Multinational firms and neocolonialism succeed in permeating capitalist economic relations into peripheral noncapitalist societies, thereby stimulating international migration from the latter to the former.

Nondemographic Theoretical Perspectives—Social and Institutional

Disciplines other than economics have also contributed theoretical perspectives, including the following:

Social network theories: These focus on elements that perpetuate migration even if the initiating forces have waned or disappeared, and complement economic and demographic theories addressing initiation of international migratory movements. The social networks are transnational ties between migrants and their relatives and neighbors in the countries of origin, networks that reduce the risk and lower the cost of further migrations and thereby perpetuate them and even increase their volume.

Institutional theories: Here the focus is on social and business institutions that emerge to serve the needs of migrants. These institutions may be for-profit or nonprofit, and their activities may be legal, "twilight," or frankly illegal, including immigration lawyers, immigration "consultants," labor contractors, and people smugglers, for example.

One important source of difference that prevails in this tapestry of theoretical perspectives is the relative emphasis upon push factors related to circumstances in countries of origin, versus pull factors in countries of destination. Neoclassical perspectives, of both the micro and macro variety, address both. The new economics and world systems theoretical traditions tend to emphasize push factors, while the dual labor market perspective emphasizes pull. Meanwhile, the social network and institutional theories focus on the space between push and pull, that is, the intermediaries and other connections between origin and destination countries.

One very promising approach in recent years is based upon eclectic combinations of different theoretical perspectives that raise hypotheses about migrations of the past that can then be subjected to empirical testing. An influential effort of this kind concluded that demographic differentials, economic differentials, and network factors were all likely important factors underlying movement of more than 50 million persons out of Europe during the nineteenth and early twentieth centuries:

> Rates of natural increase at home and income gaps between home and overseas destinations were both important, while industrialization (independent of its influence on real wages) made a moderate contribution. Our results also support the arguments of those who stress the influence of "friends and relatives" among previous emigrants abroad. (Hatton and Williamson 1994:557)

THE POTENTIAL AND THE ACTUAL

Eclectic theoretical approaches offer real promise in understanding the factors that increase or lower the potentials for international migration, and also its persistence even after such potential has declined. What they cannot tell us, however, is whether such potential will actually result in substantial migratory movements. This is a distinction with an important difference, but one that is often blurred in interpretation. In many theoretical discussions of international migration, rising potential is in effect equated to rising reality. Compare the neoclassical macroeconomic conclusion of the World Bank's 2006 Global Economic Prospects ("It is likely that the number of people who wish to migrate from developing to high-income countries will rise over the next two decades" [World Bank 2006:28]), with that penned by a supporter of the social network view ("Current theoretical and empirical knowledge . . . suggests that, if anything, migratory flows will grow throughout the world," Massey 1999:318).

It is precisely here, at the boundary between the potential and the actual, that the role of the state in initiating, selecting, restraining, and ending international migration movements becomes critical. It is also here that social science theories of international migration have been weakest: in the words of one leading researcher, "it is remarkable that the role of states in shaping international migration has been largely ignored by immigration theorists" (Zolberg 2000:71)

For some who equate potential with actual, the state is simply too weak to affect international migratory flows significantly, driven as they are by overwhelmingly strong economic, demographic, and social forces. There is much in the way of evidence to indicate that this view is a mistaken one.

In many cases, actions by governments of origin countries promote the export of migrant labor. These actions may be formal policies or informal practices, and may be acknowledged explicitly or not. Many examples can be found, and in all world regions: in Asia (Philippines, Bangladesh, India, Vietnam, Turkey, Pakistan, Indonesia, South Korea), in the Middle East (Jordan, Yemen, Egypt), in Latin America and the Caribbean (Mexico, Dominican Republic, El Salvador, Guatemala, Nicaragua, Barbados), in Africa (Morocco, Tunisia), and there are many others as well.

It is also rather clear that actions and inactions by governments have led to large out-migrations as consequences of military actions, domestic violence, political and ethnic persecution, human rights abuse, economic stagnation, even mass starvation. Consider, for example, situations in Asia (Afghanistan, Myanmar, Turkey, North Korea), in the Middle East (Iraq, Kuwait, Turkey), in Latin America and the Caribbean (Nicaragua, Guatemala, El Salvador, Cuba, Haiti), in Africa (Rwanda, Burundi, Zaire, Mozambique, Sudan, Somalia), in Europe (Kosovo, Bosnia, Croatia, and indeed most of the European continent in the period before, during, and after World War II).

Policies and actions by governments also constrain inflow or outflow of international migrants, directly in the form of border and interior controls, and indirectly through use of diplomatic, economic, or military instruments. All governments insist on their right to control entry of nonnationals into their territories. Some (for example, members states of the European Union) have agreed to take joint actions of this kind along common external borders, and some provisions of international law also prohibit states from forcibly returning officially recognized refugees to their home countries (especially the United Nations Convention Relating to the Status of Refugees [1951] and its associated Protocol [1967]).

Of course simply asserting a state's right to control entry by nonnationals does not imply that such controls will be effectively exercised: many states are too weak to do so, and some (such as the United States for the past few decades) have been unable, for domestic political reasons, to pursue effective enforcement of laws and practices.

Almost all states exercise direct controls over entry at their land borders, airports, and seaports. These familiar instruments of state action include routine inspections of border crossers and other entrants by immigration inspectors, border police, or similar organizations. Some states also use regular or reserve military forces and coast guards for such a purpose.

Almost all states also exercise indirect controls that extend well beyond their own borders. These include the ubiquitous passports and visa requirements that were innovations of the large wave of international migration a century ago. More recently states have imposed sometimes-stringent sanctions that penalize carriers (e.g., airline and shipping firms) if they fail to assure that each passenger has the passport and visa required for entry. States also often cooperate in exchanging information about networks of smugglers and others who facilitate unauthorized migratory movements.

With respect to claims for asylum and refugee states, states have also taken measures to expedite asylum claims, to exclude "manifestly unfounded" claimants, to negotiate return agreements with origin countries' governments, and to create lists of "safe countries" to which asylum claimants may be returned without violating international agreements.

In short, actions by states are normal, even ubiquitous, in initiating, selecting, restraining, and ending international migration movements. Their effectiveness, of course, varies considerably from place to place and time to time, but it would be a serious mistake to ignore them in theoretical treatments of international migration. There can be little doubt that even among origin countries with large out-migrations of their nationals, such movements would have been far larger had there not been controls over entry in the countries of destination. As but one obvious case, the percent who have emigrated from Puerto Rico to the mainland United States is far higher than that from the neighboring Dominican Republic, even though the latter is considerably poorer and more unstable politically; it seems obvious that the primary reason is that Puerto Ricans are U.S. citizens by birth, and therefore face no restrictions on their migration to the mainland United States.

Empirically, there are only a handful of emigration countries from which more than 10 percent of the population has departed: the rather special circumstances of Cuba, Haiti, Afghanistan (until recently at least), and Rwanda offer some insight into the rareness of such experiences. Even countries such as Mexico, which are well known as large exporters of people, report that less than 10 percent of their native-born populations live abroad. Notwithstanding the very large, and apparently increasing, disparities in economic well-being among and within countries, the overwhelming majority of even desperately poor people seemingly do not migrate internationally. This fact may be due to lack of information or access to migration opportunities, or to reluctance to leave family and friends behind. Yet governmental actions are self-evidently also important factors.

SUMMARY AND CONCLUSIONS

Demography is a distinct and long-established discipline that is intrinsically linked to other disciplines such as economics, sociology, political science, and some parts of biology and statistics.

While some nondemographers seem to believe that demography is a field that is rather lacking in theory, this is a quite incorrect perception. In at least one important domain of demography—formal demography—there is a large body of mathematical and statistical theory; indeed formal demography is not only highly theoretical, it is theoretical in ways that might be more familiar to mathematicians and physicists than to social scientists. With respect to international migration, however, formal demography typically simplifies reality in extreme ways by simply assuming a "closed population," that is, zero migration.

The other primary domain of demography, social demography, seeks to better understand the factors that affect the primary demographic forces of fertility, mortality, and migration. Until quite recently, international migration did not receive much attention from social demographers; fertility was their primary focus, with mortality second and migration third. Theorizing about international migration among demographers often reflected such emphases. Demographic research writings on high fertility often suggested that rapid demographic increase in poor countries would increase the push factors underlying international migration from lower- to higher-income countries. Demographic writings on low fertility also pointed to the possible increase in pull factors that would result.

There is now a wealth of social demographic theories about international migration, but none of these has yet succeeded in explaining the realities and complexities of international migration patterns. For many demographers, the best way forward is an eclectic embrace of theoretical perspectives from demography, economics, and other social sciences.

There are at least seven such schools of migration theory, five from economics, the remainder from sociology and political science. These include neoclassical macroeconomic, neoclassical microeconomic, the so-called new economics of migration, dual labor market, world systems theories, social network theories, and institutional theories. It is fair to say that none of these has attracted a consensus that sees it as offering a coherent and convincing explanation of the international migration phenomenon.

Indeed, the most promising use of such perspectives has been in eclectic combinations, which together suggest hypotheses about past migration trends and patterns that can be subjected to empirical testing. Such eclectic condominia of theories promise to increase our understanding of factors that increase or lower the potentials for international migration, and the persistence of such migratory movements even after such potential has declined.

What they cannot tell us, however, is whether argued potential that favors international migration will actually result in substantial migratory movements. It is all too common to see interpretations that blur this critical distinction by, in effect, assuming that a rising potential favoring international migration will result in rising actual migratory flows.

The state plays a key role in affecting this complicated relationship between the potential and the actual. Indeed, states engage in essentially all stages of international migratory movements: they initiate, restrain, and end them, and while they are underway they select from among potential migrants. Yet in most cases social science theorists of international migration have paid insufficient attention to these roles played by states, in some cases because they see the state as ineffectual in affecting what they consider to be powerful global flows. Yet it is evident that many governments act effectively to promote the export of their own nationals, whether formally and explicitly or informally and implicitly. Actions and inactions by states also have self-evidently produced large-scale out-migrations resulting from violence, persecution, or economic failure.

In sum, nearly all states act to regulate inflow or outflow of international migrants, directly in the form of border and interior controls, and indirectly through use of diplomatic, economic, or military instruments. There is of course much variability in their effectiveness in doing so, but it is a serious theoretical and empirical mistake to ignore state actions in research on international migration.

NOTES

1. Some portions of this chapter draw upon previous work appearing in Michael S. Teitelbaum (2001), pp. 1–11.
2. Useful summaries appear in Massey et al. (1993), Sharon Stanton Russell (1995), and Neil Howe and Richard Jackson (2006), pp. 21–29.
3. For a discussion, see Zolberg (2000).

REFERENCES

Bongaarts, J., and R. A. Bulatao, eds. 2000. *Beyond Six Billion: Forecasting the World's Population*. Washington, D.C.: National Academy Press.
Castles, S., and M. J. Miller. 1993. *The Age of Migration: International Population Movements in the Modern World*. New York: Guilford Press.

Cornelius, Wayne A., Philip L. Martin, and James F. Hollifield, eds. 1994. *Controlling Immigration: A Global Perspective*. Stanford, CA: Stanford University Press.

Hatton, Timothy J., and Jeffrey G. Williamson. 1994. "What Drove the Mass Migrations from Europe?" *Population and Development Review* 20: 553–59.

Hatton, T. J., and J. G. Williamson. 1998. *The Age of Mass Migration: Causes and Economic Impact*. New York: Oxford University Press.

Howe, Neil, and Richard Jackson. 2006. "Long-Term Immigration Projection Methods: Current Practice and How to Improve It," Center for Strategic International Studies, CSIS, CRR WP 2006-3, manuscript released June 2006, pp. 21–29.

Massey, Douglas S., J. Arango, G. Hugo, A. Kouaouci, A. Pellegrino, and J. E. Taylor. 1993. "Theories of International Migration: A Review and Appraisal," *Population and Development Review* 19: 431–66.

Massey, Douglas S., J. Arango, G. Hugo, A. Kouaouci, A. Pellegrino, and J. E. Taylor. 1994. "International Migration Theory: The North American Case," *Population and Development Review* 20: 699–751.

Ravenstein, E. G. 1885. "The Laws of Migration." *Journal of the Statistical Society of London* 48(2): 167–235.

_____. 1889. "The Laws of Migration." *Journal of the Royal Statistical Society* 52(2): 241–305.

Russell, Sharon Stanton. 1995. "International Migration: Implications for the World Bank, Human Resources Development and Operations Policy." Working Paper No. 54. Washington, D.C.: World Bank.

Russell, Sharon Stanton, and Michael S. Teitelbaum. 1992. "International Migration and International Trade." World Bank Discussion Paper No. 160. Washington, D.C.: World Bank.

Salt, J. 2005. "Current Trends in International Migration in Europe." Strasbourg: Council of Europe. Available at http://www.geog.ucl.ac.uk/mru/docs/current_trends_2004.pdf.

Smith, James P., and Barry Edmonston, eds. 1997. *The New Americans: Economic, Demographic, and Fiscal Effects of Immigration*. Washington, D.C.: National Academy Press.

Teitelbaum, Michael S., "Right vs. Right: Immigration and Refugee Policy in the United States," *Foreign Affairs* 59 (1), (fall 1980): 21–59.

_____. 1992. "Advocacy, Ambivalence, Ambiguity: Immigration Policy and Prospects in the United States." *Proceedings of the American Philosophical Society* 136: 208–25.

_____. 1999. "International Migration as a Pivotal Issue," in Robert Chase, Emily Hill, and Paul Kennedy, eds, *The Pivotal States: A New Framework for U.S. Policy in the Developing World*, 270–289. New York: W.W. Norton.

_____. "The Role of the State in International Migration." *Brown Journal of World Affairs* VIII(2), (summer/fall 2001): 1–11.

United Nations Population Division. 2001. *Replacement Migration: Is It a Solution to Declining and Ageing Populations?* New York: United Nations.

Weil, Patrick. 1998. "The State Matters: Immigration Control in Developed Countries," preliminary unedited version prepared for Population Division, Department of Economic and Social Affairs, United Nations, ESA/P/WP/146: 18. New York: United Nations.

Weiner, Myron, and Michael S. Teitelbaum. 2001. *Political Demography, Demographic Engineering*. New York and Oxford: Berghahn Books.

World Bank. 2006. *Global Economic Prospects 2006: Economic Implications of Remittances and Migration*. Washington, D.C.: World Bank.

Zolberg, Aristide R. 2000. "Matters of State: Theorizing Immigration Policy," in Philip Kasinitz, Charles Hirschman, and Josh De Wind, eds., *The Handbook of International Migration: The American Experience*, pp. 71–93. New York: Russell Sage Foundation.

CHAPTER 3

Are Immigrants Favorably Self-Selected?

An Economic Analysis

Barry R. Chiswick

INTRODUCTION

The authors of several essays in this volume, including Hasia R. Diner, Susan Hardwick, and Barbara Schmitter Heisler (Chapers 1, 6, 4), express regret regarding the virtual absence of theory in the studies of migration in their respective fields, that is, history, geography, and sociology. The research in their fields is far too often group or time and place specific, with little use of theory to motivate the analysis or to generalize the findings. This criticism is seldom leveled at economics. Indeed, all too often historians, sociologists, and other social scientists complain that economics is much too focused on formalism, with too little interest in specific groups or time and place.[1]

Economics is about the real world in which we live. It is about the study of the choices or opportunities that people have. It is concerned with the allocation of scarce resources (and all resources are scarce), including time, among alternative uses. It is concerned with how individuals, families, business enterprises, and other institutions use these scarce resources for their benefit—whether conceptualized as maximizing utility for individuals, maximizing profits for business firms, or maximizing social welfare for society.

The basic methodology of economics is the scientific method, that is, to develop models based on maximizing behavior, to derive hypotheses from these models, to then test these hypotheses, and if the hypotheses are found to be inconsistent with the data, to revise the model. Hypotheses are maintained only to the extent that they are consistent with the data, that is, the real world. Two guiding principles are Okkam's Razor, that simple models are to be preferred to complex ones, and that theory by itself can tell what might be, but that empirical analysis is needed to know what is.

This chapter uses the methodology of economics to address questions raised by Haisia Diner: "Who moves? Why do some human beings get up and shift residence? Why do others stay put?" It focuses on the determinants of selectivity from the *supply side* of migration, that is, the differential incentive among individuals for migration based on their ability, skills, and motive for migration. Another determinant of the characteristics of migrants, particularly for international migrants, is the *demand side* as represented by the mechanism for allocating immigration visas, and the enforcement of immigration law. Recent research demonstrates how the criteria used to ration the limited number of immigration visas among the much larger number of potential visa applicants can substantially influence the quality of the actual immigration flow—their ability, schooling, skills, health, occupational status and earnings (see, for example, Beach, Green, and Worswick 2007; Chiswick, Lee, and Miller 2006; Chiswick and Miller 2006). A fuller discussion of the determinants and consequences of the demand side, the visa allocation process, is beyond the scope of this chapter.

It is often said that immigrants are different from the people that they leave behind in the origin and the people they join in the destination. They are sometimes described as more aggressive, risk taking, forward looking, and avaricious or entrepreneurial, and sometimes as healthier. Sometimes they are described as fleeing the poverty, repression, and claustrophobia of the place where they were born and raised, and sometimes as being attracted or pulled by the magnet of the wealth ("streets lined with gold"), opportunities, freedom, and anonymity of where they settle.

Economic migrants are those who move from one place of work and residence to another, either within a country or across international boundaries, primarily because of their own economic opportunities. These opportunities may be in the form of earnings, employment, training, or other economic benefits for themselves or their descendants. Their motivations are distinct from those of refugees and those who move because of the migration decisions of others. One of the standard propositions in the migration literature is that economic migrants tend to be favorably *self-selected* on the basis of skills, health, and other characteristics. That is, economic migrants are described as tending, on average, to be more able, ambitious, aggressive, entrepreneurial, healthier, or otherwise have more favorable traits than similar individuals who choose to remain in their place of origin. The favorable selectivity on the basis of labor market and other characteristics would be less intense among those for whom motives other than economic considerations are most important in their migration decision, such as *tied movers* (those who move because of other family members), refugees (those who move because of real or imagined fears concerning their safety and freedom), and *ideological migrants* (those who move voluntarily for political, religious, or other ideological reasons).

Whether migrants are favorably selected or not is important for understanding the economic, historic, demographic, and sociological consequences of migration for the sending (origin) and receiving (destination) regions, as well as for the migrants themselves. The more highly favorably selected are migrants, the more successful will be their adjustment in the destination and the more favorable their impact on the destination economy and society. Moreover, the more highly favorably selected are the migrants the greater, in general, will be the adverse effect of their departure on their origin. As a consequence, the extent of the favorable selectivity of migrants will affect the impact of migration, and as a result the immigration policies of the destination and emigration policies of the origin, as well as other policies that have indirect effects on the incentives to migrate.[2] Immigration history, and as a result, the histories of the origin and destination regions, are thereby influenced by the degree of selectivity of migrants.

This chapter first develops the human capital model for migration, which serves as the focal point for the discussion of immigrant selectivity ("The Human Capital Migration Model"). It then considers ("Alternative Models") alternative specifications of the migration model, or deviations from the simple human capital model, that are relevant for the issue of migrant selectivity. A review of some of the existing literature forms the basis for the discussion of the empirical testing of the model of migrant selectivity. The chapter closes with a summary and conclusion.

THE HUMAN CAPITAL MIGRATION MODEL

Consider a simple human capital model of investment as applied to migration (Becker 1964; Sjaastad 1962). Assume that wages in the origin and destination do not vary with the level of labor market experience. That is, for simplicity of exposition, it is assumed there is no on-the-job training and there are no postmigration human capital investments. Also assume that there is a very long (infinite) work life, and that all the costs of migration occur in the first period.[3] These migration costs include foregone earnings (C_f) and direct or out-of-pocket costs (C_d). The indirect or foregone earnings costs are the value of the time devoted to the migration process. The direct or out-of-pocket costs include the expenditure of money for goods and services that are purchased because of the migration. Migration costs are defined broadly to include not merely the airfare or bus ticket and the time in transit, but the full costs of relocating and adjusting, both consumption and labor market activities, from the origin to the destination.[4]

It is easy to show that given these assumptions, the rate of return from migration (r) can then be written (approximately) as:

$$r = \frac{W_b - W_a}{C_f + C_d} \tag{3.1}$$

where W_b represents earnings in the destination and W_a represents earnings in the origin. Migration occurs if the rate of return from the investment in migration (r) is greater than or equal to the *interest cost of funds* for investment in human capital (i). The interest cost of funds for an individual is the person's cost of borrowing or lending money from the capital market. The lower the interest costs of funds is the greater the person's wealth and access to the capital market.[5]

Assume first that there are two types of workers—low-ability and high-ability workers—and that these ability levels are known without cost to the workers and potential employers.[6] The more able may have more innate ability or merely more schooling. Ability may have many dimensions, including ambition, intelligence, learning speed, decision-making proficiency, entrepreneurial skills, aggressiveness, tenacity, health, and so forth.

Let r_l be the rate of return from migration to a low-ability person and let r_h be the rate of return to a high-ability person. If the low- and high-ability individuals have the same interest cost of funds, the person with the higher rate of return from migration will have the greater propensity to migrate. As a first step, assume that in the origin (a) and destination (b) wages are 100K percent higher for the more able than the less able, that is, the ratio of wages in the destination to wages in the origin is independent of level of ability. Then,

$$W_{b,h} = (1+k)W_{b,1}$$

$$\text{and} \tag{3.2}$$

$$W_{a,h} = (1+k)W_{a,1}$$

It is assumed that direct costs, which are the out-of-pocket costs associated with migration, do not vary with ability, $C_{d,h} = C_{d,1}$. For example, the airfare is the same regardless of the person's ability. Also assume that greater ability has no effect on efficiency in migration, but because it raises the value of time in the origin, it does raise the value of foregone earnings. Then $C_{f,h} = (1 + k)$ $C_{f,1}$, where C_f is the foregone earnings. The rate of return from migration for the high-ability person can be written as:

$$r_h = \frac{(1+k)W_{b,1} - (1+k)W_{a,1}}{(1+k)C_{f,1} + C_d} = \frac{W_{b,1} - W_{a,1}}{C_{f,1} + \dfrac{C_d}{(1+k)}} \tag{3.3}$$

Thus, the rate of return to the high-ability person (r_h) is greater than the rate of return to the low-ability person (r_l) as long as earnings increase with ability ($k > 0$) and there are positive out-of-pocket costs of migration ($C_d > 0$). If the rate of return (r) from the investment is greater for the high-ability person, and if the interest cost of funds (i) is the same, the high-ability person would have a greater economic incentive to migrate. This is what is meant by positive selectivity in migration. The smaller are the direct costs of migration (C_d) relative to the wage premium for higher levels of ability ($1 + k$), the smaller is

$$\frac{C_d}{(1+k)},$$

and hence the smaller is the differential in the rate of return to those of higher ability relative to those of lesser ability. If there were no out-of-pocket costs associated with migration (C_d equals zero), then $r_h = r_l$, and there would be no selectivity in migration on the basis of ability. Alternatively, suppose there was no labor market premium for a higher level of ability or a particular dimension of ability ($k = 0$). That is, this dimension of ability was not relevant in the labor market. For example, having a higher level of ability playing the board game Monopoly may have no effect on labor market earnings ($k = 0$). Then, $r_h = r_l$, and there is no selectivity in migration on the basis of this dimension of ability.

The preceding model assumed that greater ability enhances efficiency in the labor market in both the origin and destination. Now let us add another assumption: The more able are also more efficient in migration. Just as higher ability enhances productivity in the labor market, these same characteristics may enhance efficiency in investment in human capital. The same investment in migration may require fewer units of time and/or fewer units of out-of-pocket costs for the more able. This may arise if the more able are better decision makers. For example, they know how to find the cheapest airfares.

Since the opportunity cost of migration (C_f) is the product of time units (t) involved in migration multiplied by the value of time in the origin (W_a), opportunity costs can be written as $C_f = tW_a$. Efficiency can be expressed as the more able needing fewer time units to accomplish the same task ($t_h < t_l$). Then, $C_{f,l} = t_l W_{a,l}$ and $C_{f,h} = t_h W_{a,h} = t_h(1 + k) W_{a,l}$, where $t_h < t_l$. This implies relatively lower costs for the more able, and strengthens the argument that r_h is greater than r_l.

Note that even if there are no out-of-pocket costs ($C_d = 0$), if the more able are more efficient in using time, relative skill differentials that do not vary across regions generate favorable selectivity in migration. That is, if $C_d = 0$, and $t_h < t_l$, using equation (3.3), when $C_{f,l} = t_l W_{a,l}$ and $C_{f,h} = t_h (1 + k)W_{a,l}$, then it follows that $r_h > r_l$.

The more able may also be more efficient in utilizing out-of-pocket expenditures ($C_{d,h} < C_{d,l}$) incurred in migration, just as they are more efficient in other activities. If direct costs exist and they are smaller for the more able ($C_{d,h} < C_{d,l}$), the difference in the rate of return from migration is even greater than if there were no ability differences in using the out-of-pocket expenditures required for migration. If $C_{d,h} = (1+\lambda)C_{d,l}$ where λ is a direct cost efficiency parameter, and is negative ($\lambda < 0$), then

$$r_h = \frac{W_{b,1} - W_{a,1}}{C_{f,1} + \dfrac{C_{d,1}(1+\lambda)}{(1+k)}} \tag{3.4}$$

and r_h is larger relative to r_i the greater the efficiency in handling direct costs (the more negative is λ).

Thus, a human capital model that assumes relative skill differentials are the same in the origin and destination generates favorable selectivity of migration in the supply of migrants if there are out-of-pocket (direct) costs that are not proportional to wages. This favorable selectivity is more intense if those who are more able in the labor market are also more efficient (able) in the migration process, either in using their own time or in using out-of-pocket expenditures.

It is reasonable to assume, however, that migrants will differ in the combination of their own time (forgone earnings) and purchased inputs (direct costs) in the migration and readjustment process. The greater the value of forgone earnings (wages) and the greater a person's efficiency in using purchased inputs relative to their own time, the greater will be the relative use of purchased inputs over their own time. Thus, high-ability migrants may appear to spend more dollars on the migration process (out-of-pocket expenditures) and to use less time than those of lesser ability.[7]

The model can be extended to consider situations in which the relative wage differentials are not the same across countries. Assume that there are no direct costs of migration ($C_d = 0$), and that ability (human capital) does not affect efficiency in time use in migration ($t_h = t_l$). Then,

$$r_1 = \frac{W_{b,1} - W_{a,1}}{tW_{a,1}} = \frac{1}{t}\left(\frac{W_{b,1}}{W_{a,1}} - 1\right) \tag{3.5}$$

and

$$r_h = \frac{W_{b,h} - W_{a,h}}{tW_{a,h}} = \frac{1}{t}\left(\frac{W_{b,h}}{W_{a,h}} - 1\right) \tag{3.6}$$

Then the ratio of wages in the destination relative to the origin determines migration incentives. If the ratio of wages is the same, the rates of return are the same and there is no selectivity in migration on the basis of skill. If the ratio of wages across regions is greater for those of high ability, that is, W_b/W_a is greater for h than for l, those of high ability have a greater incentive to migrate. If, on the other hand, the ratio of wages across regions is greater for those of low ability, they would have a greater propensity to migrate, other things being the same.

To take an oversimplified example, suppose the wages of low-skilled workers in the United States and Sweden were the same, but highly skilled workers earned relatively more in the United States than in Sweden. Then $\frac{W_{b,1}}{W_{a,1}} = 1$ for the low skilled and $\frac{W_{b,h}}{W_{a,h}} > 1$ for the highly skilled, and highly skilled workers would move from Sweden to the United States. If, on the other hand, the wages of low-skilled workers in the United States were higher than those in Mexico $\left(\frac{W_{b,1}}{W_{a,1}} > 1 \right)$, but the wages of highly skilled workers were the same $\left(\frac{W_{b,h}}{W_{a,h}} = 1 \right)$, then the low skilled from Mexico would move to the United States. There would be favorable or positive selectivity among migrants to the United States from Sweden and unfavorable or adverse selectivity from Mexico.

Several implications follow from this human capital model regarding the favorable selectivity of economic migrants, that is, those basing their migration decision on the conventionally measured rate of return from migration. The larger the out-of-pocket costs of migration, the lower the propensity to migrate, the lower is the propensity for immigrants to return to their origin, and the greater is the propensity for favorable selectivity in migration. This propensity for favorable selectivity is intensified if those who are more efficient in the labor market are also more efficient in the migration and adjustment process. This effect occurs if migrants are more efficient in using their own time, in using purchased inputs, or in combining their time and purchased inputs. If those with more human capital, for example, those with more schooling and greater proficiency in destination language skills, are more efficient in obtaining and interpreting information and in making decisions (greater allocative efficiency), they would be more efficient in the migration process (Schultz 1975).

The favorable selectivity of migrants is even greater if the relative wage differential between the destination and origin (the ratio of wages in the destination to those in the origin) is greater for the high-ability workers. The favorable selectivity is less intense if the ratio of wages in the destination to those in the origin is smaller for those with high ability. Only if this latter effect is sufficiently large to offset the favorable selectivity effects of out-of-pocket costs and greater efficiency in the migration process will there be no selectivity in migration. In this framework, for there to be negative selectivity in migration even more compressed wage differentials across regions are required for those with high ability relative to those with low ability.

ALTERNATIVE MODELS

Several alternatives to the simple human capital model presented previously have appeared in the literature to address the issue, either directly or indirectly, of the favorable selectivity of migrants. These include models based on asymmetric information, temporary migration, the Roy model, and noneconomic determinants of migration.

Asymmetric Information

Katz and Stark (1984, 1987) present a model of asymmetric information. Suppose potential migrants know their true productivity and employers in the origin have, over time, learned the workers' true productivity. Employers in the destination, however, cannot differentiate between high-ability and low-ability migrants. Employers in the origin pay workers wages in accordance with the worker's true productivity since this is known to them, while those in the destination pay workers according to the expected (average) productivity of migrants. High-ability workers will experience a smaller wage differential and higher foregone earnings than low-ability workers, and they will therefore have a smaller incentive to migrate. If employers can never detect true ability differences among migrant workers, there would be adverse selection. The increase in low-ability migration relative to high-ability migration would drive down the expected wage of migrants in the destination, further discouraging high-ability migration.

Employers in the destination would, of course, have an incentive to develop tests or other techniques for distinguishing high-ability from low-ability workers. The lower the cost and the shorter the time interval for identifying ability, the lower the adverse selection effect from asymmetric information. Asymmetric information would appear to be most compelling for low-skilled jobs with a short duration (tenure on the job) that do not involve repeat occurrences. High-wage jobs would warrant investment in information about ability, if only through a trial investment/working period. This might take the form of hiring immigrant workers at low wages until true ability levels are revealed. High-ability workers would be willing to take these jobs as they know that their true ability will be revealed over time, while low-ability workers would avoid these jobs for the same reason. Employers would then be able to discern the ability level of workers for jobs that have a long tenure or that involve repeat occurrences.

Short-Term Migrants

The model developed previously assumed, for simplicity, that workers remained in the destination for a long period of time, and implicitly assumed that there is no location-specific human capital. Suppose, however, there is a short expected duration in the destination because of high expectations of voluntary return migration (guest worker or sojourner migration) or involuntary return migration (deportations of illegal aliens) (Chiswick 1980, 1986b). Then migrants who made investments in destination-specific human capital would experience a capital loss when they leave the destination, and their origin-specific human capital would have depreciated during their absence from the origin. Therefore, sojourner migrants or illegal aliens, who are concerned about apprehensions and deportations, would tend to avoid country-specific human capital investments and would tend to invest in internationally transferable human capital or very little human capital.

To the extent that there is an incompatibility between country-specific and internationally transferable human capital, which is increased by location-specific occupational licensing and certifications for professional and skilled jobs, temporary migrants would tend to have lower levels of both forms of human capital. This is intensified if country-specific human capital depreciates during absence from the country. This would result in lower skill levels among sojourner migrants and illegal aliens than among long-term (permanent) legal migrants. This would give the appearance of less positive self-selectivity among short-term migrants (guest workers, sojourners, and illegal aliens) compared to permanent legal migrants.

This is consistent with analyses of illegal aliens in the United States, which indicate they are disproportionately low-skilled workers, as measured by their level of educational attainment, English language proficiency, occupational status, and earnings. Illegal aliens appear to have lower earnings than workers with legal rights to work who otherwise have similar characteristics, presumably because of their limited job mobility, their shorter expected duration in the destination, and their lower level of unmeasured human capital (see, for example, Rivera-Batiz 1999; Kossoudji and Cobb-Clark 1998).

The Roy Model—Relative Skill Differentials

In a series of studies on selectivity in migration, Borjas (1987, 1991) presents the Roy model (Roy 1951) as an alternative to the human capital model.[8] It is implicitly assumed that all migration costs are a constant proportion of foregone earnings, that there are no fixed (out-of-pocket) costs, and that ability has no effect on efficiency in migration. As a result, migration incentives are a function of the ratio of wages in the destination to those in the origin (the Roy model), as shown above in equations (3.5) and (3.6). This application of the Roy model is actually a special case of the human capital model.

If the wages of highly skilled workers are similar across countries, a larger relative skill differential (wages of highly skilled to low-skilled workers) in the lower-income origin implies a smaller skill differential for more highly skilled workers, and hence a smaller incentive for them to migrate compared to lower-skilled workers. The reverse follows if there is a smaller relative skill differential in the origin. Borjas (1987:552) writes, "If the income distribution in the sending country is more unequal than that of the United States (and the correlation in earnings is positive and strong), emigrants will be chosen from the lower tail of the income distribution in the country of origin." This is not quite correct. As shown above, a larger skill differential in the origin than in the destination does not necessarily imply negative selectivity, but rather only less favorable (positive) selectivity.

In an empirical test of the Roy model considering migration to the United States, Borjas (1987) regresses initial immigrant earnings and the improvement in immigrant earnings, as well as the emigration rate from the origin, on a measure of relative income inequality in the origin. The measure of relative inequality Borjas used is the "[r]atio of household income of the top 10 percent of the households to the income of the bottom 20 percent of the households" (Borjas 1987:545). This actually does not test for the effect of household income inequality on positive or negative selectivity in international migration, but only for whether inequality in income in the origin is associated with a greater or lesser degree of selectivity, after controlling for other variables that reflect the effects of positive immigrant selectivity on earnings in the United States. Moreover, this measure of household income inequality may be poorly related to the relevant variable, relative skill differentials. Controlling for other variables, the coefficient on the inequality variable is not statistically significant in analyses of immigrant earnings in the United States, and in half of the specifications has a positive rather than the expected negative sign. Contrary to the conclusion, the test does not offer support for the hypothesis that immigrants from countries with greater skill differentials are drawn from the least able members of the origin labor force.[9]

In his reply to the Jasso and Rosenzweig (1990) critique of his paper, Borjas (1990:306) repeats, "If earnings between the United States and the source country are positively and strongly correlated, positive selection is observed whenever the United States has more income inequality than the source country and negative selection is observed otherwise." In his new empirical test Borjas (1990:307) uses as his measure of relative skill differentials a dummy variable for whether the origin country has an income distribution more unequal than the United States. The t-ratio of -1.8 is at the margin of statistical significance, although Borjas asserts confidently that his prediction is "confirmed by the results" (Borjas 1990:308). It is not clear why he changed the measure of inequality to a dichotomous variable or whether this measure of inequality in this and in the earlier study reflects skill differentials or other dimensions of household income inequality, such as the inequality in human capital and other assets, or differences in household (especially female) labor supply. Moreover, the marginal t-ratio for inequality is in contrast to the very high t-ratios for the effect on immigrant earnings in the United States of country of origin per capita income ($t = 6.4$) and the refugee variable, as measured by whether the origin is a communist country ($t = -3.6$).

Noneconomic Migrants

Conventionally defined economic variables are not the only determinants of migration. People also move for *noneconomic* reasons, including accompanying or joining family members (*tied mover*), for real or perceived threats to their freedom or safety because of their class, religion, race, or other characteristics (refugees), and as voluntary migrants for ideological (including religious) reasons.[10] The favorable selectivity for labor market success would be expected to be less intense among those for whom migration is based primarily on factors other than their own labor market success. Studies of tied movers and refugees in comparison to economic migrants indicate that the former have higher unemployment rates and lower earnings than statistically comparable economic migrants (Mincer 1978; Chiswick 1978, 1979, 1980, 1982). The earnings disadvantages of tied movers and refugees are greater initially and diminish with duration of residence, but generally do not disappear.

Empirical Studies of Selectivity: Migrants and Return Migrants

A variety of studies have been conducted to test directly for the favorable selectivity of migrants.[11] A series of studies on internal migration in the United States and Canada have found that migrants tend to have higher levels of schooling than nonmigrants who remain in the place of origin, and that the use of selectivity correction techniques indicates that they would have had higher earnings in the origin than nonmovers (see, for example, Islam and Choudhury 1990; Robinson and Tomes 1982; DaVanzo 1976; Vandercamp 1972; Gabriel and Schmitz 1995; Bailey 1993).

An analysis of the earnings of black internal migrants in the United States is instructive (Chiswick 1980; Long and Hansen 1977; Long and Heltman 1975; Masters 1972). Using data from the 1960 and 1970 U.S. Censuses it has been found that black male migrants from the South to states outside of the South display similar earnings patterns as immigrants. The census provides data on state of birth, state of residence 5 years before, and current state of residence. Adult black men born in the South, but who have lived outside of the South less than 5 years, earn significantly less that those born outside of the South, other things being the same. On the other hand, those born in the South who have lived outside the South 5 or more years earn significantly more than statistically similar black men who were born in and remained in the non-Southern states. These findings are consistent with favorable selectivity in migration, with a period of adjustment required in the new (non-South) labor market.

Nearly all of the studies of the selectivity of migrants focus on the level of earnings or schooling of migrants compared to nonmigrants in the origin or destination. Two exceptions are studies by Tidrick (1971) and Finifter (1976). Tidrick conducted a survey among Jamaican university students about their intention to emigrate and whether they would encourage others to emigrate. Using cross-tabulations she shows that both propensities were higher, the higher the social class of the student's family and the higher the student's level of ability. Finifter (1976) reports the findings from a series of Gallup Polls conducted in the United States from 1946 to 1971 that included a question on potential interest in emigrating among Americans. The propensity to express an interest in emigrating from the United States was greater among males, the currently unemployed, those "dissatisfied with the institutions of the American political system" (ideological emigrants), and those with a higher level of education, and declined with age (Finifter 1976:34–35). Both studies find a positive selectivity in the expressed interest in emigrating.

There is less research on the issue of the selectivity of the emigration of in-migrants, of which a special case is return migrants, that is, those who return to their origin. Migrants have a higher propensity for a subsequent move than do nonmigrants, other variables being the same. The former have already demonstrated a propensity to move, and have less human and social capital specific to the initial destination. Return migrants may have human and social capital specific to the origin that has not fully depreciated in their absence. Migrants may depart for a number of reasons, including new information about even better opportunities elsewhere, because ex post there is a realization that the destination did not live up to their expectations, or because economic or political circumstances in the origin or in the destination have changed. Moreover, they may depart because the initial move was intended to be temporary (sojourners), perhaps because they are target earners in the destination, or moving to an initial destination facilitates moving to the ultimate objective (destination) as in stepwise migration. These arguments and the statistical analyses suggest that on average migrants who subsequently emigrate will be somewhat less favorably selected than the original flow of economic migrants, but they appear to be more favorably selected than those who never moved.

DaVanzo (1976) finds that for internal migration in the United States the return migrants respond to many of the same economic incentives as did the original migrants. Long and Hansen's (1977) study of black return migrants to the South suggests that both the original and return migration were selective in favor of those with more schooling. Rogers (1982) cites data indicating a variety of motives for return migration, including an original intention that the initial migration is only temporary. In an analysis of short-term interprovincial return migrants in Canada, Vanderkamp (1972) suggests that they were the less successful migrants. In a study of internal migration in the United States using the National Longitudinal Survey of Youth, Bailey (1993) finds a larger positive effect of a college education on initial migration than on return migration. He interprets this as implying that those with higher levels of education not only have higher rates of migration, but also make fewer errors in their initial migration, suggesting greater efficiency in migration.

Using data from a longitudinal survey of immigrants, Beenstock (1996) studied the return migration of immigrants in Israel. Return migration was greatest among those from the high-income Western democracies who were less successful in adjusting to Israel, among those who migrated as young adults and who did not have children. Return migrants had a lower proficiency in Hebrew (a destination-specific skill) and higher unemployment, other things being the same, before they departed. Immigrants to Israel from high-income Western democracies, primarily ideological migrants, have a high opportunity cost of remaining in Israel.

On the other hand, two recent studies suggest an absence of selectivity in out-migration among immigrants. In another longitudinal study of immigrants in Israel, Beenstock, Chiswick, and Paltiel (2005) analyzed a matched sample of respondents from the 1983 and 1995 Censuses of Israel. Other variables being the same, the earnings in 1983 of those still living in Israel in 1995 were greater than those who died in the intervening 12 years, but did not differ from those known to have emigrated. This suggests no net selectivity in the emigration of immigrants. In a study using the Longitudinal Survey of Immigrants to Australia (LSIA), Chiswick and Miller (2006) find that there was no selectivity in the health status of immigrants who left Australia in the first 3.5 years after immigration.

The Earnings of Migrants and the Children of Immigrants

One of the persistent findings regarding immigrants to the United States is the improvement in their earnings with duration in this country, and that after a period of adjustment of about 15 years, male economic migrants earn about the same and subsequently earn more than adult men born in the United States of the same racial/ethnic origin, level of schooling, and other measure characteristics (see Chiswick 1979, 1980, 1986a).[12] Among refugees, on the other hand, initial earnings are lower than among economic migrants, but the rate of improvement is greater and the gap diminishes over time, although it does not disappear with duration of residence. Equally striking is that the native-born children of immigrants (second-generation Americans) tend to earn more than the native-born with native-born parents (third- and higher-generation Americans) (Chiswick 1977, 1980, 1986b). Other things the same, within racial and ethnic groups, this earnings advantage is about 5 to 10 percent, or the earnings equivalent of about one extra year of schooling.

These earnings advantages of immigrants and their native-born children occur in spite of the disadvantages of a foreign origin, including less country-specific knowledge or information and poorer proficiency in English, especially among the immigrant parents.[13] These findings for international and internal migrants are consistent with the hypothesis that economic migrants are favorably self-selected for ability or human capital investment, and that refugees are less intensely favorably selected. When the favorable selectivity of economic migrants just outweighs the disadvantages of a "foreign" origin (less-destination-specific human capital, discrimination, etc.), the earnings of immigrants equal those of the native born, and then surpass them. Some of this favorable self-selectivity is transmitted to the immigrant's native-born children, although presumably with a regression to the mean, that is, the effect is dampened across generations.

Thus, the native-born children of immigrants, the second generation, have advantages transmitted from their favorably selected parents (e.g., high ability and motivation), and unlike their parents, the advantages of growing up in the destination culture, language, school system, and economy. Compared to native-born children of native-born parents, the advantages derived from the favorable selectivity of their parents outweigh the disadvantages of their parents' foreign origins. Yet presumably due to a "regression to the mean," across generations there is a diminution of the favorable traits of the immigrant ancestors.

SUMMARY AND CONCLUSIONS

This chapter has explored the theoretical issues and the empirical literature regarding the selectivity of migrants. The analytical framework adopted is equally applicable to internal and international migrants. The analyses indicate a tendency toward the favorable self-selection (supply) of migrants for labor market success on the basis of a higher level of ability broadly defined. The favorable selectivity is more intense: the greater the out-of-pocket (direct) costs of migration, the greater the effect of ability on lowering the costs of migration, and the smaller the wage differences by skill in the lower income origin than in the higher income destination. Favorable selectivity for labor market success can be expected to be less intense for noneconomic migrants, such as refugees, tied movers, and ideological migrants, and for sojourners (short-term migrants) and illegal aliens.

The theoretical analysis in this chapter applies only to the supply of migrants. The determinants of the demand for migrants are also relevant for international migration as all nation–states have selection criteria for those they will admit. Among countries for whom entry restrictions are binding, the criteria for rationing immigration visas will influence the degree of favorable selectivity of those who actually immigrate. Selection criteria can ration visas on one or more characteristics that enhance labor market earnings, such as schooling level, professional qualifications, age, and destination language proficiency, among other criteria. Alternatively, criteria can be used that are seemingly independent of skill level, such as kinship ties, refugee status, and lotteries.

There will be a tendency for immigrants to be favorably selected under any given selection criteria. Among those who would supply themselves as immigrants, a skill-based system for rationing immigration visas will result in a higher-ability immigrant population than would rationing visas on the basis of other criteria (Chiswick and Miller 2006; Beach, Green, and Worswick, 2007). The overall favorable selectivity of immigrants, therefore, depends on the favorable selectivity of the supply of immigrants and the criteria used to ration admissions.

NOTES

1. I am reminded of the bumper sticker that read: "The real world is just a special case."
2. It has come to be widely accepted that sovereign states have the legal right to regulate who may enter their country, under what circumstances and conditions, and for how long. Some, however, contest this proposition and argue for unrestricted rights to immigrate. It has also come to be widely accepted that sovereign states do not have the right to prevent individuals, whether citizens or not, from freely emigrating. Thus, individuals are not considered "bound to the land" as they were under serfdom or as property of their country of residence.
3. Under reasonable discount rates, increases in earnings received far into the future, say starting in 20 years, have a small present value. The length of the effective life can be considered infinite if the decision maker takes into account the higher earnings their descendants would receive if raised in the destination rather than in the origin. The sharp fall off of migration, and other human capital investments, with age among adults has less to do with the finiteness of the working life than with the rise in the opportunity cost of time with human capital investment, including on-the-job training or labor market experience, location-specific investments, and the incentive to make the most productive human capital investments (for which the internal rate of return is greater than the discount rate) sooner rather than later.
4. An analysis of the adjustment process is beyond the scope of this paper. The adjustments relevant for the labor market include investments in schooling, on-the-job training, information, language, and friendship and social networks, among other factors. See, for example, Chiswick (1978), Chiswick and Miller (1992), and Khan (1997).
5. The interest cost of funds (or the discount rate) would be the person's borrowing rate if at the margin the person is a borrower, and is the lending rate if this is what the person does at the margin. The rate depends on the person's wealth and rate of time preference for consumption in the present relative to the future. Discount rates may therefore vary across individuals and by age for the same individual (see Hirshleifer 1958). For a model of the supply and demand for funds for investments in human capital, see Becker and Chiswick (1966).

6. Although for simplicity of exposition the discussion will be in terms of labor market earnings and ability, it can easily be extended to include efficiency in consumption. For the same nominal earnings, greater efficiency in consumption enhances real earnings.

7. A high-ability (high earnings) migrant from New York to California may fly, while a low-ability (low earnings) migrant is more likely to drive or take a bus or train. This constitutes a substitution away from a relatively more expensive means of migrating. Out-of-pocket costs are frequently measured by distance. See, for example, Schwartz (1973).

8. For a comment and reply on issues other than those raised here, see Jasso and Rosenzweig (1990) and Borjas (1990).

9. Cobb-Clark (1993), however, does find a marginally significant negative relationship between income inequality in the origin and the earnings of immigrants in some of her equations in her study of immigrant selectivity among women in the United States. The effect is more pronounced for women than for men, perhaps because the women are more likely to be tied movers. Since the inequality measure is household income inequality, it is unclear whether female labor supply effects in the origin and destination are determining this relationship.

10. For the classic study of tied movers and tied stayers, see Mincer (1978). It is sometimes difficult to distinguish between ideological migrants and refugees. Many of the earliest settlers in the United States came for a fuller expression of their religious beliefs, and not necessarily because of persecution, and hence would be ideological migrants. For a study of ideology and emigration from the United States in the post–World War II period, see Finifter (1976). Americans who went to the Soviet Union in the interwar period to build the new Soviet state were ideological migrants. North American Jewish immigrants in Israel would also be an example of ideological migrants (Beenstock 1996). While the latter earn more than other immigrants in Israel, overall and other variables the same, their real earnings are lower than they would have received in the United States (Chiswick 1998).

11. See, for example, DaVanzo (1983), DaVanzo and Morrison (1986), Herzog and Schlottmann (1983), Long and Hansen (1977), Shumway and Hall (1996), Vandercamp (1972), and Yezer and Thurston (1976).

12. Borjas (1985) argues that the appearance of a rise in earnings with duration of residence in cross-sectional data is due to a decline in the quality of more recent cohorts of immigrants. He does not deny the higher ability of earlier cohorts. Using a variety of methodologies, Chiswick (1980, 1986a), Duleep and Regets (1996, 1997a, 1997b), and La Londe and Topel (1992) show that Borjas (1985) misinterpreted the data, and that there is no evidence of a decline in the earnings of immigrants relative to natives over successive cohorts during the post–World War II period, other variables being the same. By focusing on immigrant earnings at arrival, Borjas (1985) confused the steepening of human capital earnings profiles for immigrants and natives (a higher return to various types of skill) due to a rise in the rate of return on human capital and a reduction in the transferability of the skills of immigrants due to a shift in source countries of origin (from Canada and Europe to Latin America and Asia) with a decline in immigrant quality (ability). For a similar earnings catch-up at the turn of the century, see Blau (1980). For an analysis of the catch-up in terms of employment and unemployment, see Chiswick and Hurst (1998). Lindstrom and Massey (1994) show that the emigration of the foreign born does not distort the assimilation of immigrants observed in the U.S. Census.

13. Among native-born men, those who speak a language other than or in addition to English at home, and who are disproportionately second-generation Americans, have lower earnings, other measured variables the same, than the native born who speak only English at home (Chiswick and Miller 1998). This may be due to their being more closely tied to their immigrant/ethnic enclave and labor market.

REFERENCES

Bailey, Adrian. 1993. "A Migration History, Migration Behavior and Selectivity," *Annals of Regional Science* 27: 315–26.

Beach, Charles, Alan Green, Christopher Worswick. 2007. "Impact of the Point System and Immigrant Policy Levers on Skill Characteristics of Canadian Immigrants," *Research in Labor Economics* 27 (forthcoming).

Becker, Gary S. 1964. *Human Capital.* New York: NBER.

Becker, Gary S. and Barry R. Chiswick. 1996. "Education and the Distribution of Earnings," *American Economic Review* 56 (Supplement): 358–69.

Beenstock, Michael. 1996. "Failure to Absorb: Remigration by Immigrants into Israel," *International Migration Review* 30: 950–78.

Beenstock, Michael, Barry R. Chiswick, and Ari Paltiel. 2005. "Endogenous Assimilation and Immigrant Adjustment in Longitudinal Data," IZA—Institute for the Study of Labor, Discussion Paper No. 1840, November 2005.

Blau, Francine D. 1980. "Immigration and Labor Earnings in Early-Twentieth-Century America," in Julian L. Simon and Julie DaVanzo, eds., *Research in Population Economics* 2: 21–41.

Borjas, George J. 1985. "Assimilation, Changes in Cohort Quality and the Earnings of Immigrants," *Journal of Labor Economics* 3: 463–89.

Borjas, George J. 1987. "Self-Selection and the Earnings of Immigrants," *American Economic Review* 77: 531–53.

Borjas, George J. 1990. "Self-Selection and the Earnings of Immigrants: Reply," *American Economic Review* 80: 305–08.

Borjas, Geroge J. 1991. "Immigration and Self-Selection," in John Abowd and Richard Freeman, eds., *Immigration, Trade and the Labor Market*, 29–76. Cambridge: NBER.

Chiswick, Barry R. 1977. "Sons of Immigrants: Are They at an Earnings Disadvantage?" *American Economic Review* 67: 376–80.

Chiswick, Barry R. 1978. "The Effect of Americanization on the Earnings of Foreign-Born Men," *Journal of Political Economy* 86: 897–922.

Chiswick, Barry R. 1979. "The Economic Progress of Immigrants: Some Apparently Universal Patterns," in William Fellner, ed., *Contemporary Economic Problems, 1979*, 357–99. Washington, D.C.: American Enterprise Institute.

Chiswick, Barry R. 1980. *An Analysis of the Economic Progress and Impact of Immigrants.* National Technical Information Service, No. PB80-200454. Report prepared for the Employment and Training Administration, U.S. Dept. of Labor.

Chiswick, Barry R. 1982. *The Employment of Immigrants in the United States.* Washington, D.C.: American Enterprise Institute.

Chiswick, Barry R. 1986a. "Is the New Immigration Less Skilled than the Old?" *Journal of Labor Economics* 4: 168–92.

Chiswick, Barry R. 1986b. "Human Capital and the Labor Market Adjustment of Immigrants: Testing Alternative Hypothesis," *Research in Human Capital and Development* 4: 1–26.

Chiswick, Barry R. 1998. "Hebrew Language Usage: Determinants and Effects on Earnings Among Immigrants in Israel," *Journal of Population Economics* 11: 253–71.

Chiswick, Barry R., and Michael Hurst. 1998. "The Labor Market Status of Immigrants: A Synthesis," in Hermann Kurthen et al., eds., *Immigration, Citizenship and the Welfare State in Germany and the United States: Immigrant Incorporation*, 73–94. Stamford, CT: JAI Press.

Chiswick, Barry R., and Paul W. Miller. 1992. "Language in the Immigrant Labor Market," in Barry R. Chiswick, ed., *Immigration, Language, and Ethnicity: Canada and the United States*, 229–96. Washington, D.C.: American Enterprise Institute.

Chiswick, Barry R., and Paul W. Miller. 1998. "The Economic Cost to Native-Born Americans of Limited English Language Proficiency," report prepared for the Center for Equal Opportunity, August.

Chiswick, Barry R., and Paul W. Miller. 2006. "Language Skills and Immigrant Adjustment: The Role of Immigration Policy," in Deborah Cobb-Clark and Siew-Ean Khoo, eds. *Public Policy and Immigrant Settlement*, 121–48. Cheltenham, U.K.: Edward Elgar.

Chiswick, Barry R., Yew Liang Lee, and Paul W. Miller. 2006. "Immigrant Selection Systems and Immigrant Health," IZA–Institute for the Study of Labor, Discussion Paper No. 2345.

Cobb-Clark, Deborah A. 1993. "Immigrant Selectivity and Wages: The Evidence for Women," *American Economic Review* 83: 986–93.

DaVanzo, Julie. 1976. "Difference between Return and Non-Return Migration: An Econometric Analysis," *International Migration Review* 10: 13–27.

DaVanzo, Julie. 1983. "Repeat Migration in the United States: Who Moves Back and Who Moves On?" *Review of Economics and Statistics* 65: 552–59.

DaVanzo, Julie, and P. Morrison. 1986. "The Prism of Migration: Dissimilarities between Return and Onward Movers," *Social Science Quarterly* 67: 113–26.

Duleep, Harriet O., and Mark C. Regets. 1996. "The Elusive Concept of Immigrant Quality: Evidence from 1970–1990," Discussion Paper PRIP-UI-41, Program for Research on Immigration Policy. Washington, D.C.: Urban Institute.

Duleep, Harriet O., and Mark C. Regets. 1997a. "Measuring Immigrant Wage Growth Using Matched CPS Files," *Demography* 34: 239–49.

Duleep, Harriet O., and Mark C. Regets. 1997b. "The Decline in Immigrant Entry Earnings: Less Transferable Skills or Lower Ability?" *Quarterly Review of Economics and Finance* 37 (Special Issue on Immigration): 89–208.

Finifter, Ada W. 1976. "American Emigration," *Society* 13: 30–36.

Gabriel, Paul E., and Susanne Schmitz. 1995 "Favorable Self-Selection and the Internal Migration of Young White Males in the United States," *Journal of Human Resources* 30: 460–71.

Herzog, Henry W., and Alan M. Schlottmann. 1983. "Migrant Information, Job Search and the Remigration Decision," *Southern Economic Journal* 50: 43–51.

Hirshleifer, Jack. 1958. "On the Theory of Optimal Investment Decisions," *Journal of Political Economy* 66: 329–52.

Islam, Muhammed N., and Saud A. Choudhury. 1990. "Self-Selection and Interprovincial Migration in Canada," *Regional Science and Urban Economics* 20: 459–72.

Jasso, Guillermina, and Mark R. Rosenzweig. 1990. "Self-Selection and the Earnings of Immigrants: Comment," *American Economic Review* 80: 298–304.

Katz, Eliakim, and Oded Stark. 1984. "Migration and Asymmetric Information: Comment," *American Economic Review* 74: 533–34.

Katz, Eliakim, and Oded Stark. 1987. "International Migration under Asymmetric Information," *Economic Journal* 97 (387): 718–26.

Khan, Aliya H. 1997. "Post-Migration Investments in Education by Immigrants in the United States," *Quarterly Review of Economics and Finance* 37 (Special Issue on Immigration): 285–313.

Kossoudji, Sherrie A., and Deborah A. Cobb-Clark. 1998. "Coming Out of the Shadows: Learning About Legal Status and Wages from the Legalized Population," Department of Economics and School of Social Work, University of Michigan, xerox.

LaLonde, Robert J., and Robert H. Topel. 1992. "The Assimilation of Immigrants in the U.S. Labor Market," in George J. Borjas and Richard B. Freeman, eds., *Immigration and the Work Force: Economic Consequences for the United States and Source Areas*, 67–92. Chicago: University of Chicago Press.

Lindstrom, David, and Douglas Massey. 1994. "Selective Emigration, Cohort Quality and Models of Immigrant Assimilation," *Social Science Research* 23: 325–49.

Long, Larry H. 1974. "Poverty Status and Receipt of Welfare among Migrants and Nonmigrants in Larger Cities," *American Sociological Review* 39 (1): 46–56.

Long, Larry H., and Kristin A. Hansen. 1977. "Selectivity of Black Return Migration to the South," *Rural Sociology* 42 (3): 317–31.

Long, Larry H., and Lynne R. Heltman. 1975. "Migration and Income Differences between Black and White Men in the North," *American Journal of Sociology* 80 (6): 1391–1409.

Masters, Stanley H. 1972. "Are Black Men from the South to the Northern Cities Worse Off than Blacks Already There?" *Journal of Human Resources* 7: 411–23.

Mincer, Jacob. 1978. "Family Migration Decisions," *Journal of Political Economy* 86: 749–73.

Rivera-Batiz, Francisco L. 1999. "Undocumented Workers in the Labor Market: An Analysis of the Earnings of Legal and Illegal Mexican Immigrants in the United States," *Journal of Population Economics* 12: 91–116.

Robinson, Chris, and Nigel Tomes. 1982. "Self-Selection and Interprovincial Migration in Canada," *Canadian Journal of Economics* 15: 474–502.

Rogers, Rosemarie. 1982. "Return Migration in Comparative Perspective," Fletcher School of Law and Diplomacy, Tufts University, mimeo.

Roy, A. D. 1951. "Some Thoughts in the Distribution of Earnings," *Oxford Economic Papers* 3: 135–46.

Schultz, Theodore W. 1975. "The Value of the Ability to Deal with Disequilibrium," *Journal of Economic Literature* 13: 827–46.

Schwartz, Aba. 1973. "Interpreting the Effect of Distance on Migration," *Journal of Political Economy* 81: 1153–69.

Schwartz, Aba. 1976. "Migration, Age, and Education," *Journal of Political Economy* 84: 701–20.

Shumway, J. Matthew, and Greg Hall. 1996. "Self Selection, Earnings and Chicano Migration: Differences between Return and Onward Migrants," *International Migration Review* 30: 979–94.

Sjaastad, Larry A. 1962. "The Costs and Returns of Human Migration," *Journal of Political Economy* 70 (Supplement): 80–93.

Tidrick, Kathryn. 1971. "Need for Achievement, Social Class and Intention to Emigrate in Jamaican Students," *Social and Economic Studies* 20: 52–60.

Vandercamp, John. 1972. "Return Migration: Its Significance and Behavior," *Western Economic Journal* 10: 400–65.

Yezer, Anthony M., and L. Thurston. 1976. "Migration Patterns and Income Change: Implications for the Human Capital Approach to Migration," *Southern Economic Journal* 42: 693–702.

CHAPTER 4

The Sociology of Immigration

From Assimilation to Segmented Assimilation, from the American Experience to the Global Arena

Barbara Schmitter Heisler

Theory and research in international migration have centered on two basic sets of questions: Why does migration occur, and how is it sustained over time? What happens to the migrants in the receiving societies and what are the economic, social, and political consequences of their presence? While sociologists have historically focused primarily on the second set of questions, in the context of the "age of migration" (Castles and Miller 1993) they have also paid increasing attention to the first set.

Compared with other social sciences, immigration research and theory have a long history in sociology. Harking back to the beginnings of the discipline in the United States, immigration and its consequences were among the central themes pursued by the Chicago School of Sociology.[1] The assimilation perspective, pioneered by its members in the 1920s and 1930s and refined by their students in the following three decades, remained the dominant sociological paradigm until the late 1960s. Postulating the assimilation of immigrants as the eventual outcome of "all the incidental collision, conflict and fusions of peoples and cultures" resulting from migration (Park 1928), the assimilation perspective could not explain the persistence of racial inequality and conflict, and the "resurgence" of ethnicity in the 1960s.[2]

Beginning in the 1980s, when immigration once again became a pressing issue in the United States as well as a new reality in many advanced industrial countries, in particular in Europe, research on immigration has virtually exploded. While the research has generated a variety of new conceptual frameworks and models, immigration remains primarily a "data-driven field" (Portes 1997),[3] and although immigration and its consequences have become international concerns, throughout the 1970s, 1980s, and early 1990s, much of the theoretically informed work by sociologists has focused primarily on the

United States, the sine qua non of immigration countries.[4] While the United States continues to be a main "laboratory" for research and theorizing, more recent efforts have also embraced more comparative and transnational perspectives.[5] The division of labor between sociologists who study American immigration and those engaging in more comparative work has narrowed since the publication of the first edition of this essay 6 years ago (Schmitter Heisler 2000), but has not disappeared.

The purpose of this article is to provide a broad overview of the development and current state of theorizing in sociology with particular attention to more recent attempts to talk across disciplines.[6] Given that the field is characterized by considerable diversity, I organize my discussion around the major theoretical frameworks. My discussion is informed by the conviction that a fuller understanding of the multifarious and increasingly important issues raised by international migration and its consequences calls for increased comparative and interdisciplinary analyses and vigorous debates across disciplines.

THE AMERICAN EXPERIENCE: ASSIMILATION AND ITS DISCONTENTS

Given the historical role of immigration (and the related topic of race and ethnic relations) in American society and American sociology, scholars of American immigration have been located at the center of the sociological enterprise. Although they have developed a variety of new theories and models in the past 25 years, the basic questions guiding their research have not differed substantially from those asked by the sociologists who first devoted systematic attention to immigration. As sociological theory of immigration and immigrant incorporation has moved away from the assimilation perspective of the 1970s, the models and concepts have changed since Robert Park first formulated his race relations cycle (Park and Burgess 1921)[7] and W. I. Thomas and Florian Znaniecki wrote their seminal work *The Polish Peasant in Europe and America* (1927). Yet while the concepts may have changed from assimilation to integration or incorporation, and to segmented assimilation, the primary focus of research and the main questions asked by students of the American experience have not changed considerably. While more recent work has been more deliberately policy oriented, the driving research questions continue to center on the processes of immigrant assimilation/integration (or lack of incorporation as the case may be). What has changed is the conceptualization of these processes.[8]

More specifically, we can identify several conceptual and analytic changes in the past 25 years: (1) a shift from focusing on immigrants and their efforts to adapt to their new environment toward focusing on the interaction between immigrants and the structure of American society; (2) a shift from an undifferentiated and amorphous conceptualization of American society to a conceptualization that takes into account existing economic (in particular, labor market), ethnic and class structures and inequalities; (3) a shift from focusing primarily on cultural variables to emphasizing structural/economic variables, in particular labor markets and social and human capital and social networks and organizations; and (4) a shift from a single dominant model identifying the steps or stages in the process of incorporation (that is, assimilation) to the coexistence of several models, projecting and explaining a variety of conditions and possible outcomes.

These changes represent both earlier responses to the apparent failure of the assimilation model to explain the "resurgence" of ethnicity and the persistence of racial inequality and conflict in the late 1960s and 1970s, and more recent responses to understanding the new challenges posed by the new, post–1965 immigration. Although the newer models vary considerably among themselves, they are decidedly more structural, focusing less on the immigrants themselves (e.g., on "the anguish of becoming American," Agueros et al. 1971), and more on the process of interaction between host society structures and institutions and the characteristics of newcomers. While the assimilation perspective portrayed American society as a rather amorphous, homogeneous entity—an absorbent sponge—the newer theories give shape to this amorphous entity, pointing out that the sponge is structured and that the structure itself is subject to change. Finally, the claims made by the newer models tend to be more modest and less sweeping.

While earlier research by Reeves Kennedy (1944, 1952), Herberg (1956), and in particular, Glazer and Moynihan (1963) raised questions concerning the Chicago School's optimistic contention that immigrants, and especially their children, would eventually move up the occupational hierarchy, lose their cultural distinctiveness, and blend into the dominant culture, sociologists did not seriously challenge this assimilationist trajectory until the late 1960s and early 1970s.[9] The challenges took place within the context of a more general paradigm shift from the dominant functionalist perspective to conflict theory and the empirical realities indicating the persistence of racial and ethnic inequality and conflict.[10]

Although the assimilation perspective is frequently attributed to Robert Park,[11] the "canonical" assimilation perspective (Kivisto 2004) was later fleshed out by his students Floyd Warner and Leo Srole (1945)[12] and in particular Milton Gordon (1964).[13] Gordon's influential multidimensional model represents the most developed and least overtly normative attempt to outline the assimilation perspective. Although Gordon identified several barriers to the assimilation process, the barriers identified were those associated with primary group affiliations. The larger institutional structures (e.g., labor markets, political and educational institutions) considered significant barriers by the postassimilation models were hardly considered important. In keeping with one of the perspective's greatest shortcomings, Gordon took for granted what immigrants were assimilating to, namely, middle-class American cultural patterns, which in turn remained largely unaffected, barring some minor changes at the margins, such as food or recreational patterns (Alba and Nee 1997).[14] In line with the then dominant functionalist perspective on social mobility, Gordon perceived eventual assimilation and upward mobility solely in terms of the movement of individuals. He did not consider the possibility that entire groups may be moving or that ethnic boundaries themselves may be shifting over time, that is, his focus remained on the immigrant adapting to American society, while the latter remained largely unchanged.[15]

While the idea of a single "melting pot" had been questioned by Reeve Kennedy (1944, 1952) and Herberg (1956) in the 1940s and 1950s and subjected to further empirical analysis in the early 1960s (Glazer and Moynihan 1963), and earlier critics of "straight-line assimilation" (Gans 1973, 1992) noted that rather than disappearing, ethnicity and ethnic identity may go through periods of recreation (Greeley 1977; Yancey, Erikson, and Juliani 1976), the post-assimilation literature on immigrant incorporation suggests the existence of multiple melting pots, processes, stages, and modes of incorporation/exclusion. Unlike the "triple melting pot" identified by Glazer and Moynihan in the 1960s, more recent conceptualizations of the process of incorporation are less defined in religious/cultural terms, but in terms of economic activity, industry, labor markets, and socioeconomic position. Instead of identifying the cultural/ethnic characteristics of groups as a hindrance to their smooth assimilation into the American mainstream, identifying ethnicity as a resource, these models highlight the continued importance of immigrant (ethnic) economic activity and organization in the context of an ever changing society. In the context of what Rogers Brubaker has called the "massive differentialist turn" (2001), the new literature identifies the ethnic community not as a station on the way to eventual assimilation, but as a distinct mode of immigrant incorporation.[16]

IMMIGRANT ECONOMIC ACTIVITY, ETHNIC ORGANIZATION, AND IMMIGRANT COMMUNITIES

Taking their initial cues from the experiences of Asian immigrants, Edna Bonacich's *middleman minority model* (Bonacich 1973; Bonacich and Modell 1980) and Ivan Light's (Light 1972; Light and Bonacich 1988) *ethnic entrepreneur/ethnic economy model* represent the pioneering work in this area. More recent models are the *ethnic niche model* and the *ethnic enclave economy model*. While the fact that some immigrant groups (in particular Chinese, Japanese, and Jews) were overrepresented in small business activity had long been established (Glazer and Moynihan 1963), middleman minority theory provided systematic answers to this fact. Eschewing a more obvious cultural explanation for the presence of middleman minorities, Bonacich identifies the systematic exclusion of some immigrants from mainstream employment as the main cause for their position as small-scale traders and merchants, drawing much needed attention to the persistent economic and racial inequalities in American society.[17] Positioned between mainstream producers and consumers, middleman minorities occupy a distinctive class position "that is of no special use to the ruling class." They act as go-betweens to more subordinate groups (Bonacich 1980:14–15), while they also have few intrinsic ties to the larger community (Zhou 2004).

Although Bonacich linked the success of middleman minorities to their social solidarity, as a Marxist she was more concerned with their distinctive class position. Using the middleman minority model in their 1980 study of Japanese Americans, Bonacich and Modell found that the social solidarity that had helped to establish success in the first generation was eroding in the second generation, suggesting that this mode of incorporation could be conceptualized as a stepping-stone toward eventual assimilation, albeit over several generations.

Less indebted to a Marxist perspective, Light's immigrant (ethnic) entrepreneur model (1979, 1984) more directly underlines the immigrant nature of ethnic enterprise, where the very experience of immigration produces a reactive solidarity (that did not exist before immigration), which in turn becomes a resource for members of the group. Ethnic resources (in contrast to class or bourgeois resources) are the sociocultural and demographic features of the group. These typically include an entrepreneurial heritage (values and attitudes), a multiplex of social networks, and the presence of underemployed and disadvantaged co-ethnic workers (Light and Rosenstein 1995).

Based on research in the Cuban community in Miami, Alejandro Portes and his colleagues and students (Portes and Bach 1985; Wilson and Portes 1980; Portes and Manning 1986; Portes and Rumbaut 1990) developed the ethnic enclave economy model in the late 1980s. In contrast to the previous two models, the ethnic enclave economy model is rooted in dual labor market theory (Edwards, Reich, and Gordon 1975; Piore 1979). Dual, or segmented, labor market theory postulates the existence of two separate and distinct labor markets—a primary labor market of good jobs, decent wages, and secure employment, and the secondary labor market of unskilled jobs, poor wages, and insecure employment. Lacking the necessary skills for primary labor market employment and facing discrimination, immigrants are typically confined to employment in the secondary labor market where they are exploited as cheap labor, and in stark contrast to the assimilation perspective, have few opportunities for social mobility. For some immigrant groups, however, the employment in the enclave economy offers some protection from the vicissitudes of the secondary labor market, and a variety of advantages in terms of language and training opportunities and an alternative path to social mobility (Portes and Bach 1985).[18] It is important to note that the enclave economy is more than an employment system; it is an alternative to the secondary labor market. As actions and activities are governed by "bounded solidarity" and "enforceable trust," the enclave economy includes a cultural component.[19]

The characteristics of the ethnic enclave economy differ from those associated with middleman minorities and immigrant entrepreneurs. Unlike the previous two models, an ethnic enclave economy is characterized by the spatial concentration of the immigrant group and by considerable within-group stratification that give rise to clustered networks of businesses owned by group members. While ethnic business initially serves the culturally defined needs of co-ethnics, it branches out to serve the larger community. The key elements of ethnic enclaves are spatial clustering (Portes and Jensen 1989) and sectoral specialization (e.g., Cubans in Miami were found to be in five manufacturing sectors). Thus, the ethnic enclave is economically diversified, including all types of business, trade, and industrial production. Success depends on the size of the ethnic group, their level of entrepreneurial skills, and their capital resources.

Building on Stanley Lieberson's (1980) pioneering historical study of ethnic succession in urban labor markets, Roger Waldinger and his associates developed the ethnic niche model (Waldinger 1996; Waldinger and Bozorghmer 1996). The model is based on the observation that the concentration of immigrant employment is not limited to trade (as is the case for middleman minorities), or trade and small business (as is the case for ethnic enterprise), or trade and a variety of businesses (as is the case for the ethnic enclave economy), but may also include employment in the public sector.

As is the case for the previous models, occupational ethnic niches develop from the interaction between the immigrant group and the larger society. The creation of niches does not require immigrant entrepreneurs. Ethnic niches emerge when a group is able to colonize a particular sector of employment in such a way that members have privileged access to new job openings, while restricting outsiders. Ethnic niches emerge in every market economy where jobs are ranked according to the principles of desirability and availability.[20] In the United States, these rankings have been strongly influenced by a racial and ethnic pecking order, creating a queue. Immigrants are typically located at the bottom of the queue. Changes in the economy affect the queue, creating vacancies for social mobility and new spaces for new immigrants. Waldinger's research in New York and Los Angeles seems to demonstrate the continued importance of niches as a dimension of immigrant employment (Waldinger 1994; Bailey and Waldinger 1991).

By focusing on ethnicity as a resource, and stressing the central importance of networks in shaping the process of immigrant incorporation, middleman minorities, immigrant niches and enclave economy models give testimony to the sociological proposition that economic behavior is shaped by the overarching social structures in which people are embedded. Yet, these models do not capture the full diversity of the immigrant experience in the United States today.

Building on his ongoing work, Portes' typology of "modes of incorporation" represents an important attempt to capture this diversity (1995, see also Portes and Rumbaut 1990). Moving from the macro to the mid level of the social structure, the typology identifies three levels of immigrant reception, the level of government policy, the level of civil society and public opinion, and the level of the immigrant community. At the first level he identifies three possible policy responses, labeled *receptive, indifferent,* and *hostile,* where the receptive category applies to refugees who receive resettlement assistance, legal immigrants fall into the indifferent category, and the hostile category applies to populations whose entry and residence meet active opposition. At the second level, each of the three government reception categories is divided into *prejudiced* and *nonprejudiced* reception, where prejudiced reception is accorded to nonwhite groups (the majority of recent immigrants), while white immigrants enjoy nonprejudiced reception. At the third level, Portes distinguishes between *strong* and *weak* ethnic communities. Strong communities are characterized by geographic concentrations and more diversified occupational structures, including significant numbers of entrepreneurs (i.e., ethnic enclaves), whereas weak ethnic communities are either small or predominantly composed of manual workers.

This model yields twelve different contexts of immigrant incorporation. The location of an immigrant group in a specific context shapes the limits and possibilities of individual and group action. Thus, for example, the context of legal Mexican immigrants is shaped by indifferent policies of government reception, prejudiced responses from civil society and public opinion, and a weak ethnic community. Like Mexicans, Korean immigrants confront indifferent government reception and prejudiced responses from civil society, but they benefit from strong ethnic communities. As immigrant destinies depend on the specific context of incorporation, this model helps explain why Mexican immigrants (and most immigrants from Central America and the Caribbean) tend to occupy low socioeconomic positions and are less likely to be upwardly mobile.

While Portes's typology does not identify assimilation as a mode of incorporation, two of his categories suggest such an outcome: (1) the category created by "receptive government policy, non-prejudiced societal reception and weak co-ethnic community," and (2) "indifferent government policy and non-prejudiced reception and weak co-ethnic community" (Portes 1995b: 226). Examples for the first category are "Hungarian and Other Small Eastern European Refugee Groups" and for the second "Argentines." What about nonrefugee European immigrants who have continued to immigrate to the United States after World War II? Most of them would surely fall at least into the latter category.

THE RETURN OF ASSIMILATION

While the concept of assimilation had a decidedly negative press throughout the 1970s, 1980s, and early 1990s, beginning in the mid-1990s several scholarly voices have called for its rehabilitation (Morawska 1994; Brubaker 2001). The most forceful and thoroughly articulated of these voices have been those of Richard Alba and Victor Nee, who have argued that assimilation took place in the past and still frequently happens today.

Discarding the model's ideological baggage rooted in Anglo conformity and naïve images of the melting pot (Alba and Nee 1997), and the proposition that assimilation is a universal, inevitable, and straight-line outcome, Alba and Nee have advanced a new way of thinking about assimilation.

Building on the behavioral assumptions of the new institutionalism in sociology (Alba and Nee 2003:37), Alba and Nee's "new theory of assimilation" (1997, 2003) incorporates insights and findings from the postassimilation literature, in particular the recognition that the actions of immigrants are shaped by host society institutions and the social capital and networks of immigrant groups. Assimilation, defined as "the attenuation of distinctions based on ethnic origin" (2003:38) proceeds incrementally involving a variety of mechanisms at different levels (individuals, groups, networks), where the particular sets of mechanisms vary across racial and ethnic groups. What matters most is that the boundary between immigrants and the "mainstream"[21] is not fixed (as the traditional assimilation perspective suggested), but changes over time, as boundaries may become blurred or shift entirely.

In contrast to the old assimilation model, Alba and Nee's new assimilation model does not claim that assimilation is either universal or inevitable. Recognizing that American culture is mixed and that elements of minority cultures are absorbed into the mainstream, the new assimilation theory demonstrates the perspective's relevance for understanding immigration and its consequences in contemporary American society.[22] As such it remains part of "the theoretical tool kit" (Alba and Nee 1997:863).

While Alba and Nee argue that assimilation remains a viable and often unexpected and unplanned outcome for many immigrants, by adding the adjective *segmented*, and focusing specifically on the fate of the second generation, assimilation has also returned in a different, decidedly more pessimistic guise. Although Herbert Gans (1992) was first to outline several distinct paths for the children of the new immigrants, including downward mobility, the concept *segmented assimilation* was first introduced by Portes and Zhou in their 1993 seminal article. Focusing on the children of immigrants (the second generation), the segmented assimilation hypothesis has attracted considerable attention (see also Portes 1995a). Explicitly recognizing the unequal and stratified characteristics of American society, the segmented assimilation hypothesis holds that the paths taken by children of recent (post-1965) immigrants differ. Depending on their parents' social class, the children of immigrants may assimilate into different segments of the existing class structure. Thus, children of middle-class immigrants who can take advantage of the opportunities offered by American society (in particular educational opportunities and associated opportunities for upward mobility) are likely to become assimilated into the middle class. The children of lower-class immigrants, the vast majority of whom are visible minorities, may face a different trajectory. Unlike the past, when unskilled blue-collar jobs were available for the children of immigrants unable or unwilling to pursue social mobility through education, these types of jobs have disappeared in the new service economy. Encountering discrimination in schools, where they also have contact with an urban subculture that rejects education as the domain of the dominant group, and rejecting the dead-end jobs of their parents, the children of these immigrants are in danger of joining the urban underclass consisting of African Americans and Puerto Ricans in a "new rainbow underclass" located "at the bottom of society" (Portes and Rumbaut 2001:45).

GLOBALIZATION, CITIZENSHIP, AND TRANSNATIONALISM

While they have been exported and applied to other societies (in particular in Europe), the above models have been deeply rooted in the American experience. The increased salience of transnational migration around the world, including many European countries, has provided the impetus for several different approaches. Less concerned with the process of immigrant incorporation in one country (for example, the United States), but explaining the causes and consequences of immigration beyond the confines of a single country, these theories represent responses to the recognition that mass migration is self-perpetuating, transforming, and systemic.

Beginning in the 1980s, working more deductively from the perspective of world systems theory and related globalization theories, some sociologists have linked the new global migrations and their consequences to the increasing penetration of the capitalist mode of production, arguing that the new international migration is a direct consequence of globalization, including economic markets, cultural transfers, and social ties (Morawska 1990; Petras 1981; Portes and Walton 1981; Sassen 1988, 1991). Here, the dislocation of labor in semiperipheral and peripheral countries, created by the increasing penetration of the capitalist mode of production in peripheral countries accompanied by new demands for cheap labor in the core countries, are identified as the chief sources of mass migration. Although the causes of migration may be primarily economic, in a globalized economy, once set in motion migration patterns are sustained and perpetuated by "well-established regional networks of trade, production, investment and communication" (Massey et al. 1998). The technological revolution, which has facilitated travel and communication across national borders, also supports the maintenance and expansion of transnational social networks created by the migrants themselves. Mass migration becomes self-sustaining and has significant political consequences for core countries and for the traditional system of nation–states.

Within the broader context of ever more rapid globalization, more recent work has focused on conceptualizing the consequences of migration in the advanced industrial countries, where mass migration challenges state sovereignty, signaling a loss of control over state borders, and traditional conceptualizations of state membership (citizenship) and belonging. As nation (defined in terms of belonging) and state (defined in terms of territory) become increasingly decoupled, national belonging and identity are increasingly detached from their historic moorings (Sassen 1996).[23] In this process, the legal/political position of citizenship that has tied the individual to the state has also been transformed.

An evolving literature on citizenship focusing on the various understandings of citizenship as a legal status, as a possession of rights, and as a political activity and a form of collective identity (Bosniak 2000) has involved scholars from several disciplines, including law (Schuck 1998), political science and political philosophy (Smith, 2003; Kymlika 1995; Bauböck1994), anthropology (Ong 1999), and sociology. Not surprisingly, the literature on citizenship is very diverse and includes normative as well as empirically based work. Focusing on how migration and globalization have changed the nature and condition of citizenship as we knew it, scholars have identified a variety of new types of citizenship. While some, for example, "cultural citizenship" (Kymlika and Norman 1994; Turner 1993) remains based in the nation–state, others such as "flexible citizenship" (Ong 1999), "diasporic citizenship" (Laguerre 1998), and "transnational citizenship" (Bauböck 1994) are located in two or more states simultaneously. "Fragmented citizenship" (Wiener 1997) is located at the supranational (European Union) level. "Postnational citizenship" (Soysal 1994, 1997; see also Jacobson 1996) is located primarily outside the nation–state.[24] While they have touched on all four understandings of citizenship, their contributions have tended to focus on citizenship as rights and to a lesser degree on participation (which has been more in the domain of political scientists) and identity (the primary domain of anthropologists).

Sociologists first drew attention to the role of citizenship (civil, political, and social) in the European context. In the United States, where political citizenship for the children of immigrants has been based on the principles of jus soli and naturalization has been relatively easy for legal immigrants, questions of citizenship had not been an issue and had been simply taken for granted.[25]

Migration to European countries with different principles of citizenship, imposing more significant barriers to naturalization (although varying from country to country) and restrictions on birthright citizenship, gave rise to comparative studies of citizenship as a mechanism for social and political inclusion/exclusion of newcomers (Schmitter 1979; Brubaker 1989, 1992; Faist 1995).

Here the theoretical focus has been primarily on how immigration transforms host societies and only secondarily on the immigrants themselves.[26] The main questions are less directly concerned with assimilation/incorporation or non-assimilation/exclusion than those raised in the American context. Focusing on the structure of political communities, they ask how given social and political structures affect immigrant incorporation/inclusion and how immigrants in turn affect the structure of political communities.

These earlier approaches have drawn on T. H. Marshall's (1964) original conception of three types of citizenship, civil, political, and social, paying particular attention to national differences in citizenship configurations (Schmitter 1979; Brubaker 1989, 1992; Faist 1995). Taking Marshall's proposition that within the modern nation–state the civil, political, and social rights gained by citizens had been crucial to fostering the integration of previously excluded groups[27] as her starting point in a comparative study of Germany and Switzerland (countries with significant barriers to political citizenship), Schmitter argued that the more extensive social citizenship rights characteristic of Germany would foster a greater degree of economic and social integration in that country (1979). In contrast, Brubaker, comparing France and Germany (countries with different, and according to Brubaker opposing citizenship regimes), emphasized the determining role of historically developed political citizenship regimes, republican and inclusionary in France, and ethnic and exclusionary in Germany. While Schmitter, following Marshall, identified partial membership (social and civil rights without full political rights) as a step toward full membership (political rights), coining the concept of *denizenship*, Hammar (1985) identified a new type of citizenship derived from the extensive social and civil rights accorded to immigrants in European welfare states. For Brubaker, the inclusion of immigrants necessitated their full access to political citizenship.[28]

Reaching beyond the Marshallian framework and the "container model" of society, sociologists have increasingly focused on the transformation of citizenship beyond the confines of the nation–state. Focusing primarily on Western Europe, Yasemin Soysal identified the new international human rights regime, as an alternative, nonnational, citizenship-based source of rights for immigrants (1994). Arguing that refugee and human rights conventions signed by states have codified an international system based on the inviolability of the rights inherent in the "modern person," which is independent of rights inherent in a particular state, she identified a new type of citizenship, *postnational citizenship*. Legitimized by an international human rights discourse, rights and identities become increasingly decoupled from national citizenship, and the rights component of citizenship is reconfigured as the universal right of personhood, which is independent of nationality.[29]

Although the postnational citizenship model gained considerable attention as a thoughtful and innovative contribution to the literature, Soysal's central proposition that the international human rights regime was rendering nationally located citizenship rights increasingly irrelevant has not received much support. In particular, her central proposition that "the logic of person-hood supersedes the logic of national citizenship" (1994:64) remains speculative.[30] Recent comparative empirical studies by Koopmans and Stratham (1999, 2000), who studied the process of immigrant claims making in several European countries, demonstrate that immigrants in these countries who predominantly direct their claims at the national states in which they live, and not at the human rights regimes, are ultimately dependent on the very nation–states that support them.

Embedded in the larger theoretical perspective of world theory, Soysal conceptualized postnational citizenship at the intersection of migration and an evolving human rights regime. Building on her earlier work on globalization and global cities, Saskia Sassen has argued that the decoupling of state and nation engendered by the larger processes of globalization has denationalized some segments of national citizenship, a process that leads to *denationalized citizenship*. The forces that contribute to this transformation are located in the global economy where increasing competition between capitalist countries has forced them to cut back on their welfare states. At the same time massive waves of immigrants, in particular undocumented immigrants and other groups (e.g., refugees) who may live in the state but are not members of the state, challenge the congruence between state and nation from below (Sassen 2002, 2006). In Sassen's conceptualization, denationalized citizenship and postnational citizenship represent different, not mutually exclusive, trajectories, where the former emerges from the transformation of the national itself and the latter from the transformation of the international realm.[31]

Although political theorist, Rainer Bauböck, identified *transnational citizenship* in terms of the rights of immigrants who are citizens of one state but live in another (1994), what has come to be known as "the transnational turn" entered sociology "under the transnational banner of anthropologists" (Morawska 2005:214). In contrast to Soysal (and Bauböck), who based her observations primarily on the European experience, early conceptualizations of immigrant transnationalism emerged from ethnographic research of the activities of immigrant groups in the United States. As such it was part of the critique of "the unilinear assimilationist paradigm of classical migration research" (Levitt and Glick Schiller 2004:1005). Focusing primarily on the social and economic activities linking migrants in the United States with their sending countries, early conceptualizations of transnationalism were not connected to the larger debates concerning the challenges and survival of the nation–state in political sociology and political science, or the transformation of citizenship as an institution.[32]

As it was first conceptualized by Nina Linda Basch, Nina Glick Schiller, and Christina Szanton-Blanc in the mid-1990s, the ideas and concepts associated with immigrant transnationalism were both vague and overly generalizing. Transnationalism often appeared as a catchall phrase for a variety of sustained border crossing ties. Now engaging migration scholars from several disciplines, including sociology, in the United States and in Europe, several waves of scholarship have helped refine the original concepts while also limiting their applications. Going beyond conceptual and typological refinements, sociologists have begun to consider how immigrant transnationalism might illuminate, complement, or oppose more traditional forms of immigrant incorporation (Portes, Guarnizo, and Haller 2002; Morawska 2003b; Kivisto 2003; Snel, Engbersen, and Leerks 2006). Yet, while some sociologists have found considerable merit in the transnational perspective (Portes 1997, 1999, 2001; Castles 2002), others remain deeply skeptical (Alba and Nee 2003; Waldinger and Fitzgerald 2004).

The maintenance of home country ties and the semisettled condition of immigrants seemed hardly surprising in the European case where most host countries had not encouraged (and often discouraged) permanent settlement (Heisler and Schmitter Heisler 1986), and many sending states actively supported the maintenance of ties (Schmitter Heisler 1984, 1985).[33] In the United States, Massey et al.'s (1987) pioneering research also identified the persistence and growing importance of ties between Mexican immigrants and their Mexican communities of origin (see also Smith 1995).[34]

While it could be argued that migration between Mexico and the United States represents a special case, ethnographic research involving several different immigrant communities (Dominicans, Haitians, Salvadorans, Filipinos, Brazilians) suggested that the maintenance of home country ties was a pervasive practice among contemporary immigrants in the United States, that called for a new analytic perspective and a new conceptual framework: *immigrant transnationalism*. As formulated by Linda Basch, Nina Glick Schiller, and Susan Blanc-Szanton, immigrant transnationalism refers to the process by which immigrants "maintain, build and reinforce multiple linkages with their countries of origin" (1994:6; see also Glick Schiller, Basch, and Blanc-Szanton 1995). Reaching beyond both sending and receiving countries, and seemingly deterritorialized, these linkages give rise to a new social formation, the transnational community, and a new identity, the transnational identity.

The vagueness of the original concepts, and the ethnographic methodology employed by rapidly proliferating research on transnationalism, transmigrants, transnational communities, and transnational social spaces, gave the initial impression that immigrant transnationalism was not only new (representing a significant break with the past),[35] but also widespread (a widely shared characteristic of contemporary immigrants) and primarily involving the grassroots activities of migrants operating simultaneously both "here" and "there," seemingly without any constraints from existing social and political institutions or international and multinational agreements.

While recognizing the empirical reality that many contemporary immigrants engage in a variety of transnational activities (for example, they send remittances; engage in frequent travel and communication back and forth; create informal associations, including hometown associations; they may vote in home country elections while politicians from their home countries may campaign in host countries), such activities per se need not imply a new and different conceptualization. For such a conceptualization to be useful, it needs to be specified and contextualized.

Much of the more recent work toward this goal has been in the form of additional research, more systematic description, and the construction of typologies. Thus, recognizing that transnational activities could occur at different levels involving different types of actors, Smith and Guarnizo (1998) identified the transnational activities of migrants as "transnationalism from below," contrasting it with the "transnationalism from above" practiced by governments, NGOs (nongovernmental organizations), and international capital and businesses. Similarly, Portes distinguished three types of transnational actors, international (embassies, export organizations, travel and exchange programs), multinational (United States, global corporations, global religious activities), and transnational actors. The latter is limited to nongovernmental political, economic, and sociocultural activities, such as hometown associations, individual businesses that export and import goods from home countries, grassroots charities, and so forth (Portes 2001:187).

Focusing on the frequency and depth of immigrant transnational activities, José Itzigsohn et al. (1999) differentiate between *broad transnationalism* referring to more sporadic involvement and *narrow transnationalism* referring to frequent, sustained, and institutionalized transnational economic, political, social, and cultural activities. Similarly, Portes (2003) distinguishes between broad transnationalism, which includes both regular and occasional activities, and *strict transnationalism*, which refers to regular participation only. Levitt (2001a,b) distinguishes between *core* and *expanded* transnational practices. Core transnational practices can be both comprehensive in the sense that they involve many different activities, and selective in that they involve only one activity, for example politics, but not economic or social activities. Expanded transnationalism is more periodic and occasional.[36]

In addition to specifying the levels, types, and frequency of transnational activities, sociologists have attempted to define the meaning of transnational community and transnational social fields.[37] In line with his earlier research on networks and enclave economies, Portes and his collaborators have stressed the structural/morphological dimensions of the transnational community as a system of networks, institutions, and relationships that connects people in host and receiving countries, including those who are not migrants (Portes, Guarziona, and Landolt 1999; Levitt 2001a). Others stress the cultural and symbolic dimensions of transnational communities. Faist conceptualizes the transnational community as one of three types of social spaces created by "relatively stable, long lasting and dense sets of ties, reaching beyond and across the border of sovereign states" (2000:3), transnational kinship groups, transnational circuits, and transnational communities. Kinship groups are based on reciprocity within the family and may involve remittances of household family members and are typically short-lived; transnational circuits are based on exchanges of goods, people, and information. Transnational communities are based on social solidarity, shared ideas, beliefs, and symbols, and may be bilocal (involving only two localities) or multilocal, involving several localities.

In contrast to Levitt and Glick Schiller (2004), who have identified the diaspora as a building block for transnational communities, Faist identifies the diaspora as an example of the transnational community. Going beyond the usual technological and economic explanations given for the emergence of transnational communities, Faist draws attention to the constraints and opportunities imposed by host and sending countries and the relationships between them. By bringing politics (both domestic and international) into the equation, he also draws attention to the fact that the formation of a transnational community is contingent and context specific. Beyond the technologies that facilitate the transnational activities of migrants, there are a variety of political and social realities that differ substantially from case to case and from place to place.

Moving beyond the debate about the proper conceptualization of transnationalism and associated concepts, sociologists have begun to consider possible connections between transnational social spaces and other sociological models. Drawing on the larger literature of the sociology of space and the sociology of community, Kivisto has asked how transnational communities might differ from other types of immigrant and ethnic communities in the past and present (2003:15). Based on research comparing several Latin immigrant groups, finding that regular transnational activities are fairly common among immigrant entrepreneurs, Portes et al. conclude that transnational entrepreneurship represents a form of economic adaptation (Portes, Guarnizo, and Haller 2002).

Several scholars have begun to explore the connections between assimilation and enduring transnational ties often identified as "incompatible" or "binary" (Levitt and Glick Schiller 2004). Positing that "transnational involvements of immigrants and their children and their assimilation into the host society typically are concurrent," Morawska has used data and findings from five empirical case studies in the United States to explore the different constellations of macro- and micro-level circumstances that are likely to produce different varieties of transnationalism-with-assimilation combinations. Each of the case studies represents different contexts and combinations of transnational involvement and assimilation in the lives of immigrants in the United States and the variations practiced by their American-born children. Her examination of these cases reinforced the idea that combinations of assimilation/transnationalism are context dependent, they are "contingent on different constellations of features of the economies, politics, and cultures of sender and receiver societies and local communities and of the immigrants (or second generation) themselves" (2003b:162).[38]

A recent study in The Netherlands also throws some preliminary light on the proposition that integration and transnational activities go hand in hand (Snel, Engbersen, and Leerks 2006). The authors surveyed three hundred immigrants from a variety of countries (the United States, Japan, Iraq, the former Yugoslavia, Morocco, and the Dutch Antilles) and found that migrant groups such as Moroccans, who are considered to be poorly integrated into Dutch society, are not more involved in transnational activities and do not have stronger identification with the country of origin than other groups. While research on this topic is in its infancy, and the jury on transnationalism and its relations to other models is still out (Kivisto 2005), it holds some promise for the construction of new middle-range models in the future.[39]

CONCLUSION: TALKING ACROSS DISCIPLINES

Although the above discussion is far from comprehensive, it gives testimony to the considerable vitality of the sociology of immigration. Sociologists have built on previous work and, responding to changing conditions, they have explored new directions—they have also talked across disciplines. Yet such talks have been dominated by the transnationalism debates.

While each of the theories and models discussed above has been subject to theoretical, conceptual, and empirical criticisms, in this chapter I have purposely refrained from critiquing them. Instead, I would like to conclude with a constructive note by asking how we might advance from here.

As Thomas Hammar (2001) has pointed out, research on migration should be interdisciplinary. Talking across disciplines ideally should promote interdisciplinarity. Writing about the state of the art in immigration theory almost 10 years ago, Alejandro Portes argued that it would be futile to attempt a grand theory in the field (1997:810). Similarly, it may also be futile to attempt an interdisciplinary theory of migration. For better or for worse, theory remains deeply embedded in a particular discipline's conceptual and analytic language, methodological approach, and epistemological assumptions (Morawska 2003a), a fact that has been clearly revealed in the vigorous interdisciplinary discussions of transnationalism.[40] Although these discussions have not produced a theory of transnationalism (Faist 2004), they have been fruitful. They have contributed to sharpening the original concepts, and most importantly perhaps, they have contextualized and broadened the analytic framework from the micro-level analysis of anthropologists to the macro-level analysis generally favored by political sociologists and political scientists. Discussions concerning the "newness" of transnationalism have raised a new awareness of past forms of transnational activities among historians, while at the same time they have drawn attention to the often ahistorical and decontextualized conceptualizations of anthropologists. Finally, the interdisciplinary dialogue between anthropologists and sociologists has also begun to address several questions I raised in the first edition of this volume, as scholars have explored the relationship between transnationalism and other modes of immigrant incorporation/exclusion, in particular the relationship between assimilation and transnationalism (Schmitter Heisler 2000:89–90).

Overall, however, sociologists who have focused on the American experience have been reluctant to talk across disciplines.[41] Waters attributes such reluctance to the fact that "immigration is at the very core of American sociology" (1999:1264). This very fact has been an advantage and a disadvantage for the sociology of immigration. The advantage has been that American sociologists of immigration have been able to build on a long tradition of research. The disadvantage has been that such tradition has also placed limits on the sociological imagination and the potential promises of comparative research. By engaging in an interdisciplinary dialogue, sociologists have developed a greater awareness of these limits and they have begun to consider them.[42]

While I would not go so far as to replace the nation–state with the concept of *social field*, I do agree that the fact that many immigrants' lives today incorporate activities, routines, and institutions located both in a destination country and transnationally needs to be theorized and explored (Levitt and Glick Schiller 2004:1003). Yet, as Adrian Favell has pointed out, transnationalism "may not lead to expansive new public spheres" and "'political community' beyond the nation–state." It could also "speed the fragmentation and differentiation of political arenas" (Favell 2000:218).

Similarly, recent developments in the area of citizenship rights give increasing support to the claim made by political scientists that citizenship rights remain primarily in the domain of the nation–state. European states in particular have sought to reaffirm their authority through new systems of managed migration, increasingly rejecting multiculturalism (in the United Kingdom and The Netherlands) and stressing the role of the state in promoting the integration of newcomers (The Netherlands and Germany). Whatever their long-term development, the work on transnationalism and citizenship gives testimony to and provides new insights into the extraordinary complexity of immigration processes at the beginning of the twenty-first century.

Yet, to more fully understand these complexities, sociologists must follow the lead of political scientists and geographers and engage in more comparative research. Just as migration is inherently interdisciplinary, it is also inherently comparative. Just as the continued in-depth studies of the American case have generated new insights and new ways of thinking about that case, the systematic comparative study of the new immigrant societies in Europe has the potential for adding significant empirical knowledge, analytic depth, a wealth of additional insights, and perhaps new theoretical frameworks.

Research on immigration in Europe has exploded in recent years. While the recent literature includes a plethora of edited volumes comparing immigration among European countries and to a lesser degree between the United States and specific European countries (for example, Germany, France, The Netherlands, the United Kingdom), much of the sociological literature on immigrant integration remains under the spell of the American experience (Favell 2001). While political scientists such as Freeman (1995, 2004) and Hollifield (1998/99, 2000, 2004; Joppke 1998) have relied on comparative analysis, theoretically informed sociological work often continues to rely on concepts and theories developed in the American context (e.g., ethnic community, ethnic enterprise, and even segmented assimilation).

This approach has imposed limits on potential theoretical insights that may be gained from the experiences of other societies. First, by using the concepts and models developed from the American experience, researchers take for granted the structural characteristics of American society, assuming implicitly that they are the same as those of other advanced industrial countries, an assumption that we know to be incorrect. Second, and related, there is a built-in tendency to use the American case as an ideal type, judging other cases by how much they conform to that case. Existing differences are either disregarded or seen as not fitting the model. Yet it is exactly these differences that might point the way to a different way of thinking and a novel approach.[43]

NOTES

1. We may also mention Max Weber's research on the conditions of rural peasants and Polish migrant workers east of the Elbe River in Germany. For a summary, see Bendix 1962:14–30.
2. In a 1993 article Nathan Glazer argues that "the failure of assimilation to work on blacks as on immigrants, owing to the strength of American discriminatory and prejudiced attitudes and behavior toward blacks, has been responsible for throwing the entire assimilatory ideal and program into disrepute" (122).
3. Two years later Portes reiterated the idea that a quest for a grand theory of migration would be misguided (1999).
4. Favell has called sociology "the most American-centered discipline" (2004).
5. See, for example, Volume 38 (2004), Number 2 of the *International Migration Review*, edited by Alejandro Portes and Josh DeWind, in particular their article "A Cross-Atlantic Dialogue: The Progress of Research and Theory in International Migration."
6. I am using the term theory rather loosely to include typologies, frameworks, and models that do not meet the strict definition of theory. For a good discussion of these issues, see Portes 1997.

7. The race relations cycle was based on the idea that immigrant groups, and by implication ethnic and racial groups more generally, typically go through several phases—contact, competition and conflict, accommodation, assimilation—where the end product is a melting with the larger society. In the final phase, group members acquire "the memories, sentiments and attitudes of other persons or groups, and, by sharing their experience and history, are incorporated with them in a common cultural life (Park and Burgess 1921:735).

8. The main laboratory for empirical observations, which had moved from Chicago to New York in the 1950s and 1960s, now also includes the new centers of immigration, Los Angeles and Miami.

9. In the 1950s interest in immigration and immigrants began to wane and all but disappeared in the 1960s, and in the context of the Civil Rights Movement, sociologists turned to the study of race and ethnic relations (Pedraza 1999).

10. At the time the challenges were not engendered by new waves of immigrants (in the 1960s interest in immigration had all but disappeared and the full effects of the 1965 immigration law were not felt until the 1980s). Indeed, until about World War II, assimilation was discussed primarily in the context of Europeans (Glazer 1993).

11. For a thoughtful discussion of Park's work on assimilation, see Kivisto 2004. In this article Kivisto argues that much of Park's view of assimilation has been misconstrued. For example, although Park and his followers held that assimilation was inevitable and desirable, Park also recognized that "physical traits," not cultural differences, might present a stumbling block to the smooth assimilation of racial minorities.

12. Warner and Srole's study of Yankee City (1945) saw the future of ethnic groups limited and likely to disappear as they "will be quickly absorbed" (295–96). In this process they must "unlearn their cultural traits" and "successfully learn the new way of life necessary for full acceptance" (285).

13. See also the discussion in Alba and Nee (2003:3–6)who attribute some of the intellectual sins that have become associated with the assimilation perspective to Warner and Srole and Gordon (2003:3–6) and argue with considerable justification that the Chicago School's earlier conceptualizations of assimilation were more flexible and open ended (10–11).

14. Gordon's seven-stage model had the advantage of lending itself to operationalization, but as Alba and Nee point out, the focus on primary group integration overlooks the larger social processes.

15. Much of the failure of the assimilation model can be attributed to the conventional assimilation model's ideological underpinnings of Anglo-conformity, naïve images of the "melting pot" (Alba and Nee 1997), and the assumption of what Herbert Gans has called "straight-line" assimilation (1973).

16. Although Whyte's (1943) landmark study of the organizational structures and networks of an Italian immigrant community detailed the persistence of ethnic community, in the wake of post–World War II economic expansion and suburbanization the traditional immigrant/ethnic communities of eastern and southern European immigrants had declined and in line with the prevailing assimilationist perspective, they were expected to disappear.

17. As Glazer (1993) noted, the assimilation perspective had focused almost exclusively on white European immigrants, ignoring racial minorities and non-European (i.e., Asian) immigrants.

18. Empirically, there is considerable debate concerning the claim made by ethnic enclave economy theorists that employees fare better in the enclave economy than in the secondary labor market. For a review of the empirical studies, see Light et al. 1994.

19. Building on the work of Granovetter (1985, 1990), Portes and Sensenbrenner (1993) identified two main sources of social capital for immigrant communities: "bounded solidarity" (principled group behavior that emerges from Portes and Sensenbrenner's situational circumstances and is independent of earlier shared values) and "enforceable trust" (where group goals govern economic behavior).

20. Waldinger defines ethnic niches as "an industry, employing at least one thousand people, in which a group's representation is at least 150 percent of its share of total employment (1996:95).

21. Alba and Nee define the mainstream as "that part of society within which ethnic and racial origins have at most minor impacts on life chances or opportunities"(2003:12).

22. Several historians have argued that assimilation theory is useful in understanding past processes (Kazal 1995 and Barkan 1995). Anticipating criticisms that assimilation may have become a reality for European ethnic groups of the past, but hardly applies to new immigrants confronting different circumstances today, Alba and Nee make three important points. First, it is difficult to project the future of migration patterns. Second, we do not know whether assimilation would have taken place in the absence of a halt to further mass immigration between the 1920s and 1965. Third, as they are socially constructed, racial distinctiveness and perceptions change over time. South Asians and Caribbeans are examples.

23. Political scientists such as Freeman (1996) and Joppke (1998) tend to disagree with the two theses underlying the globalization perspective: the thesis of declining sovereignty and the thesis of pervasive restrictionism.

24. Citizenship is a contested concept. See Jonathan Fox (2005) for an excellent review of the varieties of transnational citizenship. See also Favell 2000.

25. This changed in the 1980s when undocumented immigration to the United States increased rapidly.

26. This is not the case for a host or primarily descriptive empirical studies of various immigrant groups.

27. Marshall was primarily concerned with the incorporation of the working class. See Heisler and Schmitter Heisler 1991.

28. Kymlicka and Norman (1995) used the concept of multicultural citizenship. Multicultural citizenship is nationally bounded, but represents accommodations made by liberal states no longer assimilating their immigrants but respecting (and promoting) their ethnic identities instead. Multicultural citizenship provides rights to individuals as members of culturally defined groups to be represented as a group in the polity. The duty of the state is to protect individuals as members of groups.

29. Although he did not use the term postnational citizenship, David Jacobson made a similar argument comparing Europe and the United States. Although border control and sovereignty issues are apparent in all advanced industrial societies, theories stressing the links between immigration and emerging human rights regimes seem to work better in the European than in the American context.

30. For a succinct critique see Joppke 1998.

31. New types of citizenship include postnational citizenship, transnational citizenship, cultural citizenship (Bauböck 1994), diasporic citizenship (Laguerre 1998) and flexible citizenship (Ong 1999), fragmented citizenship (Wiener 1997), urban citizenship (Isin 2000), and documentary citizenship (Sadiq 2006).

32. Many of the transnational activities of immigrants have been facilitated by increases in the practice of dual citizenship, as many sending countries have changed their laws to permit dual citizenship in order to facilitate the transnational activities of their citizens abroad.

33. It had also been observed in studies of immigrants to the United States at the turn of the last century (Foester 1919; Piore 1979; Hoerder 1985). The question of whether transnationalism is old or new has been hotly debated by historians, sociologists, and anthropologists. For a discussion see Portes et al. (1999) and Barkan (2006). While even the proponents of the transnationalist perspective are willing to concede that transnational activities have been part of immigrant life in the past, most observers would agree that transnational activities today are quantitatively and qualitatively different than they were in the past.

34. Linda Basch and her collaborators defined "transnationalism as the process by which immigrants forge and sustain multi-stranded social relations that link their societies of origin and settlement" (1994:6).

35. The question of whether transnationalism was new or old engendered a lively debate with historians, who argued that there was nothing new about transnationalism (Foner 1997).

36. Levitt makes further distinctions between rural-to-urban transnationalisms and urban-to-urban transnationalisms (2000b).

37. Kivisto reminds us that the concept of community is itself notoriously vague and contested (2003).

38. She identified five cases of immigrant and six modes of second-generation transnationalism/assimilation variations and more than forty factors that shape their possible combinations.

39. Morawska suggests three steps toward this goal: exploring diversity, identifying patterns of similarities and differences in transnationalism/assimilation combinations and constructing models from the information of the two preceding steps (2003b:164–65).

40. I agree with Morwaska that "learning about different analytic strategies applied in particular disciplines" can lay a groundwork for interdisciplinary research" (2003:632) but whether such research will generate interdisciplinary theory is another question.

41. Alejandro Portes is a notable exception.

42. For example, recent talking across disciplines has contributed to raising sociologists' awareness of their inherent methodological nationalism (Wimmer and Glick Schiller 2004).

43. For an elaboration in the area of immigrant integration, see Schmitter Heisler, forthcoming. On the more empirical level, more comparative research is well suited for testing and refining conceptualizations of citizenship and transnationalism. In the area of transnationalism, the permutations and possibilities of home country and sending country relations, the context of the European Union, and the fact that some of the same immigrant nationalities are found in several countries (in particular Turks) allows for the testing and analyses of a variety of context-specific propositions about transnational activities, transnational social spaces, and about the relationship between transnationalism and assimilation.

REFERENCES

Agueros, Jack, et al. 1971. *The Immigrant Experience: The Anguish of Becoming American*. New York: Dial Press.

Alba, Richard, and Victor Nee. 1997. "Rethinking Assimilation Theory for a New Era of Immigration," *International Migration Review* 31: 826–74.

———. 2003. *Remaking the American Mainstream: Assimilation and Contemporary Immigration*. Cambridge, MA: Harvard University Press.

Bailey, Thomas, and Roger Waldinger. 1991. "Primary, Secondary, and Enclave Labor Markets: A Training System Approach," *American Sociological Review* 56: 432–45.

Barkan, Elliot. 1995. "Race, Religion, and Nationality in American Society: A Model of Ethnicity—From Contact to Assimilation," *Journal of American Ethnic History* 14: 38–101.

———. 2006. "Introduction: Immigration, Incorporation, Assimilation, and the Limits of Transnationalism," *Journal of American Ethnic History*. 25:7–32.

Basch, Linda, N. Glick-Schiller, and C. Blanc-Szanton. 1994. *Nations Unbound: Transnational Projects, Post-Colonial Predicaments, and Deterritorialized Nation–States*. Langhorne, PA: Gordon and Breach.

Bauböck, Rainer. 1994. *Transnational Citizenship: Membership and Rights in International Migration*. Aldershot, U.K.: Edward Elgar.

———. 2003. "Towards a Political Theory of Migrant Transnationalism," *International Migration Review* 37: 700–23.

Bendix, Reinhard. 1962. *Max Weber, an Intellectual Portrait*. Garden City, NY: Doubleday.

Bonacich, Edna. 1973. "Theory of Middleman Minorities," *American Sociological Review* 38: 583–94.

———. 1980. "Class Approaches to Ethnicity and Race," *Insurgent Sociologist* 10: 9–23.

Bonacich, Edna, and John Modell. 1980. *The Economic Basis of Ethnic Solidarity: Small Business in the Japanese American Community*. Berkeley and Los Angeles: University of California Press.

Bosniak, Linda. 2000. "The State of Citizenship: Citizenship Denationalized," *Indiana Journal of Global Legal Studies* 7: 447–510.

Brubaker, Rogers, ed. 1989. *Immigration and the Politics of Citizenship in Europe and North America*. Lanham, MD: University Press of America.

———. 1992. *Citizenship and Nationhood in France and Germany*. Cambridge, MA: Harvard University Press.

———. 2001. "The Return of Assimilation? Changing Perspectives on Immigration and Its Sequels in France, Germany and the United States," *Ethnic and Racial Studies* 24: 531–548.

Castles, Stephen. 2002. "Migration and Community Formation under Conditions of Globalization," *International Migration Review* 36: 1143–68.

Castles, Stephen, and Mark Miller. 1998. *The Age of Migration: International Population Movements in the Modern World*. 2nd ed. New York: Guilford Press.

Edwards, Robert, Robert Reich, and David Gordon. 1975. *Labor Market Segmentation*. Lexington, MA: D.C. Heath.

Faist, Thomas. 1995. *Social Citizenship for Whom? Young Turks in Germany and Mexican Americans in the United States*. Aldershot, U.K.: Avebury.

_____. 1998. "Transnational Social Spaces out of International Migration: Evolution, Significance and Future Prospects," *Archive Européenne Sociologique* 39: 213–47.

_____. 2000. "Transnationalization in International Migration. Implications for the Study of Citizenship and Culture," *Ethnic and Racial Studies* 23: 189–222.

_____. 2004. "Toward a Political Sociology of Transnationalization: The State of the Art in Migration Research," *European Journal of Sociology* 45: 331–66.

Favell, Adrian. 2000. "To Belong or Not to Belong: The Postnational Question," in Will Kymlicka and Wayne Norman, eds., *Citizenship in Diverse Societies*, pp. 209–27. Oxford: Oxford University Press.

_____. 2001. "Integration Policy and Integration Research in Europe: A Review and Critique," in Alexander Aleinikoff and Douglas Klusmeyer, eds., *Citizenship Today: Global Perspectives and Practices*, pp. 349–99. Washington, D.C.: Carnegie Endowment for International Piece.

_____. 2004. "Book Review. Europe without Borders: Remapping Territory, Citizenship and Identity in the Transnational Age," *Social Forces* 20: 871–74.

Fitzgerald, David. 2004. "Beyond 'Transnationalism': Mexican Hometown Politics at an American Labour Union," *Ethnic and Racial Studies* 27: 228–47.

_____. 2006. "Toward a Theoretical Ethnography of Migration," *Qualitative Sociology* 29: 1–24

Foerster, Robert. 1919. *The Italian Emigration of Our Times*. Cambridge, MA: Harvard University Press.

Foner, Nancy. 1997. "What Is New About Transnationalism: New Immigrants Today and at the Turn of the Century," *Diaspora* 6: 355–76.

Fox, Jonathan. 2005. "Unpacking 'Transnational Citizenship,'" *Annual Review of Political Science* 8: 171–201.

Freeman, Gary. 1995. "Modes of Immigration Politics in Liberal Democratic States," *International Migration Review* 29: 881–902.

_____. 2004. "Immigrant Incorporation in Western Democracies," *International Migration Review* 38: 945–69.

Gans, Herbert. 1973. "Foreword," in Neil Sandberg, ed., *Ethnic Identity and Assimilation: The Polish Community*, pp. vii–xiii. New York: Praeger.

_____. 1992. "The Second Generation Decline: Scenarios for the Economic and Ethnic Futures of Post-1965 American Immigrants," *Ethnic and Racial Studies* 15: 173–92.

Glazer, Nathan. 1993. "Is Assimilation Dead?" *Annals of the American Academy of Political and Social Sciences* 530: 122–36.

Glazer, Nathan, and Daniel Patrick Moynihan. 1963. *Beyond the Melting Pot: The Negroes, Puerto Ricans, Jews, and Italians of New York City*. Cambridge, MA: MIT Press.

Glick-Schiller, Nina, Linda Basch, and Christina Blanc-Szanton. 1995. "From Immigrant to Transmigrant: Theorizing Transnational Migration, *Anthropological Quarterly* 68: 48–63.

Gordon, Milton. 1964. *Assimilation in American Life*. New York: Oxford University Press.

Granovetter, Mark. 1985. "Economic Action and Social Structure: The Problem of Embeddedness," *American Journal of Sociology* 91: 481–510.

_____. 1990. "The Old and New Economic Sociology: A History and Agenda," in R. Friedland and A. F. Robertson, eds., *Beyond the Market Place*, pp. 89–112. New York: Aldine de Gruyter.

Greeley, Andrew. 1977. *The American Catholic: A Social Portrait*. New York: Harper and Row.

Guarnizo, Luis, and Michael P. Smith. 1998. "The Locations of Transnationalism," in Michael P. Smith and Louis Guarnizo, eds., *Transnationalism from Below*, vol. 6, pp. 3–34. Comparative Urban and Community Research. New Brunswick, NJ: Transactions Publishers.

Hammar, Thomas. 1985. *European Immigration Policy*. New York: Cambridge University Press.

———. 1990. *Democracy and the Nation State: Aliens, Denizens and Citizens in a World of International Migration*. Aldershot, U.K.: Avebury.

———. 2001. "The Ugly Duckling and the Academy." Academy for Migration Studies in Denmark (AMID), Working Papers Series 2/2001.

Heisler, Martin, and Barbara Schmitter Heisler, eds. 1986. *From Foreign Workers to Settlers? Transnational Migration and the Emergence of New Minorities*. The Annals of the American Academy for Political and Social Science. Beverly Hills, CA: Sage.

———. 1991. "Citizenship—Old, New and Changing: Inclusion, Exclusion and Limbo for Ethnic Groups and Migrants in the Modern Democratic State," in Jürgen Fijalkowski, Hans Merkens, and Folker Schmidt, eds., *Dominant National Cultures and Ethnic Identities*, vol. 1, pp. 91–128. Berlin: Free University.

Herberg, Will. 1956. *Protestant-Catholic-Jew*. New York: Anchor Books.

Hoerder, Dirk, ed. 1985. *Labor Migration in the Atlantic Economies: The European and North American Working Classes during the Period of Industrialization*, part III, "Acculturation Twice: Return Migration," pp. 353–434. Westport, CT: Greenwood Press.

Hollifield, James. 1998/99. "Migration, Trade, and the Nation–State: The Myth of Globalization," *UCLA Journal of International Law and Foreign Affairs* 3: 595–636.

———. 2000. "The Politics of International Migration: How Can We 'Bring the State Back In?'" in Caroline Brettell and James Hollifield, eds., *Migration Theory: Talking across Disciplines*, pp. 137–86. New York: Routledge.

———. 2004. "The Emerging Migration State," *International Migration Review* 38: 885–912.

Isin, Engin, ed. 2000. *Democracy, Citizenship and the Global City*. New York: Routledge.

Itzigsohn, José et al. 1999. "Mapping Dominican Transnationals: Narrow and Broad Transnational Practices," *Ethic and Racial Studies* 22: 316–339.

Itzigsohn, José. 2000. "Immigration and the Boundaries of Citizenship," *International Migration Review* 34: 1126–54.

Jacobson, David. 1996. *Rights across Borders: Immigration and the Decline of Citizenship*. Baltimore, MD: Johns Hopkins University Press.

Jacobson, Matthew. 1995. *Special Sorrows: The Diasporic Imagination of Irish, Polish and Jewish Immigrants in the United States*. Cambridge, MA: Harvard University Press.

Joppke, Christian. 1998. "Immigration Challenges the Nation State," in Christian Joppke, ed., *Challenge to the Nation–State: Immigration in Western Europe and the United States*, pp. 5–44. Oxford: Oxford University Press.

Kazal, Russell. 1995. "Revisiting Assimilation: The Rise, Fall and Reappraisal of a Concept in American Ethnic History," *American Historical Review* 100: 437–72.

Kennedy, Ruby Jo Reeves. 1944. "Single or Triple Melting Pot? Intermarriage Trends in New Haven, 1870–1940," *American Journal of Sociology* 49: 331–39.

———. 1952. "Single or Triple Melting Pot? Intermarriage in New Haven, 1870–1915," *American Journal of Sociology* 58: 56–59.

Kivisto, Peter. 2003. "Social Spaces, Transnational Immigrant Communities, and the Politics of Incorporation," *Ethnicities* 3: 5–28.

———. Peter. 2004. "What Is the Canonical Theory of Assimilation? Robert Park and His Predecessors," *Journal of the History of the Behavioral Sciences* 40: 149–63.

———. 2005. "The Revival of Assimilation in Historical Perspective," in Peter Kivisto, ed. *Incorporating Diversity: Rethinking Assimilation in a Multicultural Age*, pp. 3–32. Boulder, CO: Paradigm.

Koopmans, Ruud, and Paul Stratham. 1999. "Challenging the Liberal Nation State? Postnationalism, Multiculturalism and the Collective Claims Making of Migrants and Ethnic Minorities in Britain and Germany," *American Journal of Sociology* 105: 652–96.

———. 2000. *Challenging Migration and Ethnic Relations Politics: Comparative European Perspectives*. Oxford, U.K.: Oxford University Press.

Kymlicka, Will. 1995. *Multicultural Citizenship: A Liberal Theory of Minority Rights*. Oxford: Clarendon Press.

Kymlicka, Will, and Wayne Norman 1994. "The Return of the Citizen: A Survey of Recent Work on Citizenship Theory," *Ethics* 104: 352–81.

Laguerre, Michel. 1998. *Diasporic Citizenship: Haitian-Americans in Transnational America*. New York, NY: St. Martin's Press.

Levitt, Peggy. 2001a. *Transnational Villagers*. Berkeley: University of California Press.

Levitt, Peggy. 2001b. "Transnational Migration: Taking Stock and Future Directions," *Global Networks* 1: 195–216.

Levitt, Peggy, and Nina Glick Schiller. 2004. "Conceptualizing Simultaneity: A Transnational Social Field Perspective of Society," *International Migration Review* 38: 1003–39.

Lieberson, Stanley. 1980. *A Piece of the Pie: Blacks and Immigrants Since 1880*. Berkeley and Los Angeles: University of California Press.

Light, Ivan. 1972. *Ethnic Enterprise in America: Business and Welfare among Chinese, Japanese, and Blacks*. Berkeley and Los Angeles: University of California Press.

———. 1979. "Disadvantaged Minorities in Self-Employment," *International Journal of Comparative Sociology* 20: 31–45.

———.1984. "Immigrant and Ethnic Enterprise in North America," *Ethnic and Racial Studies* 7: 195–216.

Light, Ivan, and Edna Bonacich. 1988. *Immigrant Entrepreneurs: Koreans in Los Angeles, 1965–1982*. Berkeley and Los Angeles: University of California Press.

Light, Ivan, and Carolyn Rosenstein. 1995. *Race, Ethnicity and Entrepreneurship in Urban America*. New York: De Gruyter.

Light, Ivan, et al. 1994. "Beyond the Ethnic Enclave Economy," *Social Problems* 41: 65–80.

Marshall, T. H. 1964. *Class, Citizenship and Social Development*. Garden City, NY: Anchor Books.

Massey, Douglas, et al. 1987. *Return to Aztlan: The Social Process of International Migration from Mexico*. Berkeley and Los Angeles: University of California Press.

_____. 1994. "An Evaluation of International Migration Theory," *Population and Development Review* 20: 699–751.

_____. 1998. *World in Motion: Understanding International Migration at the End of the Millennium.* Oxford: Clarendon Press.

Meyer, John, John Boli, George Thomas, and Francisco Ramirez. 1997. "World-Society and the Nation–State," *American Journal of Sociology* 103: 144–81.

Morawska, Ewa. 1990. "The Sociology and Historiography of Immigration," in Virginia Yans-McLaughlin, ed., *Immigration Reconsidered: History, Sociology, and Politics*, pp. 187–240. New York: Oxford University Press.

_____. 1994. "In Defense of the Assimilation Model," *Journal of American Ethnic History* 13: 76–87.

_____. 2003a. "Disciplinary Agendas and Analytic Strategies of Research on Immigrant Transnationalism: Challenges of Interdisciplinary Knowledge," *International Migration Review* 37: 611–640.

_____. 2003b. "Immigrant Transnationalism and Assimilation: A Variety of Combinations and the Analytic Strategy it Suggests," in Christian Joppke and Ewa Morawska, eds., *Toward Assimilation and Citizenship: Immigrants in Liberal National States*, pp. 133–76. Houndmills: Palgrave.

_____. 2005. "The Sociology and History of Immigration: Reflections of a Practitioner," in Michael Bommes and Ewa Morawska, eds., *International Migration Research: Constructions, Omission and the Promises of Interdisciplinarity*, pp. 203–39. Aldershot: Ashgate.

Ong, Aiwa. 1999. *Flexible Citizenship: The Cultural Logics of Transnationalism.* Durham, NC: Duke University Press.

Park, Robert. 1928. "Human Migration and the Marginal Man," *American Journal of Sociology* 33: 881–93.

Park, Robert, and Ernest Burgess. 1921. *Introduction to the Science of Sociology.* Chicago: University of Chicago Press.

Pedraza, Siliva. 1999. "Assimilation or Diasporic Citizenship," *Current Sociology* 28: 377–81.

Petras, Elizabeth. 1981. "The Global Market in the Modern World Economy," in Mary Kritz et al., eds., *Global Trends in Migration: Theory and Research on International Population Movements*, pp. 44–63. New York: Center for Migration Studies.

Piore, Michael. 1979. *Birds of Passage.* New York: Cambridge University Press.

Portes, Alejandro. 1995a. "Children of Immigrants: Segmented Assimilation and Its Determinants," in Alejandro Portes, ed., *The Economic Sociology of Immigration*, pp. 248–79. New York: Russell Sage.

_____. 1995b. "Economic Sociology and the Sociology of Immigration: A Conceptual Overview," in Alejandro Portes, ed., *The Economic Sociology of Immigration*, pp. 1–41. New York: Russell Sage.

_____. 1997. "Immigration Theory for a New Century: Some Problems and Opportunities," *International Migration Review* 31: 799–825.

_____. 1998. "Divergent Destinies: Immigration, the Second Generation, and the Rise of Transnational Communities," in Peter Schuck and Rainer Münz, eds., *Paths to Inclusion: The Integration of Migrants in the United States and Germany*, pp. 33–57. New York: Berghahn Books.

_____. 1999. "Immigration Theory for a New Century: Some Problems and Opportunities," in C. Hirschman, P. Kasinitz, and J. de Wind, eds., *Handbook of International Migration: The American Experience*, pp. 21–33. New York: Russell Sage Foundation.

_____. 1999. "Introduction: The Debates and Significance of Migrant Transnational-
ism," *Global Networks* 1: 181–193.

_____. 2003. "Theoretical Convergencies and Empirical Evidence in the Study of
Immigrant Transnationalism," *International Migration Review* 37: 874–92.

Portes, Alejandro, and Robert Bach. 1985. *Latin Journey: Cuban and Mexican Immigrants in the United States.* Berkeley and Los Angeles: University of California
Press.

Portes, Alejandro, and Luis Guarnizo. 1991. *Capitalistas del Trópico: La Inmigración
en los Estados Unidos y el Desarrollo de la Pequeña Empresa en la República
Dominicana.* Facultad Latinoamericana de Ciencias Sociales, Programa Repub-
lica Dominicana, Johns Hopkins University.

Portes, Alejandro, Luis Guarnizo, and William Haller. 2002. "Transnational Entrepreneurs: An Alternative Form of Immigrant Economic Adaptation," *American
Sociological Review* 67: 278–98.

Portes, Alejandro, L. E. Guarnizo, and P. Landolt. 1999. "The Study of Transnationalism: Pitfalls and Promise of an Emergent Research Field," *Ethnic and Racial
Studies* 22: 217–37.

Portes, Alejandro, and Leif Jensen. 1989. "What's an Ethnic Enclave? The Case for
Conceptual Clarity," *American Sociological Review* 52: 768–71.

Portes, Alejandro, and Robert Manning. 1986. "The Immigrant Enclave: Theory and
Empirical Examples," in Susan Olzak and Joane Nagel, eds., *Competitive Ethnic
Relations*, pp. 47–66. New York: Academic Press.

Portes, Alejandro, and Rubén Rumbaut. 1990. *Immigrant America: A Portrait.* Berkeley and Los Angeles: University of California Press.

Portes, Alejandro, and Rubén Rumbaut. 2001. "Introduction: Ethnogenesis—Coming
of Age in Immigrant America," in Alejandro Portes and Rubén Rumbaut, eds.,
Ethnicities: Children of Immigrants in America, pp. 1–19. Berkeley: University
of California Press.

Portes, Alejandro, and Julia Sensenbrenner. 1993. "Embeddedness and Immigration:
Notes on the Social Determinants of Economic Action," *American Journal of
Sociology* 98: 1320–50.

Portes, Alejandro, and John Walton. 1981. *Labor, Class and the International System.*
New York: Academic Press.

Portes, Alejandro, and Min Zhou. 1993. "The New Second Generation: Segmented
Assimilation and Its Variants among Post-1965 Immigrant Youth," *Annals of the
American Academy of Political and Social Sciences* 535: 74–96.

Sadiq, Kamal. 2006. "Have Documents, Will Travel: Illegal 'Citizenship' in Developing Countries." Paper presented at the International Studies Association Annual
Meeting, San Diego, CA.

Sassen, Saskia. 1988. *The Mobility of Capital and Labor.* Cambridge, MA: Cambridge
University Press.

_____. 1991. *The Global City: New York, London, Tokyo.* Princeton, NJ: Princeton
University Press.

_____. 1996. *Losing Control? Sovereignty in an Age of Globalization.* New York:
Columbia University Press.

_____. 2002. "The Repositioning of Citizenship: Emergent Subjects and Spaces of
Politics," *Berkeley Journal of Sociology* 46: 4–25.

_____. 2006. *Territory, Authority, Rights: From Medieval to Global Assemblages.*
Princeton, NJ: Princeton University Press.

Schmitter Heisler, Barbara. 1979. *Immigration and Citizenship in West Germany and Switzerland*, unpublished Ph.D. dissertation, Department of Sociology, University of Chicago.

———. 1984. "Sending States and Immigrant Minorities: The Case of Italy," *Comparative Studies in Society and History* 26: 325–34.

———. 1985. "Sending Countries and the Politics of Emigration and Destination," *International Migration Review* 19: 469–84.

———. 2006. "Transatlantic Discourse? Reflections on Comparing Immigration and Immigrant Integration in the United States and Germany," in Hermann Kurthen, Stefan Immerfall, and Antonio Menendez, eds., *Safeguarding German-American Relations in the New Century: Understanding and Accepting Mutual Differences*, pp. 153–172. Lanham, MD: Lexington Books.

Schuck, Peter. 1998. *Citizens, Strangers and In-Betweens: Essays on Immigration and Citizenship*. Boulder, CO: Westview Press.

Smith, Robert. 1995. *Los Ausentes Siempre Presentes: The Imagining, Making, and Politics of Transnational Community between Ticuani, Puebla, Mexico and New York City*, unpublished Ph.D. dissertation, Department of Sociology, Columbia University.

———. 1998. "Transnational Localities: Community, Technology and the Politics of Membership within the Context of Mexico–U.S. Migration," in Michael Peter Smith and Luis G. Guarnizo, eds., *Transnationalism from Below*, vol. 6, pp. 196–238, Comparative Urban and Community Research. New Brunswick, NJ: Transaction Publishers.

Smith, Michael Peter, and Luis Guarnizo, eds. 1998. *Transnationalism from Below*. New Brunswick, NJ: Transaction Publishers.

Smith, Rogers. 2003. *Stories of Peoplehood: The Politics and Morals of Political Membership*. Cambridge: Cambridge University Press.

Snel, Erik, Godfried Engbersen, and Arjen Leerkes. 2006. "Transnational Involvement and Social Integration," *Global Networks* 6: 285–308.

Soysal, Yasemin. 1994. *Limits to Citizenship: Migrants and Postnational Membership in Europe*. Chicago: University of Chicago Press.

———. 1997. "Changing Parameters of Citizenship and Claims-Making: Organized Islam in European Public Spheres," *Theory and Society* 26: 509–27.

Thomas, W. I., and Florian Znaniecki. 1927. *The Polish Peasant in Europe and America*. New York: Alfred A. Knopf.

Turner, Bryan. Ed. 1993. *Citizenship and Social Theory*. London: Sage Publications.

Waldinger, Roger. 1994. "The Making of an Immigrant Niche," *International Migration Review* 28: 3–30.

———. 1996. *Still the Promised City? African-Americans and New Immigrants in Post-Industrial New York*. Cambridge, MA: Harvard University Press.

Waldinger, Roger, and Mehdi Bozorgmehr, eds. 1996. *Ethnic Los Angeles*. New York: Russell Sage.

Waldinger, Roger, and David Fitzgerald. 2004. "Transnationalism in Question," *American Journal of Sociology* 109: 1177–95.

Warner, Lloyd, and Leo Srole. 1945. *The Social System of American Ethnic Groups*. New Haven, CT: Yale University Press.

Waters, Mary. 1999. "Sociology and the Study of Immigration," *American Behavioral Scientist* 42: 1264–67.

Weber, Max. 1965 [1922]. *The Theory of Social and Economic Organization*, translated by A. M. Henderson and T. Parsons, part I, pp. 88–115. New York: Free Press.

Weil, Patrick. 1998. *The State Matters: Immigration Control in Developed Countries.* New York: United Nations, Department of Social and Economic Affairs, Population Division.

Whyte, William Foote. 1943. *Street Corner Society: The Social Structure of an Italian Slum.* Chicago: University of Chicago Press.

Wiener, Antje. 1997. "Making Sense of the New Geography of Citizenship: Fragmented Citizenship in the European Union," *Theory and Society* 24: 529–60.

Wilson, Kenneth, and Alejandro Portes. 1980. "Immigrant Enclaves: An Analysis of the Labor Market Experience of Cubans in Miami," *American Journal of Sociology* 86: 296–319.

Wimmer, Andreas, and Nina Glick Schiller. 2004. "Methodological Nationalism and Beyond: Nation Building, Migration and the Social Sciences. *Global Networks* 2: 301–34.

Yancey, William, Eugene Erikson, and Richard Juliani. 1976. "Emergent Ethnicity: A Review and Reformulation," *American Sociological Review* 41: 391–402.

Zhou, Min. 2004. "Revisiting Ethnic Entrepreneurship: Convergencies, Controversies, and Conceptual Advancements," *International Migration Review* 38: 1040–74.

CHAPTER 5

Theorizing Migration in Anthropology
The Social Construction of Networks, Identities, Communities, and Globalscapes
Caroline B. Brettell

In the late 1920s, while conducting fieldwork in Manus, New Guinea, Margaret Mead made note of the fact that young boys spent two, five, sometimes seven years away from their villages working for the white man. "This is the great adventure to which every boy looks forward. For it, he learns pidgin, [and] he listens eagerly to the tales of returned work boys" (Mead 1930:119). Similarly, 52 percent of the Chambri (Tchambuli) men between the ages of fifteen and forty-five were working as migrant laborers and therefore absent from the Papua, New Guinea, village where Mead was living in 1933. Despite these observations, Mead's ethnographic descriptions of life in New Guinea at this time are largely portraits of discrete and timeless cultures unaffected by the outside world.[1] This mode of representation was characteristic of the anthropology of Mead's time and of the functionalist paradigm that shaped much anthropological analysis until 1960. It was an anthropology that contained a "sedentarist bias" (Malkki 1995:208) and a rooted definition of culture, both of which explain why anthropology, by comparison with a range of other social science disciplines, did not give the study of migration high priority as an area of research until the late 1950s and early 1960s. As anthropologists progressively rejected the idea of cultures as discretely bounded, territorialized, relatively unchanging, and homogenous units, thinking and theorizing about migration became increasingly possible.

Ultimately, of course, anthropologists had to pay attention to migration because in those regions of the world that had traditionally been their arenas for ethnographic fieldwork—Africa, Oceania, and increasingly Latin America and the Caribbean—people were beginning to move in significant numbers from the countryside to the growing urban centers of the underdeveloped and developing world. In the city these rural villagers were finding employment as unskilled or semiskilled workers and living in neighborhoods with people of their own ethnic group or home community. The interest in migrants and migration grew in conjunction with the growth of both peasant studies and urban anthropology as anthropologists began to focus on peasants or "tribesmen" in cities (Mangin 1970; P. Mayer 1961; Plotnicov 1967; Sanjek 1990).

Since the 1970s, migration studies within anthropology have expanded significantly both with respect to the questions examined and the cross-cultural coverage.[2] Research has been extended to the populations of Europe, the United States, Australia, Southeast Asia, and the Middle East. Increasingly, international migrants, as well as those moving from town to town or city to city, have come under consideration (Trager 2005). Numerous ethnographic monographs have been published—for example, on Jamaicans, Sikhs, Pakistanis, Indians, and Barbadians in England (Bhachu 1985; Foner 1979; Hall 2002; Gmelch 1992; Werbner 1990; Raj 2003); the Senegalese in Italy (Carter 1997); the Portuguese, Algerians, and Caribbeans in France (Brettell 1995; Silverstein 2004; Beriss 2004); Dominicans, Brazilians, Mexicans, Vietnamese, West Africans, Indians, Chinese, and Salvadorans in the United States (Grasmuck and Pessar 1991; Margolis 1994; Chavez 1992; Zloniski 2006; Nash and Nguyen 1995; Stoller 2002; Rangaswamy 2000; Guest 2003; Mahler 1995a); Palestinians in Honduras (Gonzalez 1992); Yemeni Jews in Israel (Gilad 1989); the Yoruba in north Ghana (Eades 1980); Japanese descent Brazilians in Japan (Linger 2001; Tsuda 2003); and Shanghai Chinese in Hong Kong and London (Watson 1975)—culminating in a case studies series edited by Nancy Foner that includes volumes on Haitians (Stepick 1998), Asian Indians (Lessinger 1995), Hmong (Koltyk 1998), Vietnamese (Freeman 1995), and Soviet Jews (Gold 1995) in the United States.[3]

In anthropology, as in other disciplines, theorizing about migration has been shaped by a particular epistemology that generates a specific set of questions. For anthropology, a discipline sensitive to place but also comparative in its perspective, these questions have focused less on the broad scope of migration flows than on the articulation between the place whence a migrant originates and the place or places to which he or she goes. This includes exploration of how people in local places respond to global processes. Equally, anthropology's focus on culture, which includes the study of the interaction between beliefs and behavior, of corporate groups, and of social relationships, has resulted in an emphasis in migration studies on adaptation and culture change, on forms of social organization that are characteristic of both the migration process and the immigrant community, and on questions of identity and ethnicity. In this chapter, I address the anthropological perspective on migration, beginning with a discussion of the formulation of typologies and moving from there to theories of articulation between sending and receiving societies, to a discussion of the social organization of migration and processes of adaptation and change that includes a consideration of the relationship between gender and migration, and finally to an analysis of connections between theorizing migration and theorizing identity and ethnicity.[4]

THE FORMULATION OF TYPOLOGIES

Since its beginnings as a comparative and cross-cultural science, anthropology has relied on typologies as a way to theorize about similarity and difference. Anthropologists have delineated distinct and diverse kinship and marriage systems, classified forms of religious behavior and belief, and distinguished between different types of economic exchange or political organization. Springing from this tradition, Nancie Gonzalez (1961) offered an early formulation of five types of migratory wage labor and looked at the impact of each of these on family organization. She argued that migration would be "reflected in social organization in different ways depending on the nature of the socio-cultural system affected as well as the type of migration itself" (Gonzalez 1961:1278). The five types of migration identified by Gonzalez, based largely on her research in the Caribbean region, were "seasonal," "temporary non-seasonal," "recurrent," "continuous," and "permanent." Gonzalez's typology underscores the fact that population movements, especially those across international boundaries, cannot be defined exclusively as one-way and definitive. In the African context, anthropologists identified some migrants as weekly commuters, others as seasonal and circular movers, and still others as temporary sojourners or permanently displaced (Du Toit 1975). In the Asian context, similar variations in rural-urban migration patterns were identified in terms of the degree of commitment to the city (McGee 1975). All of these types encompass theories about the motivations for migration, about how migration is shaped by local, regional, national, and international economies, about the linkages between sending and receiving societies, and about the relationship between migration on the one hand and family structure and household strategies on the other.

Gonzalez later added "conflict migration" (Gonzalez 1989, 1992) to the list of types of migration to describe population movement that is stimulated by violent conflict in the home society. Others have referred to "enforced migration" (Indra 1999). These concepts raise questions of whether and how to differentiate between migrants and refugees. The latter are assumed to be people who leave their home region involuntarily, but their experiences, once abroad, are not unlike those of migrants with the exception of their inability to return readily and freely to their homeland. Malkki (1995:496) has argued that "refugees do not constitute a naturally self-delimiting domain of anthropological knowledge," and that they can be theorized in much the same way as other displaced peoples (see also Ong 2003). Du Toit (1990) has made a similar suggestion and called, in addition, for consideration of those involuntary migrants displaced by planned relocations.

If typologies delineate various migration strategies, then they also serve to identify differing immigration policies of receiving societies and their relationship to the migrant experience (Caspari and Giles 1986; Goodman 1987). Thus the post–World War II German concept of *Gastarbeiter* (guest worker) came into common use to describe a particular approach to foreign labor reminiscent of the United States *bracero* program (Rhoades 1978b; Mandel 1989, 1990, 1991, 1994). In addition, the categories of undocumented migrant worker or illegal alien have become well known within the United States (Chavez 1990, 1991, 1992, 1994; Chock 1991; Coutin 2005), in post–World War II Europe (as the illegal or clandestine immigrant), and in a host of countries in the developing world. It is important to emphasize that anthropologists, who perceive the disjunction between the ideal and the actual as a fundamental characteristic of human experience, tend to look at immigration policy from the perspective of the immigrant who acts, adapts, and often circumvents (Sargent and Larchanché-Kim 2006). This emphasis is equally shaped by a theoretical shift in the discipline from an emphasis on structure to an emphasis on practice (Bourdieu 1977; Ortner 1984).

Since the late 1970s, in part in association with the emergence of the multi-sited approach to fieldwork (Marcus 1995), several scholars have studied so-called return migration in different parts of the world (Kenney 1976; Rhoades 1978a; Brettell 1979; Gmelch 1983, 1992; Lockwood 1990; Stack 1996; Long and Oxfeld 2004). Gmelch (1980) has drawn attention to typologies of return migration, a basic distinction being between emigrants who intend their departure to be permanent and those who intend it to be temporary. Gmelch (1980) points out that most studies indicate that strong family ties, rather than economic factors (failure to achieve financial success), are the major incentive for return. Stack (1996:xv), for example, finds this to be the case among African Americans from northern cities who were "called back home" to the rural south. "The resolve to return home is not primarily an economic decision but rather a powerful blend of motives; bad times back home can pull as well as push. People feel an obligation to help their kin or even a sense of mission to redeem a lost community . . . or simply a breathing space, a refuge from the maelstrom." In other cases, for example Western Europe after 1973, migrants have been encouraged to return by the host society and offered specific monetary packages to do so.

Return can also be part of the initial migration strategy, albeit frequently postponed. Thus the concept of sojourner has been introduced as a distinct type of migrant. For example, Margolis (1995:31) notes that Brazilians in the United States see themselves as sojourners, target earners who are motivated "by the desire to save money to meet some specific goal back home—buy a house or apartment, a car or telephone, start a business, or perhaps return to school." The question of settler or sojourner has also been raised in connection with Mexican immigrants (Chavez 1988) and is part of a literature on migration ideology that dates back to Philpott's (1973) research on West Indian migration (see also Dahya 1973; Rubenstein 1979). In the Portuguese case (Brettell 2003b), this ideology is linked to the culturally embedded concept of *saudade*—nostalgia for the homeland. *Saudade*, Feldman-Bianco (1992:145) argues, "is a cultural construct that defines Portuguese identity in the context of multiple layers of space and (past) time."

The ideology of return is conceptually similar to what Massey et al. (1993, 1994), drawing largely on anthropological research, have referred to as the culture of migration, where migration is part of behaviors and values, a kind of rite of passage like baptism or marriage (Cohen 2004). For members of Mexican rural households, migration is a survival strategy that occurs at certain phases of a household cycle (Arizpe 1981). These peasant households control the circulation of their children in a form of relay migration. Holmes (1983) makes a similar argument in his reconceptualization of the European worker-peasant. He is able to show that migration is a strategy of great historical depth in some parts of the world, a strategy that has allowed peasant households to persist into the twentieth century. The life course or household lifecycle approach to migration is characteristic of other research in European historical anthropology (Kertzer 1984; Brettell 1986).[5] In this historical work, as well as in work with contemporary societies, anthropologists have observed a powerful relationship between different patterns of inheritance and patterns of migration (Douglass 1974; Iszaevich 1974).

Some of the research on return migration demonstrates that those who do return often remigrate, leading Margolis (1995), based on her research among Brazilian immigrants in New York City, to formulate the concept of "yo-yo migration" as yet another type. She contrasts this type of migration with cultural commuters or shuttle migrants "who regularly migrate back and forth between home and host country with no particular intention of staying in either place for good" (Margolis 1995:32). Since much of this research on return migration is conducted in both sending and receiving societies, it also examines both the impact of out-migration on those left behind and the reintegration of those who have returned after many years abroad (Philpott 1970; Taylor 1976; Gmelch 1992; Grigolini 2004). Ruth Mandel (1990) describes the pain and disorientation characteristic of adolescent Turkish returnees, and in another essay she alludes to the creation of a new ethnic category for Turks who have repatriated—*Alamanyali*, the "Germanlike" (Mandel 1989). As such, rather than being accepted and respected, they are mocked. Similar categories exist for returned Portuguese migrants, be they the *brasileiros* of the nineteenth and early twentieth centuries, or the *franceses* of more contemporary times (Brettell 1986).

Finally, there is a body of research that draws on theoretical work in cultural studies (Massey 1991; Robertson et al. 1994; Ahmed 1999) to explore the relationship between return and concepts of home. Some anthropologists have been interested in where home is located for postcolonial repatriates, labeled by Smith (2003) as "invisible migrants." Others have described the unsettled homecomings of refugees or analyzed the real or imagined homelands of diasporic populations (Falzon 2003; Markowitz and Steffansson 2004).

Anthropologists still rely on typologies to capture different migration strategies, but they also recognize that typologies generally offer a static and homogenous picture of a process that is flexible over the life course of an individual migrant or the domestic cycle of a household, varied within a population, and subject to change over time as larger contextual conditions change. Nevertheless, the typologies formulated by anthropologists have directed research to the diverse nature of the process and to the fundamental relationship between sending and receiving societies, whether conceived in the macroterms of a global economy or in the more microterms of social networks and emotional relationships that link households and individuals to both areas. They also help to achieve some of the comparative theoretical goals of the science of anthropology.[6]

ARTICULATING MICRO AND MACRO/GLOBAL AND LOCAL/IMMIGRANT AND CITIZEN

The delineation of types of migration is one way to theorize the way sending areas are articulated with receiving areas (Kearney 1986). The issue of articulation has been explored by anthropologists according to two distinct analytical approaches, one rooted in modernization theory and the other in a historical-structuralist perspective ultimately grounded in broader theory of political economy and the impact of global capitalism (Georges 1990; Kearney 1995).

Much of the early work on migration within anthropology was influenced by modernization theory and a bipolar framework for analysis that separated and opposed sending and receiving areas, and the push factors of out-migration from the pull factors of in-migration. This approach emerged, as Kearney (1986) has noted, from the folk-urban continuum model originally formulated by Robert Redfield (1941), a model that opposed city and country and contrasted two distinct ways of life, one traditional and one modern. Focusing on the motivations of individual migrants, some anthropologists working within a modernization theory framework have emphasized the rational and progressive economic decisions made in response to differentials in land, labor, and capital between where a migrant lives and the locale to which he or she has chosen to migrate. Wage labor is viewed by these individuals as offering more opportunities than subsistence farming (Mitchell 1969) and can, in fact, provide the cash needed to succeed in the rural context—to accumulate bride-price, provide a dowry, or buy a home. Others, arguing what Du Toit (1990) has recently characterized as the "bright lights" theory (Gulliver 1957; P. Mayer 1961), have emphasized less the attraction of wage jobs than the excitement of urban life, which draws young migrants, especially young men, to it.

One of the underlying assumptions of modernization theory was that the movement of people from areas that had abundant labor but scarce capital to areas that were rich in capital but short of labor would ultimately contribute to economic development in both sending and host societies. Modernization theory, in other words, encompassed an equilibrium model of development, the result of which would be a more equitable balance between resources and population pressure and the ultimate elimination of differences between rural-agrarian and urban-industrial areas. Migrants, through savings and invest-ment, would become agents of change in their home communities. However, as much of the work on emigrant remittances and return migration has demon-strated, migrant savings are often spent on conspicuous consumer items, rather than for economic investment, and the skills learned abroad cannot be easily applied to the rural home context (Rhoades 1978a; Gmelch 1980; Gregory and Cazorla 1987; Donnan and Werbner 1991; Gardner 1995). Rather than being a form of development aid given by rich countries to poor countries, population movements have often resulted in migration-dependent communities and the generation of further migration through the diffusion of consumerism (Massey et al. 1994).

Although the push and pull elements of modernization theory still prevail to order discussions of why people migrate, the shortcomings of the equilib-rium model of linear development with which modernization theory has been associated have stimulated interest in a historical-structuralist approach. This approach shifts attention from the motivations and adaptations of individual migrants to the macrolevel processes that shape and sustain population move-ments. As Lessinger (1995:71, 72) has recently phrased it, "Current research sees the impetus to migration as more complex both for individuals and for entire groups of people. Often push and pull factors operate simultaneously . . . and there is no single profile of a typical migrant."

This historical-structuralist approach draws broadly on Marxist thought and more specifically on the work of dependency theorists such as André Gunder Frank (1967), and world systems theorists such as Immanuel Waller-stein (1974). It frames migration in the context of a global economy, core-periphery relations, and the development of underdevelopment. Within this perspective, concepts such as the international division of labor or the interna-tionalization of the proletariat have emerged to describe the inequities between labor-exporting, low-wage countries and labor-importing, high-wage coun-tries. Rather than stemming migration, development encourages it because development creates inequality and raises awareness about the larger society and hence enhances a sense of relative deprivation (Gonzalez and McCommon 1989). The net economic value of migration accrued to the city and not the countryside, to the core and not the periphery.

The unit of analysis in this body of theory is not the individual migrant, but rather the global market and the way that national and international economic and public policies, and particularly capitalist development, have disrupted, displaced, or even attracted local populations, thereby generating particular migration streams. Thus Eades (1987:13) argued more than two decades ago that "the anthropology of migrant labor ... has become the anthropology of a world social order within which people struggle to make lives for themselves, sometimes helped, but much more often hindered, by the results of international flows of capital and the activities of states over which they have no control."

Dissatisfaction with what was almost exclusively, although perhaps unintentionally, a macroapproach that portrayed migrants not as active agents but as passive reactors manipulated by the world capitalist system has resulted in a new form of theorizing about the articulation between sending and receiving societies, theorizing that is rooted in the concept of transnationalism. Transnationalism, which continues the critique of bipolar models of migration (Rouse 1992), is defined as a social process whereby migrants operate in social fields that transgress geographic, political, and cultural borders (Glick Schiller, Basch, and Szanton Blanc 1992:ix; see also Basch, Glick Schiller, and Szanton Blanc 1994). As a theoretical construct about immigrant life and identity, transnationalism aptly suits the study of population movements in a world where improved modes of transportation, as well as the images that are transmitted by means of modern telecommunications, have shortened the social distance between sending and receiving societies.

Transnationalism, a concept that has attracted sociologists as much as it has anthropologists, emerged from the realization that immigrants abroad maintain their ties to their countries of origin, making "home and host society a single arena of social action" (Margolis 1995:29). From a transnational perspective, migrants are no longer "uprooted," but rather move freely back and forth across international borders and between different cultures and social systems (Sutton 1987; Georges 1990; Kearney 1991; Rouse 1991; Smith 1993, 1997; Grimes 1998; Levitt 1998b; Vertovec 1999). These migrants bring change to localized communities not only through economic remittances but also social remittances (Levitt 1998b). Glick Schiller et al. (1995:49) argue that transnationalism in anthropology is "part of an effort to reconfigure anthropological thinking so that it will reflect current transformations in the way in which time and space [are] experienced and represented" (see also Glick Schiller 2003, 2004). Those who have adopted the transnational framework have written about transnational social fields within which migrant actors operate (Glick Schiller 1997; Gamburd 2000); about transnational identities that challenge processes of immigrant assimilation or incorporation (Panagakos 2003; Koven 2004); about variations in transnational practices at both the individual and institutional level (Cohen 2001; Mankekar 2002; Riccio 2001); about transnational families (Bryceson and Vuorela 2002) and the role of gender in transnationalism (Salih 2003); and about transnational policies that foster an enduring relationship between the state and their nationals abroad (Rodriguez 1996; Harney 2002).

Transnationalism reflects the more general move in anthropology away from bounded units of analysis and localized community studies (Hannerz 1996, 1998; Ho 1993). Conceived as social action in "a multidimensional global space with unbounded, often discontinuous and interpenetrating sub-spaces" (Kearney 1995:549; see also Appadurai 1991 and Rouse 1995a), transnational-ism is closely linked with broader interests emerging from postmodernist and feminist theory to theorize space and place in new ways (Gupta and Ferguson 1992, 1997; Feld and Basso 1996). One outcome of this work is research on diasporic communities (Laguerre 1998).

Diaspora is often imprecisely defined as groups of people living outside their respective homelands.[8] Faced with this imprecision, and the challenge of "defining a traveling term in changing global conditions" (Clifford 1994), some scholars question the analytical utility of the concept, but others have used it to frame a host of interesting questions about the political and economic spaces within which diasporic communities operate (Shukla 2001; Tseng 2002; Werb-ner 2002), the process of Diaspora formation (Brodwin 2003; Watson 2004), or how a "diasporic mode of existence mediates the formation of localized cultures, identities or communities" (Fortier 2000:17; see also Gordon and Anderson 1999 and Kokot, Tololyan, and Alfonso 2004), including diasporic family or ethnic networks (Halter 2004; Olwig 2004). Still others, arguing that the real meaning of diaspora is to be found in the "trail of collective memory about another place and time" (Appadurai and Breckenridge 1989:1), empha-size the subjective meanings of displacement—in short, the nature of diasporic cultural consciousness. Finally, most recently a few anthropologists have pro-posed the concept of new cosmopolitanism to capture "diaspora in motion" and people who occupy "in-between spaces of identity, culture, and communi-cation" (Rajan and Sharma 2006:3).

Theorizing diaspora is associated more broadly with considerations of the nature of community and how people become members of a community, including analysis of so-called border cultures (Alvarez 1995; Kearney 1991) and exploration of the relevance of Anderson's (1983) concept of the "imagined community" to immigration (Chavez 1991, 1994; Smith 1993).[7] Gupta and Fer-guson (1992:11) have argued that immigrants "use memory of place to construct imaginatively their new lived world," while Chavez (1991) views the imagining of community as two pronged—both from the point of view of immigrants and from the point of view of the host society. A sense of belonging emerges among the undocumented when they have "overcome feelings of isolation, developed a network of family and friends in the local community, acquired local cultural knowledge, and reconciled themselves to the possible threat of deportation" (Chavez 1991:272). Migrants themselves describe this process in terms of an emic (that is, their own) notion of adaptation. Etically (i.e., from the analyst's point of view) Chavez draws on the idea of transition as formulated by Arnold Van Gennep to describe incorporation as a process of moving from outsider to insider. However, full incorporation, Chavez argues, requires that the larger society also "imagine" immigrants as members of their community.

Chavez's research is important because it focuses attention on issues of reception and representation of the "immigrant other," something he has carried forward into an analysis of images on the covers of news magazines and what they tell us about the politics of the nation (Chavez 2001). The topic of reception has been explored from a number of different theoretical perspectives. Judith Goode (1990) reframes the relations between newcomers and established residents in a community in Philadelphia as host-guest relations and argues that hosts welcome newcomers "if they try to learn the rules" (126). In this community some of the immigrants have more education and economic power than the established residents, a difference that generates tension. Goode points to the contested arenas and military metaphors (such as "stand the ground") that residents use to express their concern. She also describes the expectations (including being a loyal American) that they hold for newcomers. Cole (1997), in a study of immigrants in Italy, calls for theorizing immigrant reception in relation to institutional or structural racism as well as class and regional identities, while Borneman (1998) draws on discourse analysis, theories of representation, and Goffman's (1963) work on stigma and labeling to explain the negative reception of Marielitos in the United States who were classified as communists, criminals, and homosexuals.[10] Finally, Koptiuch (1996) takes the question of reception in a somewhat different direction with an incisive, critical analysis of the legal strategy of "cultural defense," which characterizes some cases involving Asian immigrants who are brought into the courtrooms of the United States. Thus the attorney for a Hmong "tribesman" brought before a judge to answer criminal charges of kidnapping and rape of a Hmong college coed argues that his client is simply carrying out the cultural ritual of marriage by capture. Criminal charges in this case were dropped in favor of a lesser sentence. But, in Koptiuch's view, this is a form of paternalist and orientalist colonial discourse applied to the empire within. "From a spectacular collapse of space, time, and subjectivity, the law takes license to retrieve a non-historical, primitivized, feminized image of Asia that facilitates . . . the denial of coevalness between Asia and the United States" (Koptiuch 1996:229). This work offers an excellent, albeit rare, example of how anthropology and the law have come together in the study of the implications of the persistence of cultural patterns among immigrants (see also Shweder 2003).

To summarize, transnationalism offers an alternative to and a critique of earlier manifestations of articulation theory that "posit a primeval state of autonomy (usually labeled precapitalist), which is then violated by global capitalism" (Gupta and Ferguson 1992:8). It has generated new ideas about the representation and incorporation of immigrants and the deterritorialization, if not the actual disintegration, of nation–states (Appadurai 1996; Gupta 1992; Hannerz 1992); and it lies behind efforts to merge migration studies with diaspora studies (Clifford 1997). Immigrants in the transnational and global world are involved in the nation-building of more than one state; thus national identities are not only blurred but also negotiated or constructed. "We live in a world where identities increasingly come to be, if not wholly deterritorialized, at least differently territorialized. Refugees, migrants, displaced and stateless peoples—these are perhaps the first to live these realities in their most complete form" (Gupta and Ferguson 1992:9).

Some anthropologists have recently argued that the transnational arrangements constructed by "ordinary migrants, their families and their friends, have undermined both the political dominance exerted by the state and its cultural authority" (Rouse 1995a:358; see also Appadurai 1996 and Kearney 1991) and are therefore beginning to address the question of citizenship from a transnational perspective. Borneman (1997), for example, in research conducted prior to recent changes in German citizenship laws, has compared the exclusion from citizenship of immigrants in Germany who are legal residents and who have become culturally and linguistically German with the inclusion of ethnic Germans who have resided elsewhere in the world, sometimes for more than two centuries, and who are in fact linguistically and cultural distinct. Glick Schiller and Fouron (2001) describe long-distance Haitian nationalists who engage in transborder citizenship and Ong (1999:112) has formulated the concept of "flexible citizenship" to capture the "strategies and effects of mobile managers, technocrats, and professionals seeking to both circumvent and benefit from different nation–state regimes by selecting different sites for investments, work, and family relocation."

Maira (2004) writes about cultural citizenship among South Asian Muslim youth in the United States. As formulated by Rosaldo and Flores (1997:57), cultural citizenship refers "to the right to be different (in terms of race, ethnicity, or native language) with respect to the norms of the dominant national community, without compromising one's right to belong, in the sense of participating in the nation–state's democratic processes." Ong (1996:737) has developed quite a different approach, defining citizenship as a "cultural process of 'subjectification', in the Foucaldian sense of self-making and being-made by power relations that produce consent through schemes of surveillance, discipline, control, and administration." And Goldring (2001), in a study of the gendering of citizenship in transnational social fields, points to differences between citizenship as formal rights and substantive citizenship practice or social citizenship. Anthropological research has expanded our understanding of the forms and meanings of citizenship and delineated the complex ways in which immigrants define their own sense of belonging (Ong 2003; Brettell 2006).

THEORIZING THE SOCIAL ORGANIZATION OF MIGRATION: KINSHIP, NETWORKS, GENDER, AND ETHNIC ENCLAVES

The anthropologist generally locates transnational processes within the lives of individuals and families and particularly in the personal, economic, and social connections that articulate the world they have left with the world they have entered (Goodson-Lawes 1993; Mahler 1995; Min 1998; Pessar 1995a; Wong 1998). In other words, if the roots of the discipline are in the study of kinship and social organization, then these roots are also at the core of migration research in anthropology and revolve in particular around the concept of social network, which gained importance as anthropologists turned their attention to the study of complex societies and urban populations (Boissevain and Mitchell 1973; Mitchell 1971, 1974).[11] Although considered by many to be no more than a tool of research and a method of analysis, in fact theories about how social relationships are forged and how social systems are constructed are at the foundation of network analysis.

In a wide range of cross-cultural contexts, anthropologists have examined the role of networks, based largely on ties of kinship and friendship, in the process of chain migration or what Wilson (1994) has recently labeled "network-mediated migration" (Butterworth 1962; Graves and Graves 1974; Kemper 1977; Fjellman and Gladwin 1985; Massey et al. 1987; Kearney and Nagengast 1989; Ho 1993; Gardner 1995; Margaret Grieco 1995; Elizabeth Grieco 1998). Often, these anthropologists have emphasized multiple destinations rather than a bipolar model linking one sending society to one receiving area (Uzzell 1976; Du Toit 1990; Ho 1993). "Network-mediated chain migration does not necessarily mean that prospective migrants or migrant families are given only one or a few options as to where they will go. . . . [Migrants . . . seek work first one place, then another, where they have kin and friends. In retrospect this can appear as a step migration pattern to an ultimate destination to which a migrant recurrently returns or where he/she finally settles in with or without his/her family" (Wilson 1994:272). Wilson goes on to argue (1994:275) that migration networks must be conceived as facilitating rather than encapsulating, as permeable, expanding, and fluid rather than as correlating with a metaphor of a rigid and bounded structure. She prefers this network approach to a market theory approach that involves immigrants in a cost-benefit analysis of the most favorable destination. Thus she concurs with the conclusion drawn by Massey et al. (1993:449) who suggest that networks can become self-perpetuating to migration because "each act of migration itself creates the social structure needed to sustain it. Every new migrant reduces the costs of subsequent migration for a set of friends and relatives, and some of these people are thereby induced to migrate, which further expands the set of people with ties abroad." The theory of network-mediated migration is quite distinct from theories rooted in the rational-choice and decision-making models preferred by some economists and political scientists. Indeed, it is only with a network-based model that Chapin (1992) could formulate her argument that lower-class emigrant tourists who return to the Azores for vacations stimulate the emigration of upper-class individuals.

Both transnationalism and the study of social networks have shifted the unit of analysis from the individual migrant to the migrant household (Briody 1987). Households and social networks mediate the relationship between the individual and the world system and provide a more proactive understanding of the migrant than that provided by the historical-structuralist framework. In other words, the effort to combine macro- and microperspectives of analysis through the filter of the household not only brings the migrant-as-decision-maker back into focus, but also reintroduces the social and cultural variables that must be considered in conjunction with economic variables. This synthetic approach permits an analysis of subtle differences between those local communities or social classes that become extensively involved in migration and those that do not. It also provides more understanding of how migration streams are perpetuated despite changes in economic and public policies that serve to constrain or halt them. Grasmuck and Pessar (1991:15, 13) have made the case most pointedly: "It is not individuals but households that mobilize resources and support, receive and allocate remittances, and make decisions about members' production, consumption and distribution of activities. . . . Social networks and households simultaneously mediate macrostructural changes, facilitate the migration response to these changes, and perpetuate migration as a self-sustaining social process."

While anthropologists, and increasingly sociologists and historians, have recognized the significance of networks of kinship and friendship to the process of migration, they have also paid a good deal of attention to and hence theorized about the role of networks in the process of settlement and adaptation in the society of immigration—that is, how networks provide social capital. Lomnitz (1977), for example, found that kinship networks were the basic units of production and consumption among rural-urban migrants in Mexico. In his work among undocumented Central Americans in Houston, Rodriguez observes the "larger the social network that serves for organizing undocumented migration, the greater are the social and economic resources that can be mustered for settlement, leading to greater household stability" (Rodriguez 1987:17; see also Buechler 1976; Brettell and Callier-Boisvert 1977; Lamphere, Silva, and Sousa 1980; Gold 1989; Benson 1990; Anwar 1995; Grieco 1998; Poros 2001; Avenarius 2002; Clarke 2004). Ho (1993) looks carefully at the sharing and reciprocity that occurs within kinship networks that cross national boundaries to create international families and a common practice of child fostering that aids migrants in achieving their goals (see also Nelson 1987; Soto 1987; Spiegel 1987). Werbner (1990), in a fascinating study of the relationship between labor migration and the gift economy, stresses the central role of networks not only in the processes of distribution and credit among Pakistani entrepreneurs in Manchester, England, but also as the foundation for complex relationships of gift exchange that bind the community together. "Through gifting migrants transform persons who are strangers into lifelong friends. Through such exchanges, not only men but whole households and extended families are linked, and exchanges initiated on the shop floor extend into the domestic and inter-domestic domain" (Werbner 1990:332; see also Werbner 1995 and White 1997). Although she does not invoke it directly, Werbner's analysis fits squarely into the interactionist theoretical approach that has its roots in Marcel Mauss's classic essay *The Gift*.[12]

Immigrant women are often at the center of these immigrant networks. They both initiate and maintain them (Smith 1976; Kossoudji and Ranney 1984; Stafford 1984; Yanagisako 1985; Zavella 1988; Aranda 2003; Curran and Rivero-Fuentes 2003). O'Connor (1990) describes the female-centered informal networks based on the Mexican tradition of *confianza* (trust) that emerge among Mexican women working in a wholesale nursery in California. These networks help immigrant women to cope successfully "with the conditions imposed by the Anglo-dominated political and economic structure" (O'Connor 1990:97), or to "discover ways to negotiate patriarchal barriers" (Hondagneu-Sotelo 1994:94). Married women in particular use them to facilitate their own migration, often without the knowledge of their husbands.

Despite Ravenstein's (1885) claim more than a century ago that women dominated short-distance population movements, women were generally ignored in the study of migration until quite recently.[13] If women were considered at all, then it was as dependents and passive followers of the initiating male migrant. Alternatively, women were the ones who waited in the countryside, assuming many of the responsibilities that had once been in the hands of men.[14] This particular conceptualization of the relationship between women and the process of migration suited modernization theory—women represented the traditional pole of the continuum and men the pole of modernity. Today it is apparent that not only are women often the first to migrate (sometimes they receive the initial job contract), but they also outnumber men in some international migration streams—for example, among Caribbean immigrants to the United States. Gender has been shown to be important in the decision to migrate (when, where, and who) as well as in the process of settlement in the receiving society. It has, as Mahler and Pessar (2006) have recently argued, been brought from the periphery to the core of migration studies.

Anthropologists have been at the forefront in theorizing about the significance of gender in migration (Phizlacklea 1983; Morokvasic 1984; Simon and Brettell 1986; Brydon 1987; Goodman 1987; Westwood and Bhachu 1988; Brettell and deBerjeois 1992; Buijs 1993; Ho 1993; Pessar 1999; Mahler 1999; Anthias and Lazarides 2000). This research focuses on the role and experiences of women in migration and on the changes that occur in family and kinship patterns as a result of migration (Kibria 1993; Foner 1997a). It examines the labor force participation of immigrant women (it is high), the impact of salaried employment on domestic roles and domestic power, health issues, and issues of political consciousness-raising. Much of this research can be squarely situated in relation to analytical models at the heart of feminist anthropology—the domestic-public model that explores women's status in relation to different spheres of activity and the model springing from Marxist feminism that addresses the interrelationship between production and repro-duction. Among the questions explored are whether wage earning serves to enhance the power and status of immigrant women within their households, whether greater sharing of household activities emerges as a result of the work obligations of women, and how changes in employment, family structure, and lifestyle affect women's own assessments of their well being (Stafford 1984; Lamphere 1987; Meintel 1987; Freidenberg et al. 1988; Fernandez-Kelly and Garcia 1990; Mills 1998; Hirsch 1999; Parrenas 2001; George 2005). Chai (1987a, 1987b), for example, explicitly applies the conceptual scheme of domes-tic/public to an analysis of Korean immigrant women in Hawaii. Middle-class and well-educated Korean women have been relegated to the domestic sphere in their home society, but as immigrants they take waged work outside the home. This wage earning "may lead to a more flexible division of labor, deci-sion making and parental responsibility, as well as to less sex segregation in social and public places" (Chai 1987b:229). Korean women who tire of the menial jobs to which they are relegated in the public domain often revert to working in family-owned businesses and construct their own public domain with its own ladder of achievement within the Korean ethnic community. Bha-chu (1988:76), in a study of the wage work of Sikh immigrant women in Brit-ain, moves "beyond the simple thesis that wage labour equals liberation" to argue that "women's increased ability to develop more self-defined roles has been aided by their increased access to cash, which has allowed them to invest and consume in their own interests and for their own benefit." She also argues that specific cultural values and social patterns have undergone radical changes as a result both of migration and women's waged labor. Although the wage work of Dominican immigrant women in the United States leads to improved domestic social relations and ideology, "these household level changes do not in turn stimulate modifications in female workers' consciousness and demands for improved conditions in the workplace" (Pessar 1984:1189). By contrast, in Stockton, California, the informal economic activities in which Cambodian refugee women engage to generate extra earnings, as well as the fact that there are more job opportunities for women in this particular local economy, pro-vide the basis for their emergent leadership roles within a community where they are the primary breadwinners (Ui 1991; see also Pessar 2001).[15]

The new sense of control that women gain as immigrants has raised ques-tions for some anthropologists about the varying attitudes of men and women toward both life abroad and return migration. While some immigrant women yearn for the homeland (Goodson-Lawes 1993), research has more often demonstrated that women are often more reluctant to return to the sending society than are migrant men because it will mean giving up some of the advantages they have gained while abroad (Barou 1996). Gmelch and Gmelch (1995), in a comparative study of returnees to several countries of origin, found that women were less satisfied than men to be "home" and had greater problems of readjustment. They suggest that this is due not to differential motivations for return but to limited employment opportunities and specific social conditions that constrain women's social relationships. Goodson-Lawes (1993), in her study of Mexican women in Mexico and California, argues that the central issue is one of authority and power. In some cases women may feel that they have more power, even if more covert than overt, in their home village: "The type and extent of feminine authority wielded may be altered with immigration and thus affects the decision to emigrate or to return. In large part this decision can be understood as the product of a tension between desired control and imagined opportunity. When the possibilities of the North surpass, in a personal equation, the need to maintain a sense of personal control, one is enticed toward the border" (Goodson-Lawes 1993:293).[16]

In general, anthropological research on immigrant women that is framed in relation to the domestic/public model, the opposition between production and reproduction, or issues of power and authority, all of which are central to feminist anthropological theory (Moore 1988, 1994), indicates a set of complex and varied responses to the necessity of balancing work and family life. In some cases greater equality between men and women is the result, in others it is not. The differences must be explained by a close examination of cultural factors (including gender ideology) and economic constraints. Pessar (1995b) has argued that the study of immigrant women challenges claims of feminist theorists about the nature of unpaid domestic work and the relationship between wage labor and women's emancipation. Drawing from postmodern feminist theory, she adopts an inner subjectivity to stress that immigrant women do not necessarily view their situation as oppressive and that in fact many forge multiple and complex identities.[17]

Working within a political-economy theoretical framework, research on how the social position of immigrant women is affected by the social, economic, and political policies of states has also been a topic of research. Some theorists have described a "triple invisibility" for migrant women based on factors of class, ethnicity, and gender (Marshall 1981; Morokvasic 1983; Lamphere 1986; Melville 1988; Segura 1989; Chavira-Prado 1992). Segmented occupational structures funnel immigrant women into a few sectors of the economy, the garment industry and domestic service in particular (Fernandez-Kelly and Garcia 1985; Repak 1995). Colen (1990) describes the West Indian household workers who had to put up with the long hours and myriad responsibilities to obtain their green cards with the help of an employer-sponsor. She argues that "a system of reproduction operates, encouraged by the state, which is highly stratified by class, race, place in a global political economy, and migration status" (Colen 1990:110). For some immigrant women the segmented labor market has meant downward mobility (Chai 1987a; Gold 1989; Margolis 1990). One Haitian woman complained, "The job I do is for an animal. It's the same day after day. I used to be a schoolteacher in Haiti. Now I'm doing a job that doesn't even require me to think" (Stafford 1984:181). Exploring the questions of gender, migration, and exploitation from a somewhat different angle, Margold (1995) describes the disintegration of self and the dismemberment of masculinity among Filipino male migrants in the Middle East who are referred to as "dogs" and "slaves," while Mills (1998) addresses how Thai female migrants negotiate gendered identities in relation to courtship and marriage in the context of the hegemonic forces of global capitalism. She concludes that "migrant women's encounters with dominant notions of Thai modernity engage them in the pursuit of new models of self-fulfillment and personal autonomy that focus their concerns on individual gendered dilemmas and choices rather than broader structures and relations of power" (Mills 1998:325).

While many immigrant women internalize the discrimination that ensues from this employment situation, others, in rarer instances, have become part of group-based political action (Ong 1987; Salzinger 1991; Giles 1991, 1992, 1993; Groves and Change 1999; Goldring 2003). Much of this work is informed by broader thinking within feminist anthropology on formal and informal strategies of resistance that is itself shaped by the work of James Scott and by Anthony Giddens' theory of agency (Giddens 1984; Scott 1985; see also L. Abu-Lughod 1990; Moore 1994; Ortner 1995). It also challenges widely accepted notions that cultural constraints and a tight-knit ethnic enclave preclude immigrant women from engaging in political and leadership activities within and on behalf of their communities.

Of particular interest is Ui's (1991) study of female leadership in the Cambodian refugee community in Stockton, California. She argues that the rapid growth of the enclave has resulted in an expansion of service programs for Cambodians, which has in turn created employment opportunities that are disproportionately filled by women. These positions become the basis for obtaining economic and social power and hence leadership roles. Her conclusion offers a hypothesis that can be tested within other immigrant communities: "Despite traditional culture and gender roles, female leadership will develop and emerge when groups are in a situation in which ethnic identity and unity are strong, the employment opportunities for women are greater than those for men, and the intervention of the welfare state is significant" (Ui 1991:175).

Ui's study indicates that the concept of the ethnic enclave, addressed quite extensively by sociologists, is also of some importance to anthropological thinking about institution building, community formation, insertion into a particular urban economy and society, and the creation of ethnic space among immigrant populations (Harbottle 1997; Herman 1979; Kwong 1997; Werbner 1987; Wong 1998). Brettell (2003c) has asked whether an ethnic enclave or community is inevitable in a broader comparative context, and points to immigration policy, laws about small business proprietorship, and the structure of cities as important variables to consider. Similarly, Werbner (1990), in research on Sikhs in Britain, addresses the question of whether and how enclave economies are formed, relating this process in some cases to the relative weight of ethnic versus class resources as principles of social organization within an immigrant community. Finally, based on research among Latinos in Washington, D.C., Pessar concludes that the emergence of social solidarity and an ethnic enclave is not inevitable and is unlikely where "immigrants do not face major hurdles to full participation in mainstream social and economic institutions" (Pessar 1995c:391). In this research on immigrant place-making, anthropologists have often drawn on the research of geographers, for whom space and place are equally important theoretical constructs.

Studies of ethnic enclaves in sociology are also linked with theories about the extent to which the ethnic economy and self-employment deter or promote immigrant incorporation and social and economic mobility. These are also questions explored by some anthropologists. Alvarez (1990), for example, challenging widely held notions that Mexican immigrants have a low level of involvement in entrepreneurship and the ethnic economy, outlines their activities in the Los Angeles produce industry. He finds it necessary to move beyond dual economy and labor market theory to anthropological theories about market hierarchies, formulated initially in the study of peasant societies in Asia and Latin America, in order to explain what has happened. Boissevain and Grotenberg (1986) have examined variables such as experience and feeling about management, access to loyal and cheap labor, a patriarchal family structure, access to capital, the ability to control the administration of credit, access to a network of contacts, ambition and willingness to take risk, and a desire for independence to explain differences in the degree of self-employment among Surinamese of various ethnic backgrounds (Hindustani, Creole, Chinese, Javanese) who reside in Amsterdam. In another essay, Boissevain and Grotenbreg (1989) address the legal constraints on the self-employment of immigrants. Their research can be situated in relation to the theoretical debate within sociology (specifically in the work of Ivan Light and Edna Bonacich 1988) between cultural background and structural conditions as explanations for rates of entrepreneurship. They conclude that the harsh analytical distinction is inappropriate.

The work on ethnic enclaves and the ethnic economy within anthropology can also be related to a separate literature within urban anthropology that focuses on "the city as context" as an important framework within which to examine the process of adaptation and institution building among immigrant populations (Rollwagen 1974a, 1974b; M. Smith 1974; Foner 1987a; Lamphere 1992; Brettell 2003d). In an attempt to "theorize the city," Low (1997) distinguishes between ethnic cities, gendered cities, and global cities. She delineates two different approaches in research on ethnic cities. One describes the ethnic city as a "mosaic of enclaves that are economically, linguistically and socially self-contained as a strategy of political and economic survival." The other focuses on ethnic groups defined "by their location in the occupational structure, their position in the local immigrant social structure, their degree of marginality, and/or their historical and racial distinctiveness as the basis of discrimination and oppression" (Low 1997:405; see also Low 1996). Low's formulations suggest a profitable new direction in research, one that reunites theories of migration and theories of urbanization. Certainly some anthropologists have moved to focus on the city as a unit of analysis in their study of immigration (Stepick et al. 2003), reflecting a broader trend across disciplines to theorize municipal responses to immigrants (Alexander 2003).

THEORIZING MIGRATION/THEORIZING ETHNICITY AND IDENTITY

Clearly, anthropological studies of ethnic enclaves and entrepreneurship among migrant populations also underscore the close connections between theorizing migration and theorizing ethnicity. Indeed, Kearney (1995:559) has observed that "at the heart of current anthropological concerns with transnationalism, identity politics, migration, and human rights is the persistence, resurgence, or de novo emergence of ethnicity at a time when, according to modernization theory, it was to have been attenuated by robust nation states." He links the growing interest in the concept of identity and by extension ethnicity to the "implosion" of the concept of culture.[18]

Anthropological consideration of ethnicity has its origins in the research of the first generation of urban anthropologists working in Africa. Seminal work such as J. Clyde Mitchell's (1957) study of the Kalela Dance in Rhodesia (now Zambia), Epstein's (1958) monograph, *Politics in an Urban African Community,* and Abner Cohen's (1969) analysis of how Hausa traders used ethnicity for their own political and economic ends, challenged the assumption that detribalization was the inevitable outcome of the movement of rural dwellers to cities—clearly another critique of modernization theory. Much of this early work wrestled with the conceptual differences between "tribe" and "ethnic group" and resulted in the delineation of three distinct theoretical approaches to the study of ethnicity.[19] The primordialist approach, which prevailed until the 1960s, argues that ethnic identity is the result of deep-rooted attachments to group and culture; the instrumentalist approach focuses on ethnicity as a political strategy that is pursued for pragmatic interests; and the situational approach, emerging from the theoretical work of Frederik Barth

(1969), emphasizes the fluidity and contingency of ethnic identity, which is constructed in specific historical and social contexts (Banks 1996).

In studies of migration by anthropologists, the latter two approaches have attracted the most attention, not only because they suit the more emergent and interactive understanding of culture and the poststructuralist emphasis on the multiple and shifting basis of self-representation (Gupta and Ferguson 1997), but also because the act of migration brings populations of different backgrounds into contact with one another and hence creates boundaries. It is the negotiation across such boundaries, themselves shifting, that is at the heart of ethnicity and the construction of migrant identities.[20] As Tseng (2002: 386) has observed, ethnic identification is "dialogic, in the sense that it is created, preserved, reaffirmed, and even rejected through a continuous set of contrasts between one's own group and others."

Ethnicity is thus theorized as a strategic response, invoked in particular situations (Durham 1989). Thus, Lyman and Douglass (1973:350) have argued that to treat ethnic identity "as a group phenomenon in which recruitment of membership is ascriptive forecloses study of the process whereby individuals make use of ethnicity as a maneuver or stratagem in working out their own life chances in an ethnically pluralistic social setting." This is precisely the approach that Rouse (1995b) takes in his study of Mixtec migrants from the *municipio* of Aguililla in central western Mexico who are residing in Redwood City, California. "Most Aguilillans who migrated . . . did not negotiate a shift from one set of identities to another but instead moved from a world in which identity was not a central concern to one in which they were pressed with increasing force to adopt understandings of personhood and collectivity that privileged notions of autonomous self-possession and a formal equivalence between the members of a group" (Rouse 1995b:370).[21] Lessinger (1995:6) follows a similar line of argument in her research on Asian Indians in the United States. "For many Indian immigrants and their children, ethnic group identity and ethnicity, have become the point of entry into U.S. society, and the vehicle for carving out a social role. . . . When Indians first migrate to the United States they think of themselves as Indians living abroad, then begin to envision themselves as Americans. Very quickly, however, they realize that U.S. society divides itself along ethnic and racial lines. A great many Indian immigrants conclude that it is preferable to develop an ethnic group identity rather than accept a racial categorization."

Negotiating race and ethnicity is also part of the Jamaican and Haitian immigrant experiences in the United States (Foner 1985, 1987; Stafford 1987) and has led several anthropologists to argue that race and ethnicity need to be considered together in any theoretical formulations of the construction of immigrant identity (Williams 1989; Goode and Schneider 1994; Banks 1996; Brettell 2007). Stepick (1998) describes how Haitian immigrant youth construct their identity in relation or in contrast to that of African Americans. He characterizes the first case as a "Haitian cover-up" and reveals some intriguing differences between boys who choose to be monocultural (either Haitian or African American) and girls who choose to be multicultural (both Haitian and African American).

Similar issues and approaches arise in research among immigrants in the European context. The identity of Sikh immigrants in Britain is crosscut by differences of class and caste as well as by differences between "twice migrants" and direct migrants (Bhachu 1993). Mandel (1989), emphasizing how social context influences the expression of identity, describes Greeks and Turks who are bitter enemies in the homeland but who join in a common purpose as immigrants in Germany. At issue, she suggests, "are the ways self and other articulate, historically and in the migratory situation, with shifting hierarchies of 'others'" (Mandel 1989:62). White (1997:754) comes to a similar conclusion, arguing that Turkish identities in Berlin "are forged from class, ethnic, and religious loyalties, from institutional and media ethnoscapes (created by Germans and by Turks themselves), from shared regularities of interpersonal expectations of generalized reciprocity, and in reaction to how Turks are defined (and redefined after reunification) by Germans." She focuses on the processual, community-building aspects of identity rather than on those that rely on fixed and external markers such as language. All these scholars of immigration suggest that ethnicity, which Ronald Cohen (1978:387) has defined (from the situational perspective) as a "series of nesting dichotomizations of inclusiveness and exclusiveness," provides a foundation for constructing social cohesion and allegiance. It organizes and legitimizes responsive action. It is the "location and reason for the maintenance of a we/they dichotomization" [that has become], in Cohen's view (1978:385), "the crucial goal of research and theorizing."

Some anthropologists have explored the symbols or ethnic markers around which such dichotomizations are formulated or constructed. Beriss (1990), for example, analyzes the so-called Foulard Affair, the 1989 incident in France in which three young girls were expelled from a school for wearing Muslim scarves in class. At the center of the conflict were the issues of French national identity and the integration of immigrants. Gross, McMurray, and Swedenburg (1996) explore the role of a musical genre, *rai,* not only in the construction of Franco-Maghrebi identities in Paris and Marseilles but also in the recasting of contemporary French identity in less exclusive and more syncretized form. Koltyk (1993) discusses how story cloths and home videos become the focus for the definition of self and the reinforcement of ethnic affiliation among Hmong refugees in the United States. Drawing on the theoretical work of Clifford and Marcus (1986), she views the videos in particular as a form of ethnic voice by which Hmong can write their own history and take control of their future, including the process by which they are integrated into American society. Finally, and in a somewhat different vein, Harbottle (1997) analyzes how

Iranian immigrants in Britain who are involved in the catering trade disguise and protect their ethnicity through their work with specific types of non-Iranian food.

Mandel (1996), in an essay that links ethnic entrepreneurship to the symbols of ethnic identity, describes shopkeepers in Kreuzberg, the "little Istanbul" of Berlin, who have used the fear of *haram* (forbidden meat) as well as that which is obligatory or permitted (*helal*) to their advantage, the result being a proliferation of shops that cater exclusively to Turks and the creation of a Muslim space in Germany that is then subdivided by religion, either Sunni or Alevi. This "commercial self-sufficiency," she argues, "is another way the migrants have recreated the place for themselves, and in their own terms. . . . In this new place, by their own actions and decisions, they are setting new precedents, as they project an agency of their own design, reshaping the Kreuzbergs of Europe into novel and heterogeneous communities" (Mandel 1996:163–64). From a more critical perspective, Kwong (1997:366) argues that within the Chinese community in New York ethnic solidarity "has increasingly been manufactured by the economic elite . . . to gain better control over their co-ethnic employees." Employers convince their employees, many of whom are illegal immigrants, that the larger society is hostile and racist. In what he views as a form of class exploitation, these co-ethnic elites control the boundaries of the ethnic community and promote ethnic identity to serve their own ends.

Within the migrant spaces such as those described above, immigrants engage in a host of community activities that become expressions of their ethnic identity. Anthropologists have been particularly interested in religious institutions and activities.[22] Ralston (1992), for example, has explored the role of religion in the formation of personal and social identity among South Asian immigrant women in Canada. In the absence of residential concentration, it is the collective activities in religious institutions that provide the context for ethno-religious consciousness. Indeed, she argues that in the context of a Canadian policy of multiculturalism religious activities may be more prominent as markers of identity abroad than they are at home. In a somewhat similar vein, Park (1989:290) suggests that many Korean immigrants "go from being non-religious to becoming believers." In New York City, where a new Korean church was founded every six days in the mid-1980s, the church provides an ethnic forum for socializing and status seeking. She contrasts the double role of Christian churches to both promote Americanization and preserve Korean identity with the emphasis on the preservation of Korean culture in Buddhist churches. In particular, Park explores the meaning of being "born again" and its links to spirit possession in Korean shamanistic ritual. Numerous other scholars, across a range of disciplines, have noted the significance of religious institutions to place-making and the construction of community among immigrant populations (Warner and Wittner 1998; Ebaugh and Chafetz 2000; Min and Kim 2002).

McAlister (1998) also explores the fusing of religious traditions in the context of transnationalism in her description of the participation of Haitian immigrants in the feast of the Madonna of 115th Street, a feast originated by Italian immigrants (Orsi 1985). Several other ethnographers have documented the survival, if not elaboration, of Afro-Caribbean, spirit-based religions such as Voodoo and Santería among West Indian immigrants in the United States (Gregory 1987; Murphy 1988; Brown 1991). Among the most interesting is Tweed's (1997) monograph on the shrine of Our Lady of Charity, which serves the Cuban community in Miami. Tensions between prescribed religion and religion as practiced, between official Catholicism and Santería rituals are apparent. But Tweed's broader argument is that Cuban exiles see the shrine in Miami as a place to express diasporic nationalism and construct a translocal identity. Levitt (1998a) also draws on ideas about translocal identity to describe a transnational religious system connecting Dominican immigrants in Boston with their home island. These religious connections are part of what she labels social remittances, the "ideas, practices, identities, and social capital that flow from receiving to sending-country communities" (Levitt 1998a:76). Religious life in the home community has changed as a result of immigrant religious life, while the Catholic Church in Boston has succeeded where political and economic organizations have failed in forging pan-ethnic coalitions.

This interest in religion is also manifested in anthropological studies of ethnic festivals. Schneider (1990) has analyzed the ethnic parades of Poles and Puerto Ricans in Philadelphia as symbolic presentations that encode ideas about being an immigrant and being an American. Parade commentators stress unity and community self-identification as messages conveyed by these events. Similarly, Kasinitz and Freidenberg-Herbstein (1987) have compared a West Indian American Day Carnival and a Puerto Rican Day Parade in New York as manifestations of ethnic pride and civic politics. Abner Cohen (1980, 1993) has studied similar festivals among West Indian immigrants in Britain. Finally, Werbner (1996) describes the processions of Muslim men to celebrate anniversaries of death and rebirth that wind their way through the streets of immigrant neighborhoods in Birmingham, Manchester, and London, England. Through these processions Muslims "stamp the earth with the name of allah" and thereby "make territorial claims in their adopted cities . . . and assert their equal cultural claims within the society" (Werbner 1996:182).[23] All of these studies challenge unidirectional theories of assimilation, add agency and fluidity to the process of adaptation, and reinforce the theory that ethnicity is culturally constructed. As Glick Schiller (1977) suggested more than 20 years ago, "ethnic groups are made, not born."

CONCLUSION

Although migrants around the globe have common experiences, migration itself is a complex and diverse phenomenon. Migrants can be differentiated by sex, class, ethnicity, the nature of their labor force participation, their reasons for migrating, the stage of the life cycle at which they move, the form of the migration (internal, international, temporary, and so on), and the nature and impact of global economic and political policies that affect population movement. A consideration of all these factors, from a comparative perspective, offers the best understanding of the process of migration and of migrant culture. It assumes that migrants act and are "acted upon" with reference to their social, cultural, and gendered locations.

But for anthropologists whose central interest is in the human dimensions of this global process and the lived experience of being a migrant, there are further considerations that guide their research. These considerations have their roots in several key concepts of the discipline that in turn ground anthropological theory. Thus, the distinction between nature and culture is at the foundation of theories of ethnicity that reject a primordial and inherent identity in favor of one that is socially constituted. The connections between society and culture, as well as an understanding of community that has both local (micro) and global (macro) dimensions help to explain how migrants as transnationals can operate in or between two (or more) worlds. An acceptance of the common disjunction between the ideal and the actual permits more complex formulations of the processes of change and adaptation that are part of being a migrant. An awareness of the differences between participant's models (the emic perspective) and observer's models (the etic perspective) lends subtlety to our knowledge of similarities and differences and solidity to our theories about the particular and the general in the experience of migration. Furthermore, an observer's model rooted in the interaction between structure and agency accepts the fact that migrants shape and are shaped by the context (political, economic, social, cultural) within which they operate, whether in the sending society or in the receiving society.[24] Finally, the holistic perspective draws anthropologists to an exploration of a range of social and cultural phenomena (religious rituals, for example) that both have an impact on and are affected by migration.

Much of what is written by anthropologists on the subject of migration may, at first glance, be dismissed as largely descriptive ethnography, but a closer examination indicates that while generally "located" in the study of a specific migrant community or population, most of this research is implicitly, if not explicitly, theoretical. If a theory is defined as "an explanation of a class of events, usually with an empirical referent, providing insight into how and what is going on, and sometimes explaining why phenomena exist" (Barrett 1997:40), then much of this ethnographic work makes a significant and sometimes unique contribution to our theoretical conversations across the disciplines.

NOTES

1. For a discussion of the essentializing character of Mead's work see Gewertz and Errington 1991. Lavie and Swedenburg (1996:2) have posed the question of what Margaret Mead would have "made of Samoan gangs in Los Angeles, or of the L.A.-Samoan gansta rap group the Boo-Yah Tribe, named after the Samoan term "boo yah!" for a shotgun blast in a drive-by shooting.

2. This turning point was marked by the theme of the 1970 volume of the proceedings of the American Ethnological Society, *Migration and Anthropology*, edited by Robert F. Spencer. Five years later, two volumes dealing with migration were the result of the World Anthropological Congress (Du Toit and Safa 1975; Safa and Du Toit 1975). In these volumes, migration was linked to urbanization and development.

3. Other volumes in this series are Margolis 1998; Min 1998; Pessar 1995; Mahler 1995b; Wong 1998; Holtzman 2000; and Adler 2004. Holtzman's volume on the Nuer has sold well because the Nuer, the subject of classic ethnographic work by the British social anthropologist E. E. Evans Pritchard, are well known among anthropologists.

4. See Foner (2003) for a recent assessment of anthropological approaches to the study of contemporary U.S. migration. See Foner (2005) and Brettell (2003a) for further discussion of the importance of the comparative perspective in the anthropological study of immigration.

5. Escobar, Gonzalez, and Roberts (1987:59) also argue that stage in the life and household cycle can also influence the place of destination. For further discussion of the historical relationship between migration and the peasant household, see Moch 1992 and Brettell 2002.

6. Arguing in support of the role of typologies in anthropological theory, Schweizer (1998:74) claims that "types are theoretical idealizations that can be illustrated by empirical cases and that are approximated by other cases belonging to a given type. The typology is refined in light of new empirical and theoretical evidence obtained by research." This contrasts with Portes's (1997:806) assessment that typologies simply "assert differences without specifying their origins or anticipating their consequences." These varying points of view speak to distinctions in the nature of both theory and method in anthropology and sociology, respectively.

7. For a collection of essays about transnationalism by scholars trained in a breadth of disciplines, see volume 37 (3) of the *International Migration Review*. Many of those scholars, who were working with return migration in the 1970s, were also thinking within a transnationalist framework although they were not using the concept itself (Brettell 2003a). Most recently, Foner (1997b) has asked what is actually new about transnationalism in a comparative analysis of immigrants to New York at the turn of the century with those in more recent decades.

8. Some scholars have addressed the conceptual distinctions between diaspora and transnational communities. Levitt (2001:203) has suggested that "Diasporas form out of transnational communities that span sending and receiving countries and out of the real or imagined connections between migrants from a particular homeland who are scattered throughout the world. If a fiction of congregation

takes hold, then a Diaspora emerges." For an attempt at a theoretical paradigm of diasporas see Shuval (2000). For its application to refugee studies, see Wahlbeck (2002); see also Vertovec 1997 and Butler 2001.

9. Alvarez (1995) cites Linda Whiteford's early work on the extended community as the first to emphasize an unbounded and cross-border community. From this point on, he suggests, "it became the task of anthropologists to clarify how people arranged and located themselves in these binational and extended communities" (Alvarez 1995:457).

10. For additional discussions see some of the essays in Lamphere 1992. For additional research on the reception and representation of immigrants in European countries see Grillo 1985, Mandel 1989, McDonogh 1992, Zinn 1994, Modood and Werbner 1997, and Riccio 2000.

11. J. A. Barnes (1954) first recognized the analytical utility of the concept of social network in his research on a Norwegian fishing community. Social networks received a good deal of attention from British social anthropologists working among urban migrants in Africa in the 1960s (Epstein 1961; Gutkind 1965; Mayer 1966; Mitchell 1971, 1974). For a more recent discussion of social network analysis as a "theory-net," see Schweizer 1998.

12. See Layton (1997) for a complete discussion of this approach within anthropology.

13. This was equally true of much historical research. Several excellent monographs focusing on immigrant women have emerged to compensate for this lack of attention (for example, Diner 1983; Friedman-Kasaba 1996; Gabaccia 1994). Most recently, several scholars (see, for example, Hondagneu-Sotelo 1994 and Mahler and Pessar 2006) have correctly argued that gender is an analytic category that should be equally applied to an understanding of men's migration. For comprehensive consideration of the theoretical role of gender in migration research across a range of disciplines, see the special issue of the *International Migration Review*, volume 40, 2006.

14. Examples of research that addresses how wives who remain behind manage remittances and maintain the reproductive and productive activities of the home community can be found in Brettell 1986, Connell 1984, Georges 1992, Hondagneu-Sotelo 1992, and Hammam 1986. See also Donnan and Werbner 1991.

15. Several volumes in the New Immigrant Series edited by Nancy Foner address gender issues. See Pessar (2003) for a more thorough development of the scholarship on gender and migration within anthropology. Recently, Hirsch (1999:1346) has argued that a focus on "the causes of women's empowerment has limited our understanding of gender and migration." We miss, she suggests, the interrelatedness of wage labor on the one hand and broader cultural and legal differences of life in the receiving society on the other. Furthermore, we tend to assume that migration is always beneficial to women and this may not be the case.

16. See Adler (2004) for a different perspective on this issue.

17. See Abu-Lughod (1993) for a good example of the postmodern feminist approach.

18. For other discussions of the concept of cultural identity, see Bammer 1994, Gupta and Ferguson 1992, Rouse 1995b, and Williams 1989.

19. For more thorough discussions than can be offered here see Banks 1996 and Jenkins 1997. Earlier reviews can be found in Cohen 1978, Reminick 1983, and Jenkins 1986; see also Wallman 1978, 1986. Cohen (1978:384), in particular, addresses the difference between "tribe" and "ethnic," the former characterized as isolated, primitive-atavistic, non-Western, bounded, systemic, and objectively identified; the latter characterized as nonisolated, contemporary, universally applicable, a unit in relation to others where the degree of systemic quality varies,

and both objectively and subjectively identified. While the traditional/modern dichotomy underlies these differences, it is nevertheless apparent how the transfer from thinking about tribes to thinking about ethnic groups was influenced by a reconceptualization of the concept of culture.

20. Wallman (1986:229–30) has argued that anthropologists looking at ethnic relations "take account of the effect of context on the marking and meaning of ethnic difference, and since it is impossible to understand contextual factors without noticing change, it is the variability of ethnic boundaries which catches the anthropologist's eye, and the logic of ethnic boundary processes which holds the profession's attention. . . . Differences between groups of people turn into ethnic boundaries only when heated into significance by the identity investments of either side." For another application of this approach see Talai 1986.

21. In what is quite apparently a challenge to an outsider perspective and to the question of rights pursued by some political scientists, Rouse (1995b) suggests that few of these Mixtec migrants construed their problems in terms of prejudice and discrimination or by recourse to the language of rights.

22. Several of the authors who have contributed monographs to the New Immigrant Series edited by Nancy Foner include sections that deal with the significance of religious institutions in the formation of community and ethnic identity. Of course this interest in religion is not unique to anthropologists. Historians have written about the role of religious institutions among immigrants in America. The book, edited by Stephen Warner and Judith Wittner (1998), includes a number of interesting chapters by scholars with diverse disciplinary backgrounds.

23. Anthropologists have also looked at the impact of returning migrants on the revitalization of festivals in the home community. See Cruces and Diaz de Roda 1992, Kenna 1992, Levitt 1998b, and Brettell 2003e. Two ethnographic films, *Mayordomia: Ritual, Gender and Cultural Identity in a Zapotec Community* and *Oaxacalifornia*, also deal with this topic. Feldman Bianco's film *Saudade*, about Portuguese immigrants in New Bedford, MA, opens with the celebration of the Day of Portugal in that community.

24. Ortner (1996:12) conceptualizes this interaction as "the challenge to picture indissoluble formations of structurally embedded agency and intention-filled structures, to recognize the ways in which the subject is part of larger social and cultural webs, and in which social and cultural "systems" are predicated upon human desires and projects."

REFERENCES

Abu-Lughod, Janet. 1975. "The End of the Age of Innocence in Migration Theory," in Brian Du Toit and Helen I. Safa, eds., *Migration and Urbanization: Models and Adaptive Strategies*, pp. 201–06. The Hague: Mouton.

Abu-Lughod, Lila. 1990. "The Romance of Resistance: Tracing Transformations of Power through Bedouin Women," *American Ethnologist* 17: 41–55.

———. 1993. *Writing Women's Worlds: Bedouin Stories*. Berkeley: University of California Press.

Adler, Rachel H. 2004. *Yucatecans in Dallas, Texas: Breaching the Border, Bridging the Distance*. Boston: Allyn and Bacon.

Ahmed, Sara. 1999. "Home and Away: Narratives of Migration and Estrangement," *International Journal of Cultural Studies* 2: 329–47.

Alexander, Michael. 2003. "Local Policies toward Migrants as an Expression of Host-Stranger Relations: A Proposed Typology," *Journal of Ethnic and Migration Studies* 29: 411–30.

Alvarez, Robert M. Jr. 1990. "Mexican Entrepreneurs and Markets in the City of Lost Angeles: A Case of an Immigrant Enclave," *Urban Anthropology* 19: 99–124.

———. 1995. "The Mexican-U.S. Border: The Making of an Anthropology of Borderlands," *Annual Review of Anthropology* 24: 447–70.

Anderson, Benedict. 1983. *Imagined Communities: Reflections on the Origins and Spread of Nationalism*. London: Verso.

Anthias, Floya, and Cabriella Lazarides, eds. 2000. *Gender and Migration in Southern Europe: Women on the Move*. New York: Berg Publishers.

Anwar, Muhammad. 1995. "Social Networks of Pakistanis in the U.K.: A Re-evaluation," in Alisdair Rogers and Steven Vertovec, eds., *The Urban Context: Ethnicity, Social Networks and Situational Analysis*, pp. 237–57. Oxford: Berg Publishers Limited.

Appadurai, Arjun. 1991. "Global Ethnoscapes: Notes and Queries for a Transnational Anthropology," in Richard Fox, ed., *Recapturing Anthropology*, pp. 191–210. Santa Fe: School of American Research Press.

———. 1996. "Sovereignty without Territoriality: Notes for a Postnational Geography," in Patricia Yaeger, ed., *The Geography of Identity*, pp. 40–58. Ann Arbor: University of Michigan Press.

Appadurai, Arjun, and Carol Breckenridge. 1989. "On Moving Targets," *Public Culture* 2: i–iv.

Aranda, Elizabeth M. 2003. "Global Care Work and Gendered Constraints: The Case of Puerto Rican Transmigrants," *Gender & Society* 17: 609–26.

Arizpe, Lourdes. 1981. "Relay Migration and the Survival of the Peasant Household," in Jorge Balan, ed., *Why People Move: Comparative Perspectives on the Dynamics of Internal Migration,* pp. 187–210. Paris: Unesco Press.

Avenarius, Christine. 2002. "Work and Social Network Composition among Immigrants from Taiwan to Southern California," *Anthropology of Work Review* 23: 3–15.

Bammer, Angelika, ed. 1994. *Displacements: Cultural Identities in Question*. Bloomington: Indiana University Press.

Banks, Marcus. 1996. *Ethnicity: Anthropological Constructions*. New York: Routledge.

Barnes, J. A. 1954. "Class and Committees in a Norwegian Island Parish," *Human Relations* 7: 39–58.

Barou, Jacques. 1996. "Portugais d'Auvergne: D'une identité villageoise à l'autre. *Revued'Auvergne* 3: 147–59.

Barrett, Stanley R. 1997. *Anthropology: A Student's Guide to Theory and Method*. Toronto: University of Toronto Press.

Barth, Frederik, ed. 1969. *Ethnic Groups and Boundaries: The Social Organization of Cultural Difference*. London: George Allen and Unwin.

Basch, Linda, Nina Glick Schiller, and Cristina Szanton Blanc. 1994. *Nations Unbound: Transnational Projects, Postcolonial Predicaments, and Deterritorialized Nation–States*. Utrecht: Gordon and Breach Publishers.

Benson, Janet E. 1990. "Households, Migration and Community Context," *Urban Anthropology* 19: 9–29.

Bentley, G. Carter. 1987. "Ethnicity and Practice," *Comparative Studies in Society and History* 29: 24–55.

Beriss, David. 1990. "Scarves, Schools and Segregation: The Foulard Affair," *French Politics and Society* 8: 1–13.

———. 2004. *Black Skins, French Voices: Caribbean Ethnicity and Activism in Urban France*. Boulder, CO: Westview Press.

Bhachu, Parminder. 1985. *Twice Migrants: East African Sikh Settlers in Britain*. London: Tavistock.

———. 1988. "Apni Marzi Kardhi Home and Work: Sikh Women in Britain," in Sallie Westwood and Parminder Bhachu, eds., *Enterprising Women: Ethnicity, Economy and Gender Relations*, pp. 76–102. London: Routledge.

———. 1993. "Twice and Direct Migrant Sikhs: Caste, Class and Identity in Pre- and Post-1984 Britain," in Ivan Light and Parminder Bhachu, eds., *Immigration and Entrepreneurship*, pp. 163–83. New Brunswick, NJ: Transaction Press.

Boissevain, Jeremy, and Hanneke Grotenberg. 1986. "Culture, Structure and Ethnic Enterprise: The Surinamese of Amsterdam," *Ethnic and Racial Studies* 9: 1–22.

———. 1989. "Entrepreneurs and the Law: Self-Employed Surinames in Amsterdam," in June Starr and Jane Collier, eds., *History and Power in the Study of Law: New Directions in Legal Anthropology*, pp. 223–51. Ithaca, NY: Cornell University Press.

Boissevain, Jeremy, and J. Clyde Mitchell, eds. 1973. *Network Analysis*. The Hague: Mouton.

Borjas, George. 1989. "Economic Theory and International Migration," *International Migration Review* 23: 457–87.

Borneman, John. 1997. "State, Territory and National Identity Formation in the Two Berlins, 1945–1995," in Akhil Gupta and James Ferguson, eds., *Culture, Power, Place: Explorations in Critical Anthropology*, pp. 93–117. Durham, NC: Duke University Press.

———. 1998. "Emigrées as Bullets/Immigration as Penetration; Perceptions of the Marielitos," in John Borneman, ed., *Subversions of International Order: Studies in the Political Anthropology of Culture*, pp. 249–72. Albany, NY: SUNY Press.

Bourdieu. Pierre. 1977. *Outline of a Theory of Practice*. Cambridge: Cambridge University Press.

Brettell, Caroline B. 1977. "Ethnicity and Entrepreneurs: Portuguese Immigrants in a Canadian City," in George Hicks and Philip Leis, eds., *Ethnic Encounters: Identities and Contexts*, pp. 169–80. Belmont, CA: Wadsworth Publishing Co.

———. 1979. "Emigrar para Voltar: A Portuguese Ideology of Return Migration," *Papers in Anthropology* 20: 1–20.

———. 1986. *Men Who Migrate, Women Who Wait: Population and History in a Portuguese Parish*. Princeton, NJ: Princeton University Press.

———. 1995. *We Have Already Cried Many Tears: The Stories of Three Portuguese Migrant Women*. Prospect Heights, IL: Waveland Press.

———. 2002. "Migration," in David I. Kertzer and Marzio Barbagli, eds., *Family Life in the Long Nineteenth Century, 1789–1913*, pp. 229–47. New Haven, CT: Yale University Press.

———. 2003a. *Anthropology and Migration: Essays on Transnationalism, Ethnicity and Identity*. Walnut Creek, CA: Altamira Press.

———. 2003b. "Emigrar para Voltar: A Portuguese Ideology of Return Migration," in *Anthropology and Migration: Essays on Transnationalism, Ethnicity and Identity*, pp. 57–74. Walnut Creek, CA: Altamira Press.

_____. 2003c. "Is the Ethnic Community Inevitable? A Comparison of the Settlement Patterns of Portuguese Immigrants in Toronto and Paris," in *Anthropology and Migration: Essays on Transnationalism, Ethnicity and Identity*, pp. 109–26. Walnut Creek, CA: Altamira Press.

_____. 2003d. "Bringing the City Back In: Cities as Contexts for Immigrant Incorporation," in Nancy Foner, ed., *American Arrivals: Anthropology Engages the New Immigration*, pp. 163–96. Santa Fe, NM: School of American Research Press.

_____. 2003e. "Emigration, the Church, and the Religious Festa in Northern Portugal," in *Anthropology and Migration: Essays on Transnationalism, Ethnicity and Identity*, pp. 75–99. Walnut Creek, CA: Altamira Press.

_____. 2006. "Political Belonging and Cultural Belonging: Immigration Status, Citizenship and Identity among Four Immigrant Populations in a Southwestern City," *American Behavioral Scientist* 50: 70–99.

_____, ed. 2007. *Crossing Borders/Constructing Boundaries: Race, Ethnicity and Immigration*. Lanham, MD: Lexington Books.

Brettell, Caroline B., and Colette Callier-Boisvert. 1977. "Portuguese Immigrants in France: Familial and Social Networks and the Structuring of Community," *Studi Emigrazione/Études Migrations* 46: 149–203.

Brettell, Caroline B., and Patricia A. de Berjeois. 1992. "Anthropology and the Study of Immigrant Women," in Donna Gabaccia, ed., *Seeking Common Ground: Multidisciplinary Studies of Immigrant Women in the United States*, pp. 41–64. Westport, CT: Greenwood Press.

Briody, Elizabeth K. 1987. "Patterns of Household Immigration into South Texas," *International Migration Review* 21: 27–47.

Brodwin, Paul. 2003. "Marginality and Subjectivity in the Haitian Diaspora," *Anthropological Quarterly* 76: 383–410.

Brown, Karen McCarthy. 1991. *Mama Lola: A Vodou Priestess in Brooklyn*. Berkeley: University of California Press.

Bryceson, Deborah, and Ulla Vuorela. 2002. *The Transnational Family: New European Frontiers and Global Networks*. Oxford: Berg.

Brydon, Lynne. 1987. "Who Moves? Women and Migration in West Africa in the 1980s," in Jeremy Eades, ed., *Migrants, Workers, and the Social Order*, pp. 165–80. London: Tavistock Publications.

Buechler, Hans Christian, and Judith-Maria Buechler, eds. 1987. *Migrants in Europe: The Role of Family, Labor, and Politics*. New York: Greenwood Press.

Buechler, Judith-Maria. 1976. "Something Funny Happened on the Way to the Agora: A Comparison of Bolivian and Spanish Galician Migrants," *Anthropological Quarterly* 49: 62–69.

Buijs, Gina, ed. 1993. *Migrant Women: Crossing Boundaries and Changing Identities*. Oxford: Berg Publishers.

Butterworth, Douglas. 1962. "A Study of the Urbanization among Mixtec Migrants from Tilaltongo in Mexico City," *America Indígena* 22: 257–74.

Butler, Kim D. 2001. "Defining Diaspora, Refining a Discourse," *Diaspora* 10: 189–219.

Callier-Boisvert, Colette. 1987. "Working-Class Portuguese Families in a French Provincial Town," in Hans Christian Buechler and Judith-Maria Buechler, eds., *Migrants in Europe: The Role of Family, Labor, and Politics*, pp. 61–76. New York: Greenwood Press.

Caspari, Andrea, and Wenona Giles. 1986. "Immigration Policy and the Employment of Portuguese Migrant Women in the U.K. and France: A Comparative Analysis," in Rita J. Simon and Caroline B. Brettell, eds., *International Migration: The Female Experience*, pp. 152–77. Totowa, NJ: Rowman & Allenheld.

Carter, Donald. 1997. *States of Grace: Senegalese in Italy and the New European Migration*. Minneapolis: University of Minnesota Press.

Chai, Alice Yun. 1987a. "Adaptive Strategies of Recent Korean Immigrant Women in Hawaii," in Janet Shristanian, ed., *Beyond the Pubic/Domestic Dichotomy: Contemporary Perspectives on Women's Public Lives,* pp. 65–100. New York: Greenwood Press.

———. 1987b. "Freed from the Elders but Locked into Labor: Korean Immigrant Women in Hawaii," *Women's Studies* 13: 223–33.

Chapin, Frances W. 1992. "Channels for Change: Emigrant Tourists and the Class Structure of Azorean Migration," *Human Organization* 51: 44–52.

Chavez, Leo. 1988. "Settlers and Sojourners: The Case of Mexicans in the United States," *Human Organization* 47: 95–107.

———. 1990. "Coresidence and Resistance: Strategies for Survival among Undocumented Mexicans and Central Americans in the United States," *Urban Anthropology* 19: 31–61.

———. 1991. "Outside the Imagined Community: Undocumented Settlers and Experiences of Incorporation," *American Ethnologist* 18: 257–78.

———. 1992. *Shadowed Lives: Undocumented Immigrants in American Society*. Fort Worth, TX: Holt, Rinehart and Winston.

———. 1994. "The Power of the Imagined Community: The Settlement of Undocumented Mexicans and Central Americans in the United States," *American Anthropologist* 96: 52–73.

———. 2001. *Covering Immigration: Popular Images and the Politics of the Nation*. Berkeley: University of California Press.

Chavez, Leo, F. Allan Hubbell, Shiraz I. Mishra, and R. Burciaga Valdez. 1997. "Undocumented Latina Immigrants in Orange County, California: A Comparative Analysis," *International Migration Review* 31: 88–107.

Chavira-Prado, Alicia. 1992. "Work, Health, and the Family: Gender Structure and Women's Status in an Undocumented Migrant Population," *Human Organization* 51: 53–64.

Chock, Phyllis. 1991. "'Illegal Aliens' and 'Opportunity': Myth-Making in Congressional Testimony," *American Ethnologist* 18: 279–94.

Clarke, Darryl Victor. 2004. *Mapping Yoruba Networks: Power and Agency in the Making of Transnational Communities*. Durham, NC: Duke University Press.

Clifford, James. 1994. "Diasporas," *Cultural Anthropology* 9: 302–38.

———. 1997. *Routes: Travel and Translation in the Late Twentieth Century*. Cambridge: Harvard University Press.

Clifford, James, and George E. Marcus, eds. 1986. *Writing Culture: The Poetics and Politics of Ethnography*. Berkeley: University of California Press.

Cohen, Abner. 1969. *Custom and Politics in Urban Africa*. London: Routledge and Kegan Paul.

———. 1980. "Drama and Politics in the Development of a London Carnival," *Man* 15: 65–87.

———. 1993. *Masquerade Politics: Explorations in the Structure of Urban Cultural Movements*. Berkeley: University of California Press.

Cohen, Jeffrey H. 2001. "Transnational Migration in Rural Oaxaca, Mexico: Dependency, Development, and the Household," *American Anthropologist* 103: 954–67.

———. 2004. *The Culture of Migration in Southern Mexico*. Austin: University of Texas Press.

Cohen, Ronald. 1978. "Ethnicity: Problem and Focus in Anthropology," *Annual Review of Anthropology* 7: 379–403.

Cole, Jeffrey. 1997. *The New Racism in Europe: A Sicilian Ethnography*. Cambridge: Cambridge University Press.

Colen, Shellee. 1990. "Housekeeping for the Green Card: West Indian Household Workers, the State, and Stratified Reproduction in New York," in Roger Sanjek and Shellee Colen, eds., *At Work in Homes: Household Workers in World Perspective*, pp. 89–118. Washington, D.C.: American Ethnological Society, Monograph #3, American Anthropological Association.

Comaroff, John. 1987. "Of Totemism and Ethnicity: Consciousness, Practice, and the Signs of Inequality," *Ethnos* 52: 301–323.

Connell, John. 1984. "Status or Subjugation? Women, Migration and Development in the South Pacific," *International Migration Review* 18: 964–83.

Coutin, Susan Bibler. 2005. "Being En Route," *American Anthropologist* 107: 195–206.

Cruces, Francisco, and Angel Diaz de Roda. 1992. "Public Celebrations in a Spanish Valley," in Jeremy Boissevain, ed., *Revitalizing European Rituals*, pp. 62–79. London: Routledge.

Curran, Sara R., and Estela Rivero-Fuentes. 2003. "Engendering Migrant Networks: The Case of Mexican Migration," *Demography* 40: 289–307.

Dahya, B. 1973. "Pakistanis in Britain: Transients or Settlers," *Race* 14: 241–77.

Diner, Hasia R. 1983. *Erin's Daughters in America: Irish Immigrant Women in the Nineteenth Century*. Baltimore, MD: The Johns Hopkins University Press.

Donnan, Hastings, and Pnina Werbner, eds. 1991. *Economy and Culture in Pakistan: Migrants and Cities in a Muslim Society*. New York: St. Martin's Press.

Douglass, William A. 1974. *Echalar and Murelaga: Opportunity and Rural Exodus in Two Spanish Basque Villages*. New York: St. Martin's Press.

Durham, William H. 1989. "Conflict, Migration, and Ethnicity: A Summary," in Nancie Gonzalez and Carolyn S. McCommon, eds., *Conflict, Migration and the Expression of Ethnicity*, pp. 138–45. Boulder, CO: Westview Press.

Du Toit, Brian. 1975. "A Decision-Making Model for the Study of Migration," in Brian Du Toit and Helen I. Safa, eds., *Migration and Urbanization: Models and Adaptive Strategies*, pp. 49–74. The Hague: Mouton.

———. 1990. "People on the Move: Rural-Urban Migration with Special Reference to the Third World: Theoretical and Empirical Perspectives," *Human Organization* 49: 305–19.

Du Toit, Brian, and Helen I. Safa. 1975. *Migration and Urbanization: Models and Adaptive Strategies*. The Hague: Mouton.

Eades, Jeremy. 1980. *The Yoruba Today*. Cambridge: Cambridge University Press.

———, ed. 1987. *Migrants, Workers, and the Social Order*. London: Tavistock Publications.

Ebaugh, Helen Rose, and Janet Saltzman Chafetz, eds. 2000. *Religion and the New Immigrants*. Walnut Creek, CA: Altamira Press.

Epstein, A. L. 1958. *Politics in an Urban African Community*. Manchester: Manchester University Press.

_____. 1961. "The Network and Urban Social Organization," *Rhodes-Livingstone Journal* 29: 29–62.

Escobar, Agustin, Mercedes Gonzalez, and Bryan Roberts. 1987. "Migration, Labour Markets, and the International Economy: Jalisco, Mexico, and the United States," in Jeremy Eades, ed., *Migrants, Workers, and the Social Order*, pp. 42–64. London: Tavistock Publications.

Falzon, Mark-Anthony. 2003. "'Bombay, Our Cultural Heart': Rethinking the Relation between Homeland and Diaspora," *Ethnic and Racial Studies* 26: 662–83.

Feld, Steven, and Keith H. Basso, eds. 1996. *Senses of Place*. Santa Fe, NM: School of American Research Press.

Feldman-Bianco, Bela. 1992. "Multiple Layers of Time and Space: The Construction of Class, Ethnicity and Nationalism among Portuguese Immigrants," in Nina Glick Schiller, Linda Basch, and Cristina Blanc Szanton, eds., *Towards a Transnational Perspective on Migration: Race, Class, Ethnicity and Nationalism Reconsidered*, pp. 145–74. New York: Annals of the New York Academy of Sciences, volume 645.

Fernandez-Kelly, Maria Patricia, and Anna M. Garcia. 1985. "The Making of an Underground Economy: Hispanic Women, Home Work and the Advanced Capitalist State," *Urban Anthropology* 14: 59–90.

_____. 1990. "Delicate Transactions: Gender, Home, and Employment among Hispanic Women," in Faye Ginsburg and Anna Lowenhaupt Tsing, eds., *Uncertain Terms: Negotiating Gender in American Culture*, pp. 183–95. Boston: Beacon Press.

Fjellman, Stephen M., and Hugh Gladwin. 1985. "Haitian Family Patterns of Migration to South Florida," *Human Organization* 44: 301–12.

Foner, Nancy. 1979. *Jamaica Farewell*. London: Routledge and Kegan Paul.

_____. 1985. "Race and Color: Jamaican Migrants in London and New York City," *International Migration Review* 19: 706–27.

_____. 1987a. "Introduction: New Immigrants and Changing Patterns in New York City," in Nancy Foner, ed., *New Immigrants in New York*, pp. 1–33. New York: Columbia University Press.

_____. 1987b. "The Jamaicans: Race and Ethnicity among Migrants in New York City," in Nancy Foner, ed., *New Immigrants in New York*, pp. 195–217. New York: Columbia University Press.

_____. 1997a. "The Immigrant Family: Cultural Legacies and Cultural Changes," *International Migration Review* 31: 961–74.

_____. 1997b. "What's New About Transnationalism? New York Immigrants Today and at the Turn of the Century," *Diaspora* 6: 355–76.

_____. 1999. "Anthropology and the Study of Immigration," *American Behavioral Scientist* 42: 1268–70.

_____. 2003. *American Arrivals: Anthropology Engages the New Immigration*. Santa Fe, NM: School of American Research Press.

_____. 2005. *In a New Land: A Comparative View of Immigration*. New York: New York University Press.

Fortier, Anne-Marie. 2000. *Migrant Belongings: Memory, Space, Identity*. Oxford: Berg Publishers.

Frank, Andre Gundre. 1967. *Capitalism and Underdevelopment in Latin America*. New York: Monthly Review Press.

Freeman. James M. 1995. *Changing Identities: Vietnamese Americans 1975–1995*. Boston: Allyn and Bacon.

Freidenberg, Judith, G. Imperiale, and M. L. Skovron. 1988. "Migrant Careers and Well-Being of Women," *International Migration Review* 22: 208–25.

Friedman-Kasaba, Kathie. 1996. *Memories of Migration; Gender, Ethnicity and Work in the Lives of Jewish and Italian Women in New York, 1870–1924*. Albany, NY: SUNY Press.

Gabaccia, Donna. 1994. *From the Other Side: Women, Gender, & Immigrant Life in the U.S. 1820–1990*. Bloomington, IN: Indiana University Press.

Gamburd, Michele Ruth. 2000. *The Kitchen Spoon's Handle: Transnationalism and Sri Lanka's Migrant Housemaids*. Ithaca, NY: Cornell University Press.

Gardner, Katy. 1995. *Global Migrants, Local Lives: Travel and Transformation in Rural Bangladesh*. Oxford: Clarendon Press.

George, Sheba Mariam. 2005. *When Women Come First: Gender and Class in Transnational Migration*. Berkeley: University of California Press.

Georges, Eugenia. 1990. *The Making of a Transnational Community: Migration, Development, and Cultural Change in the Dominican Republic*. New York: Columbia University Press.

————. 1992. "Gender, Class, and Migration in the Dominican Republic: Women's Experiences in a Transnational Community," in Nina Glick Schiller, Linda Basch, and Christina Szanton Blanc, eds., *Towards a Transnational Perspective on Migration: Race, Class, Ethnicity, and Nationalism Reconsidered*, pp. 81–99. New York: Annals of the New York Academy of Sciences.

Gewertz, Deborah, and Frederick Errington. 1991. "We Think, Therefore They Are? Occidentalizing the World," *Anthropological Quarterly* 64: 80–91.

Giddens, Anthony. 1984. *The Constitution of Society*. Cambridge: Polity Press.

Gilad, Lisa. 1989. *Ginger and Salt: Yemeni Jewish Women in an Israeli Town*. Boulder, CO: Westview Press.

Giles, Wenona. 1991. "Class, Gender and Race Struggles in a Portuguese Neighborhood in London," *International Journal of Urban and Regional Research*. 15: 432–41.

————. 1992. "Gender, Inequality and Resistance: The Case of Portuguese Women in London," *Anthropological Quarterly* 65: 67–79.

————. 1993. "Clean Jobs, Dirty Jobs: Ethnicity, Social Reproduction and Gendered Identity," *Culture* 13: 37–44.

Glick Schiller, Nina. 1977. "Ethnic Groups Are Made, Not Born: The Haitian Immigrant and American Politics," in George Hicks and Philip Leis, eds., *Ethnic Encounters: Identities and Contexts*, pp. 23–35. Belmont, CA: Wadsworth Publishing Co.

————. 1997. "The Situation of Transnational Studies," *Identities* 4: 155–66.

————. 2003. "The Centrality of Ethnography in the Study of Transnational Migration: Seeing the Wetlands Instead of the Swamp," in Nancy Foner, ed., *American Arrivals: Anthropology Engages the New Immigration*, pp. 99–128. Santa Fe, NM: School of American Research Press.

————. 2004. "Transnationality," in David Nugent and Joan Vincent, eds., *A Companion to the Anthropology of Politics*, pp. 448–67. Oxford: Blackwell Publishers.

Glick Schiller, Nina, Linda Basch, and Christina Szanton Blanc. 1992. "Transnationalism: A New Analytical Framework for Understanding Migration," in Nina Glick Schiller, Linda Basch, and Christina Szanton Blanc, eds., *Towards a Transnational Perspective on Migration: Race, Class, Ethnicity, and Nationalism Reconsidered*, pp. 1–24. New York: Annals of the New York Academy of Sciences.

————, eds. 1992. *Towards a Transnational Perspective on Migration: Race, Class, Ethnicity, and Nationalism Reconsidered*. New York: New York Academy of Sciences.

————. 1995. "From Immigrant to Transmigrant: Theorizing Transitional Migration," *Anthropological Quarterly* 68: 48–63.

Glick Schiller, Nina, and Georges Eugene Fouron. 2001. *Georges Woke Up Laughing: Long-Distance Nationalism and the Search for Home.* Durham, NC: Duke University Press.

Gmelch, George. 1980. "Return Migration," *Annual Review of Anthropology* 9: 135–59.

———. 1983. "Who Returns and Why: Return Migration Behavior in Two Atlantic Societies," *Human Organization* 42: 46–54.

———. 1992. *Double Passage: The Lives of Caribbean Migrants Abroad and Back Home.* Ann Arbor: University of Michigan Press.

Gmelch, George, and Sharon Bohn Gmelch. 1995. "Gender and Migration: The Readjustment of Women Migrants in Barbados, Ireland, and Newfoundland," *Human Organization* 54: 470–73.

Goffman, Erving. 1963. *Stigma.* Englewood Cliffs, NJ: Prentice-Hall.

Gold, Steven J. 1989. "Differential Adjustment among New Immigrant Family Members," *Journal of Contemporary Ethnography* 17: 408–34.

———. 1995. *From the Workers State to the Gold State: Jews from the Former Soviet Union in California.* Boston: Allyn and Bacon.

Goldring, Luin. 2001. "The Gender and Geography of Citizenship in Mexico-U.S. Transnational Spaces," *Identities* 7: 501–37.

———. 2003. "Gender, Status, and the State in Transnational Spaces: The Gendering of Political Participation and Mexican Hometown Associations," in Pierrette Hondagneu-Sotelo, ed., *Gender and U.S. Immigration: Contemporary Trends,* pp. 341–58. Berkeley: University of California Press.

Gonzalez, Nancie L. Solien de. 1961. "Family Organization in Five Types of Migratory Wage Labor," *American Anthropologist* 63: 1264–80.

———. 1988. *Sojourners of the Caribbean: Ethnogenesis and the Ethnohistory of the Garifuna.* Urbana: University of Illinois Press.

———. 1989. "Conflict, Migration, and the Expression of Ethnicity: Introduction," in Nancie Gonzalez and Carolyn S. McCommon, eds., *Conflict, Migration and the Expression of Ethnicity,* pp. 1–9. Boulder, CO: Westview Press.

———. 1992. *Dollar, Dove and Eagle. One Hundred Years of Palestinian Migration in Honduras.* Ann Arbor: University of Michigan Press.

Gonzalez, Nancie, and Carolyn S. McComon, eds. 1989. *Conflict, Migration and Expression of Ethnicity.* Boulder, CO: Westview Press.

Goode, Judith. 1990. "A War Welcome to the Neighborhood: Community Responses to Immigrants," *Urban Anthropology* 19: 125–53.

Goode, Judith, and J. A. Schneider. 1994. *Reshaping Ethnic and Racial Relations in Philadelphia: Immigrants in a Divided City.* Philadelphia, PA: Temple University Press.

Goodman, Charity. 1987. "A Day in the Life of a Single Spanish Woman in West Germany," in Hans Christian Buechler and Judith-Maria Buechler, eds., *Migrants in Europe: The Role of Family, Labor, and Politics,* pp. 207–19. New York: Greenwood Press.

Goodsen-Lawes, J. 1993. "Feminine Authority and Migration: The Case of One Family from Mexico," *Urban Anthropology* 22: 277–97.

Gordon, Edmund T., and Mark Anderson. 1999. "The African Diaspora: Toward an Ethnography of Diasporic Identification," *Journal of American Folklore* 112: 282–96.

Grasmuck, Sherri, and Patricia R. Pessar. 1991. *Between Two Islands: Dominican International Migration.* Berkeley: University of California Press.

Graves, Nancy B., and Theodore D. Graves. 1974. "Adaptive Strategies in Urban Migration," *Annual Review of Anthropology* 3: 117–51.

Gregory, S. 1987. "Afro-Caribbean Religions in New York City: The Case of Santeria," in Constance Sutton and Elsa Chaney, eds., *Caribbean Life in New York City: Sociocultural Dimensions*, pp. 307–24. New York: Center for Migration Studies.

Gregory, David D., and Jose Cazorla. 1987. "Family and Migration in Andalusia," in Hans Christian Buechler and Judith-Maria Buechler, eds., *Migrants in Europe: The Role of Family, Labor, and Politics*, pp. 149–88. New York: Greenwood Press.

Grieco, Margaret. 1995. "Transported Lives: Urban Social Networks and Labour Circulation," in Alisdair Rogers and Steven Vertovec, eds., *The Urban Context: Ethnicity, Social Networks and Situational Analysis*, pp. 189–212. Oxford: Berg Publishers Limited.

Grieco, Elizabeth M. 1998. "The Effects of Migration on the Establishment of Networks: Caste Disintegration and Reformation among the Indians of Fiji," *International Migration Review* 32: 704–36.

Grigolini, Silvia. 2004. "When Houses Provide More Than Shelter: Analyzing the Uses of Remittances within Their Sociocultural Context," in Lillian Traver, ed., *Migration and Economy: Global and Local Dynamics*, pp. 193–223. Walnut Creek, CA: Altamira Press.

Grillo, Ralph. 1985. *Ideologies and Institutions in Urban France. The Representation of Immigrants*. Cambridge: Cambridge University Press.

Grimes, Kimberly M. 1998. *Crossing Borders: Changing Social Identities in Southern Mexico*. Tucson: University of Arizona Press.

Gross, Joan, David McMurray, and Ted Swedenburg. 1996. "Arab Noise and Ramadan Nights: *Rai*, Rap, and Franco-Maghrebi Identities," in Smadar Lavie and Ted Swedenburg, eds., *Displacement, Diaspora, and Geographies of Identity*, pp. 119–55. Durham, NC: Duke University Press.

Groves, Julian McAllister, and Kimberly A. Chang. 1999. "Romancing Resistance and Resisting Romance: Ethnography and the Construction of Power in the Filipina Domestic Worker Community in Hong Kong," *Journal of Contemporary Ethnography* 28: 235–65.

Guest, Kenneth J. 2003. *God in Chinatown: Religion and Survival in New York's Evolving Immigrant Community*. New York: New York University Press.

Gulliver, P. H. 1957. "Nyakusa Labour Migration," *Rhodes-Livingstone Institute Bulletin* 21: 32–63.

Gupta, Ahkil. 1992. "The Song of the Non-aligned World: Transnational Identities and the Reinscription of Space in Late Capitalism," *Cultural Anthropology* 7: 63–79.

Gupta, Akhil, and James Ferguson. 1992. "Beyond 'Culture': Space, Identity and the Politics of Difference," *Cultural Anthropology* 7: 6–23.

———. 1997. "Culture, Power, Place: Ethnography at the End of an Era," in Akhil Gupta and James Ferguson, eds., *Culture, Power, Place: Explorations in Critical Anthropology*, pp. 1–29. Durham, NC: Duke University Press.

Gutkind, Peter C. W. 1965. "African Urbanism, Mobility and the Social Network," *International Journal of Comparative Sociology* 6: 48–60.

Hall, Kathleen D. 2002. *Lives in Translation: Sikh Youth as British Citizens*. Philadelphia: University of Pennsylvania Press.

Halter, Diieter. 2004. "Let It Flow: Economy, Spirituality and Gender in the Sindhi Network," in Waltraud Kokot, Khachig Tololyan, and Carolin Alfonso, eds., *Diaspora, Identity and Religion: New Directions in Theory and Research*, pp. 189–204. New York: Routledge.

Hammam, Mona. 1986. "Capitalist Development, Family Division of Labor, and Migration in the Middle East," in Eleanor Leacock and Helen I. Safa, eds. *Women's Work: Development and Division of Labor by Gender*, pp. 158–73. South Hadley: Bergin and Garvey.

Hannerz, Ulf. 1992. "The Global Ecumene as a Network of Networks," in Adam Kuper, ed., *Conceptualizing Society*, pp. 34–56. New York: Routledge.

———. 1996. *Transnational Connections: Culture, People, Places*. New York: Routledge.

———. 1998. "Transnational Research," in H. Russell Bernard, ed., *Handbook of Methods in Cultural Anthropology*, pp. 235–56. Walnut Creek, CA: Altamira Press.

Harbottle, Lynn. 1997. "Fast Food/Spoiled Identity: Iranian Migrants in the British Catering Trade," in Pat Caplan, ed., *Food, Health and Identity*, pp. 87–110. New York: Routledge.

Harney, Nicholas. 2002. "Building Italian Regional Identity in Toronto: Using Space to Make Cultural Material," *Anthropologica* 44: 43–54.

Herman, Harry Vjekoslav. 1979. "Dishwashers and Proprietors: Macedonians in Toronto's Restaurant Trade," in Sandra Wallman, ed., *Ethnicity at Work*, pp. 71–90. London: MacMillan Press Ltd.

Hirsch, Jennifer S. 1999. "En el Norte la Mujer Manda: Gender, Generation, and Geography in a Mexican Transnational Community," *American Behavioral Scientist* 42: 1332–49.

Ho, Christine G. T. 1993. "The Internationalization of Kinship and the Feminization of Caribbean Migration: The Case of Afro-Trinidadian Immigrants in Los Angeles," *Human Organization* 52: 32–40.

Holmes, Douglas. 1983. "A Peasant-Worker Model in a Northern Italian Context," *American Ethnologist* 10: 734–48.

Holtzman, Jon D. 2000. *Nuer Journeys, Nuer Lives: Sudanese Refugees in Minnesota*. Boston: Allyn and Bacon.

Hondagneu-Sotelo, Pierrette. 1992. "Overcoming Patriarchal Constraints: The Reconstruction of Gender Relations among Mexican Immigrant Men and Women," *Gender and Society* 6: 393–415.

———. 1994. *Gendered Transitions: Mexican Experiences of Immigration*. Berkeley: University of California Press.

Indra, Doreen, ed. 1999. *Engendering Forced Migration: Theory and Practice*. New York: Berghahn Books.

Iszaevich, Abraham. 1974. "Emigrants, Spinsters, and Priests: The Dynamics of Demography in Spanish Peasant Societies," *Journal of Peasant Studies* 2: 292–312.

Jenkins, Richard. 1986. "Social Anthropological Models of Inter-ethnic Relations," in John Rex and Dick Mason, eds., *Theories of Race and Ethnic Relations*, pp. 170–85. Cambridge: Cambridge University Press.

———. 1997. *Rethinking Ethnicity: Arguments and Explorations*. Thousand Oaks, CA: Sage Publications.

Kasinitz, P., and J. Freidenberg-Hjerbstein. 1987. "The Puerto Rican Parade and West Indian Carnival: Public Celebrations in New York City," in Constance Sutton and Elsa Chaney, eds., *Caribbean Life in New York City: Sociocultural Dimensions*, pp. 327–49. New York: Center for Migration Studies.

Kearney, Michael. 1986. "From the Invisible Hand to Visible Feet: Anthropological Studies of Migration and Development," *Annual Review of Anthropology* 15: 331–404.

———. 1991. "Borders and Boundaries of State and Self at the End of Empire," *Journal of Historical Sociology* 4: 52–74.

———. 1995. "The Local and the Global: The Anthropology of Globalization and Transnationalism," *Annual Review of Anthropology* 24: 547–65.

Kearney, Michael, and Carole Nagengast. 1989. *Anthropological Perspectives on Transnational Communities in Rural California*. Davis, CA: California Institute for Rural Studies.

Kemper, Robert V. 1977. *Migration and Adaptation: Tzintzuntzan Peasants in Mexico City*. Beverly Hills, CA: Sage Publications.

Kenna, Margaret E. 1992. "Mattresses and Migrants: A Patron Saint's Festival on a Small Greek Island over Two Decades," in Jeremy Boissevain, ed., *Revitalizing European Rituals*, pp. 155–72. London: Routledge.

Kenney, Michael. 1976. "Twentieth Century Spanish Expatriate Ties with the Homeland: Remigration and its Consequences," in Joseph B. Aceves and William A. Douglass, eds., *The Changing Faces of Rural Spain*, pp. 97–122. New York: Schenkman.

Kertzer, David I. 1984. *Family Life in Central Italy, 1880–1910*. New Brunswick, NJ: Rutgers University Press.

Kibria, Nazli. 1993. *Family Tightrope: The Changing Lives of Vietnamese Americans*. Princeton, NJ: Princeton University Press.

Kokot, Waltraud, Khachig Tololyan, and Carolin Alfonso, eds., 2004. *Diaspora, Identity and Religion: New Directions in Theory and Research*. New York: Routledge.

Koltyk, Jo Ann. 1993. "Telling Narratives through Home Videos: Hmong Refugees and Self-Documentation of Life in the Old and New Country," *Journal of American Folklore* 106: 435–49.

———. 1998. *New Pioneers in the Heartland: Hmong Life in Wisconsin*. Boston: Allyn and Bacon.

Koptiuch, Kristin. 1996. "Cultural Defense and Criminological Displacements: Gender, Race, and (Trans)nation in the Legal Surveillance of U.S. Diaspora Asians," in Smadar Lavie and Ted Swedenburg, eds., *Displacement, Diaspora, and Geographies of Identity*, pp. 215–33. Durham, NC: Duke University Press.

Kossoudji, Sherrie A., and Susan I. Ranney. 1984. "The Labor Market Experience of Female Migrants: The Case of Temporary Mexican Migration to the U.S," *International Migration Review* 18: 120–43.

Koven, Michele. 2004. "Transnational Perspectives on Sociolinguistic Capital among Luso-Descendants in France and Portugal," *American Ethnologist* 31: 270–90.

Kwong, Peter. 1997. "Manufacturing Ethnicity," *Critique of Anthropology* 17: 365–87.

Laguerre, Michel S. 1998. *Diasporic Citizenship: Haitian Americans in Transnational America*. New York: St. Martin's Press.

Lamphere, Louise. 1986. "From Working Daughters to Working Mothers: Production and Reproduction in an Industrial Community," *American Ethnologist* 13: 118–30.

———. 1987. *From Working Daughters to Working Mothers: Immigrant Women in a New England Community*. Ithaca, NY: Cornell University Press.

———, ed. 1992. *Structuring Diversity: Ethnographic Perspectives on the New Immigration*. Chicago: University of Chicago Press.

Lamphere, Louise, Filomena M. Silva, and John P. Sousa. 1980. "Kin Networks and Strategies of Working-Class Portuguese Families in a New England Town," in Linda Cordell and Stephen Beckerman, eds., *The Versatility of Kinship*, pp. 219–49. New York: Academic Press.

Lavie, Smadar, and Ted Swedenburg. 1996. "Introduction: Displacement, Diaspora, and Geographies of Identity," in Smadar Lavie and Ted Swedenburg, eds., *Displacement, Diaspora, and Geographies of Identity*, pp. 1–25. Durham, NC: Duke University Press.

Layton, Robert. 1997. *An Introduction to Theory in Anthropology*. Cambridge: Cambridge University Press.

Lessinger, Johanna. 1995. *From the Ganges to the Hudson: Indian Immigrants in New York City*. Boston: Allyn and Bacon.

Levitt, Peggy. 1998a. "Local-level Global Religion: The Case of U.S.-Dominican Migration," *Journal for the Scientific Study of Religion* 37: 74–89.

———. 1998b. "Social Remittances: Migration Driven Local-Level Forms of Cultural Diffusion," *International Migration Review* 32: 926–48.

———. 2001. "Transnational Migration: Taking Stock and Future Directions," *Global Networks* 1: 195–216.

Light, Ivan, and Edna Bonacich. 1988. *Immigrant Entrepreneurs: Koreans in Los Angeles, 1965–1982*. Berkeley and Los Angeles: University of California Press.

Linger, Daniel Touro. 2001. *No One Home: Brazilian Selves Remade in Japan*. Stanford, CA: Stanford University Press.

Lockwood, Victoria S. 1990. "Development and Return Migration to Rural French Polynesia," *International Migration Review* 24: 347–71.

Lomnitz, Larissa. 1977. *Networks and Marginality: Life in a Mexican Shantytown*. New York: Academic Press.

Long, Lynellyn D., and Ellen Oxfeld. 2004. *Coming Home? Refugees, Migrants, and Those Who Stayed Behind*. Philadelphia: University of Pennsylvania Press.

Low, Setha M. 1996. "The Anthropology of Cities: Imagining and Theorizing the City," *Annual Review of Anthropology* 25: 383–409.

———. 1997. "Theorizing the City: Ethnicity, Gender, and Globalization," *Critique of Anthropology* 17: 403–09.

Lyman, Stanford M., and William A. Douglass. 1973. "Ethnicity: Strategies of Collective and Individual Impression Management," *Social Research* 40: 344–65.

Mahler, Sarah J. 1995a. *American Dreaming: Immigrant Life on the Margins*. Princeton, NJ: Princeton University Press.

———. 1995b. *Salvadorans in Suburbia: Symbiosis and Conflict*. Boston: Allyn and Bacon.

———. 1999. "Engendering Transnational Migration: A Case Study of Salvadorans," *American Behavioral Scientist* 42: 690–719.

Mahler, Sarah J., and Patricia R. Pessar. 2006. "Gender Mattes: Ethnographers Bring Gender from the Periphery toward the Core of Migration Studies," *International Migration Review* 40: 27–63.

Maira, Sunaina. 2004. "Youth Culture, Citizenship and Globalization: South Asian Muslim Youth in the United States after September 11th," *Comparative Studies of South Asian, Africa and the Middle East* 24: 18–30.

Malkki, Liisa H. 1995. "Refugees and Exile: From 'Refugee Studies' to the National Order of Things," *Annual Review of Anthropology* 24: 495–523.

Mandel, Ruth. 1989. "Ethnicity and Identity among Guestworkers in West Berlin," in Nancie L. Gonzalez and Carolyn S. McCommon, eds., *Conflict, Migration, and the Expression of Ethnicity*, pp. 60–74. Boulder, CO: Westview Press.

———. 1990. "Shifting Centers and Emergent Identities: Turkey and Germany in the Lives of Turkish Gastarbeiter," in Dale Eickelman and James Piscatori, eds., *Muslim Travelers: Pilgrimage, Migration, and the Religious Imagination*, pp. 153–71. Berkeley: University of California Press.

————. 1991. "Foreigners in the Fatherland: Turkish Immigrants Workers in Germany," in G. Guyerin-Gonzales and C. Strikwerda, eds., *The Politics of Immigrant Workers: Labor Activism and Migration in the World Economy since 1830*. New York: Holmes and Meier.

————. 1994. "'Fortress Europe' and the Foreigners Within: Germany's Turks," in Victoria A. Goddard, Josep R. Llobera, and Cris Shore, eds., *The Anthropology of Europe: Identities and Boundaries in Conflict*, pp. 113–24. Oxford: Berg Publishers.

————. 1996. "A Place of Their Own: Contesting Spaces and Defining Places in Berlin's Migrant Community," in Barbara Daly Metcalf, ed., *Making Muslim Space in North America and Europe*, pp. 147–66. Berkeley: University of California Press.

Mangin, William. 1970. *Peasants in Cities: Readings in the Anthropology of Urbanization*. Boston: Houghton Mifflin Company.

Mankekar, Purnima. 2002. "India Shopping: Indian Grocery Stores and Transnational Configurations of Belonging," *Ethnos* 67: 75–98.

Marcus, George. 1995. "Ethnography in/of the World System: The Emergence of Multi-sited Ethnography," *Annual Review of Anthropology* 24: 95–117.

Margold, Jane A. 1995. "Narratives of Masculinity and Transnational Migration; Filipino Workers in the Middle East," in Aihwa Ong and Michael G. Peletz, eds., *Bewitching Women, Pious Men; Gender and Body Politics in Southeast Asia*, pp. 274–98. Berkeley: University of California Press.

Margolis, Maxine. 1990. "From Mistress to Servant: Downward Mobility among Brazilian Immigrants in New York City," *Urban Anthropology* 19: 215–30.

————. 1994. *Little Brazil: An Ethnography of Brazilian Immigrants in New York City*. Princeton, NJ: Princeton University Press.

————. 1995. "Transnationalism and Popular Culture: The Case of Brazilian Immigrants in the United States," *Journal of Popular Culture* 29: 29–41.

————. 1998. *An Invisible Minority: Brazilians in New York City*. Boston: Allyn and Bacon.

Markowitz, Fran, and Anders H. Steffansson. 2004. *Homecomings: Unsettling Paths of Return*. Lanham, MD: Lexington Books.

Marshall, Paule. 1981. "Black Immigrant Women in Born Girls, Brownstones," in Delores Mortimer and Roy S. Bryce Laporte, eds., *Female Immigrants in the United States*, pp. 1–13. Washington, D.C.: Smithsonian Press.

Massey, Doreen. 1991. "A Place Called Home?" *New Formations: Journal of Culture/Theory/Practice* 17: 133–45.

Massey, Douglas, Rafael Alarcon, Jorge Durand, and Humberto Gonzalez. 1987. *Return to Aztlan: The Social Process of International Migration from Western Mexico*. Berkeley: University of California Press.

Massey, Douglas S., Joaquin Arango, Graeme Hugo, Ali Kouaouci, Adela Pellegrino, and J. Edward Taylor. 1993. "Theories of International Migration: A Review and Appraisal," *Population and Development Review* 19: 431–66.

————. 1994. "An Evaluation of International Migration Theory: The North American Case," *Population and Development Review* 20: 699–751.

Mayer, Adrian C. 1966. "The Significance of Quasi-groups in the Study of Complex Societies," in Michael Banton, ed., *The Social Anthropology of Complex Societies*, pp. 97–122. London: Tavistock.

Mayer, Philip. 1961. *Townsmen or Tribesmen*. Cape Town: Oxford University Press.

McAlister, Elizabeth. 1998. "The Madonna of 115th Street Revisited: Vodou and Haitian Catholicism in the Age of Transnationalism," in R. Stephen Warner and Judith G. Witnner, eds., *Gatherings in Diaspora. Religious Communities and the New Immigration*, pp. 123–60. Philadelphia, PA: Temple University Press.

McDonogh, Gary. 1992. "The Face behind the Door: European Integration, Immigration, and Identity," in Thomas Wilson, ed., *Cultural Change and the New Europe*, pp. 143–65. Newbury Park, CA: Sage Publications.

McGee, T.G. 1975. "Malay Migration to Kuala Lumpur City: Individual Adaptation to the City," in Brian Du Toit and Helen I. Safa, eds., *Migration and Urbanization: Models and Adaptive Strategies*, pp. 143–78. The Hague: Mouton.

Mead, Margaret. 1930. *Growing Up in New Guinea*. New York: Mentor Books.

Meintel, Deidre. 1987. "The New Double Workday of Immigrant Workers in Quebec," *Women's Studies* 13: 273–93.

Melville, Margarita. 1988. *Mexicans at Work in the United States*. Houston, TX: Mexican American Studies Program, University of Houston.

Mills, Mary Beth. 1998. "Gendered Encounters with Modernity: Labor Migrants and Marriage Choices in Contemporary Thailand," *Identities* 5: 301–34.

Min, Pyong Gap. 1998. *Changes and Conflicts: Korean Immigrant Families in New York*. Boston: Allyn and Bacon.

Min, Pyong Gap, and Jung Ha Kim, eds. 2002. *Religions in Asian America: Building Faith Communities*. Walnut Creek, CA: Altamira Press.

Mitchell, J. Clyde. 1957. "The Kalela Dance: Aspects of Social Relationships among Urban Africans in Northern Rhodesia," *Rhodes Livingstone Papers*, no. 27. Manchester: Manchester University Press.

_____. 1969. "Structural Plurality, Urbanization and Labour Circulation in Southern Rhodesia," in J. A. Jackson, ed., *Migration*, pp. 156–80. Cambridge: Cambridge University Press.

_____. 1971. *Social Networks in Urban Situations*. Manchester: Manchester University Press.

_____. 1974. "Social Networks," *Annual Review of Anthropology* 3: 279–99.

Moberg, Mark. 1996. "Transnational Labor and Refugee Enclaves in a Central American Banana Industry," *Human Organization* 55: 425–35.

Moch, Leslie Page. 1992. *Moving Europeans: Migration in Western Europe since 1650*. Bloomington: Indiana University Press.

Modood, Tariq, and Pnina Werbner, eds. 1997. *The Politics of Multiculturalism in the New Europe: Racism, Identity and Community*. London: Zed Books Limited.

Moore, Henrietta. 1988. *Feminism and Anthropology*. Minneapolis: University of Minnesota Press.

_____. 1994. *A Passion for Difference*. Bloomington, IN: Indiana University Press.

Morokvasic, Mirjana. 1983. "Women in Migration: Beyond the Reductionist Outlook," in Annie Phizacklea, ed., *One Way Ticket: Migration and Female Labour*, pp. 13–31. London: Routledge and Kegan Paul.

_____. 1984. "Birds of Passage Are also Women," *International Migration Review* 18: 886–907.

Murphy, Joseph. 1988. *Santeria: An African Religion in America*. Boston: Beacon Press.

Murray, Colin. 1981. *Families Divided: The Impact of Migrant Labour in Lesotho*. Cambridge: Cambridge University Press.

Nash, Jesse W., and Elizabeth Nguyen. 1995. *Romance, Gender, and Religion in a Vietnamese-American Community: Tales of God and Beautiful Women*. Lewiston: The Edward Mellen Press.

Neale, Rusty, and Virginia Neale. 1987. "As Long as You Know How to do Housework: Portuguese-Canadian Women and the Office-Cleaning Industry in Toronto," *Resources for Feminist Research* 16: 39–41.

Nelson, Nici. 1987. "Rural-urban Child Fostering in Kenya: Migration, Kinship Ideology, and Class," in Jeremy Eades, ed., *Migrants, Workers, and the Social Order*, pp. 181–98. London: Tavistock Publications.

O'Connor, Mary. 1990. "Women's Networks and the Social Needs of Mexican Immigrants," *Urban Anthropology* 19: 81–98.

Olwig, Karen Fog. 2004. "Place, Movement and Identity: Processes of Inclusion and Exclusion in a 'Caribbean' Family,'" in Waltraud Kokot, Khachig Tololyan, and Caroline Alfonso, eds., *Diaspora, Identity and Religion: New Directions in Theory and Research,* pp. 53–71. New York: Routledge.

Ong, Aihwa. 1987. *Spirits of Resistance and Capitalist Discipline: Factory Women in Malaysia.* Albany, NY: SUNY Press.

———. 1996. "Cultural Citizenship as Subject-Making: Immigrants Negotiate Racial and Cultural Boundaries in the United States," *Current Anthropology* 37: 737–62.

———. 1999. *Flexible Citizenship: The Cultural Logics of Transnationality.* Durham, NC: Duke University Press.

———. 2003. *Buddha is Hiding: Refugees, Citizenship, the New America.* Berkeley: University of California Press.

Orsi, Robert Anthony. 1985. *The Madonna of 115th Street: Faith and Community in Italian Harlem, 1880–1950.* New Haven, CT: Yale University Press.

Ortner, Sherry. 1984. "Theory in Anthropology since the Sixties," *Comparative Studies in Society and History* 26: 126–66.

———. 1995. "Resistance and the Problem of Ethnographic Refusal," *Comparative Studies in Society and History* 37: 173–93.

———. 1996. "Making Gender: Toward a Feminist, Minority, Postcolonial, Subaltern, etc., Theory of Practice," in Sherry Ortner, *Making Gender: The Politics and Erotics of Culture*, pp. 1–20. Boston: Beacon Press.

Panagakos, Anastasia. 2003. "Downloading New Identities: Ethnicity, Technology, and Media in the Global Greek Village," *Identities: Global Studies in Culture and Power* 10: 201–19.

Park, Kyeyoung. 1989. "'Born Again': What Does it Mean to Korean-Americans in New York City," *Journal of Ritual Studies* 3: 287–301.

Parrenas, Rachel S. 2001. *Servants of Globalization: Women, Migration, and Domestic Work.* Stanford, CA: Stanford University Press.

Pessar, Patricia R. 1984. "The Linkage between the Household and Workplace of Dominican Women in the U.S.," *International Migration Review* 18: 1188–1211.

———. 1995a. *A Visa for a Dream: Dominicans in the United States.* Boston: Allyn and Bacon.

———. 1995b. "On the Homefront and in the Workplace: Integrating Immigrant Women into Feminist Discourse," *Anthropological Quarterly* 68: 37–47.

———. 1995c. "The Elusive Enclave: Ethnicity, Class, and Nationality among Latino Entrepreneurs in Greater Washington, D.C.," *Human Organization* 53: 383–92.

———. 1999. "Engendering Migration Studies: The Case of New Immigrants in the United States," *American Behavioral Scientist* 42: 565–600.

———. 2001. "Women's Political Consciousness and Empowerment in Local, National and Transnational Contexts: Guatemalan Refugees and Returnees," *Identities: Global Studies in Culture and Power* 7: 461–500.

_____. 2003. "Anthropology and the Engendering of Migration Studies," in Nancy
Foner, ed., *American Arrivals: Anthropology Engages the New Immigrants*, pp.
75–98. Santa Fe, NM: School of American Research Press.

Philpott, Stuart B. 1970. "The Implications of Migration for Sending Societies: Some
Theoretical Considerations," in R. F. Spencer, ed., *Migration and Anthropology*,
pp. 9–20. Seattle, WA: American Ethnological Society.

_____. 1973. *West Indian Migration*. London: London School of Economics
Monograph.

Phizalacklea, Annie. 1983. *One Way Ticket: Migration and Female Labour*. London:
Routledge and Kegan Paul.

Plotnicov, Leo. 1967. *Strangers to the City: Urban Man in Jos, Nigeria*. Pittsburgh, PA:
University of Pittsburgh Press.

Poros, Maritsa. 2001. "The Role of Migrant Networks in Linking Local Labour Markets: The Case of Asian Indian Migration to New York and London," *Global
Networks: A Journal of Transnational Affairs* 1: 243–60.

Portes, Alejandro. 1997. "Immigration Theory for a New Century: Some Problems and
Opportunities," *International Migration Review* 31: 799–825.

Raj, Dhooleka S. 2003. *Where Are You From? Middle-Class Migrants in the Modern
World*. Berkeley: University of California Press.

Rajan, Gita, and Shailja Sharma. 2006. "New Cosmopolitanisms: South Asians in the
United States at the Turn of the Twenty-First Century," in Gita Rajan and Shailja
Sharma, eds., *New Cosmopolitanisms: South Asians in the U.S.*, pp. 1–36. Stan-
ford, CA: Stanford University Press.

Ralston, Helen. 1992. "Religion in the Life of South Asian Immigrant Women in Atlantic Canada," *Research in the Social Scientific Study of Religion* 4: 245–60.

Rangaswamy, Padma. 2000. *Namasté America: Indian Immigrants in an American
Metropolis*. Philadelphia: Pennsylvania State University Press.

Ravenstein, E.G. 1885. "The Laws of Migration," *Journal of the Royal Statistical Society* 48: 167–277.

Redfield, Robert. 1941. *The Folk Culture of Yucatan*. Chicago: University of Chicago Press.

Reichert, Joshua S. 1981. "The Migrant Syndrome: Seasonal U.S. Wage Labor and
Rural Development in Central Mexico," *Human Organization* 40: 56–66.

Reminick. Ronald. A. 1983. *Theory of Ethnicity: An Anthropologist's Perspective*.
Lanham, MD: University Press of America.

Repak, Terry A. 1995. *Waiting on Washington: Central American Workers in the
Nation's Capital*. Philadelphia, PA: Temple University Press.

Rex, John. 1997. "The Nature of Ethnicity in the Project of Migration," in Montserrat
Guibernau and John Rex, eds., *The Ethnicity Reader: Nationalism, Multiculturalism, and Migration*, pp. 269–82. London: Polity Press.

Rhoades, Robert E. 1978a. "Intra-European Migration and Rural Development: Les-
sons from the Spanish Case," *Human Organization* 37: 136–47.

_____. 1978b. "Foreign Labor and German Industrial Capitalism 1871–1978: The
Evolution of a Migratory System," *American Ethnologist* 5: 553–75.

Riccio, Bruno. 2000. "The Italian Construction of Immigration: Sedentarist and Cor-
poratist Narratives facing Transnational Migration in Emilia-Romagna," *The
Anthropological Journal on European Cultures* 9: 53–74.

_____. 2001. "From 'Ethnic Group' to 'Transnational Community'? Senegalese
Migrants' Ambivalent Experiences and Multiple Trajectories," *Journal of Ethnic and Migration Studies* 27: 583–99.

CAROLINE B. BRETTELL 156

Robertson, George, Melinda Mash, Lisa Tickner, J. Bird, B. Curtis, and T. Putnam, eds.
1994. *Travelers' Tales: Narratives of Home and Displacement.* London: Routledge.
Rodriguez, Nestor. 1987. "Undocumented Central Americans in Houston: Diverse
Populations," *International Migration Review* 21: 4–26.
———. 1996. "The Battle for the Border: Notes on Autonomous Migration, Transna-
tional Communities, and the State," *Social Justice* 23: 21–38.
Rollwagen, Jack. 1974a. "Introduction: The City as Context: A Symposium," *Urban
Anthropology* 4: 1–4.
———. 1974b. "The City as Context: The Puerto Ricans of Rochester," *Urban Anthro-
pology* 4: 53–9.
Rosaldo, Renato. 1988. "Ideology, Place, and People Without Culture," *Cultural
Anthropology* 3: 77–87.
Rosaldo, Renato, and William V. Flores. 1997. "Identity, Conflict, and Evolving Latino
Communities: Cultural Citizenship in San Jose, California," in William V.
Flores and Rina Benmayor, eds., *Latino Cultural Citizenship: Claiming Iden-
tity, Space, and Rights,* pp. 57–96. Boston: Beacon Press.
Rouse, Roger. 1991. "Mexican Migration and the Social Space of Postmodernism,"
Diaspora 1: 1–23.
———. 1992. "Making Sense of Settlement: Class Transformation, Cultural Strug-
gle, and Transnationalism among Mexican Migrants in the United States," in
Nina Glick Schiller, Linda Basch, and Christina Szanton Blanc, eds., *Towards a
Transnational Perspective on Migration: Race, Class, Ethnicity, and Nationalism Reconsidered,* pp. 25–52. New York: Annals of the New York Academy of
Sciences.
———. 1995a. "Thinking through Transnationalism: Notes on the Cultural Politics of Class Relations in the Contemporary United States," *Public Culture* 7:
353–402.
———. 1995b. "Questions of Identity: Personhood and Collectivity in Transnational
Migration to the United States," *Critique of Anthropology* 15: 351–80.
Rubenstein, Hymie. 1979. "The Return Ideology in West Indian Migration," *Papers in
Anthropology* 20: 21–38.
Safa, Helen I. 1975. "Introduction," in Helen I. Safa and Brian Du Toit, eds., *Migration
and Development: Implications for Ethnic Identity and Political Conflict,* pp.
1–13. The Hague: Mouton.
Safa, Helen I., and Brian Du Toit, eds. 1975. *Migration and Development: Implica-
tions for Ethnic Identity and Political Conflict.* The Hague: Mouton.
Salih, Ruba. 2003. *Gender in Transnationalism: Home, Longing and Belonging
Among Moroccan Migrant Women.* New York: Routledge.
Salzinger, Leslie. 1991. "A Maid by Any Other Name: The Transformation of 'Dirty
Work' by Central American Immigrants," in Michael Burawoy, et al., eds., *Eth-
nography Unbound: Power and Resistance in the Modern Metropolis,* pp. 139–
60. Berkeley: University of California Press.
Sanjek, Roger. 1990. "Urban Anthropology in the 1980s: A World View," *Annual
Review of Anthropology* 19: 151–86.
Sargent, Carolyn, and Stephanie Larchanché-Kim. 2006. "Liminal Lives: Immigra-
tion Status, Gender, and the Construction of Identities among Malian Migrants
in Paris," *American Behavioral Scientist* 50: 9–26.
Schneider, Jo-Anne. 1990. "Defining Boundaries, Creating Contacts: Puerto Rican
and Polish Presentation of Group Identity through Ethnic Parades," *Journal of
Ethnic Studies* 18: 33–57.

Schweizer, Thomas. 1998. "Epistemology: The Nature and Validation of Anthropological Knowledge," in H. Russell Bernard, ed., *Handbook of Methods in Cultural Anthropology*, pp. 39–87. Walnut Creek, CA: Altamira Press.

Scott, James. 1985. *Weapons of the Weak: Everyday Forms of Peasant Resistance.* New Haven, CT: Yale University Press.

Segura, Denise A. 1989. "Chicanas and Immigrant Women at Work: The Impact of Class, Race and Gender on Occupational Mobility," *Gender and Society* 3: 37–52.

Shukla, Sandhya. 2001. "Locations for South Asian Diasporas," *Annual Review of Anthropology* 30: 551–72.

Shuval, Judith T. 2000. "Diaspora Migration: Definitional Ambiguities and a Theoretical Paradigm," *International Migration* 38: 41–56.

Shweder, Richard A. 2003. "The Moral Challenge in Cultural Migration," in Nancy Foner, ed., *American Arrivals: Anthropology Engages the New Immigration*, pp. 259–94. Santa Fe, NM: School of American Research Press.

Silverstein, Paul. 2004. *Algeria in France: Transpolitics, Race and Nation.* Bloomington: Indiana University Press.

Simon, Rita James, and Caroline B. Brettell. 1986. *International Migration: The Female Perspective.* Totowa, NJ: Rowman and Allanheld.

Smith, Andrea, ed., 2003. *Europe's Invisible Migrants.* Amsterdam: University of Amsterdam Press.

Smith, M. Estellie. 1974. "A Tale of Two Cities: The Reality of Historical Differences," *Urban Anthropology* 4: 61–72.

———. 1976. "Networks and Migration Resettlement: Cherchez la Femme," *Anthropological Quarterly* 49: 20–7.

Smith, Robert. 1993. "Los Ausentes Siempre Presentes: The Imagining, Making and Politics of a Transnational Community between New York City and Ticuani, Puebla." Papers on Latin American and Iberian Studies. New York: Columbia University.

———. 1997. "Transnational Migration, Assimilation, and Political Community," in Margaret E. Crahan and Alberto Vourvoulias-Bush, eds., *The City and the World: New York's Global Future*, pp. 110–32. New York: Council on Foreign Relations.

Soto, Isa Maria. 1987. "West Indian Child Fostering: Its Role in Migrant Exchanges," in Constance Sutton and Elsa Chaney, eds., *Caribbean Life in New York City: Sociocultural Dimensions*, pp. 131–49. New York: Center for Migration Studies.

Spiegel, Andrew. 1987. "Dispersing Dependents: A Response to the Exigencies of Labour Migration in Rural Transkei," in Jeremy Eades, ed., *Migrants, Workers, and the Social Order*, pp. 113–29. London: Tavistock Publications.

Stack, Carol. 1996. *Call to Home: African Americans Reclaim the Rural South.* New York: Basic Books.

Stafford, Susan Buchanan. 1984. "Haitian Immigrant Women: A Cultural Perspective," *Anthropologica* 26: 171–89.

———. 1987. "The Haitians: The Cultural Meaning of Race and Ethnicity," in Nancy Foner, ed., *New Immigrants in New York*, pp. 131–58. New York: Columbia University Press.

Stepick, Alex. 1998. *Pride against Prejudice: Haitians in the United States.* Boston: Allyn and Bacon.

Stepick, Alex, Guillermo Grenier, Max Castro and Marvin Dunn. 2003. *This Land Is Our Land: Immigrants and Power in Miami.* Berkeley: University of California Press.

Stoller, Paul. 2002. *Money Has No Smell: The Africanization of New York City*. Chicago: University of Chicago Press.

Sutton, Constance. 1987. "The Caribbeanization of New York City and the Emergence of a Transnational Sociocultural System," in Constance Sutton and Elsa Chaney, eds., *Caribbean Life in New York City: Sociocultural Dimensions*, pp. 15–30. New York: Center for Migration Studies.

Talai, V. 1986. "Social Boundaries within and between Ethnic Groups: Armenians in London," *Man* 21: 251–70.

Taylor, Edward. 1976. "The Social Adjustment of Returned Migrants to Jamaica," in Frences Henry, ed., *Ethnicity in the Americas*, pp. 213–30. The Hague: Mouton.

Trager, Lillian, ed. 2005. *Migration and Economy: Global and Local Dynamics*. Walnut Creek, CA: Altamira Press.

Tseng, Yen-Fen. 2002. "From 'Us' to "Them': Diasporic Linkages and Identity Politics," *Identities: Global Studies in Culture and Power* 9: 383–404.

Tsuda, Takeyuki. 2003. *Strangers in the Ethnic Homeland: Japanese Brazilian Return Migration in Transnational Perspective*. New York: Columbia University Press.

Tweed, Thomas A. 1997. *Our Lady of the Exile: Diasporic Religion at a Cuban Catholic Shrine in Miami*. New York: Oxford University Press.

Ui, Shiri. 1991. "Unlikely Heroes: The Evolution of Female Leadership in a Cambodian Ethnic Enclave," in Michael Burawoy, et al., eds., *Ethnography Unbound: Power and Resistance in the Modern Metropolis*, pp. 161–77. Berkeley: University of California Press.

Uzzell, Douglas. 1976. "Ethnography of Migration: Breaking Out of the Bipolar Myth." Houston, TX: Rice University, Program of Development Studies.

Vertovec, Steven. 1997. "Three Meanings of Diaspora, Exemplified among South Asian Religions," *Diaspora: A Journal of Transnational Studies* 6: 277–300.

———. 1999. "Conceiving and Researching Transnationalism," *Ethnic and Racial Studies* 22: 447–62.

Wahlbeck, Osten. 2002. "The Concept of Diaspora as an Analytical Tool in the Study of Refugee Communities," *Journal of Ethnic and Migration Studies* 28: 221–39.

Wallerstein, Immanuel. 1974. *The Modern World-System: Capitalist Agriculture and the Origins of the European World Economy in the Sixteenth Century*. New York: Academic Press.

Wallman, Sandra. 1978. "The Boundaries of Race: Processes of Ethnicity in England," *Man* 13: 200–17.

———. 1986. "Ethnicity and the Boundary Process in Context," in John Rex and David Mason, eds., *Theories of Race and Ethnic Relations*, pp. 226–45. Cambridge: Cambridge University Press.

Warner, R. Stephen, and Judith G. Wittner, eds. 1998. *Gatherings in Diaspora: Religious Communities and the New Immigration*. Philadelphia, PA: Temple University Press.

Watson, James. 1975. *Emigration and the Chinese Lineage: The Mans in Hong Kong and London*. Berkeley: University of California Press.

Watson, James, ed. 1977. *Between Two Cultures*. Oxford: Basil Blackwell.

———. 2004. "Virtual Kinship, Real Estate, and Diaspora Formation—The Man Lineage Revisited," *Journal of Asian Studies* 63: 893–910.

Werbner, Pnina. 1987. "Enclave Economies and Family Firms: Pakistani Traders in a British City," in Jeremy Eades, ed., *Migrants, Workers, and the Social Order*, pp. 213–33. London: Tavistock Publications.

_____. 1988. "Taking and Giving: Working Women and Female Bonds in a Pakistani Immigrant Neighbourhood," in Sallie Westwood and Parminder Bhachu, eds., *Enterprising Women: Ethnicity, Economy, and Gender Relations*, pp. 177–202. London: Routledge.

_____. 1990. *The Migration Process: Capital, Gifts, and Offerings among British Pakistanis*. New York: Berg Publishers.

_____. 1995. "From Commodities to Gifts: Pakistani Migrant Workers in Manchester," in Alisdair Rogers and Steven Vertovec, eds., *The Urban Context: Ethnicity, Social Networks and Situational Analysis*, pp. 213–36. Oxford: Berg Publishers Limited.

_____. 1996. "Stamping the Earth with the Name of Allah: Zikr and the Sacralizing of Space among British Muslims," in Barbara Daly Metcalf, ed., *Making Muslim Space in North America and Europe*, pp. 167–85. Berkeley: University of California Press.

_____. 2002. "The Place which is Disapora: Citizenship, Religion and Gender in the Making of Chaordic Transnationalism," *Journal of Ethnic and Migration Studies* 28: 119–34.

Westwood, Sallie, and Parminder Bhachu, eds. 1988. *Enterprising Women: Ethnicity, Economy, and Gender Relations*. London: Routledge.

White, Jenny. 1997. "Turks in the New Germany," *American Anthropologist* 99 (4): 754–69.

Whiteford, Linda. 1979. "The Borderland as an Extended Community," in F. Camara and Robert Van Kemper, eds., *Migration across Frontiers: Mexico and the United States*, pp. 127–37. Albany: Institute for MesoAmerican Studies, State University of New York at Albany.

Whitten, Norman E. Jr. 1975. "Jungle Quechua Ethnicity: An Ecuadorian Case Study," in Helen I. Safa and Brian Du Toit, eds., *Migration and Development: Implications for Ethnic Identity and Political Conflict*, pp. 145–74. The Hague: Mouton.

Williams, Brackette F. 1989. "A Class Act: Anthropology and the Race to Nation across Ethnic Terrain," *Annual Review of Anthropology* 18: 401–44.

Wilson, Tamar Diana. 1992. "Theoretical Approaches to Mexican Wage Labor Migration," *Latin American Perspectives* 20: 98–129.

_____. 1994. "What Determines Where Transnational Labor Migrants Go? Modifications in Migration Theories," *Human Organization* 53: 269–78.

Wong, Bernard. 1998. *Ethnicity and Entrepreneurs: The New Chinese Immigrants in the San Francisco Bay Area*. Boston: Allyn and Bacon.

Yanagisako, Sylvia. 1985. *Transforming the Past: Tradition and Kinship among Japanese Americans*. Stanford, CA: Stanford University Press.

Yelvington, Kevin A. 1991. "Ethnicity as Practice? A Comment on Bentley," *Comparative Studies in Society and History* 33: 158–68.

Zavella, Patricia. 1988. "Abnormal Intimacy: The Varying Work Networks of Chicana Cannery Workers," *Feminist Studies* 11: 541–57.

Zinn, Dorothy Louise. 1994. "The Senegalese Immigrants in Bari: What Happens When the Africans Peer Back," in Rina Benmayor and Andor Skotnes, eds., *Migration and Identity*, pp. 53–68. Oxford: Oxford University Press.

Zloniski, Christian. 2006. *Janitors, Street Vendors, and Activists. The Lives of Mexican Immigrants in Silicon Valley*. Berkeley: University of California Press.

CHAPTER 6

Place, Space, and Pattern

Geographical Theories in International Migration

Susan W. Hardwick

INTRODUCTION

The field of geography is a complex discipline that involves research in both the human geography and physical geography domains.[1] Human geographers are defined by their specialization in a particular subfield such as political geography, cultural geography, economic geography, and urban geography; scholars who study international migration are known as *population geographers*. The latter focuses on studies of the interrelated socioeconomic, cultural, political, and environmental processes that help shape the spatial patterns of various populations on Earth. Geographers' interest in the dynamics of space and place, in fact, has long been the core defining framework of both human and physical aspects of the discipline.

An emphasis on the spatial relationships of comparative ethnic, racial, and immigrant groups lies at the heart of work by population geographers interested in international migration. As a result, research questions related to topics such as (1) the formation and evolution of ethnic enclaves in metropolitan areas; (2) changing segregation rates of various groups; (3) assimilation patterns and processes; and (4) residential, commercial, and employment patterns of comparative groups have dominated the literature for many decades. This long-term tradition of positivistic empirical work (for example, analyzing the spatial patterns of particular groups through time using census data) is one of the primary reasons population geographers have been seated relatively recently at the theoretical table.

A gathering of human geographers at the University of St. Andrews six years ago, however, set the stage for deepening the ongoing debate related to theory in population geography. The goal of this international meeting was to find new ways to (re)theorize population geography and stimulate debate about how the subfield might find and test innovative ways to more theoretically ground studies of migration from a spatial perspective. As this conference and an ever increasing number of publications in recent years attest, just as research on international migration by scholars trained in related disciplines has expanded exponentially during the past two decades, so too has the use of theory by human geographers interested in conducting research on migration on a variety of scales.

After many decades of empirically focused positivist work on the geography of immigration, publications calling for scholars to open up the discussion about the value of theorizing the "new" population geography began in earnest in the 1990s (see, for example, Findlay and Graham 1991; Graham and Boyle 2001; Halfacree 1995; Halfacree and Boyle 1993; Lawson 2000; McKendrick 1999; Silvey 2004; and White and Jackson 1995). Despite an overdependence on quantitative data sets such as census records (which may result in overly empirical and even atheoretical outcomes), these early calls for the use of theory in migration studies from a geographical perspective laid the foundation for the more recent expansion of a set of more integrated and deepened theoretical approaches in our discipline.

Key debates argued at the St. Andrews conference were published in a special issue of the *International Journal of Population Geography* in 2001.[2] The authors of these papers debated and explored the potential power of integrating several strands of theory to enrich research on the geography of migration. They suggested, for example, that the synthesizing of theories such as transnationalism (Bailey 2001) and diaspora (Boyle 2001) "to provide bridges between population geography and new (and more theoretical) human geography" (Boyle 2001:431) could help "provide a space of interconnection between migration geography and contemporary debates in human geography" (Laoire 2003:276).

But what theories best apply to studies of migration set within a spatial/geographical framework? And how might these theories, or some combination of them, be used most effectively in geographic studies of migration? This chapter provides preliminary answers to these overarching questions and lays a foundation for encouraging geographers to consider the application of a more expansive theoretical framework in their work. In the spirit of this volume, I build on Graham's call that "population geography would do well to enhance its own identity as *geography* by re-engaging with wider debates in human geography and the social sciences more generally" (2000:269–70).

Four years after population geographers interested in migration studies at the St. Andrews conference debated the use of theory in migration research, a special issue of *Population, Space, and Place* focused on theory building in the post–Trewartha era in geography.[3] When geographer Glenn Trewartha presented his presidential address to the discipline's flagship organization, the Association of American Geographers, as long ago as 1953, he declared that population geographers were still primarily descriptive scholars who tended to "treat human beings in terms of numbers almost exclusively," and that they were becoming marginalized in the discipline as a whole (1953:74, 96). These concerns remained true for most of the next four decades as migration scholars in geography continued to do primarily empirical and descriptive work (even though research grounded in critical social theory has been well underway elsewhere in the field for at least three decades).

Despite this rather late start, human geographers interested in studies of international migration from a theoretical perspective have begun to "see the theoretical light" during the past decade and a half. However, finding ways to theorize the subfield in a meaningful and cohesive way still has a long way to go. To help provide an overview of current theories in migration geography, in this chapter I discuss work accomplished to date that is grounded in the following interrelated theoretical strands: (1) sociospatial theory; (2) transnationalism, social networks, and "networks of ethnicity"; and (3) critical race theory and whiteness studies. I then make recommendations for expanding the role of theory more widely in work conducted by population geographers, including frameworks used by feminist and diaspora scholars. The chapter concludes with a discussion of some approaches to synthesizing place, space, and theory that have the power to enhance the development of new theories that may be useful in expanding work on international migration more broadly across the disciplines.

SOCIOSPACIAL THEORIES IN GEOGRAPHY: SPATIALITY, ASSIMILATION, AND HETEROLOCALISM

One of the defining features of work in the field of human geography is the analysis of the spatial patterns of immigrants through time. Studies that focus on patterns and processes are, in fact, one of the key cornerstones of the discipline. For more than a century, geographers interested in immigration have documented the residential patterns of new immigrants to understand more about migration and settlement decision making, immigrant's propensity (or not) to reside in close proximity to others from their homeland, and the relationship between these shifting spatial patterns and immigrant identities, assimilation experiences, multiethnic household distributions, and incorporation (see, for example, Hoelscher 1998; Johnston, Poulsen, and Forrest 2003; Kaplan 1998; McHugh 1989; Ostergren 1988; and Wong 1999).

The quest to understand this ever-shifting residential domain built upon work accomplished by the Chicago School of Sociology where immigrant residential patterns, especially in urban areas, were closely related to their ability to master the English language and increase their socioeconomic status. Upward mobility brought on by linguistic and economic change then made it possible for (white) groups to move outward from their original settlement site in the central city to the suburbs. These and other moves toward spatial assimilation, according to the Chicago School model, made it possible for foreign-born residents in the city to work their way out of downtown ghetto enclaves to a new life in more affluent suburbs (Park, Burgess, and McKenzie 1925). While this early work held promise in terms of relating spatial patterns and social and economic processes, it was dependent on the basic *invasion-succession model* of immigrant assimilation, which was most applicable to (1) European groups who were able to blend into the suburban mainstream, and (2) pre–1970s-era metropolitan areas. In the post–1970s era of immigration to North American metropolitan areas, however, new incoming groups of immigrants are just as likely to settle in the suburbs upon their arrival in the United States as they are to reside in downtown neighborhoods.

These dramatic changes in immigrant settlement patterns during the past 30 years have provided geographers and other scholars with fertile ground for ongoing work analyzing the residential patterns of various groups. However, the analysis of these mapped patterns is now linked closely to larger questions about urban space and the interrelated social, economic, and political processes that shape it. Geographers such as Li and Siu's work (1998) on permanent and temporary migration in China; research on international migration and the change in women's roles in rural Bangladesh accomplished by Hadi (2001); Jones's study of the ongoing segregation of ancestry groups in urban Texas (2003) and McHugh's analysis of the redistribution of Hispanics in the United States (1989); work on transnational women migrants in southern and Southeast Asia (Boyle 2002); research by Hardwick on the relationship between Russian immigrant patterns and their acculturation in cities located on the North American Pacific Rim (1993, 2003); and the study of Sydney, Australia's recent ethnic patterns and their relationship to the segregation rates of selected immigrant groups by Forrest and Johnston (2001) are all examples of this type of work. Analyzing the shifting residential patterns of immigrants has remained important in geographical studies of migration in recent years, but only as one piece of a larger and more theoretical puzzle that links these spatial questions with other related processes and issues.

Adding to the literature on the comparative spatiality of immigrant groups, geographers such as William Frey (1995, 1996) have pointed out that in today's metropolitan areas, sharp disparities often exist between white populations and racial and ethnic minorities. He called these patterns *demographic balkanization* inferring that there are well-bounded and often harsh special divisions among these groups. A subsequent critique of the use of this metaphor, however (see Ellis and Wright 1998), posited that invoking the term balkanization to describe the spatial patterns of foreign-born groups in U.S. society may create a negative perception, viewpoint, and/or theory about the placing of immigrant groups in American cities. They argue that "the term balkanization is associated with ethnic territorial conflict . . . and [thus] carries with it an implicit and deeply negative commentary on current immigrants in the United States" and that "the deployment of the term balkanization sounds a false alarm that warns of a Yugoslavian fate for the United States produced by an immigrant-induced break-up of a unified nation with a common culture" (686).

Even though the balkanization metaphor may tread on dangerous meta-phorical ground, Frey's work provides yet another reminder that studies of the relationship between the spatial segregation and the assimilation of immigrant groups remains a key theme in the theoretical literature in geography. Despite the ongoing suburbanization of immigrants in the first decade of the twenty-first century, questions related to these themes have largely been examined in downtown enclaves where foreign-born residents tend to live in close proximity to co-ethnics from their homeland. In contrast to this enclave-based emphasis in the literature, however, today's suburban metropolis is a place where migrants from outside the United States more often settle in a more dispersed pattern during their earliest years of settlement instead of in immigrant-rich parts of the downtown area.

In the late 1990s, geographers Zelinsky and Lee formulated a new theory called *heterolocalism* to help explain the significance of these dispersed (and often suburban) immigrant patterns and their relationship to the maintenance of ethnic identity (1998, 2001). Heterolocalism suggests that the greatly improved connectivity in urban areas, brought on by improvements in transportation and communication technologies in recent decades, has increased the potential accessibility of residential space, thereby making it possible for certain ethnic and racial groups to maintain their identities through time no matter where they live. Thus, despite a lack of residential propinquity after initial settlement, ethnic ties remain strong at varying scales of analysis including the neighborhood, urban, regional, national, and even international level. In essence then, heterolocalism provides an alternative theory to help explain and link the spatial patterns of immigrants with their assimilation rates and ethnic identities.

According to Zelinsky (2001:133), the theory of heterolocalism encompasses the following criteria:

1. There is an immediate and prompt spatial dispersion of heterolocal immigrants within the host country.
2. Residence and work place are usually widely separated, and frequently there is also a lack of spatial overlap between residence on the one hand and shopping districts and sites of social activity on the other.
3. Despite the lack of spatial propinquity, strong ethnic community ties are maintained via telecommunications, visits, and other methods at the metropolitan, regional, national, and even international scale.
4. Heterolocalism is a time-dependent phenomenon so that although we can detect some partial manifestation in earlier periods of time, its full development is conceivable only under the socioeconomic and technological conditions established in the late 20th century.
5. As is the case of other models, heterolocalism can exist in both metropolitan and nonmetropolitan settings.

6. In contrast to other models, heterolocalism has implications for socio-spatial behavior at the transnational and even global scale.

At its most foundational level, the theory of heterolocalism provides a "way in" to analyze the relationship between residential spatial patterns and ethnic identity. In addition, this theory has also made a contribution to the theoretical discussions in human geography that center on the importance of analyzing other types of sociospatial patterns of immigrants beyond their places of residence. While most geographers have focused on immigrant residential patterns as a point of departure, research on the relationship between places of work, church patterns, and the social spaces of immigrants are also proving useful in helping unravel the structures, patterns, and processes influencing assimilation.

Places of employment have been of particular importance in understanding the economic and social ties that help shape urban immigrant landscapes. According to Zelinsky, "among the least advantaged segments of the urban population such as working-class African Americans or Latinos, we find a general situation quite unlike that of Asian Indians and other heterolocal groups, but separation nonetheless between home and job. The former may be clustered in well-defined neighborhoods, but a large percentage of full or part-time employees, especially domestic workers, gardeners, and casual laborers, earn wages by the day or hour almost anywhere within the metropolitan area" (Zelinsky 2001:138).

The thinking of Ellis and Wright (2004) expanded our understanding of the importance of analyzing and theorizing employment patterns as they relate to residential patterns. Their research comparing native-born and the largest immigrant groups in the Los Angeles metropolitan area revealed that differences in segregation rates between home and work can be very large in the case of Mexican and native-born residents. These comparative groups, they found, live in very different parts of the city but are likely to work in the same census tracts (although this pattern is much better developed among all groups of native-born men and immigrant women). These findings give credence to the authors' argument that the emphasis in past geographic work on the analysis of residential patterns of immigrants "creates false impressions of urban areas' ethnic and racialized spaces as fixed and misleadingly characterizes residential neighborhoods as the exclusive domain of those who live, rather than work, in them" (620).

The locations and roles of religious institutions, social clubs, businesses, and other immigrant gathering places as sites of ethnic identity and cultural maintenance have been the focus of other work on immigration by geographers. A recent analysis of the relationship between the business and church networks of refugees in the Pacific Northwest, for example, provides evidence that the residential patterns of certain groups may have little to do with the location of their other activity spaces in the city (Hardwick and Meacham 2005) (see Figure 6.1).

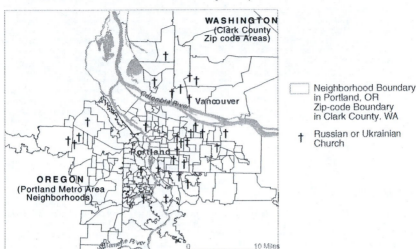

FIGURE 6.1 Portland-Vancouver Area Churches Serving Russian-Speaking Residents (Immigrant and Refugee Organization, CENSUS Tiger/Line 2000 and Slavic Directory, 2002.)

In another study emphasizing the location and role of religious institutions in immigrant communities, Beattie and Ley (2003) documented the changing role of immigrant churches through time in Vancouver, British Columbia. Their contribution helped provide further impetus for a more nuanced study of the relationship among the spatial patterns of churches and the meanings of distinctive cultural landscape and values and helped theorize and problematize the analysis of spatial patterns. These geographers "see religious landscape forms (or map distributions) not as unproblematic social facts but as social constructions embodying meanings to be revealed through hermeneutic method, meanings that both create landscapes and also perpetuate existing cultural values and social and political relationships" (3).

In sum, population geographers interested in furthering our understanding of the relationship among spatial patterns and assimilation and ethnic identity have pushed the theoretical boundaries of how to most effectively analyze immigrant space and place in recent years by offering these and other critiques and expansions of traditional Chicago School assimilation models. Wright, Ellis, and Parks (2005), for example, argued for a completely revised theory of spatial assimilation based on the experiences and patterns of recent immigrant groups (see Figure 6.2). Their work provides a comparison of the dramatic differences between immigrant space in the past and present. In this

Conventional Spatial Assimilation Theory	Modified Spatial Assimilation Theory
1. The intertwined processes of acculturation assimilation - the adoption of English as a second language plus mainstream values and customs - and socioeconomic mobility help drive spatial assimilations: the relocation of immigrants to neighborhoods with better amenities.	1. a. Immigrants arrive with varying degrees of economic resources and skills. Some will be more able to acquire more housing and live in better neighborhoods immediately, or very soon after arrival. Others will move into better housing and neighborhoods if they make economic progress. b. Acculturation may not enhance economic mobility. Following segmented assimilation theory, acculturation may in fact retard economic progress and prolong isolation in poorer ethnic neighborhoods, at least for nonwhite immigrants. Alternatively, ethnic neighborhoods may offer advantages of selective acculturation for nonwhite groups. Consequently, the degree of a group's spatial concentration is not necessarily an indicator of its assimilative progress.
2. Better neighborhoods tend to be suburban areas with high percentages of whites. Proximity to whites is a proxy indicator of assimilative progress because whites tend to live in better housing and neighborhoods with more amenities. Proximity to whites is also an indicator of reduced social distance with the dominant group. The relocation of immigrants to neighborhoods with better amenities folds into Gordon's idea of "structural assimilation," and "the large scale entrance into cliques, clubs, and institutions of the host society in a primary group level." (1964, p. 71).	2. Better neighborhoods may be suburban areas with high percentages of whites But they may also be mixed or primarily nonwhite neighborhoods, and not necessarily suburban. The key is improvements in housing and neighborhood quality - not proximity to whites in suburban locations.
3. Immigrants initially settle in ethnic concentrations in central areas of cities where housing is relatively inexpensive with access to low wage jobs in manufacturing and services. Spatial assimilation involves dispersion from these areas to suburban white neighborhoods. (This dispersion is accompanied by a weakening in ethnic division of labor.)	3. Immigrants' initial settlement is affected by their contacts with co-ethnics, the availability of employment, skills, and personal wealth. This leads some groups to move into ethnic neighborhoods in central cities; others move directly to suburbs. Subsequent dispersion is not necessarily suburban in orientation to or toward whites; dispersion is better thought of as moves to better housing and neighborhoods. Dispersion could be toward pan-ethnic neighborhoods, either by choice or constraint.

FIGURE 6.2 Comparison of Conventional and Modified Spatial Assimilation Theories (Wright, Ellis, and Parks 2005.)

newly revised assimilation model, integration into mainstream white society may not enhance economic mobility, and in fact may retard economic progress and prolong isolation in poor ethnic neighborhoods, especially for nonwhite immigrants. While some higher-income neighborhoods may be suburban (as in traditional models of assimilation), they may not have a high percentage of white residents, but instead may be mixed or nonwhite. And these diverse neighborhoods may not even be suburban, as the straight-line assimilation argument would predict. According to this recast spatial assimilation theory, "a key objective for spatially oriented assimilation research should now be to unpack the relationships between assimilation at different scales and different places" (134).

Building on this revised and expanded model, population geographers and other scholars have found that while today's metropolitan areas do still have distinctive immigrant settlement nodes, many are so ethnically mixed that they cannot be identified as an ethnic enclave in any traditional sense as they were in the past. In places ranging from Queens, New York (called one of the most diverse populations in the world by Khandelwal in 1995) to Sacramento, California, for example (see Dingemans and Datel 1995), "a general tendency in the new metropolis is for immigrants to live in areas where they combine with other nonwhite ethnic groups to create multiethnic communities" (Skop and Li 2003:116). Lower-income immigrants may be forced to reside in marginalized spaces located on the periphery of urban areas, such as Mexicans who live in outlying *colonias* in Laredo, Texas, and Hmong who reside in apartments and small rental homes on the edge of Fresno, California (Miyares 1997).

Wei Li's conceptualization of immigrant *ethnoburbs*, or "suburban ethnic clusters of residential areas and business districts in large metropolitan areas," presents yet another spatial form that is increasingly common in today's metropolis (1998:482). According to her findings in Monterey Park, California, ethnoburbs are most often located in former white-dominated bedroom communities in the inner suburban ring of large cities. The economic, social, and cultural bonds that develop in these kinds of clustered immigrant communities, where one group forms a solid majority, provide a source of support that often leads to enhanced upward mobility for many of these already successful immigrants (Skop and Li 2003:118).

As this large body of prior work indicates, residential, religious, economic, and other patterns may be theorized in a variety of ways. Whether shaped by individual agency or by overarching political, economic, and/or social structures, the spatial patterns of immigrant groups are created and maintained by a set of nested processes and relationships.

TRANSNATIONALISM, SOCIAL NETWORKS, AND NETWORKS OF ETHNICITY

Along with anthropologists and other migration scholars, human geographers have also contributed to a growing body of literature on globalization, transnational connectivity, and the activities and patterns of transnational communities in recent years.[4] For the past two decades, in a variety of disciplines and contexts, migration theorists have been engaged in an ongoing debate about ways to best understand and analyze a world in motion brought on by the drama of migration—and many have come to depend on transnational theory in one way or another (see Brettell, this volume). Some scholars argue that political borders are now permeable sites of flexible and hybrid migrant identities (see, for example, Bailey et al. 2002; Mitchell 1997a). Others suggest that to accommodate and make sense of this ongoing and often dramatic globalizing process, it is necessary for scholars to come up with a new way to conceptualize and write about the transnational migration experience. Whether discussing transnationalism and the changing role and relevance of the state (Wright 1997); transnational communities, transmigrants, and transnational social fields (Glick Schiller et al. 1995); transnational global ethnoscapes (Appadurai 1991); transnational sojourners (Scott 2003); research methods for studying transnationalism (Hyndman and Walton-Roberts 2000); transnational methodologies (Mountz, Wright, Miyares, and Bailey 2002); or economic, social, cultural, and/or symbolic ties linking places of origin with co-ethnics who reside in new sites of residence, transnational theory and all its interrelated ramifications have clearly emerged as the buzzword of the new millennium in migration research.

Transnational relationships and linkages hold particular fascination for population geographers interested in research on global migration because transnational processes happen in distinctive places and at distinctive moments. Despite arguments that space has become deterritorialized in today's transnational world, like national political borders, space and time still exist. However, most of the current literature on transnationalism weakly theorizes space–time relationships and the impacts of space, place, and time on migrants, and fails to critically examine how migration processes shape various locales and the people who live there.[5] Geographic studies of the relational and locational situations framing the transnational experience and transnational communities are helping to fill this gap.

Migration processes shaped by the larger context of conditions in the sending country, the characteristics and events that happen during the journey in between, and the economic, political, and cultural context of the receiving society have been of particular interest to geographers. Of note are ways in which the political and social structures of distinctive places shape individual and group migration decision making about destination locales. Although transmigrants are often described in spatially interwoven terms as migrants who live in two worlds at the same time, in order to find ways to survive and ultimately even thrive in their new lives, most must make decisions and produce actions at particular times in particular places. Therefore, while their past lives may haunt migrants at times (for example, during periods of civil and military unrest or economic duress at home), most focus their energies on finding ways to survive and adjust to their new place of residence, especially in the early years. As new migrants face ongoing decisions and choices each day, it is essential to learn more about how individuals and groups find ways to adapt in situ in particular places at particular moments in time.

The study of transnational communities as distinctive places linked by a set of intense cross-border social relations that enable individuals to participate in the activities of two or more nations has been of particular importance in studies of the geography of international migration. Distinctive places, and the people who reside in them, are created by a nuanced set of circumstances, processes, and interconnections. Current research on these linked communities "connect ethnographic evidence on daily lives to broader accounts of the changing nature of economic and cultural systems . . . and thus the emerging population geographies feature landscapes of hyperconnectivity, fluidity, and dispersion" (Bailey 2001:420) making them ideal sites for geographic analysis.

In their study of the transnational relationships of Salvadoran migrants in northern New Jersey, Bailey et al. (2002) found that their legal provision of temporary protected status (TPS) permeated the everyday lives of this migrant group on both ends of the transnational circuit. Their work employed what they called a transnational mixed-methods approach to analyze the impacts of "permanent temporariness" on this group. They found that TPS status "limits the geographic, economic, social, and political ambitions of Salvadorans, [that] is increasingly resisted through acts of strategic visibility" (125) such as pursuing permanence through educational investments in the second generation, marriage, and refusing to leave the United States by going underground.

Geographers have also added to the work of scholars in other disciplines who have written about the importance of theorizing subjectivity, positionality, and awareness of the ways in which the (mobile) researcher affects the lives of (immobile) people who may reside in transnational communities (see, for example, Mountz, Miyares, Wright, and Bailey 2003). These calls for action urged scholars to heighten their sensitivity to the meanings and perceptions of feelings and actions in everyday life as particularly important points of departure for research in hyperlinked communities. Work on transnational geographies of migration, then, provides new opportunities to fill in the space–time gap that remains in much of the emerging, cross-disciplinary, and now quite vast transnational literature that all too often fails to consider scale, context, and place as key ingredients in understanding the processes involved in shaping transnational circuits.

Geographers working on immigration processes taking place in Canada have made a significant contribution to research on issues related to the geography of transnational migration in recent years. Hyndman and Walton-Roberts's (2000) research on transnational approaches to studying refugees in Canada, Sherrell and Hyndman's work with Kosovar refugees in seven cities in British Columbia (2004), and Mountz's research on the four boatloads of smuggled Chinese migrants who arrived on the west coast of Vancouver Island in the late 1990s (almost all of whom where deported soon thereafter) provide useful conceptual approaches to studying the nation–state, transnationalism, and migration. Mountz found that although Canada is often viewed as the humanitarian state (especially as compared to the United States), and the assumption that wealthy immigrants are good for the state persists within government circles, smuggled migrants remain out of the realm of possibility as potentially positive contributors to the greater good of the nation. These "narratives of disruption and difference expose inconsistencies in Canada's self-imaginings," which enable national narratives to fall apart and open up new transnational imaginaries of the nation–state in relation to global restructuring and the mediation of transnational migrations (2003:640).

Walton-Roberts's study of the impacts of transnational immigrant networks linking India and Canada (2004) argued appropriately that gender has been underplayed in many of the prior studies of transnational migration accomplished by geographers. She used Punjabi marriage migration networks to demonstrate how the practice of spousal selection has become globalized for certain diasporic communities. Her work found that "pre-existing dense social networks between Canada and India provide opportunities for mobility, but in the case of spousal migration, the process is marked by gendered inequality and the transnational extension of certain patriarchal practices" and that the "patriarchal practices in northern India have served to reinforce the position of women in society generally and in marriage processes in particular" (370). Walton-Roberts and other geographers interested in immigration, race, and place have contributed to both the emerging transnational literature and also increased our understanding of some of the ways that transnational practices and relationships are linked to insider and outsider social networks.

The concept of *networks of ethnicity* first discussed by Mitchell (2000) provides a related theoretical framework for integrating transnational discourse into geography. These economic, social, and politically constructed networks may be internal (endogenous) social connections that are specific to one or more distinctive groups or external (exogenous) networks that provide newcomers linkages with the outside world. Networks of ethnicity enhance the transfer of information among family and friends, co-workers, and co-religionists, and social networks shared by migrants with similar backgrounds may also help to cushion the impact of adjusting to life in a new place. Once in place, information that is passed back and forth within networks of ethnicity may lead to self-perpetuating chain migration flows.

Geographers interested in migrant networks such as Harner (2000), Hardwick (2003, 2006b), Mattingly (1999), and Wright and Ellis (2000b), have documented that these connections exist at different scales ranging from local to national and international and that they connect migrants and nonmigrants in origin and destination areas through ties of kinship, friendship, and shared community origin. For some groups, these ties enhance the likelihood of international migration because they lower the risks and costs of relocating to a new place. They may also transform groups into spatial or social enclaves of ethnic identity within a relatively short period of time since participation in ethnic organizations, religious rituals, festivals, and visits to co-ethnic shops and restaurants helps to consolidate attachment to migrant communities.

Of particular note in recent geographic work has been a search for appropriate qualitative methodologies to analyze social networks and networks of ethnicity. Network analysis, which became popular among quantitative scholars in the 1960s and 1970s, first began as ethnographic work in British social anthropology. However, in the field of geography, this approach soon devolved into a purely statistical analysis of socioeconomic and other variables that measured and compared characteristics of individuals, groups, and places. More recently, geographers have recast this quantitative approach to network theory through the use of qualitative methods such as structured and unstructured interviews and participant observation to analyze the relationships and linkages among social and other kinds of networks and place-based migration experiences (Hardwick 2003:167). Analyzing the social connections and networks that immigrants maintain and use through a set of embedded relationships has the potential to help scholars understand more about how social, economic, and cultural processes help shape immigrant settlement patterns, and how these interrelated processes and relationships contribute to the adjustment and adaptation of new immigrants through time and in space.

CRITICAL RACE THEORY AND WHITENESS STUDIES IN GEOGRAPHY

Another area of theoretical work now well underway in geography builds upon prior work on critical race theory and research on normalized whiteness undertaken by scholars in other fields. These studies draw upon signal contributions made by Roediger (1991) and other scholars working in the fields of sociology, anthropology, history, critical studies, literary criticism, and other related disciplines. Critical race theorists challenge the idea of race as a natural and universal classification of human experience, contending that categories such as black and white are too easily accepted as givens, and that this simplistic duality conceals the social processes that define and rank racial difference. Critical race approaches, on the other hand, stress that racial identity is socially constructed and therefore subject to contestation, negotiation, and change. Geographers who engage critical race theory have been especially interested in the ways that the material realities of the construction of race are expressed through time and in place (see, for example, Anderson 1988; Bonnett 2000, 1997; Howard 2003; Jackson 1989; Kobayashi 2003; Kobayashi and Peake 2000; Nash 2003; Peake and Ray 2001; Smith 1989; Winders 2003, 2005).[6]

For the past decade, geographers interested in theorizing issues related to race and place have addressed such topics as environmental racism (e.g., Pulido 2000); studies of some of the ways that racially coded environments, identities, cultural practices, and other cultural, social, economic, and political practices help create and maintain racial divisions in place and space (e.g., Holloway 1998; Liu 2000; McCarthy and Hague 2004); and assessing and comparing the processes shaping ethnic and racial identities and their multiplicity of expressions in time and space (e.g., Berry and Henderson 2002). Of particular concern in much of this work has been distancing current efforts from the more heavily empirical research accomplished in the past by population geographers who emphasized spatialized approaches without delving into defining and deconstructing the concept of race.

Peter Jackson sounded one of the earliest calls for geographers to move away from more simplistic approaches to understanding the constructions of race in the late 1980s. He encouraged geographers to identify the places and times that were critical to the formation of race relations as a political issue, analyze the polarization of race and the racialization of politics, examine sites of struggle and resistance in both a spatial and social sense, and survey the social geography of struggle by compiling ethnographies of the racialized experience (1989:191). In the decades since his early attention to the importance of these kinds of questions in geographic work on migration, an increasing amount of attention has been paid to understanding the relationships and processes that shape race, place, and space. Of note are semiannual research conferences on these themes sponsored by the discipline's flagship organization, the Association of American Geographers (at Howard University in 2004 and Texas State University in 2006).

The social construction of whiteness has also been of interest to critical theorists in geography in recent years. The work of Bonnett (2000, 1996) provided a launching point, a summary of research underway in other fields, and a call to action for geographers to shift their focus on the study of race to a recognition of the normalized role of whiteness in society. Building on the work of Levine (1994), who suggested that whiteness has long been the "standard against which the 'Other' is judged as inferior, deviant, exotic, or simply noteworthy" (1994:11), Bonnett and other geographers such as Ellis (2001), Hoelscher (2003), Jackson (1998), Kobayashi and Peake (2000), and McCarthy and Hague (2004) have placed whiteness and white studies firmly within the study of geography from a variety of perspectives.

One of these studies centered attention on the actions and perceptions of "wise use" activists in the rural southwestern United States as expressed through the lens of white Celtic identity (McCarthy and Hogue 2004). By claiming Celticness, this group was able to assert their membership in an identity that is strongly associated with resistance to the state and oppression, while at the same time retaining the benefits of white privilege (Peake and Kobayashi 2002). Their work adds to the growing body of theoretical literature in geography related to whiteness study in several important ways. First, it serves as a reminder that it is essential not to limit work in critical race theory and whiteness only to urban places since "spatial racialization involves not only relegation of minorities to segregated areas, but the placement of *all* people in specific but highly variable circumstances" (Kobayashi and Peake 2000:395). Second, this study points out the importance of conducting white studies in noncoastal and predominately white places because these areas have largely been overlooked in the literature to date. Finally, this analysis of Celtic whiteness provides a case study that serves as an important reminder that there is diversity in whiteness just as there is among and between other ethnic and racial groups. As Bonnett reminded us, "white identities are currently being developed and transformed in different societies around the world" (1997:97) and thus need to be deconstructed and untangled (as do the identities of other racial groups).

Similarly, Peake and Kobayashi published a call to geographers to heed recent efforts to understand not only the culture of racialization, but also the culture of whiteness as both reciprocal and formative (2002:52; Bonnett 1997, 2000). Their work reminds scholars that whiteness is an embedded aspect of analyzing landscapes as an expression of human values, cultural practices, and tastes. "Antiracist landscape analysis, therefore, requires that we tread carefully between understanding landscapes as a dominant way in which white power is played out and advocate for new power and positions (Peake and Kobayashi 2002:52). Because geographic analysis often focuses attention on the ever-changing processes that shape and reshape landscapes through time, this reminder is well placed to help bring the study of whiteness into the center of the discipline rather than locating it only on the periphery. In sum then, critical race theory and whiteness studies, when taken to the limit, may seem to devolve into the chaos of difference, but their purpose in geography has been to help demonstrate how attitudes toward race are created, sustained, and challenged in place, space, and time in real-world contexts.

CONCLUSIONS: TOWARD INTEGRATION, SYNTHESIS, AND CROSS-DISCIPLINARY WORK ON MIGRATION

As this chapter has illustrated, geographers have a relatively short history of doing theoretical work on migration. Recent contributions to transnational and spatial assimilation theories, along with work on social networks, networks of ethnicity, critical race theory, and critical whiteness studies, however, have already made significant contributions to research on international migration. Traditionally, geographers have been most interested in issues related to the spatiality of immigrant communities and the processes that shape their patterns. This fascination continues to inform much of the work underway in the subfield of population geography today (although it has been deepened and expanded considerably through the use of this more theoretical lens).

Along with the theoretical approaches discussed earlier in this chapter, feminist geographers have also played an important role in helping deconstruct some of the objectivist research on spatial mobility (see, for example, Arokiasamy 2001; Boyle and Halfacree 1999; Hadi 2001; Lawson 1999, 1998; Silvey 2004; Silvey and Lawson 1999; and Walton-Roberts 2004). The role of gender in migration decision making and the spatial and material implications of gendered migrations have emerged in recent years as important topics of concern among geographers, anthropologists (see Brettell, this volume), and other scholars interested in critical studies of migration. Feminist geographers who are engaged in migration research critically disentangle the politics of difference as they shape the processes affecting population movements through time "as well as the knowledge that is produced about these processes" (Silvey 2004:305).

Alongside this increased attention to gender issues in geography is a new emphasis on studies of migrant groups overlooked in most of the traditional migration literature such as refugees, asylees, and diasporic communities (e.g., Brah 1996; Brun 2001; Stewart 2005; and White 2002). Analyzing the spatial patterns and related processes shaping the refugee experience have in particular emerged as salient themes in the geographic literature in recent years. Hyndman's critique and deconstruction of the work of political agencies in the resettlement of refugees caused both scholars and activists to rethink the strategies used in refugee support systems worldwide (2000). Of particular concern in other work has been attention to the shifting identities and patterns of refugees in North American cities, such as Jackiewicz and Pfeifer's work on the ethnic identities of Vietnamese refugees as they are expressed through family reunions in two comparative U.S. cities (2000); Miyares study of Hmong refugee identity, space, and place in California's Central Valley (1997); and Hume and Hardwick's analysis of the impact of local refugee resettlement agencies and other support networks on the lives and patterns of African, Russian, and Ukrainian refugees in the Portland metropolitan area (2005).

The study of the geography of diaspora has taken on greater urgency in recent years as a particularly rich space for interdisciplinary work. To understand the processes shaping diasporic flows, it is necessary to understand their location in particular geographical contexts so that the complexity of specific diasporic experiences can be better understood. Because the word *diaspora* is a term taken from the Greek that implies scattering or dispersion of a population, it is surprising that geographers have not been participants in diaspora studies until recently. A collection of articles on diaspora studies from a geographic perspective published in a special issue of the *International Journal of Population* (2003) drew attention to some of the ways spatial/geographical approaches can be used to understand more about political and economic structures involved in diasporic migrations, and the intersections of gender, class, ethnicity, and nation in the formation of different groups.

Like other disciplines in the social sciences, geography is an integrative discipline grounded in approaches, models, and theories that mesh well with scholarly work in related fields. Therefore it is not surprising that recent efforts in the field to theorize the study of international migration from a geographical perspective have built upon work accomplished by migration scholars in other disciplines. As the other chapters in this book illustrate, many of the theories now being tested and refined by geographers are also central to the work of anthropologists, sociologists, and other migration scholars in related fields of study. As studies of migration, place, and space continue to expand in number and consequence in the coming years, it is important for geographers, in close consort with other scholars, to continue to document, analyze, and theorize the patterns and processes involved in international migration in the past, present, and future.

NOTES

1. This chapter was completed with the invaluable research support of Ginger Mansfield along with expert cartographic work accomplished by Grace Gardener and James E. Meacham, director of the InfoGraphics Laboratory at the University of Oregon. My ideas on the development and evolution of theory in geography have also benefited enormously from faculty colleagues in the Human Geography Writing Group in the Department of Geography at the University of Oregon—Lise Nelson, Alec Murphy, Shaul Cohen, and Peter Walker.
2. Six of the papers presented at the discussion and debate about theory in migration studies in geography at the St. Andrews conference were included in a special issue of the *International Journal of Population Geography*, volume 7, "(Re) Theorising Population Geography: Mapping the Unfamiliar," published in 2000.
3. This forum, "Fifty Years since Trewartha," was published in volume 10 of *Population, Space, and Place* (2004) and included papers by six population geographers, including an Introduction and a Postscript by Kavita Pandit (2004a, 2004b).
4. A special issue of *Antipode*, edited by Katharyne Mitchell in 1997, was one of the first publications on transnational research in geography. Mitchell's goal was to bring attention to the ways that understanding transnational processes and discourses could be studied from a geographic perspective. A second goal of this collection of articles was to "bring geography back in" at several different scales to learn more about the context of hybridity and life and landscape at the margins.
5. For an exception to this dearth of work on place-based transnational studies, see Hardwick's recent article on the lived experiences and religious and residential networks of Russian and Ukrainian immigrants and refugees on both sides of the United States–Canadian border, "The Ties that Bind: Transnational Migrant Networks at the Canadian U.S. Borderland," *The American Review of Canadian Studies* 35: 667–82.
6. See Janet Kodras, "Race and Place: Geographic Research on Race Relations in the United States," unpublished manuscript prepared on behalf of the Association of American Geographers as a contribution to former President Clinton's One America initiative.

REFERENCES

Anderson, Kay J. 1988. "Cultural Hegemony and the Race Definition Process in Chinatown," *Environment and Planning D: Society and Space* 6: 127–49.

Appadurai, Arjun. 1991. "Global Ethnoscapes: Notes and Queries for a Transnational Anthropology, in R. G. Fox, ed., *Recapturing Anthropology: Working in the Present*, pp. 191–210. Santa Fe, NM: School of American Research Press.

Arokiasamy, Perianayagam. 2001. "Gender Preference, Contraceptive Use and Fertility in India: Regional and Development Influences," *International Journal of Population Geography* 8: 49–67.

Bailey, Adrian J. 2001. "Turning Transnational: Notes on the Theorisation of International Migration," *International Journal of Population Geography* 7: 413–28.

Bailey, Adrian J., Richard A. Wright, Alison Mountz, and Ines Miyares. 2002. "(Re) Producing Salvadoran Transnational Geographies," *Annals of the Association of American Geographers* 92: 125–44.

Beattie, Laura, and David Ley. 2003. "The German Immigrant Church in Vancouver: Service Provision and Identity Formation," *Die Erde* 134: 3–22.

Berg, Lawrence D. 1993. "Racialization in Academic Discourse," *Urban Geography* 14: 194–200.

Berry, Kate A., and Martha L. Henderson, eds. 2002. *Geographical Identities of Ethnic America*. Reno: University of Nevada Press.

Bonnett, Alastair. 2000. *White Identities: Historical and International Perspectives*. Essex, England: Pearson Education Ltd.

Bonnett, Alastair. 1997. "Geography, 'Race' and Whiteness: Invisible Traditions and Current Challenges," *Area* 29: 193–99.

Bonnett, Alastair. 1996. "Constructions of 'Race,' Place, and Discipline: Geographies of 'Racial' Identity and Racism," *Ethnic and Racial Studies* 19: 864–83.

Boyle, Mark. 2001. "Towards a (Re) Theorisation of the Historical Geography of Nationalism in Diasporas: The Irish Diaspora as an Exemplar," *International Journal of Population Geography* 7: 429–46.

Boyle, Paul. 2002. "Population Geography: Transnational Women on the Move," *Progress in Human Geography* 26: 531–43.

Boyle, Paul, and Keith Halfacree, eds. 1999. *Migration and Gender in the Developed World*. London: Routledge.

Brah, A. 1996. *Cartographies of Diaspora: Contesting Identities*. London: Routledge.

Brun, C. 2001. "Reterritorializing the Relationship between People and Place in Refugee Studies," *Geografiska Annaler* 83: 15–25.

Dingemans, Dennis, and Robin Datel. 1995. "Urban Multiethnicity," *The Geographical Review* 85: 458–77.

Ellis, Mark. 2001. "What Future for Whites? Population Projections and Racialised Imaginaries in the U.S.," *International Journal of Population Geography* 7: 213–29.

Ellis, Mark, and Richard Wright. 1998. "The Balkanization Metaphor in the Analysis of U.S. Immigration," *Annals of the Association of American Geographers* 88: 686–98.

Ellis, Mark, and Richard Wright. 2004. "Work Together, Live Apart? Geographies of Racial and Ethnic Segregation at Home and at Work," *Annals of the Association of American Geographers* 94: 620–37.

Findlay, A. M., and E. Graham. 1991. "The Challenge Facing Population Geography," *Progress in Human Geography* 15: 149–62.

Forrest, James, and Ron Johnston. 2001. "The Geography of the New Ethnicity: Ethnic Residential Segregation in Metropolitan Sydney," *Tijdschrift voor Economische en Sociale Geografie* 92: 42–59.

Frey, William H. 1995. "Immigration and Internal Migration 'Flight' from U.S. Metropolitan Areas: Toward a New Demographic Balkanization," *Urban Studies* 32: 733–57.

Frey, William H. 1996. "Immigration, Domestic Migration, and Demographic Balkanization: New Evidence for the 1990s," *Population and Development Review* 22: 741–63.

Glick Schiller, Nina, Linda Basch, and Cristina Szanton Blanton. 1995. "From Immigrant to Transmigrant: Theorizing Transnational Migration," *Anthropological Quarterly* 68: 48–63.

Graham, Elspeth. 2000. "What Kind of Theory for What Kind of Population Geography?" *International Journal of Population Geography* 6: 257–72.

Graham, Elspeth, and Paul Boyle. 2001. "(Re) Theorising Population Geography: Mapping the Unfamiliar," *International Journal of Population Geography* 7: 389–94.

Hadi, Abdullahel. 2001. "International Migration and the Change in Women's Position among the Left-Behind in Rural Bangladesh," *International Journal of Population Geography* 7: 53–61.

Halfacree, Keith H. 1995. "Household Migration and the Structuration of Patriarchy: Evidence from the USA," *Progress in Human Geography* 19: 159–82.

Halfacree, Keith H., and P. J. Boyle. 1993. "The Challenge Facing Migration Research: The Case for Biographical Research," *Progress in Human Geography* 17: 333–48.

Hardwick, Susan W. 1993. *Russian Refuge: Religion, Migration, and Settlement on the North American Pacific Rim.* Chicago: University of Chicago Press.

Hardwick, Susan W. 2003. "Migration, Embedded Networks, and Social Capital: Towards Theorizing North American Ethnic Geography," *International Journal of Population Geography* 9: 163–79.

Hardwick, Susan W. 2006a. "The Ties that Bind: Transnational Migrant Networks at the Canadian-U.S. Borderland," *American Review of Canadian Studies* 35: 667–82.

Hardwick, Susan W. 2006b. "The Geography of Whiteness: Russian and Ukrainian 'Coalitions of Color' in the Pacific Northwest," in John Frazier, ed. *Race, Ethnicity, and Place in a Changing America*, pp. 329–39. Albany, NY: State University of New York Press.

Hardwick, Susan W., and James E. Meacham. 2005. "Heterolocalism, Networks of Ethnicity, and Refugee Communities in the Pacific Northwest: The Portland Story," *Professional Geographer* 57: 539–57.

Harner, J. 2000. "The Mexican Community in Scottsdale, Arizona," *Yearbook of the Association of Pacific Coast Geographers* 26: 29–46.

Hoelscher, Steven D. 1998. *Heritage on Stage: The Invention of Ethnic Place in America's Little Switzerland.* Madison: University of Wisconsin Press.

Hoelscher, Steven D. 2003. "Making Place: Making Race: Performances of Whiteness in the Jim Crow South," *Annals of the Association of American Geographers* 93: 657–86.

Holloway, S. 1998. "Exploring the Neighborhood Contingency of Race Discrimination in Mortgage Lending in Columbus, Ohio," *Annals of the Association of American Geographers* 88: 252–76.

Howard, David. 2003. "Reappraising Race: Dominicans in New York," *International Journal of Population Geography* 9: 337–50.

Hume, Susan E., and Susan W. Hardwick. 2005. "Migration, Culture, and Place: The Impacts of Refugee Resettlement on the Portland Urban Area," *Geographical Review* 95: 189–209.

Hyndman, Jennifer. 1997. "Border Crossings," *Antipode* 29: 149–76.

Hyndman, Jennifer. 2000. *Managing Displacement: Refugees and the Politics of Humanitarianism.* Minneapolis: University of Minnesota Press.

Hyndman, Jennifer, and Margaret Walton-Roberts. 2000. "Interrogating Borders: A Transnational Approach to Refugee Research in Vancouver," *Canadian Geographer* 3: 244–58.

Jackiewicz, Edward L., and M. Pfeifer. 2000. "Refugee Resettlement, Family Reunion, and Ethnic Identity: Evolving Patterns of Vietnamese Residence in Two American Metropolitan Areas," *North American Geographer* 2: 9–32.

Jackson, Peter. 1989. "Geography, Race, and Racism," in Richard Peet and Nigel Thrift, eds. *New Models in Geography: The Political-Economy Perspective*, pp. 176–95. London: Unwin Hyman.

Jackson, Peter. 1998. "Constructions of Whiteness in the Geographical Imagination," *Area* 30: 99–106.

Johnston, Ron, Michael Poulsen, and James Forrest. 2003. "Ethnic Residential Concentration and a 'New Spatial Order:' Exploratory Analysis of Four United States Metropolitan Areas, 1980–2000," *International Journal of Population Geography* 9: 39–56.

Jones, Richard C. 2003. "The Segregation of Ancestry Groups in San Antonio," *Social Science Journal* 40: 213–32.

Kandelwal, Madhulika S. 1995. "Indian Immigrants in Queens, New York City: Patterns of Spatial Concentration and Distribution," in Peter van der Veer, ed., *Nation and Migration: The Politics of Space in the South Asian Diaspora*, pp. 178–96. Philadelphia: University of Pennsylvania Press.

Kaplan, David. 1998. "The Spatial Structure of Urban Ethnic Economies," *Urban Geography* 19: 489–501.

Kobayashi, Audrey. 2003. "The Construction of Geographical Knowledge—Racialization, Spatialization," in Kay Anderson, Mona Domosh, Nigel Thrift, and Steve Pile, eds., *Handbook of Cultural Geography*, pp. 544–56. London: Sage.

Kobayashi, Audrey, and Linda Peake. 2000. "Racism Out of Place: Thoughts on Whiteness and an Antiracist Geography in the New Millennium," *Annals of the Association of American Geographers* 90: 392–403.

Laoire, Caitriona Ni. 2003. "Editorial Introduction: Locating Geographies of Diaspora," *International Journal of Population Geography* 9: 275–80.

Lawson, Victoria. 1998. "Hierarchal Households and Gendered Migration: A Research Agenda," *Progress in Human Geography* 22: 32–53.

Lawson, Victoria. 1999. "Questions of Migration and Belonging: Understandings of Migration under Neoliberalism in Ecuador," *International Journal of Population Geography* 5: 261–76.

Lawson, Victoria A. 2000. "Arguments within the Geographies of Movement: The Theoretical Potential of Migrants' Stories," *Progress in Human Geography* 24: 173–89.

Levine, J. 1994. "The Heart of Whiteness: Dismantling the Master's House," *Voice Literary Supplement* 128: 11–16.

Li, Si-Ming, and Yat-Ming Sui. 1998. "A Comparative Study of Permanent and Temporary Migration in China: The Case of Dongguan and Meizhou, Guangdong Province," *International Journal of Population Geography* 3: 63–82.

Li, Wei. 1998. "Los Angeles's Chinese Ethnoburb: From Ethnic Service Center to Global Economy Outpost," *Urban Geography* 19: 502–17.

Liu, L. Y. 2000. "The Place of Immigration in Studies of Geography and Race," *Social and Cultural Geography* 1: 170–82.

Mattingly, D. J. 1999. "Job Search, Social Networks, and Local Labor-Market Dynamics: The Case of Paid Household Work in San Diego, California," *Urban Geography* 20: 46–74.

McKendrick, John. 1999. "Multi-Method Research: An Introduction to Its Application in Population Geography," *Professional Geographer* 51: 40–50.

Mitchell, Katharyne. 2000. "Networks of Ethnicity," in E. Sheppard and Trevor J. Barnes, eds., *A Companion to Economic Geography*, pp. 392–407. London: Blackwell Publishers.

Mitchell, Katharyne. 1997a. "Transnational Discourse: Bringing Geography Back In," *Antipode* 29 (2): 101–14.

Mitchell, Katheryne. 1997b. "Different Diaporas and the Hype of Hybridity," *Environment and Planning D: Society and Space* 15: 533–53.

McCarthy, J., and E. Hague. 2004. "Race, Nation, and Nature: The Cultural Politics of 'Celtic' Identification in the American West," *Annals of the Association of American Geographers* 94: 387–408.

McHugh, Kevin E. 1989. "Hispanic Migration and Population Redistribution in the United States," *Professional Geographer* 41: 429–39.

Miyares, Ines. 1997. "Changing Perceptions of Space and Place as Measures of Hmong Acculturation," *Professional Geographer* 49: 214–24.

Mountz, Alison. 2003. "Human Smuggling, the Transnational Imaginary, and Everyday Geographies of the Nation–State," *Antipode* 35: 622–44.

Mountz, Alison, Ines Miyares, Richard A. Wright, and Adrian J. Bailey. 2003. "Methodologically Becoming: Power, Knowledge, and Politics in the Field," *Gender, Place, and Culture* 10: 29–46.

Mountz, Alison, Richard Wright, Ines Miyares, and Adrian J. Bailey. 2002. "Lives in 'Limbo': Temporary Protected Status and Immigrant Identities," *Global Networks: A Journal of Transnational Affairs* 2 (4): 335–56.

Nash, Catherine. 2003. "Cultural Geography: Anti-Racist Geographies," *Progress in Human Geography* 27: 637–48.

Naved, Ruchira T. 2001. "The Effects of Migration and Work on Marriage of Female Garment Workers in Bangladesh," *International Journal of Population Geography* 7: 91–104.

Nogle, June Marie. 1997. "Internal Migration Patterns for U.S. Foreign-Born, 1985–1990," *International Journal of Population Geography* 2 (4): 1–13

Ostergren, Robert C. 1988. *A Community Transplanted: The Trans-Atlantic Experience of a Swedish Immigrant Settlement in the Upper Middle West, 1835–1915.* Madison: University of Wisconsin Press.

Pandit, Kavita. 2004a. "Introduction: The Trewartha Challenge," *Population, Space, and Place* 10: 277–78.

Pandit, Kavita. 2004b. "Postscript: Looking Back, Looking Forward," *Population, Space, and Place* 10: 309.

Park, Robert E., Ernest W. Burgess, and Roderick D. McKenzie, eds. 1925. *The City.* Chicago: University of Chicago Press.

Peake, Linda, and Audrey Kobayashi. 2002. "Policies and Practices for an Antiracist Geography at the Millennium," *Professional Geographer* 54: 50–61.

Peake, Linda, and Brian Ray. 2001. "Racializing the Canadian Landscape: Whiteness, Uneven Geographies and Social Justice," *Canadian Geographer* 45: 180–86.

Pulido, Laura. 2000. "Rethinking Environmental Racism: White Privilege and Urban Development in Southern California," *Annals of the Association of American Geographers* 90: 12–40.

Roediger, D. 1991. *The Wages of Whiteness: Race and the Making of the American Working Class.* London: Verso.

Scott, Gwen G. 2003. "Situating Fijian Transmigrants: Towards Racialised Transnational Social Spaces of the Undocumented," *International Journal of Population Geography* 9: 181–98.

Sherrell, Kathy, and Jennifer Hyndman. 2004. "Global Minds, Local Bodies: Kosovar Transnational Connections beyond British Columbia," Vancouver Centre of Excellence for Research on Immigration and Integration in the Metropolis (RIIM). Vancouver: The Metropolis Project.

Silvey, Rachel. 2004. "On the Boundaries of a Subfield: Social Theory's Incorporation into Population Geography," *Population, Space, and Place* 10: 303–08.

Silvey, Rachel, and Victoria Lawson, 1999. "Placing the Migrant," *Annals of the Association of American Geographers* 89: 121–32.

Skop, Emily, and Wei Li. 2003. "From the Ghetto to the Invisiburb," in John W. Frazier and F. Marqui, eds., *Multicultural Geographies*. New York: Academic Publishing.

Smith, Susan J. 1989. "Race and Racism," *Urban Geography* 10: 593–603.

Stewart, Emma. 2005. "Exploring the Vulnerability of Asylum Seekers in the U.K.," *Population, Space, and Place* 2: 499–512.

Trewartha, Glenn. 1953. "A Case for Population Geography," *Annals of the Association of American Geographers* 42: 71–97.

Walton-Roberts, Margaret. 2004. "Transnational Migration Theory in Population Geography: Gendered Practices in Networks Linking Canada and India," *Population, Space, and Place* 10: 361–73.

Winders, Jamie. 2003. "White in All the Wrong Places: White Rural Poverty in the Postbellum U.S. South," *Cultural Geographies* 10: 45–63.

Winders, Jamie. 2005. "Changing Politics of Race and Region: Latino Migration to the U.S. South," *Progress in Human Geography* 29: 683–99.

White, A. 2002. "Organic Functionalism, 'Community,' and Place: Refugee Studies and the Geographical Constitution of Refugee Identities," *Geoforum* 33: 73–83.

White, P., and Peter Jackson. 1995. "(Re) Theorising Population Geography," *International Journal of Population Geography* 1: 111–23.

Wong, David W. S. 1998. "The Spatial Patterns of Ethnic Integration in the United States," *Professional Geographer* 50: 13–30.

Wong, David W. S. 1999. "A Geographical Analysis of Multiethnic Households in the United States," *International Journal of Population Research* 5: 31–48.

Wright, Richard. 1997. "Transnationalism, Nationals, and International Migration: The Changing Role and Relevance of the State," in L. Staeheli, J. Kodras, and C. Flint, eds., *State Devolution in America: Implications for a Diverse Society*. Thousand Oaks, CA: Sage Publications.

Wright, Richard, Adrian J. Bailey, Ines Miyares, and Alison Mountz. 2000. "Legal Status, Gender, and Employment among Salvadorans in the U.S.," *International Journal of Population Geography* 6: 273–86.

Wright, Richard, and Mark Ellis. 2000a. "The Ethnic and Gender Division of Labor Compared among Immigrants to Los Angeles," *International Journal of Urban and Regional Research* 24: 583–601.

Wright, Richard, and Mark Ellis. 2000b. "Race, Region, and the Territorial Politics of Immigration in the U.S.," *International Journal of Population Geography* 6: 197–211.

Wright, Richard, Mark Ellis, and Virginia Parks. 2005. "Re-Placing Whiteness in Spatial Assimilation Research," *City and Community* 4: 111–35.

Zelinsky, Wilbur. 2001. *The Enigma of Ethnicity*. Iowa City: University of Iowa Press.

Zelinsky, Wilbur, and Barrett A. Lee. 1998. "Heterolocalism: An Alternative Model of the Sociospatial Behaviour of Immigrant Ethnic Communities," *International Journal of Population Geography* 4: 281–98.

CHAPTER 7

The Politics of International Migration
How Can We "Bring the State Back In"?
James F. Hollifield

In the disciplines and subdisciplines associated with the study of politics and government, including political science, public policy, public administration, and international relations, migration is a rapidly emerging field of study. Yet compared to the other social sciences—especially sociology, history, and economics—political scientists came late to the study of migration. From the standpoint of intellectual history, it is interesting to ask why political scientists and scholars of international relations were so late to focus on the topic of international migration. This is especially surprising in a country like the United States, where immigration has had an enormous impact on politics and government.

I offer a historical and a theoretical explanation for the lack of interest in migration among (American) students of politics. The historical explanation lies in the long gap between the end of the third wave of immigration in the 1920s, when the famous Chicago School of Sociology (Park 1928; for a review, see Heisler in this volume) was dominant, and the beginning of the fourth wave in the 1970s and 1980s. During this 50- to 60-year period, levels of immigration, both legal and illegal, were at historical lows; and from the end of World War II until the 1980s, immigration policy was largely confined to the realm of *low politics*, which is to say that it was considered to be a domestic issue that did not rise to the level of foreign policy or *high politics*. At a theoretical level, especially in the field of international relations, the Cold War was dominant, and migration did not directly affect the balance of power, the East-West struggle, or the nature of the international system, with the exception of refugees (Zolberg, Suhrke, and Aguayo 1989; Teitelbaum 1980, 1984; Tichenor 2002; Zolberg 2006). This is not to say that immigration and refugee policy was unimportant during the period from the end of the third to the beginning of the fourth wave—one need only look at major policy reforms, such as the National Origins Quota Act (1924), McCarran-Walter (1952), Hart-Celler

(1965), and the Refugee Act (1980), all major pieces of legislation—but that levels of immigration were at historic lows and immigration had little direct impact on American politics and society. The Cold War also created "strange bedfellow" coalitions between economic liberals (Republicans) on the right and political or civil rights liberals (Democrats) on the left, making it easier to pass major immigration legislation than in earlier periods of American history. These rights-markets coalitions held together until the end of the Cold War, helping to pass Hart-Celler (1965), the 1986 Immigration Reform and Control Act (IRCA), and the 1990 Immigration Act (Hollifield, Hunt, and Tichenor 2006; Hollifield and Zuk 1998).

If immigration was not a topic of great interest among students of American politics during the Cold War period, it was nonetheless important in the study of comparative politics, especially among Europeanists. Again the reason is largely historical—many countries in Western Europe (France, Switzerland, Germany, The Netherlands, and Belgium, to name a few) opened their doors to immigrants, guest workers, and refugees as early as the 1950s, with the result that by the 1970s immigration was a hot political issue, which attracted the attention of scholars of comparative politics. One of the earliest and most influential studies of immigration in Western Europe was written by two political sociologists, Stephen Castles and Godula Kosack, *Immigrant Workers and Class Structure in Western Europe* (1973). They argued that immigrants (and guest workers) were necessary for the survival of advanced capitalist societies because they provided an "industrial reserve army" of labor. This study was followed by the now classic works of political scientists Gary Freeman (1979) and Mark Miller (1981) looking at issues of immigration, race, and ethnic politics in Western Europe. Despite these early studies in comparative politics, migration remained on the margins of the discipline of political science in the United States until the 1990s.

Given the paucity of theorizing about the politics of international migration, it is therefore not surprising that migration theory tends to be dominated by economic or sociological explanations. Push-pull and cost-benefit analyses are closely associated with neoclassical economics, whereas networks and transnationalism are analytical concepts derived primarily from world systems theory and most often studied in sociology and anthropology. As pointed out above, political scientists were not totally absent from the study of immigration and international migration in the early postwar period. I will cite here a number of distinguished political scientists in this field, who are today considered pioneers. But only recently, in the 1980s and 1990s, has the field of study begun to emerge, which we might call the *politics of international migration*, and theorists are scrambling to see how we can "bring the state back in" to social scientific analyses of migration.[1]

This chapter treats three major themes or questions that have emerged in the study of the politics of international migration. The first major theme revolves around the question of *control*, that is, the role of the nation–state in establishing rules of entry and exit. To what extent can states control their borders? What are the factors that define the capacity and limits of control (Brochmann and Hammar 1999; Cornelius, Martin, and Hollifield 1994; Freeman 1995; Hollifield 1992a, 1999a)? These questions lead directly to the second major theme of this chapter—the impact of migration on international relations. How does migration affect the sovereignty and *security* of the nation–state (a question that has gained new urgency after the terrorist attacks of September 11, 2001)? What are the possibilities for controlling or managing migration at the international, as opposed to the domestic, level? What are the relationships among migration, national security, and foreign policy (Rudolph 2006; Teitelbaum 1980; Weiner 1993)? And why do states "risk migration" and accept "unwanted immigrants" (Hollifield 1998; Hollifield 2004; Joppke 1998a; Martin 1994b)? The third theme to be explored is intricately related to the first two. It revolves around the issue of *incorporation*, specifically the impact of immigration on citizenship, political behavior, and the polity itself (Freeman 2004). How do emigration and immigration affect the political behavior of individuals, natives as well as migrants? What role does the state play in incorporating immigrants into society and the economy? And what is the relationship between social and political citizenship? These questions lead inevitably to discussions of national identity, citizenship, and rights, which are at the heart of the way in which every polity defines itself (Brubaker 1992; Schuck 1998; Schmitter 1979; Turner 1993).

The final section of the chapter links these three themes (control, security, and incorporation) together, focusing on political explanations for international migration and the role of the state in encouraging or discouraging migration. Demarcating the politics of international migration is a first and essential step to talking across the disciplines.

FRAMING THE QUESTION

The movement of individuals across national boundaries challenges many of the basic assumptions that social scientists make about human behavior—for example, that individuals tend to be risk averse, that they are always in need of community, or as Aristotle put it, "man is a social animal." If individuals move long distances, leaving their families and communities behind and crossing national, ethnic, or cultural boundaries, then there must be some extraordinary forces compelling them to do this. Hence, many social scientists, especially economists, begin their study of international migration by pointing out that the vast majority of the world's population is in fact sedentary. At the end of the twentieth century only 125 million people—roughly equivalent to the population of Japan, according to estimates by the International Organization for Migration—lived outside of their country of origin; hence international migration is the exception rather than the rule. Why then should we bother to study it, if most people are born, live, and die in the same geographic area, if not in the same village?

The answer to the "so what" question is not straightforward. The best answer I can offer is that international migration provokes a sense of crisis and has been steadily increasing as a result of social and economic forces that seem to be beyond the control of states and communities (Massey 1998; Sassen 1996). An anthropologist or sociologist might call it a fear of the other, of the unknown, and of those who are different (Barth 1969; Lévi-Strauss 1952; Schnapper 1998). In this sense, xenophobia could be considered a basic human instinct. An economist or a demographer might argue that international migration places a strain on resources. It can cause a hemorrhage of scarce human capital—a brain drain—from the sending society, if the brightest and most talented people leave their home countries (Bhagwati 1976). If, however, those leaving are the most destitute, least educated, and have low levels of human and social capital, then they may pose a threat for the receiving society. Some economists and demographers have argued in Malthusian terms, that even the wealthiest societies have a limited amount of space (land) and capital, which should be preserved for the national or indigenous population. Overpopulation and overcrowding can strain urban infrastructures and cause environmental damage, while saturated urban labor markets can drive down wages, hurting those who are at the bottom of the social ladder (Bouvier 1992). In those receiving societies with highly developed welfare states, there is a fear that immigrants will become public charges, placing an unfair burden on the public purse (Borjas 1990). Of course, the same arguments can be made in reverse: migration poses no threat to either the sending or receiving society; it is in fact a boon, providing remittances for the sending society and an influx of human capital and entrepreneurial talent for the receiving society (Chiswick 1982; Russell 1986; Simon 1989). In either case, the focus is on the abundance or scarcity of resources, the social or human capital of migrants and how well they integrate into the receiving society.

THE MIGRATION "CRISIS" IN HISTORICAL PERSPECTIVE

In the last decades of the twentieth century, international migration has been increasing in every region of the globe, feeding the fears of some political and intellectual elites, who give voice to a sense of crisis—a crisis that is as much political as social and economic. Yet the political aspect of international migration has, until recently, received little attention from political scientists, perhaps because the "crisis" is so recent, or because migration is viewed as essentially an economic and sociological phenomenon.

It might be wise, however, to remind ourselves that migration is *not* a new phenomenon in the annals of human history. Indeed, for much of recorded history and for many civilizations, the movement of populations was not unusual. Only with the advent of the nation–state in sixteenth- and seventeenth-century Europe did the notion of legally tying populations to territorial units and to specific forms of government become commonplace (Moch 1992). State building in Europe entailed consolidating territory, centralizing authority, controlling the nobility, imposing taxes, and waging warfare (Tilly 1975). The institutions of nationality and citizenship, which would become the hallmarks of the modern nation–state, did not develop fully until the nineteenth and twentieth centuries (Koslowski 1999). Again, the reason for this development, particularly in Europe, was closely related to warfare, to the beginnings of conscription and more fully developed systems of taxation. Modern warfare took on the characteristic of pitting one people against another, nationalism intensified, and political elites cultivated among their populations a sense of nationalism or of belonging to a nation and a state (Kohn 1962). The expansion of the European system of nation–states through conquest, colonization, and then decolonization spread the ideals of sovereignty, citizenship, and nationality to the four corners of the globe (Krasner 1999; Said 1993).

In the nineteenth and twentieth centuries, passport and visa systems developed and borders were increasingly closed to nonnationals, especially those deemed to be hostile to the nation and the state (Noiriel 1988; Torpey 1998). Almost every dimension of human existence—social-psychological, demographic, economic, and political—was reshaped to conform to the dictates of the nation–state (Hobsbawm 1990). In looking at recent migration "crises," it is important to keep in mind *la longue durée*, to put these "crises" into historical perspective. Historians have a better understanding of what constitutes a crisis and what forms of human behavior are unique and unusual.[2] From a historical perspective, the migration crises of the late twentieth century pale by comparison with the upheavals associated with the industrial revolution, the two world wars, and decolonization, which resulted in genocide, irredentism, the displacement of millions of people, and the radical redrawing of national boundaries, not only in Europe but also around the globe (Said 1993). This process, which Rogers Brubaker calls the "un-mixing of peoples," has been repeated with the end of the Cold War and the breakup of the Soviet Empire, Czechoslovakia, and Yugoslavia (Brubaker 1996). Does this mean that the latest waves of migration do not rise to the level of a crisis, threatening the political and social order in various regions of the globe?

In *The Global Migration Crisis* (1995), Myron Weiner argues that the increase in international migration in recent decades poses a threat to international stability and security. This is especially true in those areas of the globe where nation–states are most fragile—the Balkans, Transcaucasia, the Middle East, or the great lakes region of Africa, for example. But Weiner extends this argument to the Western democracies as well, pointing out that the rise in xenophobic and nationalist politics in Western Europe indicates that even the most advanced industrial democracies risk being destabilized politically by a "massive" influx of unwanted immigrants, refugees, and asylum seekers. Weiner postulates that there are limits on how many foreigners a society can absorb. Samuel Huntington has argued that in the post–Cold War era, failure to control American borders is the single biggest threat to the national security and identity of the United States (Huntington 1996, 2004). Weiner and Huntington echo the sentiments of the historian Arthur Schlesinger Jr., who sees immigration and the rise of multiculturalism as an existential threat to society, leading potentially to the *Disuniting of America* (1992). In this line of reasoning, nation–states are being threatened by globalization from above and multiculturalism from below.

Whether international migration in the late twentieth century poses a dramatic threat to the sovereignty and integrity of nation–states remains an open question. But clearly the latest waves of migration have led to political crises in many countries in both the developed and developing world. As a result, a new literature in political science is emerging, with a range of research questions, some of which are similar to the questions posed about migration in other social science disciplines. Not surprisingly, at the heart of the political science literature on international migration are concerns about the institutions of sovereignty and citizenship (Fuchs 1990; Rudolph 2006; Shanks 2000; Smith 1997). If we accept the Weberian definition of sovereignty—which flows more or less directly from the Treaty of Westphalia of 1648—a state can exist only if it has a monopoly of the legitimate use of force in a given territorial area. In this way, states have some protection from interference in their internal affairs (Weber 1947; Krasner 1999). It would then follow that the ability or inability of a state to control its borders and hence its population must be considered the sine qua non of sovereignty (Hollifield 2005). With some notable exceptions—such as the international refugee regime created by the 1950 Geneva Convention in the aftermath of World War II (Goodwin-Gill 1996)—the right of a state to control entry and exit of persons to and from its territory is an undisputed principle of international law (Shaw 1997). But this political and legal principle, which is one of the cornerstones of the international legal system, immediately raises another question or puzzle: Why are some states willing to accept rather high levels of immigration (or emigration for that matter), when it would seem not to be in their interest to do so (Cornelius, Martin, and Hollifield 1992a; Hollifield 1994; Hollifield 2004; Joppke 1998b)? Does this influx pose a threat to the institutions of sovereignty and citizenship (Pickus 1998; Rudolph 2006; Schuck 1998; Shanks 2000)?

The sovereignty or security issue, then, immediately spills over into a more specific question of migration control, and a large and growing body of literature seeks to address this question. Here, political scientists, sociologists, anthropologists, and economists begin to step on each others' toes, with historians and demographers more or less on the sidelines. To understand the difficulties of controlling (or regulating) international migration, it is essential to understand why individuals move in the first place. Economists and sociologists have developed elaborate models to explain international migration, favoring such factors as demand-pull, supply-push, and relative deprivation on the economic dimension (Stark 1991; Todaro 1976) and transnationalism, networks, and social capital on the sociological dimension (Faist 2000; Levitt 2001; Massey et al. 1993, 1998; Portes 1996).

Only recently have political scientists begun to formulate hypotheses about the political dimension of international migration and specifically the role of the state. For Aristide Zolberg—who was among the first to try to insert political variables into the equation—by any measure, the state does matter and has the capacity, if not always the will, to regulate migration flows and stocks. Zolberg's argument is that social scientists can measure and observe the independent effect of state policies for controlling entry and exit (Zolberg 1981, 1999). But, even if we accept this argument prima facie—that politics and the state matter—it does not explain *how* they matter. To understand how politics affects international migration requires us, in the first instance, to theorize about politics and the state. This is an essential first step—to agree on some of the categories and concepts that will constitute our independent variables. The next step is to search for a consensus on the dependent variables: What exactly is it that we are trying to explain? The final step, which is the principal subject of this chapter, is to open a dialogue with migration scholars in the other social sciences, so that we can talk across the disciplines, see if the objects of our inquiry are the same, and see whether our research findings are complementary or contradictory. A new generation of scholars in political science has begun to do the research that will be needed to fill the gap that exists in the migration literature, bringing to bear theories of politics, sorting out dependent from independent variables, and addressing what I see as three major areas of inquiry: the politics of control, national security, and incorporation/citizenship.

THE POLITICS OF CONTROL

Many political scientists would agree that at its most basic level politics involves "control, influence, power, or authority." If we add to this definition Weber's concerns about legitimacy and the importance of controlling territory, together with Aristotle's more normative focus on issues of participation, citizenship, and justice, we have a fairly complete picture of what Robert Dahl (1991) calls the "political aspect."[3] We can see immediately how migration touches on each of these dimensions of politics: the procedural or distributional dimension—who gets what, when, and how; the legal or statist dimension, involving issues of sovereignty and legitimacy; and the ethical or normative dimension, which revolves around questions of citizenship, justice, and participation. Choosing policies to control migration leads us to ask who is making those decisions and in whose interest? Are policies being made in the interest of migrants, workers, employers, or some other group? Are these policies contributing to the national interest and security of the state and are they just? Does migration weaken or strengthen the institutions of sovereignty and citizenship? At what point should migrants become full members of society, with all the rights, duties, and responsibilities of a citizen?

As in other social sciences, but especially economics, the key concept here is one of interest. But, unlike economics, where the emphasis is on scarcity and efficiency, in the study of politics the primary emphasis is on power, influence, and authority, but with strong ethical and normative overtones, concerning justice, membership, and citizenship (Benhabib 2004; Carens 1989, 2000; Schuck 1998; Walzer 1983). In a free market, the allocation of scarce goods and resources takes place according to the logic of the marketplace, that is, the interaction of supply and demand. The exercise of power, however, takes place in the ideational, legal, and institutional confines of political systems. These range from the most autocratic (for example, North Korea), where decisions are made by a single individual, surrounded by a small clique of military or party officials, to the most democratic (for example, Switzerland), where decisions are made by "the people" according to elaborate constitutional arrangements and with safeguards often built into the system to protect individuals and minorities from the "tyranny of the majority." Obviously migration is less of a problem in North Korea than in Switzerland. Almost by definition, the more liberal and democratic a society is, the greater the likelihood that migration control will be an issue; and that there will be some level of "unwanted migration" (Boswell 2006; Hollifield 1992a, 2004; Joppke 1998b; Martin 1994b).

Not surprisingly, therefore, almost all the literature on the politics of control is focused on the receiving countries, many but not all of which are liberal democracies. Very little has been written about the politics of control from the standpoint of the sending countries (see, however, Sadiq 2005). As the world has become more open and democratic, since the end of World War II and especially since the end of the Cold War (Hollifield and Jillson 1999)—from a political standpoint, entry rather than exit is more problematic.[4] With the steady increase in immigration in the advanced industrial democracies in the postwar period (International Organization for Migration [IOM] 1996; Organization for Economic Cooperation and Development [OECD] 2005), many states began to search for ways to stop or slow the influx, while immigration injected itself into the politics of these countries. In traditional countries of immigration, especially the United States, this was not the first time that immigration had become a national political issue; but for many of the states of Western Europe, this was a relatively new phenomenon, which took politicians and the public by surprise. How would these different political systems cope with immigration? Would there be a convergence of policy responses, or would each state pursue different control policies (Brochmann and Hammar

1999; Cornelius et al. 1994, 2004; Ohliger et al. 2003)? As political scientists began to survey the politics of immigration control, a central puzzle emerged. Since the 1970s, almost all of the receiving states were trying to reassert control over migration flows, often using similar policies and in response to public opinion, which was increasingly hostile to high levels of immigration (Fetzer 2000). Yet immigration persisted and there was a growing gap between the goals of immigration policies—defined as outputs—and the results or outcomes of these policies (Hollifield 1986, 1990, 1992a). This argument has since come to be known as the *gap hypothesis* (Cornelius, et al. 1994, 2004). Moreover, if control of borders is the sine qua non of sovereignty and if states are unable to control immigration, does it not follow that the institutions of sovereignty and citizenship are threatened and that the security of the state itself is at issue (Castles and Davidson 2000; Huntington 2004; Rudolph 2006; Sassen 1996; Schuck 1998; Shanks 2000; Soysal 1994)? I shall return to these questions below.

With this puzzle and the gap hypothesis in mind and armed with a panoply of theories, political scientists set off in search of answers. Some, like Aristide Zolberg, Anthony Messina, and to a lesser extent Gary Freeman, questioned the empirical premise of the argument. Zolberg argues that liberal states have never lost control of immigration and that the migration crisis itself is much exaggerated (Zolberg 1999; also Brubaker 1994). Messina and Freeman pointed to Great Britain as a major outlier—a liberal democracy which has been efficient at controlling its borders (Freeman 1994; Messina 1996). Yet, Freeman concedes that "the goal of a theory of immigration politics must be to account for the similarities and differences in the politics of immigration receiving states and to explain the persistent gaps between the goals and effects of policies as well as the related but not identical gap between public sentiment and the content of public policy" (Freeman 1998b:2). The challenge, therefore, for political scientists is to develop some generalizable or unifying hypotheses to account for variation in (1) the demand for and the supply of immigration policy—whether greater restriction or more liberal admission policies—and (2) the outcomes or results of those policies, as measured in terms of increasing or decreasing flows and stocks. Looking at immigration from the standpoint of the politics of control, these are, in effect, two separate dependent variables.

As in any social science discipline, the choice of independent variables is driven largely by theoretical considerations and the hypotheses flowing from them. This brings us back to our definition of politics (above) and raises the broader question of how political explanations for international migration are related to economic or sociological explanations. If politics is defined primarily in terms of process and the struggle for "influence, power, and authority," then it is a relatively straightforward exercise to develop a theoretical framework for explaining the demand for and supply of immigration policy, as well as the gap between policy outputs and outcomes. This is the approach taken by Gary Freeman, who, following the work of James Q. Wilson on *The Politics of Regulation* (1980), argues that the demand for immigration policy—like any public policy in a democracy—is heavily dependent on the play of organized interests. To understand the politics of immigration control, we must be able to define the distribution of costs and benefits, which will then enable us to separate winners from losers in the policy-making process. Depending on the scarcity or abundance of productive factors (land, labor, and capital), as well as the substitutability of immigrant for native labor, the costs and benefits of immigration will be either concentrated or diffuse. From this simple factor-cost logic, we can deduce what position powerful interest groups, like organized labor and agricultural or business lobbies, are likely to take in debates over immigration policy. Again following Wilson, Freeman associates different cost-benefit distributions with specific "modes of politics," either interest group, clientelist, entrepreneurial, or majoritarian (Freeman 1995, 1998b; Wilson 1980).

Using this essentially microeconomic framework, Freeman predicts that when—as is often the case with immigration policy—benefits are concentrated and costs are diffuse, a clientelist politics will develop. The state will then be captured by powerful organized interests, who stand to benefit handsomely from expansive immigration policies—like fruit and vegetable growers in the southern and southwestern United States, the software and computer industry in the Northwest, or perhaps the construction industry in Germany or Japan. This would seem to explain why many states persist with admissionist or guest-worker policies, even during recessionary periods when the economic conjuncture would seem to dictate greater restriction. If we combine Freeman's "modes of politics" approach with the work of Jeannette Money (1999) and Alan Kessler (1998)—who argue in a similar vein that the demand for immigration policy is heavily dependent on the relative rates of return to factors and the substitutability or complementarity of immigrant and native labor—then we have a fairly complete theory of the politics of immigration control, albeit one that is heavily indebted to microeconomics and may be (like the old push-pull arguments) economically overdetermined.

The reason for this is not hard to see. If we start with a definition of politics that reduces the political process to an economic calculus, then we have in effect defined away some of the more interesting and difficult questions associated with immigration politics. In this formulation, the role of the state is particularly problematic, since the state is merely a reflection of societal interests. By focusing so exclusively on process, we lose sight of the importance of institutional and ideological variation within and among states. Freeman (1995), Money (1999), and Kessler (1998) concede that the supply of immigration policy does not always match demand. Policy outputs are heavily contingent on ideational, cultural, and institutional factors, which often distort the market interests of different groups, to such an extent that some groups (like organized labor, for example) may end up pursuing policies that would seem to be irrational, or at odds with their economic interests (Haus 1995, 1999; Watts 2002). Likewise, many employers in Western Europe were initially skeptical of the need to import labor (Hollifield 1992a; cf. Watts 2002). As Freeman puts it, the drawback of these economic models of politics "is their extreme parsimony. They leave us with generalizations about labor, landowners and capitalists; useful abstractions, surely, but probably too crude for the satisfactory analysis of immigration politics in particular countries, especially highly developed ones" (Freeman 1998b: 17). So where does this leave us with respect to our ability to advance generalizable and testable hypotheses about the politics of immigration control?

Freeman offers several solutions. One obvious way to get around the limitations of factor-endowment or factor-cost models is to disaggregate or break down factors into economic sectors, which would lead us into an industry-by-industry analysis of immigration politics. We also would want to distinguish between the political positions of skilled labor (e.g., software engineers or mathematicians) and unskilled workers (e.g., in the construction trades or service sectors). In the end, Freeman seems to retreat to a position that is a bit more ad hoc, from a theoretical and empirical standpoint. He argues that there is not that much uniformity in immigration policies among the Western democracies. He also draws a sharp distinction between the settler societies—such as the United States, Canada, or Australia—which continue to have more expansionist immigration policies, when compared to the newer countries of immigration in Western Europe. For example, Britain, France, Germany, Switzerland, and The Netherlands are still struggling to cope with the fallout from postcolonial and guest-worker migrations (Freeman 1998a; Green 2004; Joppke 1998b; Ohliger et al. 2003; Thränhardt 1996).

An alternative to Freeman's interest-based approach to the politics of immigration control can be found in my own work, which one reviewer aptly described as the "liberal state" thesis (Schmitter-Heisler 1993; cf. also Boswell 2006; Joppke 1998b). Rather than focusing on politics defined as process, which leads us into a factor-cost logic, where productive factors in the guise of interest groups are the units of analysis, my work takes the state as the unit of analysis (Hollifield 1992a, 1997a). The dependent variable also differs from that of Freeman and many other political scientists (see, for example, Money 1999), who are more interested in explaining policy outputs (the demand for and the supply of immigration policy) than in explaining policy outcomes (flows and stocks of immigrants across time and space). From a political and theoretical standpoint, it is admittedly more difficult to explain outcomes than it is to explain outputs, because we are compelled to look at a broader range of independent variables. If we want to know why individuals move across national boundaries and if we want to explain variation in those movements over time, it will not be enough just to look at policy outputs and the political process. As I pointed out in the first section of this chapter, theories of international migration have been propounded primarily by economists and sociologists. Economists have sought to explain population movements in terms of a basic push-pull logic, whereas sociologists have stressed the importance of transnationalism and social networks. What's missing from these accounts is a theory of the state and the way in which it influences population movements (Massey 1999b; Portes 1997).

The types of push and pull factors identified by scholars may vary, but the logic of looking at individual migrants as preeminently rational, utility-maximizing agents remains the same (see, for example, Stark 1991). Some economists, like George Borjas or Julian Simon, have injected important political or policy considerations into their analysis. Borjas in particular has argued that the welfare state itself can act as a powerful pull factor, which may affect the propensity to migrate. In his formulation, before the rise of the welfare state, individuals chose to emigrate on the basis of their chances for finding gainful employment. However, after the advent of generous social policies in the principal receiving countries, such as the United States, even migrants with low levels of human capital were willing to risk the move, confident in the fact that they would be cared for by the host society (Borjas 1990; cf. Chiswick in this volume, Chapter 3). Gary Freeman also argues that the logic of the modern welfare state is one of closure and that large-scale immigration may ruin public finances, bankrupt social services, and undermine the legitimacy of the welfare state (Freeman 1986; Ireland 2004). But none of these works has really elevated policy outputs and the state to the status of independent variables. Little systematic cross-national research has been done by economists, with the notable exception of scholars like Philip Martin and Georges Tapinos (Miller and Martin 1982; Tapinos 1974; also Martin et al. 2006).

Many sociologists and anthropologists have built upon the logic of push-pull, often setting up their work in direct opposition to microeconomics, in order to inject more sociological reasoning into theories of international migration. A pioneer in this regard is Douglas Massey, who was one of the first sociologists to point out the importance of social networks in linking sending and receiving societies (Massey 1987, 1998). In the same vein, Alejandro Portes has developed the notion of transnational communities to explain international migration. Portes—whose work will be discussed in greater detail in the last section of this chapter—has done extensive empirical research on the human and social capital of different immigrant groups in the United States. He seeks to explain not only why individuals emigrate but also patterns of immigrant incorporation (Portes and Bach 1985; Portes and Rumbaut 1996; Portes and Zhou 1993). Both network and social capital theory help to explain the difficulty that states may encounter in their efforts to control immigration. Kinship, informational networks, and transnational communities are in effect a form of social capital (Faist 2000). As they develop, they can substantially reduce the risks that individual migrants must take in moving from one country to another, thereby increasing the propensity to migrate. States must then find a way to intervene in or break up the networks in order to reduce emigration.

Still, by their own admission, sociologists have been unable to incorporate political variables into their analysis of international migration. Both Massey and Portes lament the absence of a political theory of international migration. Massey writes, "Until recently, theories of international migration have paid short shrift to the nation–state as an agent influencing the volume and composition of international migration" (Massey 1999b:303). Portes argues along the same lines that "detailed accounts of the process leading to major legislation . . . have not been transformed into a systematic theoretical analysis of both the external pressures impinging on the state and the internal dynamics of the legislative and administrative bodies dealing with immigration" (Portes 1997:817).

In response to this challenge, the liberal state thesis draws our attention to a third independent variable—rights—which are heavily contingent upon legal and institutional developments. Rights must be considered in any theory of international migration. Thus, in my formulation, international migration can be seen as a function of (1) economic forces (demand-pull and supply-push), (2) networks, and (3) rights (Cornelius, Martin, and Hollifield 1994; Hollifield 1992a; Hollifield, Hunt, and Tichenor 2006). Much of the variation in international migration over time can be explained in economic terms. In the post–World War II period, south–north labor migration started largely in response to demand-pull forces.[5] The major industrial democracies suffered labor shortages, from the 1940s through the 1960s, and foreign workers were brought in to meet the increasing demand for labor. In the United States, these shortages, especially in agriculture, were met in part through the *bracero* program; whereas in Western Europe, *Gastarbeiter* programs were put in place to recruit foreign workers, thus placing the imprimatur of the state on certain types of (presumably temporary) international migration. But when demand for foreign labor began to decline in the 1970s, in the wake of the first oil shock in 1973, powerful supply-push factors came into play. The populations of the sending countries (for example, Algeria, Turkey, and Mexico) were increasing rapidly, at the same time that the economies of these developing states were reeling from the first truly global recession of the postwar period. Networks helped to sustain international migration, even in countries that attempted to stop all forms of immigration, including family and refugee migration. These economic and sociological factors were the *necessary* conditions for continued migration, but the *sufficient* conditions were political and legal. In the last three decades of the twentieth century, a principal factor that has sustained international migration (both south–north and to a lesser extent east–west) is the accretion of rights for foreigners in the liberal democracies, or what I have called elsewhere the rise of "rights-based liberalism" (Cornelius, Martin, and Hollifield 1994:9–11; Hollifield 2004).

Politics affects migration, like many other social and economic phenomena, at the margins. But this does *not* mean that politics (like culture) is simply a residual variable. In any social process, it is often what happens at the margins that is of greatest importance and also the most difficult to incorporate into our analysis. To use a familiar Weberian metaphor, the speeding train of international migration is fueled by economic and sociological forces, but it is the state that acts as a switching mechanism, which can change the course of the train, or derail it altogether. In the oft-quoted words of the Swiss novelist Max Frisch, speaking of the guest-worker program in Switzerland: "We asked for workers but human beings came."

Where do rights come from, and how are they institutionalized? Unlike recent works in sociology, which see rights flowing from international organizations (such as the United Nations [UN] or the European Union [EU]) and from human rights law—a kind of postnational or transnational citizenship (Bauböck 1994; Jacobson 1996; Soysal 1994)—I argue that rights still derive primarily from the laws and institutions of the liberal state and they fall into the three categories originally enunciated by the sociologist T. H. Marshall: namely, civil, political, and social rights (Castles and Davidson 2000; Marshall 1964; Schmitter 1979). My interpretation of "rights-based liberalism" differs from Marshall's in the sense that I do not espouse the same linear and evolutionary sequence, which Marshall first identified in Great Britain. Rather, I argue that rights vary considerably, both cross-nationally and over time. Therefore, a major challenge for migration scholars is to find ways to incorporate rights, as an institutional and legal variable, into our analysis of international migration.

I have done this in two ways: first, by measuring the impact of specific policy changes (either expanding or contracting rights for immigrants and foreigners) on immigration flows, while controlling for changes in the business cycle (Hollifield 1990, 1992a; Hollifield, Hunt, and Tichenor 2006; Hollifield and Zuk 1998); and secondly, by looking specifically at how rights act, primarily through independent judiciaries, to limit the capacity of liberal states to control immigration (Hollifield 1999a, 1999b; also Joppke 2001; Morris 2002). Again, the level and unit of analysis is the state; and the method is statistical, comparative, and historical. The best way to think about how rights act to limit the capacity of states to control immigration is to envision a time-series curve of immigration flows. The United States is currently well into the fourth great wave of immigration in its history. What is driving this immigration wave? To what extent is it driven by economic or political factors? To answer these questions, Valerie Hunt, Daniel Tichenor, and I used time-series analysis to look at the effect of business cycles on immigration flows from 1890 to 1996 (Hollifield, Hunt, and Tichenor, 2006). We were able statistically to demonstrate the impact of major policy shifts on flows during this time period, net of the effects of the economic conjuncture. The most striking result of our analysis is the gradual weakening of the effect of business cycles on flows after 1945, but especially from the 1960s to the late 1990s. The impact of legislation passed after the Civil Rights Act of 1964 was so expansive that it negates the effect of business cycles, in stark contrast to the period before 1945, when flows were much more responsive to economic cycles. Thus, to explain the politics of control in Western democracies, it is crucial to take account of changes in the legal and institutional environment. It is not sufficient simply to look at winners and losers, or focus on politics defined narrowly in terms of process and interest.

From the works of Zolberg, Freeman, Hollifield, and others, we are starting to get a better picture of how politics matters in driving and channeling international migration. Two theories and their attendant hypotheses have been advanced: (1) the interest-based argument of Freeman, that states are subject to capture by powerful organized interests. These groups have pushed liberal democracies toward more expansive immigration policies, even when the economic conjuncture and public opinion would argue for restriction; and (2) the more comparative, historical, and institutional analysis—which I have summarized as the liberal state thesis—that, irrespective of economic cycles, the play of interests and shifts in public opinion, immigrants and foreigners have acquired rights and therefore the capacity of liberal states to control immigration is constrained by laws and institutions. This is not meant to imply that rights, once extended to foreigners, can never be revoked. Laws and institutions can and do change. Like any social, economic, or political variable, rights vary, cross-nationally and over time; we have seen evidence in the past 10 to 15 years that many liberal states have indeed tried to roll back immigrant rights (Hollifield 1999a, 2004). But, rights in liberal democracies have a long half-life. Once extended, it is difficult to roll them back, which may explain why many liberal states, especially in Western Europe, are so reluctant to make even small or incremental changes in immigration and refugee law. Governments fear that any move to expand the rights of foreigners could open up the floodgates and that such change (like amnesties or wholesale naturalizations) would increase the propensity to migrate.

The more procedural and rational choice theory of Freeman and the more institutional and state-centered theory of Hollifield try to explain policy outputs as well as outcomes. But Freeman tends to focus more on the demand for and supply of immigration policy, whereas Hollifield and colleagues are more focused on outcomes, that is, immigration flows. To this point, my review has barely touched on the core issues of sovereignty and citizenship. If we turn our attention from the politics of control to international relations and the politics of national security, then we can add a third hypothesis concerning the capacity of states to control migration. This is what I call the *globalization thesis*, which, in its original formulation, was developed by sociologists, although some political scientists have contributed to its elaboration and test-ing (Cornelius 1998; Koslowski 1999; Sassen 1996). Simply put, there is a process of economic globalization at work in the late twentieth century, but-tressed by transnational social networks and communities. Globalization has led to a structural demand for foreign labor (at the high and low end of the labor market) and a loss of control of borders, to the point that the institutions of sovereignty and citizenship have been transformed (Bauböck 1994; Castles and Davidson 2000; Soysal 1994). The next two sections are devoted to an examination of these powerful arguments.

MIGRATION AND INTERNATIONAL RELATIONS

With the rapid increase in transnational flows of goods, services, capital, and people in the postwar period, it is tempting to argue that migration is simply part of the inexorable process of globalization over which states have little control. Indeed there is a correlation between the rise of free trade and inter-national migration (Hatton and Williamson 1998; Sassen 1988); and the con-ventional economic wisdom is that trade can substitute for migration in the long run through a process of factor-price equalization (Krugman and Obst-feld 1997:160–65; Mundell 1957; Stolper and Samuelson 1941; Straubhaar 1988; Tapinos 1974). In the short run, however, historical and empirical studies demonstrate that free trade can lead to increased emigration, especially when disparities in wages and incomes are high, as between the United States and Mexico, for example (Faini, De Melo, and Zimmerman 1999; Martin 1993; Hollifield and Osang 2005). When backward economies are exposed to strong exogenous competitive pressures, the agricultural sector can collapse, lead-ing to a rural exodus, which will swell the population of cities and increase pressures to emigrate. Following the Heckscher-Ohlin logic we would expect emigration to continue so long as there are economic imbalances in the inter-national economy or until the process of factor-price equalization is complete (Krugman and Obstfeld 1997; Tapinos 1974). But these basic economic models, like their sociological counterparts, more often than not, ignore the political and legal realities of the Westphalian system, which is based on the principles of sovereignty and noninterference. Without arguing that these principles are eternal, absolute, and immutable, it is nonetheless important to remind our-selves that the world is divided into territorial units over which governments still exercise considerable authority (Hollifield 2005; Krasner 1999). Rather than assuming that states have lost control of their borders—overwhelmed by transnationalism and unable to regulate the movement of goods, capital, and people (Levitt 2001; Sassen 1996)—a more interesting question is to ask why states risk opening themselves to trade, foreign investment, and immigration, and why such openness has varied considerably over time (Hollifield 2004).

In looking at migration and international relations, we are concerned not just with domestic politics, the play of organized interests, and issues of state autonomy (Hollifield 1992a), but with foreign policy, national security, and the nature and structure of the international system. In addition to immigration policy, we can add to our list of dependent variables the demand for and supply of refugee policy, which is an increasingly important foreign-policy issue, especially with the end of the Cold War (Boswell 2006; Rudolph 2006; Teitelbaum 1984; Thielemann 2003; Weiner 1993, 1995; Zolberg, Suhrke, and Aguayo 1989). When and under what international systemic conditions are states willing to accept large numbers of refugees or risk large-scale labor migration (Hollifield 2004)? In asking this type of question, we are shifting the level of analysis from individuals and interest groups, to the state and the international system itself. Contending theoretical perspectives in international relations (liberalism, realism, and Marxism-Leninism) come into play, each with its own view of the state and the international system. However, the political science literature on migration and international relations (IR) is exceptionally thin, even though a number of younger (and some older) scholars have begun to turn their attention to this field of inquiry (see, for example, works by Andreas 1998, 2000; Andreas and Snyder, 2000; Greenhill 2002; Heisler 1998; Hollifield 1998, 2004; Koslowski 1999; Meyers 2004; Miller 1997; Rosenblum 2004; Rudolph 2006; Sassen 2006; Uçarer and Lavenex 2002; Weiner 1993, 1995).

How to explain the relative absence of the study of migration from one of the most important subfields in political science is indeed a mystery.[6] I argue that the answer to the mystery is historical, as well as theoretical and methodological. The period from 1945 to 1990 was dominated by the Cold War and international relations theorists tended to divide politics into two categories: high and low. In the realist formulation, high politics—the paramount subject of international relations—is concerned with national security, foreign policy, and issues of war and peace, whereas low politics is concerned with domestic issues relating to social and economic policy. In this framework, international migration, like any economic or social issue, belongs in the realm of low politics and therefore was not a subject of analyses by scholars of international relations, especially national security or foreign-policy analysts. For IR theorists wedded to the "realist paradigm," the international system, rather than the state or the individual, is the appropriate level of analysis (Waltz 1979). Unless it can be demonstrated that a social or economic phenomenon, like migration, clearly affects relations among states, to the point of upsetting the balance of power, it should be left to economists, sociologists, anthropologists, and other scholars of low politics.

But as the Cold War began to wane, during the period of detente in the 1970s, new issues forced their way onto the agenda of IR theorists. Enormous increases in the volume of trade and foreign investment in the 1950s and 1960s and the rise of multinational corporations (MNCs) drew the attention of IR theorists like Robert Gilpin, Joseph Nye, Robert Keohane, and Stephen Krasner. Efforts were made to bring the insights of IR theory to bear on solving some of the basic dilemmas of conflict and cooperation, not only in the area of international security also but in international economics. From the efforts of these and other scholars, a new subfield of international political economy (IPE) was created; and the basic, realist assumptions of IR theory—that the international system is structured by anarchy, and states are the key units of action—were relaxed (Katzenstein 1996; Keohane and Nye 1977). With the end of the Cold War in 1990 and even before, a cottage industry of new security analysis sprang up, focusing on a wide range of problems: from population control and environmental degradation, to the protection of human rights and combating terrorism. But still, despite the best efforts of some scholars (e.g., Heisler 1992; Hollifield 1992b; Weiner 1993), the issue of international migration did not make it onto the agenda of IR theorists. Only in the mid- to late 1990s, and especially after the terrorist attacks of September 11, 2001, did IR scholars begin to focus more attention on migration (Andreas and Snyder 2000; Koslowski 1999; Meyers 2004; Rosenblum 2004; Rudolph 2006). The discipline of international relations began to recognize that international population movements can have a dramatic effect on the security and sovereignty of states.[7] How then can we theorize about international migration from the standpoint of IR?

Broadly speaking, there are three schools of thought in IR that inform the study of international migration: (1) realism or neorealism; (2) transnationalism or what I call the globalization thesis, which is closely related to constructivism; and (3) liberal institutionalism and the theory of complex interdependence (Hollifield 1992b, 2000a, 2004). In these three theories, much empirical work has been done from the globalization perspective, primarily in the context of the sociology of international relations, following the works of such scholars as Mary Douglas (1986) and John Meyer (Meyer and Hannan, 1979). The students of Douglas, like Martin Heisler (1992, 1998) and of Meyer, like Yasemin Soysal (1994) and David Jacobson (1996), have been especially prolific in writing about international migration. In political science, Rey Koslowski (1999) subscribes to the basic tenets of globalization theory. He has extended his work to look at migration from a constructivist perspective, which holds that concepts such as national security or the national interest are sociological constructs (Katzenstein 1996). Constructivists argue that the national interest cannot simply be deduced, as realists would have it, from the structure of the international system or from the balance of power.

A growing body of work draws upon the insights of IPE to understand why states risk migration. Exemplars of this school include Christopher Rudolph (2006), Marc Rosenblum (2004), and Hollifield (2004). As we shall see, they differ from globalization theorists, who focus more on social networks and transnational communities and less on the state, which they want to decon-struct and de-emphasize (Faist 2000; Koslowski 1999; Sassen 1996, 2006). IPE theorists follow one of the two approaches delineated in the previous section of this chapter on the politics of control. They focus either on the play of interests (à la Freeman or Money) or on ideas, institutions, and political cul-ture (Hollifield and Rudolph) to explain why states risk migration.

Finally, the school of thought in IR which has the least to say about interna-tional migration is in fact the oldest and most venerable theory: political real-ism. Myron Weiner (1993, 1995) was the most consistent advocate in political science for a realist approach to the study of international migration. But, like IPE theorists, he tended to mix the levels of analysis, moving back and forth from the individual, to the state, to the international system. In this respect, few if any theorists have taken a purely realist approach to the study of inter-national migration. Such an approach would require us to infer the behavior of states, as reflected in their policy choices (more or less migration, greater or lesser support for the principle of political asylum), from the structure of the international system (that is, the distribution of power).

The basic assumption of political realism is that states are unitary rational actors, whose behavior is constrained by the anarchic structure of the inter-national system. States are therefore caught in a security dilemma, forced to be ever attentive to the protection of their sovereignty and searching for ways to enhance their power and capabilities. From this theoretical starting point, we can derive two simple hypotheses. (1) Migration or refugee policy (that is, rules of entry and exit) is a matter of national security, and states will open or close their borders when it is in their national interest to do so (i.e., when it will enhance their power and position in the international system). We can see rather quickly that this argument is dangerously close to being a tautology, and must be linked therefore to the second hypothesis. (2) Migration policy (the management of flows) is a function of international systemic factors, namely, the distribution of power in the international system and the relative positions of states. It is their relative position in the system and balance of power con-siderations that will determine whether states are willing to risk immigration or emigration and whether they will accept large numbers of refugees or turn them back.

We can see the attractiveness of these arguments, if we look at shifts in the politics of international migration before and after the end of the Cold War in 1990. During the Cold War, it was not in the interest of communist states to allow their people to emigrate (witness the construction of the Berlin Wall); and it was in the interest of the West to support the principle of political asylum and promote immigration from the East. With the end of the Cold War, the situation changed dramatically. Now people are freer to move (exit), but not so free to enter (Gibney 2004; Zolberg et al. 1989). Migration has been rede-fined in the West as a security issue by national security analysts like Samuel

Huntington (1996, 2004) and Christopher Rudolph (2006), whereas the economist George Borjas puts it succinctly in the title of his best-known work,
Friends or Strangers? (1990). He argues that mass migration from poor Third
World countries constitutes an economic threat, because it depletes or waters
down the human capital stock of the receiving societies, transforming them
from diamond- to hourglass-shaped societies, with lots of haves at the top and
more have-nots at the bottom. The middle class is squeezed, which fosters
social and economic conditions that are not healthy for capitalist democracies.
In *Alien Nation* (1995) the polemicist Peter Brimelow makes a security argument with clear cultural and racial overtones. He sees the influx of nonwhite
immigrants into Western societies as a cultural threat that could lead to the
political destabilization of the liberal democracies. His argument is reminiscent of the now famous quote, from 1969, by the Tory politician Enoch Powell
that, unless colored immigration to Britain is halted, there would be "rivers of
blood" in English streets (Hansen 2000). How to incorporate elements of "societal security," culture, and demography into the analysis of national security
is a major theme of recent scholarship in migration and international relations
(Rudolph 2006; Weiner and Russell 2001; Weiner and Teitelbaum 2001).

All of these works are, in effect, securitizing migration. Weiner and his
collaborators offer a sophisticated treatment of migration from the standpoint
of political realism. He and Kelly Greenhill (2002) draw our attention to the
destabilizing potential of mass refugee migrations, where the legitimacy of
states is fragile. Weiner extends his argument to include south-north and east-
west movements, hypothesizing that every society has a limited capacity to
absorb foreigners—what the former French President François Mitterrand
called a "threshold of tolerance"—and he points to xenophobic backlashes in
Western Europe as examples of the kind of security threat posed by uncontrolled migration. Greenhill shows how states can manipulate migration and
refugee movements in order to gain strategic advantage. According to this
logic, states must be prepared to intervene in conflicts that are likely to produce
large refugee flows, as the United States did in Haiti and the North Atlantic
Treaty Organizaion (NATO) in the Balkans in the 1990s. Another example is
the Mariel exodus in 1980, when Castro's Cuba succeeded in using migration
to gain advantage in the Cold War struggle with the United States.

Although it is a powerful argument—we cannot ignore the effect of structural
or systemic factors on the demand for and the supply of migration policy—the
principal weaknesses of realism are that it is politically overdetermined and
cannot account for the continued increase in world migration (flows) in the
post–Cold War era. The globalization thesis, with its strong emphasis on transnationalism, offers a compelling alternative hypothesis. Globalization arguments come in many shapes and sizes, but most are grounded in one way or
another in the world systems framework (Wallerstein 1976) and are inspired by
works in economic sociology and the sociology of international relations. But

all the globalization theorists agree on one point: the sovereignty and regulatory power of the nation–state has been weakened by transnationalism, in the form of the movement of goods, capital, or people (Levitt 2001; Sassen 1996, 2006). With respect to migration, however, the dependent variable in these arguments is the movement of people; and, in contrast to realism, the actors in international relations are not limited, if they ever were, to states. In the globalization thesis, firms, individuals, and transnational communities have found ways to bypass the regulatory authority of sovereign states. In the words of James Rosenau (1990), the world has been "indivdualized." To borrow the expression of another IR theorist, John Ruggie (1998), states have been "deterritorialized" and state agendas, following Sassen (2006), have been "denationalized."

The globalization thesis stands at the other extreme from neorealist arguments, which stress the role of the nation–state as the primary decision-making unit in international relations. In this perspective, the nation–state is no longer the sole, legitimate actor in international relations, if it ever was. Rather, the tables have been turned against the state, which is unable to control either transnational corporations—especially banks, which move vast sums of capital around the globe—or migrants, who move in search of employment opportunities. The internationalization of capital, we are told, has provoked a radical restructuring of production, as national economies move up (or down) in the international product cycle. Production itself has been decentralized with the rise of new centers of power and wealth, which Saskia Sassen (1991) has dubbed "the global city." In *Territory, Authority, Rights* (Sassen 2006) she offers a unified theory of globalization, explaining how the relationship between the individual and the state has evolved from the "medieval to the global assemblage."

According to Sassen, Portes, Faist, and others, the rise of transnational economies has resulted in the creation of transnational communities, as workers are forced to move from one state to another in search of employment, often leaving family members behind. Such communities can be found at both the high and low end of the labor market, as individuals move with more or less ease from one national society to another. A great deal of research has been done to document this practice among Mexican immigrants to the United States. Douglas Massey was one of the first migration scholars to point out the importance of transnational social networks in linking communities in the country of origin to those in the country of destination (Massey 1987; see also Levitt 2001). These kinship and informational networks helped to instill confidence in potential migrants, thus raising their propensity to migrate and, in effect, lowering transaction costs for international migration. Alejandro Portes (1996) argues that migrants have learned to use this "transnational space" as a way to get around national, regulatory obstacles to their social mobility. He goes on to point out that changes in Mexican law to permit dual nationality may reinforce this type of behavior, leading to ever-larger transnational communities (see also Fitzgerald 2000).

In the globalization thesis, the rapid decline in transaction costs and the ease of communication and transportation have combined to render national migration policies obsolete; and the entire regulatory framework of the state with respect to labor and business has been shaken by the process of globalization. To compete in the new international marketplace, business and governments in the OECD countries have been forced to deregulate and liberalize labor and capital markets. Moreover, less developed states have been thrown into debt crises, leading to the imposition of painful policies of structural adjustment, which in turn cause more migration from poor to rich states. A case in point is the financial crisis in Mexico in the mid-1990s, which led to the devaluation of the peso and a surge in emigration to the United States in the latter part of the decade (Commission on Immigration Reform 1997).

Politics and the state have been factored out of international relations in these types of globalization arguments (Waldinger and Fitzgerald 2004). Following on this apolitical logic, both trade and migration (which are closely linked) are largely a function of changes in the international division of labor, and states play at best a marginal role in determining economic and social outcomes. The prime agents of globalization are transnational corporations and transnational communities, if not individual migrants themselves. If states have such a minor role to play, any discussion of national interests, national security, sovereignty, or even citizenship would seem to be beside the point. But some sociologists have tried to bring politics and law, if not the state, back into the picture.

Recent works by Yasemin Soysal and David Jacobson focus on the evolution of rights for immigrants and foreigners. Both authors posit the rise of a kind of postnational regime for human rights wherein migrants are able to attain a legal status that somehow surpasses citizenship, which remains grounded in the logic of the nation–state. Jacobson, more so than Soysal, argues that individual migrants have achieved an international legal personality by virtue of various human rights conventions, and both authors view these developments as presenting a distinctive challenge to traditional definitions of sovereignty and citizenship (Jacobson 1996). But Soysal in particular is careful not to use the term postnational or transnational citizenship, opting instead for the expression postnational membership. Wrestling with the contradictory nature of her argument, Soysal writes: "Incongruously, inasmuch as the ascription and codification of rights move beyond national frames of reference, postnational rights remain organized at the national level . . . the exercise of universalistic rights is tied to specific states and their institutions" (Soysal 1994:157).

Another sociologist, Rainer Bauböck, is less circumspect. He argues simply that, given the dynamics of economic globalization, a new transnational/political citizenship is necessary and inevitable (Bauböck 1994). Bauböck draws heavily on political and moral philosophy, especially Kant, in making his argument in favor of transnational citizenship. Like Soysal, he relies on the recent history of international migration in Europe and the experience of the European Community/Union to demonstrate that migration has accompanied the process of economic growth and integration in Europe. These guest workers and other migrants achieved a rather unique status as transnational citizens. What all three of these authors (Soysal, Jacobson, and Bauböck) are attempting to do is to give some type of political and legal content to world systems and globalization arguments. But like Saskia Sassen (1996, 1999, 2006), they see the nation–state as essentially outmoded and incapable of keeping pace with changes in the world economy.

What do these theories tell us about migration policy (the opening and closing of societies) and the more or less continuous rise in international migration in the postwar period? At first blush, they would seem to account rather well for the rise in migration. Even though the globalization arguments, which draw heavily upon world systems theory, are more often than not neo-Marxist and structuralist in orientation, they share many assumptions with conventional, neoclassical (push-pull) theories of migration. The first and most obvious assumption is that migration is caused primarily by dualities in the international economy. So long as these dualities persist, there will be pressures for individuals to move across national boundaries in search of better opportunities. But whereas many neoclassical economists (like the late Julian Simon) see this as pareto optimal—creating a rising tide that will lift all boats—many globalization theorists (like Sassen and Portes) view migration as further exacerbating dualities both in the international economy and in national labor markets. This variant of the globalization thesis is close to the Marxist and dual labor market arguments that capitalism needs an industrial reserve army to surmount periodic crises in the process of accumulation (Bonacich 1972; Castells 1975; Castles and Kosack 1973; Piore 1979). As migration networks become more sophisticated and transnational communities grow in scope and complexity, migration should continue to increase, barring some unforeseen and dramatic fall in the demand for immigrant labor. Even then, some theorists, like Wayne Cornelius, would argue that the demand for foreign labor is "structurally embedded" in the more advanced industrial societies, which cannot function without access to a cheap and pliable foreign workforce (Cornelius 1998).

The second (crucial) assumption that globalization theorists share with neoclassical economists is the relatively marginal role of the state in governing and structuring international migration. States can act to distort or delay the development of international markets (for goods, services, capital, and labor), but they cannot stop it. With respect to migration, national regulatory regimes and municipal law in general simply must accommodate the development of international markets for skilled and unskilled workers. To talk about the opening and closing of societies, or rules of exit and entry, is simply a non-starter in a "global village." Likewise, citizenship and rights can no longer be understood in their traditional national contexts (Castles and Davidson 2000). If we take the example of postwar West Germany, nationality and citizenship laws date from 1913 and, until the reforms of 1999, they retained kinship or blood (*jus sanguinis*) as the principal criterion for naturalization (Brubaker 1992; Green 2004). But this very restrictionist citizenship regime did not prevent Germany from becoming the largest immigration country in Europe. Globalization theorists, like Portes, Soysal, and Castles can explain this anomaly by reference to the structural demand for foreign labor in advanced industrial societies, the growth of networks and transnational communities, and the rise of postnational membership, which is closely tied to human rights regimes—what Soysal calls universal personhood. National citizenship and regulatory regimes would seem to explain little in the variation of migration flows or the openness (or closure) of German society.

What can we retain from globalization, as opposed to neorealist, arguments? The biggest shortcoming of the globalization thesis—in contrast to realism—is the weakness or in some cases the absence of any political explanation for migration. The locus of power and change is in society and the economy. There is little place for states and national regulation in this framework. Almost everything is socially and economically determined, and contingency is removed from history (Waldinger and Fitzgerald 2004). By contrast, neoliberal arguments focus on institutions and the state and they share many assumptions with neorealism. Both neoliberal and neorealist theories are heavily rationalist and stress the primacy of interests, the major difference being that neoliberals want to disaggregate the "national interest" and to look at the multiplicity of social and economic groups, which compete to influence the state. For neoliberals, both national and international politics can be reduced to an economic game and ultimately to a problem of collective action. To understand this (means-ends) game, all that is needed is to correctly identify the interests and preferences of social, economic, and political actors (Milner 1997). Not surprisingly, neoliberal theorists focus almost exclusively on politics and policy in liberal states, where the competition among groups is relatively open and unfettered by authoritarianism and corruption. Studying competition among groups at the domestic level, as well as the allocational and distributional consequences of policy, presents a clearer picture of why states behave the way they do in the international arena, whether in the areas of trade, finance, or migration.

Since this approach incorporates both economic and political analysis, it has come to be called international political economy (IPE). IPE theorists are interested in the connections between domestic/comparative and international politics. In addition to focusing on domestic interests, they also stress the importance of institutions in determining policy outcomes. For one of the original IPE theorists, Robert Keohane, international institutions hold the key to explaining the puzzle of conflict and cooperation in world politics, especially with the weakening of American hegemony in the last decades of the twentieth century. Along with Joseph Nye, Keohane argued that increases in economic interdependence in the postwar period have had a profound impact on world politics, altering the way states behave and the way in which they think about and use power (Keohane and Nye 1977). In the nuclear age and with growing interdependence, it became increasingly difficult for states to rely on traditional military power in order to guarantee their security. National security was tied more and more to economic power and nuclear weapons fundamentally altered the nature of warfare. The challenge for states (especially liberal states) was how to construct a new world order to promote their national interests that were tied ever more closely to international trade and investment, if not to migration (Hollifield 2004).

In the first two decades after World War II, this problem was solved essentially by the United States, which took it upon itself to reflate the world economy and to provide liquidity for problems of structural adjustment. This approach was dubbed "hegemonic stability" (Gilpin 1986); and with the gradual decline of American economic dominance in the 1970s, the problem arose of how to organize world markets in the absence of a hegemon. The answer would be found, according to Keohane and others, in multilateralism and the building of international institutions and regimes (like the General Agreement on Tariffs and Trade [GATT] and the International Monetary Fund [IMF]) to solve the problems of international cooperation and collective action (Keohane 1984; Ruggie 1993). As the Cold War waned in the 1980s, the entire field of international relations shifted dramatically away from the study of national security toward the study of international economics, especially issues of trade and finance. In the last decades of the twentieth century, even domestic politics, according to IPE theorists, has been thoroughly internationalized (Keohane and Milner 1996).

Despite the fact that international migration would seem to lend itself to neoliberal/IPE arguments (migration has a strong political-economic dimension and it clearly contributes to the internationalization of domestic politics), very little has been written about it from this perspective (see, however, Hollifield 1992b, 1998, 2000a, 2004). The reasons for this are fairly simple. Until recently, there was little demand for international cooperation (or policy) in the area of migration, with the major exception of managing refugee flows (Gibney 2004; Teitelbaum 1984; Thielemann 2003). The dependent variable in this framework is the demand for and supply of international policy, in the form of regimes. Even for the relatively weak refugee regime (United Nations High Commission for Refugees [UNHCR]), the numbers were modest until the 1980s and the incentives for cooperation among liberal states were closely linked to the Cold War and the bipolar structure of the international system.

From the late 1940s through the 1970s, liberal states had little incentive to cooperate or to build regimes for managing labor migration because there was an unlimited supply of (unskilled) labor available, which could be recruited through bilateral agreements with the sending countries (Martin et al. 2006). The German *Gastarbeiter* (1960s) and the American *bracero* (1940s to the 1960s) programs are classic examples of these types of bilateral accords (Calavita 1992; Rogers 1985).

With the major exception of the European Union and the Schengen system (Geddes 2000, 2003; Guiraudon 1998; Thielemann 2003; Uçarer and Lavenex 2002), the situation did not change that much in the 1980s and 1990s, despite the end of the Cold War. There is still an unlimited and rapidly growing supply of cheap labor available in developing countries. What has changed, however, are the goals of immigration and refugee policies among the OECD states. The demand now is for policies to control, manage, or stop migration and refugee flows (Ghosh 2000). The cold-war refugee regime, specifically the UNHCR, has come under enormous pressure to manage various refugee crises. Existing international organizations for dealing with economic migration, such as the International Organization for Migration (IOM) and the International Labour Office (ILO) in Geneva, have not been besieged by demands for action. Western Europe, however, developed its own regional regime for migration—the Schengen and Dublin systems. Otherwise, there has been little effort to regulate international migration on a multilateral basis.

What can neoliberal or IPE arguments tell us about the development of international migration during the postwar period and the willingness of states to risk exposing their economies to the exogenous pressures of trade and migration? The first major hypothesis that we can derive from neoliberal theory is that states are more willing to risk opening their economies to trade (and by extension migration) if there is some type of international regime (or hegemonic power) that can regulate these flows and solve collective action and free-rider problems. However, there is no regime for regulating migration that comes close to the type of regime that exists for trade (GATT/WTO [World Trade Organization]), or for international finance (IMF/World Bank). Yet, we know that migration has increased steadily throughout the postwar period, in the absence of a regime or any type of effective multilateral process. Again, the EU and Schengen constitute important exceptions. If we accept the neorealist assumptions that states are unitary, sovereign actors, capable of closing as well as opening their economies, then other (political) factors must be at work, driving the increases in migration and maintaining a degree of openness to migration, at least among the advanced industrial democracies (Hollifield 2000a).

A second (powerful) hypothesis can be derived from neoliberal theory. The maintenance of a relatively open (nonmercantilist) world economy is heavily dependent on coalitions of powerful interests in the most dominant, liberal states. In *Resisting Protectionism* (1988), Helen Milner—a prominent neoliberal theorist—demonstrates how advanced industrial states in the 1970s were able to resist the kind of beggar-thy-neighbor policies that were adopted in the 1920s and 1930s. She argues that growing interdependence (multinationality and export dependence) helped to solidify free trade coalitions among the OECD states in the postwar period, thus preventing a retreat into protectionism following the economic downturns of the 1970s and 1980s. Government leaders in a range of industrial nations were willing (and able) to resist strong political pressures for protectionism in the 1970s in large part because a powerful constellation of business interests contributed to a substantial realignment within these societies. In some cases polities themselves were creatively redesigned by political entrepreneurs to facilitate the maintenance and strengthening of these new (free-trade) coalitions (Lusztig 1996). Of course, free-trade interests were bolstered by the existence of an international trade regime (GATT) in the 1970s.

From a neoliberal/IPE perspective, the central question with respect to migration is: How did proimmigration coalitions in the key OECD states form, and will they be able to maintain legal immigration regimes with the end of the Cold War and in the absence of a strong international migration regime? We cannot discount the importance of international systemic constraints, like the end of the Cold War, which clearly has had an impact on political coalitions and alignments in all of the liberal democracies (Meyers 2004). The end of the Cold War has had a profound impact on coalitions supporting open migration policies, even more so than in the area of trade. The major difference between trade and migration is in the nature and types of the coalitions that form to support or oppose them. Although related, in the sense that strong economic liberals tend to support both free trade and more open migration policies (Hollifield, Hunt, and Tichenor 2006), there is a much stronger legal, ideational, and cultural dimension involved in the making of promigration coalitions than is the case with free-trade coalitions, which tend to be based more narrowly on economic interests. Free-trade policies clearly have important political and social effects, but the arguments about comparative advantage and tariff policies tend to be heavily economic, and the interests are organized by economic sector or along class lines. With respect to trade, individuals and groups tend to follow their market interests. But in the making of migration policies, this is not always the case.

If a state can be sure of reciprocity—that other states will abide by the most-favored nation (MFN) principle—then it is easier to convince a skeptical public to support free trade. With migration, by contrast, economic arguments (about the costs and benefits of migration) tend to be overshadowed by political, cultural, and ideological arguments. National identities and founding myths, what I have called elsewhere "national models," come into play in the making and unmaking of coalitions for admissionist or restrictionist migration policies (Hollifield 1997a, 1997b; cf. King 2005). Debates about migration in the liberal-democratic (OECD) states revolve as much, if not more so, around issues of rights, citizenship, and national identity than around issues of markets (cf. infra). The coalitions that form to support more open migration policies are often rights-markets coalitions. Debates about sovereignty and control of borders are reduced to debates about national identity—a fungible concept that reflects values, morality, and culture, rather than a strictly instrumental, economic calculus.

THE POLITICS OF INCORPORATION, CITIZENSHIP, AND NATIONAL IDENTITY

If we take a neoliberal approach to understanding the rise of international migration in the postwar era, then we are thrown back onto an analysis of three factors, which together drive national migration policies. The first of these factors is *ideational, historical, and cultural.* Migration policy, especially in the big three liberal republics (the United States, France, and Germany), is heavily influenced by national or founding myths, which are codified in citizenship and nationality laws. These myths about the national identity are fungible, subject to manipulation, and involve strong elements of symbolic politics (Chavez 2001; King 2005). They are reflected in constitutional law and can be analyzed from a historical, sociological, legal, and political standpoint (Bade 2000; Hollifield 1997a, 1997b; Noiriel 1988; Schuck 1998; Shanks 2000; Smith 1997; Tichenor 2002; Weil 1991, 2002; Zolberg 2006). They also can be the subject of political struggle and heated partisan debates; and the institutions of sovereignty and citizenship, like the economy, are subject to exogenous shocks. Immigration, as Gary Freeman (1979), Myron Weiner (1995), Martin Schain (1988), Rey Koslowski (1999), Jeannette Money (1999), and others (Givens 2005; Lahav 2004; Norris 2005;) have pointed out, can change the composition of societies, alter political coalitions, disrupt the party system, and transform citizenship and the national identity. The argument therefore can be made, following Koslowski and Money, that migration contributes to the internationalization of local and domestic politics. Multiculturalism is the functional equivalent of multinationalism. If the rise of multinational corporations—as Milner and others have argued—contributed to the creation of new free-trade coalitions, then the rise of immigration and multiculturalism has contributed to political realignments in the liberal democracies. As foreigners gain a legal foothold in liberal societies, rights accrue to them and they become political actors capable of shaping both policy and polity (Hollifield 1992a; Ireland 1994, 2004; Miller 1981; Schmitter 1979). Conversely, immigration can increase diversity and radically alter the composition of societies, provoking a radical, populist backlash. For this reason, the politics of incorporation is closely linked to issues of race (Bleich 2003; Skerry 2000), religion (Fetzer and Soper 2005; Klausen 2005), and social class (Lamont 1998, 2000).

But to understand immigration politics we must also look at the *play of organized interests*. As Gary Freeman argues, businesses that are dependent on foreign labor—whether skilled, as in the case of the software industry, or unskilled, as in the case of construction trades or agriculture—can form powerful lobbies. Under the right conditions, these lobbies can capture parts of the state in order to maintain access to a vital input (Freeman 1995). The political and economic history of Western states, since the late nineteenth century when the transaction costs of migration were drastically reduced, is replete with examples of businesses working with, around, through, or against the state to import labor (Cornelius, Martin, and Hollifield 1994; Cornelius, Tsuda, Martin, and Hollifield 2004). Economic interests are always at play in the making of migration policy, because the profits to be had from importing labor are great (demand-pull forces are strong) and there is an abundant supply of cheap labor available. Cutting off access to foreign labor for businesses that are heavily dependent upon it is the same thing as imposing high tariffs on imported raw materials. The industries affected will howl (Cornelius 1998). Both policies are protectionist and have profound allocational effects.

In the postwar period, the third and most important factor in immigration politics is *institutional and legal*. Again to quote Max Frisch, "We asked for workers but human beings came." Unlike capital or goods, migrants, qua individuals and sometimes qua groups (e.g., Cubans in the United States, ethnic Germans and Jewish immigrants in Germany) can acquire legal rights and protections under the aegis of liberal constitutions and statutory law. Even when they are not admitted immediately to full citizenship, migrants acquire the rights of membership, which can (depending upon the state) include basic civil rights, a package of social or welfare rights and political rights (Geddes and Favell 1999; Hammar 1990; Hollifield 2000b; Layton-Henry 1990; Morris 2002; Schuck 1998). What is important to keep in mind, however, is that these rights are anchored in national legal systems. Although they may flow from constitutional law, they also depend upon increasingly fragile political coalitions, involving left- and right-wing liberals. With the end of the Cold War, these "strange bedfellow" coalitions have become more difficult to sustain, even in the area of political asylum, a principle which is supported in international law (Gibney 2004; Goodwin-Gill 1996; Shaw 1997; Zolberg, Suhrke, and Aguayo 1989). As the coalitions weaken, we would expect to see a concomitant decline in support for admissionist immigration and refugee policies (Hollifield, Hunt, and Tichenor 2006).

But rights have a very long half-life in liberal democracies. Once they are extended and institutionalized, it is extremely difficult to roll them back. Most democracies—especially those like the United States, France, and Germany, which have universalist (egalitarian), republican traditions and strong elements of separation of powers—have a variety of institutional/judicial checks that limit the ability of executive and legislative authorities to change individual

rights. To understand the "limits of immigration control" in liberal democracies, as well as the mix of internal and external strategies for control, we
must have a clear understanding of the evolution of rights-based politics and of
the way in which rights are institutionalized (Cornelius et al. 1994; Hollifield
1998; Morris 2002). Even if rights-markets coalitions supporting immigration
weaken, this does not mean that migration and refugee policies will change
overnight or that liberal states can quickly and effectively seal their borders.

The neoliberal approach requires us, in the first instance, to look at international institutions and regimes and secondly at the types of coalitions that
form to support more open migration regimes. I have identified three factors
that influence coalition building: (1) ideational and cultural factors, which are
closely linked to formal-legal definitions of citizenship; (2) economic interests, which are linked to factor proportions and intensities, that is, land, labor,
capital ratios; and (3) rights, which flow from liberal-republican constitutions.
Although we have seen a good deal of theorizing in political science about the
second factor and how it affects immigration policy (outputs) and actual flows
(outcomes), less has been written about the first and third factors. Certainly
there is a burgeoning literature on the politics of citizenship, focused on a
wide range of issues, such as nationality, naturalization, ethnicity, and identity.
Political scientists, along with sociologists, have contributed heavily to debates
about the changing nature of citizenship (Brubaker 1989, 1992; Fuchs 1990;
Turner 1993; Pickus 1998, 2005; Smith 1997). But no attempt has been made
to link the literature on citizenship with an even broader range of sociological
and economic work on incorporation (see, for example, Favell 1998; Freeman
2004; Kurthen, Fijalkowski, and Wagner 1998; Portes and Rumbaut 1996).
Instead, we have seen the emergence of a small but growing literature on the
politics of immigration, by which I mean the effect that immigration has on
public opinion, political behavior in general, and voting in particular (De la
Garza and DeSipio 1996; DeSipio 1996; Fetzer 1996, 2000). Much of the literature on the politics of immigration is comparative in nature, with a regional
focus on Western Europe. Many of the works in this field are more interested
in the rise of radical right-wing, xenophobic, and anti-immigrant political
movements, than in understanding the politics of immigration and citizenship (see, for example, Betz 1994; Givens 2005; Kitschelt 1995; Layton-Henry
1992; Messina 1989; Minkenberg 1992; Money 1999; Norris 2005; Schain
1990; Thränhardt 1993, 1996; Wihtol de Wenden 1988). With respect to the
tremendously important role that rights play in defining citizenship—who is
and is not a foreigner—most of the work has been done by legal scholars, like
Peter Schuck (1998), Alexander Aleinikoff and David Martin (1995), or Stephen Legomsky (1987) in the United States, Danièlle Lochak (1985) in France,
or Kay Hailbronner (1984; Hailbronner, Martin, and Motomura 1997) in Germany. Two notable exceptions are Patrick Weil, the French political scientist
and historian who has written the most comprehensive work on the politics of

immigration, the rights of foreigners, and a history of nationality in France (Weil 1991, 2005), and the British sociologist Lydia Morris (2002), who has developed a comparative framework for understanding the evolution of rights for foreigners and immigrants in Europe (cf. Janoski 1998).

If my analysis is correct—that ideas and institutions play a vital role in determining outputs (the demand for and supply of immigration and refugee policy) and outcomes (the level of flows and stocks)—then it is in the area of immigration politics, involving issues of incorporation, sovereignty, and citizenship where the most work remains to be done (for an overview, see Freeman 2004). Many questions barely have been posed, but are begging for an answer. (1) What is the relationship between the politics of immigration and incorporation? (2) Is there a link between social and political incorporation? (3) How does the rate of social and economic incorporation affect political behavior and the institutions of sovereignty and citizenship? All of these questions strike at the heart of the state-society relationship and presuppose that immigration has the effect of upsetting or transforming this relationship, which leads inexorably to policy reform and institutional change.

But before we can understand the impact of immigration on the state (and how we can bring the state back into our analysis), we must understand the impact of immigration on society. Theories about the social impact of immigration fall into fairly recognizable categories, and each of these theoretical perspectives tends to inform the way in which political scientists think about the political impact of immigration. I would divide these theories into four categories. First is the Smithian or liberal view, which holds that market-oriented societies are incredibly dynamic and capable of absorbing large numbers of immigrants, who, because they tend to self-select, will contribute to the human capital stock and to the overall wealth of society. The works of Julian Simon and Barry Chiswick best reflect this perspective (Chiswick 1982 and in this volume, Chapter 3; Simon 1989). Scholars working in this tradition generally accept the proposition that immigrants will assimilate, within one or two generations (Gordon 1964; Fuchs 1990). Ethnic identity and ethnic politics should fade quickly as individuals are absorbed into the mainstream of the political and social life of the host country. From this perspective, there is no need for positive discrimination, affirmative action, or bilingual education policies that may prolong the process of acculturation and exacerbate ethnic tensions. If problems arise with the assimilation of immigrants, then naturalization or "Americanization" would be the obvious long-term remedy (Pickus 1998, 2005; Skerry 1993).

A second theoretical perspective—at the opposite extreme of Smithian liberalism—is the neo-Malthusian view that every society has limited resources (especially land) and a limited number of jobs. From this perspective, any immigration may be harmful to some or all segments of society and the environment. Some level of immigration may be safe, but a large or uncontrolled influx of foreigners is not in the interests of society. This perspective seems most often shared by demographers (e.g., Bouvier 1992; Coleman 1992), economists (Borjas 1990; Martin 1994a), and by some political scientists (Teitelbaum and Weiner 1995; Weiner 1995). A third perspective is informed by the Marxist notion (already discussed above) that capitalist economies need an industrial reserve army, composed primarily—but not exclusively—of foreign or immigrant workers, in order to overcome periodic crises of accumulation (Bonacich 1972; Castells 1975). In this view, immigration only heightens class conflict and will contribute to a further politicization and ethnicization of the working class (Castles and Kosack 1973; Faist 1995; Miles 1982; Rath 1988; Rex and Moore 1967). Finally, a fourth perspective is what I would call, for lack of a better term, the Durkheimian view, that immigration, like the process of modernization itself, may contribute to a sense of alienation, leading to the fragmentation or even dissolution of society. This perspective is often shared by social or political geographers and demographers, who point to the spatial impacts of immigration. A large concentration of foreigners in specific locales can exacerbate class, ethnic, and racial tensions (Clark 1997; Money 1999; Tribalat 1995).

From the Smithian perspective, the institution of citizenship and the regulatory powers of the liberal state should be dynamic enough to respond to the challenges posed by international migration. The strongest polities are those with strong civil societies and a well-developed "national model" or founding myth around which to organize debates about immigration control and incorporation (Hollifield 1997). The American political scientist and historian Lawrence Fuchs, argues in Tocquevillian fashion that the strength of American civic culture has helped the United States to overcome racial, ethnic, and even class divisions, leading to what he calls a kind of "voluntary pluralism" (Fuchs 1990; cf. King 2005). In effect, Fuchs is arguing for American exceptionalism, where the strengths of liberal-republican ideals and institutions have created a pluralist and centrist politics, gradually excluding the extremist politics of the Right or the Left that one finds in other political systems, particularly in Europe. The American conception of citizenship, with its emphasis on individual rights and responsibilities and its aversion to "old-world" notions of class and ethnicity, is most compatible with a liberal society and economy and therefore most open to immigration (Pickus 2005; Ueda 2006).[8] Since the adoption of the Fourteenth Amendment, access to citizenship is automatic for anyone born on American territory and naturalization is relatively easy for newcomers who arrive legally in the United States (Schuck 1998). Immigration, as Rogers Brubaker (1989) and others have pointed out, is part of the American tradition of nationhood, whereas in Europe the formation of nation–states did not coincide with waves of immigration. With the partial exception of France (Hollifield 1994, 1999b), European societies from the sixteenth through the nineteenth centuries were exporting rather than importing people (Moch 1992). Most of these European emigrants went to the Americas, with the idea of leaving the "old world" behind forever.

This is the American founding myth, which stood in sharp contrast to European traditions, until the latter half of the twentieth century, when we have seen a rise of immigration in Western Europe and a marked convergence in immigration and citizenship laws and practice (Cornelius, Martin, and Hollifield 1994; King 2005; Thränhardt 1996). The American political theorist Rogers Smith, while remaining firmly ensconced in the liberal-republican tradition, has criticized the narrow reading of American history offered by Fuchs and others. Smith finds that there are multiple traditions in American liberalism, some more egalitarian than others. For much of the history of the American Republic, ascriptive, hierarchic, and racist views were preferred over more egalitarian or Tocquevillian views (King 2000; Smith 1997). Clearly racism, through slavery and the Jim Crow system—an American version of apartheid—was built into the American political system from the beginning. In the nineteenth and first half of the twentieth centuries, racism also played a prominent role in the making of immigration and naturalization policy and in the construction of American national identity, from the Chinese Exclusion Act through the National Origins Quota System (Kettner 1978; King 2000; Zolberg 2006). In the post–World War II period, however, both the United States and the immigrant receiving states of Western Europe have moved away from this ascriptive, exclusionary, or particularistic approach to immigration and naturalization, in favor of more egalitarian policies (Cornelius, Martin, and Hollifield 1994; Joppke 2005; Tichenor 2002). In 1999, the German government changed German nationality law, making it possible for anyone born in Germany who has at least one parent who has been in the country for eight years to gain automatic German citizenship. This reform was the culmination of decades of political struggle and debate and was fiercely contested right up to the moment of its passage (Green 2004). Among the liberal democracies, Britain would seem to be the glaring exception to this rule of convergence in citizenship policy and practice. Race has remained a prominent feature of immigration policy making in Britain throughout the postwar era (Bleich 2003; Freeman 1979; Hansen 2000; Layton-Henry 1992; Messina 1996).

Remaining within the Smithian/liberal-republican tradition, the jurist Peter Schuck (1998) has written extensively on the evolution of American citizenship, carefully documenting changes in law and policy and their effects on immigration and incorporation. Schuck and his coauthor, Rogers Smith, criticized American naturalization policy for contributing to the "devaluation" of American citizenship (cf. Pickus 2005; Schuck and Smith 1985). Their main concern was that newcomers had little incentive to naturalize and that as a consequence American society and ultimately the polity itself was being weakened. This concern for the solidarity of society and community is echoed in the works of other political theorists, like Michael Walzer (1983) and Joseph

Carens (1989), who argue that openness to immigration must be tempered by a willingness on the part of the receiving society quickly to integrate and care for newcomers. To show how expansive and adaptive liberal thinking about citizenship can be, the Canadian political theorist Will Kymlicka (1995) argues that liberal states even can function in a multiethnic or multicultural setting. A uniform (legal) citizenship is not, in his view, inconsistent with the recognition of minority and group rights. The biggest theoretical stretch of all is the argument advanced by the sociologists Yasemin Soysal (1994) and David Jacobson (1996), who see the possibility of a postnational citizenship, where rights flow from international law, organizations, and regimes (cf. Joppke 2001).

Each of these liberal theorists places great emphasis on ideas and institutions for understanding the impact of immigration on the state-society relationship. Each also points to the contradictions and tensions within liberal theory; but none of them, with the exceptions of Peter Schuck and Daniel Tichenor, seek to include in their theoretical framework more economic or interest-based explanations for the supply of and demand for immigration policy (Hollifield, Hunt, and Tichenor 2006; Schuck 1998; Tichenor 2002). For most of these political theorists, citizenship is a dependent rather than an independent variable. So there would be no reason to try to link the evolution of rights with changes in immigration policy (outputs) or actual levels of immigration (outcomes). Both Fuchs and Smith, for example, are writing about American political and social development, rather than about immigration per se. But both are intensely interested in how newcomers have fared in different periods of American history and how their identities and legal status have been shaped by the evolution of the institution of citizenship. The issue of incorporation lies just beneath the surface in many of these works on citizenship. But it is not clear how to make the link between the politics of incorporation, immigration control, and citizenship.

Sociologists, like Alejandro Portes and Ruben Rumbaut (1996) and Min Zhou (Portes and Zhou 1993), focus on immigration (that is, the process of immigrating), settlement, and incorporation. They see citizenship not so much as an institution but as a process whereby newcomers are able to adapt to their new social and political environment, with some groups adapting more quickly than others, depending on their levels of social and human capital. They take issue with scholars, like Glazer and Moynihan (1970) or Fuchs (1990), who see assimilation as a more or less linear process where ethnic identities and attachments fade quickly over time. Instead, they note an increasing tendency toward segmented assimilation, whereby immigrant groups (and especially the second generation) suffer from new forms of discrimination that may delay or impede acculturation and assimilation. The unevenness of the process is linked, in their view, to the advent of postindustrial society, which places a great premium on education and human capital. Earlier waves of unskilled immigrants were able to find employment in traditional manufacturing industries. Their children either followed in the parents' footsteps or (more likely) got a better education and moved into high-skilled jobs. This is the traditional pattern of assimilation as outlined by Gordon (1964) and Alba and Nee (1997). Today, however, according to Portes and Rumbaut (1996), many immigrant groups in postindustrial economies have found themselves trapped in an endless cycle of poverty and discrimination. But despite the difficulties of finding adequate employment, immigrants continue to arrive in the United States in great numbers (legally or illegally) because of poorer opportunities in the countries of origin and because social networks help to sustain high levels of immigration. Many members of the first and second generations find themselves excluded from the mainstream of social and economic life, ostracized or stigmatized by dominant groups in the host society. They are thus denied the benefits of citizenship (Lamont 1998, 2000). As a result, they retreat into ethnic enclaves (or ghettos) in search of community, which can lead to deviant behavior, such as joining gangs. This pattern of segmented assimilation reinforces ethnic identity and makes it more difficult for newcomers to incorporate politically (Favell 1998).

In this analysis, we can see how the optimistic, liberal view of immigration, incorporation, and citizenship begins to give way to a more Durkheimian, if not Malthusian or Marxist view of the impact of immigration on state and society. As newcomers "fail" to assimilate, a political backlash will build and natives—especially those more marginal members of the majority ethnic group—will come to see immigrants as a threat, demanding that the state do something to alleviate "the problem." Analyses of voting in the California ballot initiative Proposition 187 point to social class as a major predictor of voting outcomes, and higher levels of education and income were correlated with a higher "no" vote (Hollifield and Martin 1996). At the same time, individuals belonging to an ethnic minority or in some other way culturally marginalized (e.g., being young or female) were less likely to support the initiative (Fetzer 1996). The passage of Proposition 187 together with the Illegal Immigration and Immigrant Responsibility Act, approved in 1996 by the U.S. Congress and which severely curtailed immigrant access to certain social programs like Supplemental Security Income (SSI), contributed to a wave of naturalizations in the mid- to late 1990s. A decade earlier Peter Schuck had been writing about the "devaluation of citizenship," but by the end of the 1990s, he was writing about the "revaluation of citizenship" (Schuck 1998), and in the first decade of the twenty-first century, citizenship has become a focus of political inquiry (Pickus 2005).

The newcomers in the United States were naturalizing in great numbers and beginning to organize and participate in a wider range of political activities. Louis DeSipio finds that, while political participation of first-generation immigrants in the United States is low, it is substantially higher for the second generation but still lower than that of natives. He is cautiously optimistic that new immigrants and their children will not descend into a kind of political ghetto (DeSipio 1999). Likewise, comparative studies of immigrant political behavior show the resilience of the institutions of the liberal state and demonstrate how immigrants are able to take advantage of opportunity structures open to them in the political process. Immigrants then become players in redefining the institution of citizenship itself (Feldblum 1999; Ireland 1994, 2004; Miller 1981).

A legitimate question of cause and effect can be raised regarding what triggers such a change in political attitudes and behaviors, in the native as well as the immigrant population. The rather straightforward, Durkheimian thesis is that social change itself is driving politics (Durkheim 1964). As societies "modernize," individuals and groups are displaced. This occurred in Europe during the industrial revolution, which completely disrupted family and community life, leading to anomie and forcing individuals to seek new communities and new identities. In some societies this type of social change led to a radicalization and polarization of politics—in Germany, for example—whereas in others the institutions of the liberal state were able to control and channel these radical impulses. Britain is the most obvious example (Marshall 1964; Moore 1966). Many political and social scientists see the same thing happening with the advent of postindustrial society, which has created feelings of failure, alienation, and resentment, especially among workers in the most advanced industrial societies, many of whom see immigrants as the cause of their problems (Betz 1994; Kitschelt 1995; Norris 2005). All it takes then is some entrepreneurial (usually right-wing) politician to trigger feelings of xenophobia and racism in these segments of the population (Thränhardt 1993). It is not surprising that immigration becomes the focal point of radical right-wing politics (Mayer and Perrineau 1996; Minkenberg 1992), and in some cases, like France, the entire party system may be destabilized (Givens 2005; Schain 1988).

As the politics of immigration and incorporation intensify, political institutions in general and political parties in particular come to center stage. Demands for greater immigration control or changes in nationality or citizenship laws will be channeled through political parties and party systems (Givens 2005; Lahav 2004; Perlmutter 1996; Schain 1990). In this perspective, immigration can be understood as part of the broader phenomenon of globalization, which itself goes hand in hand with the advent of postindustrial society. Social movements, opposed to globalization and multiculturalism, may spring up in the native populations, resulting in a new politics of national identity and citizenship, driven in part by the demand for participation by new immigrant groups (Ireland 1994; Kastoryano 1997). Fierce debates have occurred over whether new immigrant groups should be entitled to special rights and privileges, or whether they should conform to a more individualistic pattern of incorporation (Carens 2000; Feldblum 1999; Freeman 2004; Kymlicka 1995; Skerry 1993).

As during the industrial revolution, how a society manages this type of change is heavily dependent on the strength of its institutions, especially the welfare state, which is much stronger and better developed today than in the nineteenth century (Bommes and Halfmann 1998; Ireland 2004; Kurthen, Fijalkowski, and Wagner 1998; Marshall 1964). It is important to note, however, that the level and unit of analysis in these works has shifted, from the state to the individual or the group. In such analyses of political behavior, political scientists are not so concerned with predicting state-level responses to immigration, as with understanding the impact of immigration on the attitudes of individuals and groups in society.

In the analysis of the politics of immigration, the whole panoply of variables for predicting voting behavior (Miller and Shanks 1996; Norris 2005) comes into play. They can be arrayed along two dimensions: one focused on social class, the other on culture and ethnicity. Hypotheses for explaining the support for anti-immigrant parties and social movements or ballot initiatives, like California's Proposition 187 and English-only movements, tend to stress one or the other dimension (Citrin, Reingold, and Green 1990; Espenshade and Calhoun 1993; Hollifield and Martin 1996; Mayer and Perrineau 1996; McClain and Karnig 1990). The question is whether the roots of xenophobic politics lie primarily in the realm of economic interests or cultural beliefs and attitudes. Scholars are divided in their answer to this question: some stress the importance of ethnicity as a mobilizing factor (Fetzer 2000; Schmitter-Heisler 1986; Tolbert and Hero 1996); others continue to focus on class as the driving force in immigration politics (Bach 1986; Hollifield and Martin 1996; Lamont 1995, 2000; Norris 2005; Rath 1988). In the general literature on voting in the United States, very little attention has been paid to the impact of immigration on political behavior.[9] Perhaps because immigration has had a much more visible impact on politics in Western Europe, the European voting literature is more extensive (see, for example, Betz 1994; Givens 2005; Mayer and Perrineau 1996; Lahav 2004; Norris 2005).

An alternative to the Smithian or Durkheimian arguments draws heavily on social geography and has a distinctive Malthusian ring to it. This is the idea that the spatial concentration of immigrants triggers a xenophobic reaction in the native population, which fears being overwhelmed by "the other." According to Jeannette Money (1998, 1999; cf Favell 1998), limits on resources and space, especially at the local level, will trigger xenophobic and nativist politics. The intensity of local reactions against immigration, as happened in the town of Dreux, France, in the early 1980s, or in Southern California in the early 1990s, forced immigration onto the national political agenda (Clark 1997; Tribalat 1995). Martin Schain (1988, 1990) has analyzed how the French National Front began to make inroads in local politics, often at the expense of the communists, playing on the xenophobic feelings of the native working class vis-à-vis North African immigrants who were having difficulties in acculturating and assimilating. Tolbert and Hero (1996) look at the subtle interplay of class, race, and ethnicity in local voting patterns for and against Proposition 187 in California. In the mid-1990s, it appeared that the California ballot initiative would succeed in putting nativist politics back on the top of the agenda in American politics. But as quickly as the issue inserted itself onto the California agenda, it disappeared as the business cycle in the state improved. The "Golden State" once again found its Midas touch, which would seem to indicate that economic interests play a crucial role in the rise and decline of immigration politics (Hollifield and Martin 1996).

Nevertheless, as I pointed out above, it would be a mistake to reduce immigration politics to the simple play of economic interests. Coalitions that form for or against immigration are held together not simply by narrow calculations of the costs and benefits that accrue to a specific class or group. Rather policy and politics in this area are driven in no small measure by attitudes and beliefs shaped by national cultures and histories. This is why identity politics in the advanced industrial democracies can quickly overwhelm clientelist politics, driving immigration policy either in a more expansive direction (as in the cases of the United States and Germany) or toward greater restriction (as in Britain). Concerns over citizenship, identity, sovereignty, and incorporation can override the market interests of specific groups or classes, creating "strange bedfellow" coalitions, most often of right-wing (free-market or economic) liberals and left-wing (political) liberals—what I have called elsewhere "rights-markets coalitions" (Hollifield 1992; Hollifield, Hunt, and Tichenor 2006). What is it that holds these coalitions together?

In the American case, it was the strange conjuncture of the Cold War—with its emphasis on national security and the need to resurrect the very old notion of the United States as a land of asylum or refuge—and the civil rights movement. Taken together, they dramatically expanded the civil and social rights of minorities, including immigrants (Tichenor 1994, 1996; Zolberg 2006). In the German case, the Cold War also played a role. But more important is what Markovits and Reich (1997) call the politics of collective memory, which helped to shape a new German model of citizenship. This model was based in the first instance on the famous social market economy (*Sozialmarktpolitik*), meaning a strong commitment to the welfare state and to the maintenance of social solidarity in the face of rapid social and economic change. In the second instance, the model derives from the overwhelming burden of German history and the experiences of the Holocaust and the Second World War. In both cases "ideas, institutions and civil society" have worked to limit the capacity for immigration control (Hollifield 1997a, 1997b, 1999a, 2004). In neither case were markets for immigrant or foreign labor functioning in a political, cultural, or ideational void. In the German or American cases, any attempt to understand policy outputs or outcomes purely in terms of interest or clientelist politics will not get us very far. This does not mean that powerful anti-immigrant forces were absent in either the German or the American cases; merely that they were unable to overcome strong proimmigration coalitions, built on the dual dynamic of markets and rights.

So where does this leave us with respect to our understanding of the politics of international migration and our ability to theorize about this complex phenomenon? I would like to conclude this chapter by summarizing the various theories and hypotheses reviewed above, with an eye to describing how we can bring politics and the state into or "back into" our analysis of migration. I also will discuss what I see as the major avenues for future research.

CONCLUSION: AVENUES FOR FUTURE RESEARCH

Simply asserting that politics and the state matter in the analysis of international migration does not help us in constructing a theory of the politics of international migration. The challenge for political scientists is to demonstrate how the state and politics matter and to develop theories of international migration that incorporate political variables. Few serious social scientists, irrespective of their home discipline, would disagree with the proposition that politics matters. The trick, as one colleague put it to me, is to bring politics into the analysis in a "nonstylized way."[10] Before we can get to the richness or power of political explanations for migration, we must be clear about the models we are using, as well as the levels and units of analysis. Only then will we be able to develop generalizable and testable propositions.

In the current literature, what is an independent variable for some—the supply of and the demand for immigration policy—is a dependent variable for others. We can therefore identify an immediate schism between those who see their objective as explaining policy, *tout court*, or what I call policy outputs, and those who have a somewhat broader objective of explaining policy outcomes, in this case international migration itself. Most works, however, focus on explaining immigration rather than international migration, for reasons that I have outlined in the first section of this chapter. The receiving countries really are calling the shots with respect to international migration, and not surprisingly, much greater attention is given to the politics of immigration (rules of entry) than to the politics of emigration (rules of exit). This points to an immediate gap in the literature, since, with very few exceptions (Russell 1986; Sadiq 2005; Shain 1989; Weiner 1995), scholars have focused most of their attention on political, economic, and social conditions in the liberal, receiving states. One, perhaps false, assumption is that immigration is permanent. But with the rise of transnational communities and dual nationality, this may be even less true today than it was in earlier periods. Clearly more research needs to be done on the politics of emigration and the increasingly transnational nature of migration, one indicator of which is dual nationality (Faist 2000).

By contrast, in the study of the politics of immigration, we have only scratched the surface. Much of the literature takes the supply of and the demand for immigration policy as the dependent variable, focusing heavily on the play of organized interests to explain why some states are willing at certain points in time to "risk migration," while others remain closed. Freeman's "modes of politics" approach offers a neat typology for explaining how powerful, proimmigration coalitions form and prevent liberal democracies from reducing immigration, even when the economic conjuncture would seem to dictate greater closure (Freeman 1995). Freeman's is basically a "capture argument," that liberal states are vulnerable to capture by powerful organized interests. If we combine his approach with a factor-cost model (Money 1999), then we have a more complete theory of the political economy of immigration, albeit one heavily indebted to microeconomics. In this construction, politics is defined primarily by the play of interests.

In the liberal state thesis, I offered a more cultural and institutionalist approach to answering the question of why states are willing to risk migration, even in the face of a negative economic conjuncture. In this approach, politics is defined more in institutional and legal terms, with a heavy focus on the evolution of rights as the key variable for explaining openness or closure (Hollifield 1992, 1999a; Hollifield, Hunt, and Tichenor 2006). In most of my work, the dependent variable is immigration and policy is an independent variable. The unit of analysis is the state, while the method is comparative, historical, and statistical; and the analysis is done at a macrolevel, using aggregate data. In this framework, the principal challenge is to understand the development of rights (as an independent variable), in their civil, social, and political dimensions. The liberal state is key to understanding immigration and rights are the essence of the liberal state. One problem with this approach, however, is that liberal states are caught in a dilemma. International economics (markets) push liberal states toward greater openness for efficiency (allocational) reasons; whereas domestic political and legal forces push the same states toward greater closure, to protect the social contract and to preserve the institutions of citizenship and sovereignty (Hollifield 1992, 2004). How can states escape from this dilemma or paradox?

Some political scientists, like Myron Weiner (1995), argue that states cannot escape from this dilemma; therefore, migration must be understood in the context of political realism. For Weiner, migration is simply another of the many security threats that states must face in an international system, structured by anarchy, where states are the sole/unitary actors. Here, the dependent variables are the rules of entry and exit (supply of and demand for migration policy) and the principal independent variable is national security. In Weiner's framework, migration is above all else a foreign policy issue and the international system or the state—as opposed to individuals or groups—are the appropriate levels of analysis. In making migration policy, states face fundamental, structural constraints that are dictated by the nature of the international system. As in Freeman's theory, politics is defined primarily in terms of the play of interest, but at the international rather than the domestic level.

As with most interest-based arguments in political science, we do not have to look very far to find alternative hypotheses that place more stress on institutions and ideas, if not culture. The globalization thesis has it that states are not the sole/unitary actors in the international system and the dilemma in which they find themselves is a result of a process of social and economic change, over which states have little control (Sassen 1996, 2006). Migration is simply one of several transnational forces that buffet states and societies, leading inevitably to the erosion of sovereignty and the system of nation–states. Few if any political scientists would accept the globablization thesis in its purest form, because it is so apolitical. Most would agree that states remain very much at the center of international relations. But, unlike the political realists, those international relations theorists who take a liberal institutionalist approach accept the fact that economic and social change have led to growing interdependence and states have found ways to cooperate and solve coordination problems. The way in which they have done this is through international law and organization and the building of international regimes and institutions.

Liberal institutionalists themselves are split between those who see the rise in migration primarily as a function of the growth of international human rights regimes (Jacobson 1996; Soysal 1994) and those who see the "possibility" for further cooperation among liberal states in building such a regime. As someone who subscribes to the latter view, I argue that in the final analysis rights still derive from the liberal constitutions (and power) of national states (Hollifield 1998, 2000a; Joppke 2001). Here, politics is defined more in terms of ideas and institutions than in terms of interest. Much work, however, remains to be done in the area of migration and international relations. Scholars have only just begun to specify the conditions under which states may cooperate to solve the problem of unwanted or uncontrolled migration (Ghosh 2000; Hollifield 2000a). Not surprisingly, a great deal of attention is being lavished by political scientists on the experience of the European Union, as it attempts to grapple with the rights of third-country nationals (Geddes 2000, 2003; Guiraudon and Lahav 2000; Ireland 2004; Lahav 2004; Uçarer and Lavenex 2002).

Once again we are thrown back onto an analysis of rights, which raises another set of questions and problems concerning the institutions of citizenship and sovereignty. It is in this area of inquiry where the most work by political scientists remains to be done and where the biggest payoff will be in theoretical terms. Is international migration really eroding the twin pillars of the international system: citizenship (the nation) and sovereignty (the state)? This is a daunting question and we can see immediately that the dependent and independent variables have been reversed. Is migration now a force that has the potential to undermine the institution of sovereignty and transform world politics, as Rey Koslowski (1999) and Yasemin Soysal (1994), inter alia, have put it? Answering this question will require us to look at the relationship between immigration and integration (or incorporation). Very few political scientists have studied immigration as an issue of sovereignty (see, however, Joppke 1998a; Rudolph 1998, 2006; Shanks 2000). Instead, more have focused on the relationship between citizenship and immigration (Fuchs 1990; Pickus 1998, 2005; Smith 1997; Tichenor 2002). Almost no one in political science has studied the relationship between immigration and incorporation—a literature dominated by sociologists and economists (see, however, DeSipio 1996; Freeman 2004). How, for example, does political incorporation (the final step to formal-legal citizenship) affect the prospects for social and economic incorporation? Does or should one precede the other? Without the data or the theoretical tools to answer these questions, we cannot begin to understand the relationship between immigration and citizenship. Yet, given the rise in immigration in the industrial democracies since 1945 and the development of more expansive notions of citizenship, this relationship is likely to preoccupy students of international migration for decades to come.

Much of the literature on citizenship tends to be atheoretical and heavily formal-legal in orientation, relying primarily on inductive/historical analysis and moral reasoning (Benhabib 2004; Carens 2000; Honig 2001). Perhaps the most highly developed body of literature in political science is that on voting. But, as in the area of international relations, little attention has been given to the issue of migration (notable exceptions include Givens 2005; Norris 2005), and few attempts have been made to integrate the literature on voting behavior with broader issues in the politics of immigration: control, national security, sovereignty, citizenship, and incorporation. Most studies of immigration, voting, and political participation have focused on the rise of extremist political parties and new social movements, again with little attention given to issues of political incorporation or citizenship (Feldblum 1999; Freeman 2004; Pickus 2005). In much of this literature, the nativist and xenophobic backlash against immigration is seen as yet another symptom of postindustrial change, with the losers in struggles over modernization (especially unskilled workers) seen to be the easiest groups to mobilize against further immigration. Jeannette Money (1999) has added a spatial dimension to the analysis, suggesting that heavy concentrations of immigrants in specific locales can exacerbate anti-immigrant politics.

While the literature on immigration, voting, and political participation holds some promise for helping us to understand how and why coalitions form—for or against immigration—it does not address the relationship between immigration and integration. Jeannette Money (1998) argues that the determinants of immigration policy are difficult to grasp because immigration is a two-dimensional policy problem. She returns to the classical distinction made by Tomas Hammar (1985); (Hollifield 2000b) between immigration and immigrant policy, arguing that issues of control elicit different types of coalitions than issues of integration or incorporation. These two issues tend to split mainstream political parties, often in very odd ways that are difficult to predict. Much more theorizing and research needs to be done on the relationship between immigration and integration in order to understand the types of coalitions that form.

In this respect, political scientists have their work cut out for them. Historians, sociologists, economists, anthropologists, and demographers have a head start in the study of international migration. These disciplines have a large body of literature and a bigger empirical base from which to work. But given the sheer number of political scientists who are now turning their attention to the study of international migration, we are closing the gap fairly quickly.

ACKNOWLEDGMENTS

Many colleagues read and commented on earlier drafts of this chapter. I would like specifically to acknowledge the invaluable feedback I received from Wayne Cornelius, Louis DeSipio, Thomas Faist, Miriam Feldblum, Gary Freeman, Barbara and Martin Heisler, Christian Joppke, Rey Koslowski, Marc Rosenblum, Rogers Smith, and Dietrich Thränhardt. Errors, of course, are mine alone.

NOTES

1. Reference here is to the seminal essay by Theda Skocpol, "Bringing the State Back In" (Evans, Rueschemeyer, and Skocpol 1985). For some recent efforts to theorize about the role of the state in international migration, see Freeman 1998b, Weil 1998, and Zolberg 1999.
2. I was once reproached by a colleague in history who said, "You political scientists just lurch from one crisis to another."
3. As defined in one of the most widely used introductory texts in political science (Dahl 1991).
4. Aristide Zolberg pointed out the hypocrisy of liberal democracies, which, throughout the period of the Cold War, worked to create a right to exit, but without a concomitant right to entry (Zolberg 1981).
5. The argument here is that international migration in the post-1945 period was stimulated by economic imbalances between the north and the south. We cannot, however, ignore the role of decolonization and refugee movements in this process. The politics of postcolonial and refugee migrations are admittedly different than the politics of labor migration (see Zolberg, Suhrke, and Aguayo 1989; Joppke 1998a).
6. An interesting exercise is to search the index of major texts in international relations. Almost never does one find even a single entry about migration, immigration, or emigration.
7. The section on Ethnicity Nationalism and Migration (ENMISA) is the fastest growing group within the International Studies Association.

8. This liberal view of citizenship underpins the modernization school of political development. At a conference on security and migration at MIT, convened by Myron Weiner, Lucian Pye was asked to comment on the rise of ethnic nationalism in the post–Cold War era. He responded that ethnic nationalism is an oxymoron. According to Pye, you either have ethnicity or nationalism. But you cannot have both, because one destroys the other.

9. If we take Miller and Shanks (1996) as the state of the art in this literature, then it is surprising to see no reference whatsoever to immigration in the entire volume and only one reference to ethnicity.

10. The quote is taken from an e-mail exchange with Robert Keohane.

REFERENCES

Alba, Richard, and Victor Nee. 1997. "Rethinking Assimilation Theory for a New Era of Immigration," *International Migration Review* 31: 826–74.

Aleinikoff, Thomas A., and David A. Martin. 1995. *Immigration Process and Policy.* St. Paul, MN: West Publishing.

Andreas, Peter. 1998. "The Escalation of U.S. Immigration Control in the Post-NAFTA Era," *Political Science Quarterly* 113/4: 591–615.

————. 2000a. *Border Games: Policing the US-Mexico Divide.* Ithaca, NY: Cornell University Press.

Andreas, Peter, and Timothy Snyder, eds. 2000b. *The Wall around the West: State Borders and Immigration Controls in North America and Europe.* Lanham, MD: Roman & Littlefield.

Bach, Robert L. 1986. "Immigration: Issues of Ethnicity, Class and Public Policy in the United States," *The Annals* 485: 139–52.

Bade, Klaus J. 2000. *Europa in Bewegung: Migration vom späten 18. Jahrhundert bis zur Gegenwart.* München: Verlag C.H. Beck.

Barth, Fredrik. 1969. *Ethnic Groups and Boundaries: The Social Organization of Culture Difference.* Boston: Little, Brown.

Bauböck, Rainer. 1994. *Transnational Citizenship: Membership and Rights in International Migration.* Aldershot, England: Edward Elgar.

Benhabib, Seyla. 2004. *The Rights of Others: Aliens, Residents and Citizens.* Cambridge: Cambridge University Press.

Betz, Hans Georg. 1994. *Radical Right-wing Populism in Western Europe.* New York: St. Martin's Press.

Bhagwati, Jagdish. 1976. *The Brain Drain and Taxation: Theory and Empirical Analysis.* New York: American Elsevier.

Bleich, Erik. 2003. *Race Politics in Britain and France: Ideas and Policymaking since the 1969s.* Cambridge: Cambridge University Press.

Bommes, Michael, and Jost Halfmann. 1998. *Migration in nationalen Wohlfahrtsstaaten.* Osnabrück: Universitätsverlag Rasch.

Bonacich, Edna. 1972. "The Split Labor Market: A Theory of Ethnic Antagonism," *American Journal of Sociology* 37: 1050–87.

Borjas, George J. 1990. *Friends or Strangers: The Impact of Immigrants on the U.S. Economy.* New York: Basic Books.

Boswell, Christina. 2006. "The Liberal Dilemma in the Ethics of Refugee Policy" in Anthony M. Messina and Gallya Lahav, eds., *The Migration Reader: Exploring Politics and Policies.* Boulder, CO: Lynne Rienner.

Bouvier, Leon F. 1992. *Peaceful Invasions: Immigration and Changing America*. Lanham, MD: University Press of America.

Brimelow, Peter. 1995. *Alien Nation: Common Sense About America's Immigration Disaster*. New York: Random House.

Brochmann, Grete, and Tomas Hammar, eds. 1999. *Mechanisms of Immigration Control: A Comparative Analysis of European Regulation Policies*. Oxford: Berg.

Brubaker, Rogers, ed. 1989. *Immigration and the Politics of Citizenship in Europe and North America*. Lanham, MD: University Press of America.

———. 1992. *Citizenship and Nationhood in France and Germany*. Cambridge, MA: Harvard University Press.

———. 1994. "Are Immigration Control Efforts Really Failing?" in Wayne A. Cornelius, Philip L. Martin, and James F. Hollifield, eds., *Controlling Immigration: A Global Perspective*. Stanford, CA: Stanford University Press.

———. 1996. *Nationalism Reframed. Nationhood and the National Question in the New Europe*. Cambridge: Cambridge University Press.

Calavita, Kitty. 1992. *Inside the State: The Bracero Program, Immigration and the INS*. New York: Routledge.

Carens, Joseph H. 1989. "Membership and Morality: Admission to Citizenship in Liberal Democratic States," in Rogers Brubaker, ed., *Immigration and the Politics of Citizenship in Europe and North America*. Lanham, MD: University Press of America.

———. 2000. *Culture, Citizenship, and Community: A Contextual Exploration of Justice as Evenhandedness*. New York: Oxford University Press.

Castells, Manuel. 1975. "Immigrant Workers and Class Struggles in Advanced Capitalism: The Western European Experience," *Politics and Society* 5: 33–66.

Castles, Stephen, and Alastair Davidson. 2000. *Citizenship and Migration: Globalisation and the Politics of Belonging*. London: Macmillan.

Castles, Stephen, and Godula Kosack. 1973. *Immigrant Workers and Class Structure in Western Europe*. London: Oxford University Press.

Castles, Stephen, and Mark Miller. 1998. *The Age of Migration: International Population Movements in the Modern World*. New York: Guilford.

Chavez, Leo R. 2001. *Governing Immigration: Popular Images and the Politics of the Nation*. Berkeley and Los Angeles: University of California Press.

Chiswick, Barry R., ed. 1982. *The Gateway: U.S. Immigration Issues and Policies*. Washington, D.C.: American Enterprise Institute.

Citirn, Jack, Beth Reingold, and Donald P. Green. 1990. "American Identity and the Politics of Ethnic Change," *Journal of Politics* 52: 1124–54.

Clark, W. A. V. 1997. "Scale Effects in International Migration to the United States," *Regional Studies* 30: 589–600.

Coleman, David A. 1992. "Does Europe Need Immigrants? Population and Work Force Projections," *International Migration Review* 26/2: 413–61.

Commission on Immigration Reform. 1997. *Binational Study on Migration between Mexico and the United States*. Washington, D.C.

Cornelius, Wayne A. 1998. "The Structural Embeddedness of Demand for Mexican Immigrant Labor: New Evidence from California," in Marcelo M. Suárez-Orozco, ed., *Crossings: Mexican Immigration in Interdisciplinary Perspectives*. Cambridge, MA: Harvard University Press.

Cornelius, Wayne A., Philip L. Martin, and James F. Hollifield, eds. 1994. *Controlling Immigration: A Global Perspective*. Stanford, CA: Stanford University Press.

Cornelius, Wayne A., Takeyuki Tsuda, Philip L. Martin, and James F. Hollifield, eds. 2004. *Controlling Immigration: A Global Perspective*, 2nd ed. Stanford, CA: Stanford University Press.

Dahl, Robert A. 1991. *Modern Political Analysis*. Englewood Cliffs, NJ: Prentice-Hall.

De la Garza, Rodolfo O., and Louis DeSipio. 1996. *Ethnic Ironies: Latino Politics in the 1992 Elections*. Boulder, CO: Westview Press.

DeSipio, Louis. 1996. *Counting on the Latino Vote: Latinos as a New Electorate*. Charlottesville: University of Virginia Press.

————. 1999. "The Second Generation: Political Behaviors of Adult Children of Immigrants in the United States," paper prepared for the annual meeting of the American Political Science Association, Atlanta, GA.

Douglas, Mary. 1986. *How Institutions Think*. Syracuse, NY: Syracuse University Press.

Durkheim, Emile. 1964. *The Division of Labor in Society*. New York: Free Press.

Espenshade, Thomas J., and Charles A. Calhoun. 1993. "An Analysis of Public Opinion toward Undocumented Immigration," *Population Research and Policy Review* 12: 189–224.

Evans, Peter B., Dietrich Rueschemeyer, and Theda Skocpol, eds. 1985. *Bringing the State Back In*. New York: Cambridge University Press.

Faini, Ricardo, Jaime De Melo, and Klaus F. Zimmerman, eds. 1999. *Trade and Migration: The Controversies and the Evidence*. Cambridge: Cambridge University Press.

Faist, Thomas. 1995. *Social Citizenship for Whom? Young Turks in Germany and Mexican Americans in the United States*. Aldershot, England: Avebury.

————. 2000. *The Volume and Dynamics of International Migration and Transnational Social Spaces*. New York: Oxford University Press.

Favell, Adrian. 1998. *Philosophies of Integration: Immigration and the Idea of Citizenship in France and Britain*. New York: St. Martin's Press.

Feldblum, Miriam. 1999. *Reconstructing Citizenship: The Politics of Citizenship and Immigration in Contemporary France*. Albany, NY: SUNY Press.

Fetzer, Joel. 1996. "Marginality, Economic Self-Interest and Voting for Proposition 187," paper prepared for the annual meeting of the American Political Science Association, San Francisco, CA.

————. 2000. *Public Attitudes toward Immigration in the United States, France, and Germany*. Cambridge: Cambridge University Press.

Fetzer, Joel S., and J. Christopher Soper. 2005. *Muslims and the State in Britain, France and Germany*. Cambridge: Cambridge University Press.

Fitzgerald, David. 2000. *Negotiating Extra-Territorial Citizenship: Mexican Migration and the Transnational Politics of Community*. La Jolla, CA: University of California, San Diego Center for Comparative Immigration Studies.

Freeman, Gary P. 1979. *Immigrant Labor and Racial Conflict in Industrial Societies: The French and British Experiences*. Princeton, NJ: Princeton University Press.

————. 1986. "Migration and the Political Economy of the Welfare State," *The Annals* 485/May: 51–63.

————. 1994. "Britain, the Deviant Case," in Wayne A. Cornelius, Philip L. Martin, and James F. Hollifield, eds., *Controlling Immigration: A Global Perspective*. Stanford, CA: Stanford University Press.

————. 1995. "Modes of Immigration Politics in Liberal Democratic States," *International Migration Review* 29/4: 881–902.

————. 1998a. "The Decline of Sovereignty? Politics and Immigration Restriction in Liberal States" in Christian Joppke, ed., *Challenge to the Nation–State*. Oxford: Oxford University Press.

————. 1998b. "Toward a Theory of the Domestic Politics of International Migration in Western Nations," South Bend, IN: Nanovic Insititute, University of Notre Dame.

_____. 2004. "Immigrant Incorporation in Western Democracies." *International Migration Review* 38/3: 945–69.

Fuchs, Lawrence H. 1990. *The American Kaleidoscope: Race, Ethnicity and the Civic Culture*. Hanover, NH: Wesleyan University and University Press of New England.

Geddes, Andrew. 2000. *Immigration and European Integration: Towards Fortress Europe?* Manchester: Manchester University Press.

_____. 2003. *The Politics of Migration and Immigration in Europe*. London: Sage Publications.

Geddes, Andrew, and Adrian Favell. 1999. *The Politics of Belonging: Migrants and Minorities in Contemporary Europe*. Aldershot, England: Ashgate.

Ghosh, Bimal, ed. 2000. *Managing Migration: The Need for a New International Regime*. Oxford: Oxford University Press.

Gibney, Matthew J. 2004. *The Ethics and Politics of Asylum: Liberal Democracy and the Response to Refugees*. Cambridge: Cambridge University Press.

Gilpin, Robert. 1986. *The Political Economy of International Relations*. Princeton, NJ: Princeton University Press.

Givens, Terri E. 2005. *Voting Radical Right in Western Europe*. Cambridge: Cambridge University Press.

Glazer, Nathan, and Daniel P. Moynihan. 1970. *Beyond the Melting Pot: The Negroes, Puerto Ricans, Jews, Italians and Irish of New York City*. Cambridge, MA: MIT Press.

Goodwin-Gill, Guy S. 1996. *The Refugee in International Law*. Oxford: Clarendon.

Gordon, Milton. 1964. *Assimilation in American Life*. New York: Oxford University Press.

Green, Simon. 2004. *The Politics of Exclusion: Institutions and Immigration Policy in Contemporary Germany*. Manchester: Manchester University Press.

Greenhill, Kelly. 2002. "Engineered Migration and the Use of Refugees as Political Weapons: A Case Study of the 1994 Cuban *Balseros* Crisis," *International Migration* 40/4: 39–72.

Guiraudon, Virginie. 1998. "Third Country Nationals and European Law: Obstacles to Rights' Expansion," *Journal of Ethnic Studies* 24/4: 657–74.

Guiraudon, Virginie, and Gallya Lahav. 2000. "A Reappraisal of the State Sovereignty Debate: The Case of Migration Control," *Comparative Political Studies* 33(2): 163–195.

Hailbronner, Kay. 1984. *Ausländerrecht*. Heidelberg: C.F. Müller.

Hailbronner, Kay, David A. Martin, and Hiroshi Motomura, eds. 1997. *Immigration Admissions: The Search for Workable Policies in Germany and the United States*. Oxford: Berghahn Books.

Hammar, Tomas, ed. 1985. *European Immigration Policy: A Comparative Study*. New York: Cambridge University Press.

_____. 1990. *Democracy and the Nation–State: Aliens, Denizens and Citizens in a World of International Migration*. Aldershot, England: Avebury.

Hammar, Tomas, Grete Bochmann, Kristof Tamas, and Thomas Faist, eds. 1997. *International Migration, Immobility and Development: Multidisciplinary Perspectives*. Oxford: Berg.

Hansen, Randall. 2000. *Immigration and Citizenship in Postwar Britain*. Oxford: Oxford University Press.

Hatton, Timothy J., and Jeffrey G. Williamson. 1998. *The Age of Mass Migration: Causes and Economic Impact*. New York: Oxford University Press.

Haus, Leah. 1995. "Openings in the Wall: Transnational Migrants, Labor Unions and U.S. Immigration Policy," *International Organization* 49/2: 285–313.

————. 1999. "Labor Unions and Immigration Policy in France," *International Migration Review* 33/3: 683–716.

Heisler, Martin O. 1992. "Migration, International Relations and the New Europe: Theoretical Perspectives from Institutional Political Sociology," *International Migration Review* 26/2: 596–622.

————. 1998. "Contextualizing Global Migration: Sketching the Socio-Political Landscape in Europe," *UCLA Journal of International Law and Foreign Affairs* 3/2: 557–93.

Hobsbawm, Eric. 1990. *Nations and Nationalism since 1780*. Cambridge: Cambridge University Press.

Hollifield, James F. 1986. "Immigration Policy in France and Germany: Outputs vs. Outcomes," *The Annals* 485/May: 113–28.

————. 1990. "Immigration and the French State," *Comparative Political Studies* 23 (April): 56–79.

————. 1992a. *Immigrants, Markets and States: The Political Economy of Postwar Europe*. Cambridge, MA: Harvard University Press.

————. 1992b. "Migration and International Relations: Cooperation and Control in the European Community," *International Migration Review* 26/2: 568–95.

————. 1994. "Immigration and Republicanism in France: The Hidden Consensus," in Wayne A. Cornelius, Philip L. Martin, and James F. Hollifield, eds., *Controlling Immigration: A Global Perspective*. Stanford, CA: Stanford University Press.

————. 1997a. *L'Immigration et L'Etat-Nation à La Recherche d'un Modèle National*. Paris: L'Harmattan.

————. 1997b. "Immigration and Integration in Western Europe: A Comparative Analysis," in Emek M. Uçarer and Donald J. Puchala, eds., *Immigration into Western Societies: Problems and Policies*. London: Pinter.

————. 1998. "Migration, Trade and the Nation–State: The Myth of Globalization," *UCLA Journal of International Law and Foreign Affairs* 3/2: 595–636.

————. 1999a. "Ideas, Institutions and Civil Society: On the Limits of Immigration Control in Liberal Democracies," *IMIS-Beiträge* 10 (January): 57–90.

————. 1999b. "On the Limits of Immigration Control in France," in Grete Brochmann and Tomas Hammar, eds., *Mechanisms of Immigration Control*. Oxford: Berg.

————. 2000a. "Migration and the 'New' International Order: The Missing Regime," in Bimal Ghosh, ed., *Managing Migration: The Need for a New International Regime*. Oxford: Oxford University Press.

————. 2000b. "Immigration and the Politics of Rights," in Michael Bommes and Andrew Geddes, eds., *Migration and the Welfare State in Contemporary Europe*. London: Routledge.

————. 2004. "The Emerging Migration State," *International Migration Review* 38: 885–912.

————. 2005. "Sovereignty and Migration," in Matthew J. Gibney and Randall Hansen, eds., *Immigration and Asylum from 1900 to the Present, Volume Two*. Santa Barbara, CA: ABC-CLIO.

Hollifield, James F., Valerie F. Hunt, and Daniel J. Tichenor. 2006. "Immigrants, Markets and the American State: The Political Economy of U.S. Immigration," in Marco Giugni and Florence Passy, eds., *Dialogues on Migration Policy*. Oxford: Lexington Books.

Hollifield, James F., and Calvin Jillson, eds. 1999. *Pathways to Democracy: The Political Economy of Democratic Transitions*. New York: Routledge.

Hollifield, James F., and David L. Martin. 1996. "Strange Bedfellows? Immigration and Class Voting on Prop 187 in California," paper prepared for the American Political Science Association, San Francisco, CA.

Hollifield, James F., and Thomas Osang. 2005. "Trade and Migration in North America: The Role of NAFTA," *Law and Business Review of the Americas* 11/3-4: 327–60.

Hollifield, James F., and Gary Zuk. 1998. "Immigrants, Markets and Rights," in Hermann Kurthen, Jürgen Fijalkowski, and Gert G. Wagner, eds., *Immigration, Citizenship and the Welfare State in Germany and the United States*. Stamford, CT: JAI Press.

Honig, Bonnie. 2001. *Democracy and the Foreigner*. Princeton, NJ: Princeton University Press.

Huntington, Samuel P. 1996. "The West: Unique, Not Universal," *Foreign Affairs* 75/6: 28–46.

———. 2004. *Who Are We? The Challenges to America's Identity*. New York: Simon & Schuster.

IOM. 1996. *Foreign Direct Investment, Trade, Aid and Migration*. Geneva: International Organization for Migration.

Ireland, Patrick. 1994. *The Policy Challenge of Ethnic Diversity: Immigrant Politics in France and Switzerland*. Cambridge, MA: Harvard University Press.

———. 2004. *Becoming Europe: Immigration, Integration and the Welfare State*. Pittsburgh, PA: University of Pittsburgh Press.

Jacobson, David. 1996. *Rights across Borders: Immigration and the Decline of Citizenship*. Baltimore, MD: Johns Hopkins University Press.

Janoski, Thomas. 1998. *Citizenship and Civil Society*. New York: Cambridge University Press.

Joppke, Christian, ed. 1998a. *Challenge to the Nation–State: Immigration in Western Europe and the United States*. Oxford: Oxford University Press.

———. 1998b. "Why Liberal States Accept Unwanted Migration," *World Politics* 50/2: 266–93.

———. 2001. "The Legal-Domestic Sources of Immigrant Rights: The United States, Germany and the European Union," *Comparative Political Studies*, 34/4: 339–66.

———. 2005. *Selecting by Origin: Ethnic Migration in the Liberal State*. Cambridge, MA: Harvard University Press.

Kastoryano, Riva. 1997. *La France, l'Allemagne et leurs immigrés: négocier l'identité*. Paris: Armand Colin.

Katzenstein, Peter J., ed. 1996. *The Culture of National Security: Norms and Identity in World Politics*. New York: Columbia University Press.

Keohane, Robert O.1984. *After Hegemony: Cooperation and Discord in the World Economy*. Princeton, NJ: Princeton University Press.

Keohane, Robert O., and Helen V. Milner. 1996. *Internationalization of Domestic Politics*. New York: Cambridge University Press.

Keohane, Robert O., and Joseph S. Nye. 1977. *Power and Interdependence: World Politics in Transition*. Boston: Little, Brown.

Kessler, Alan E. 1998. "Distributional Coalitions, Trade and the Politics of Postwar American Immigration," paper prepared for the American Political Science Association, Boston, MA.

Kettner, James H. 1978. *The Development of American Citizenship, 1608–1870*. Chapel Hill: University of North Carolina Press.

King, Desmond. 2000. *Making Americans: Immigration, Race and the Diverse Democracy.* Cambridge, MA: Harvard University Press.

———. 2005. *The Liberty of Strangers: Making the American Nation.* New York: Oxford University Press.

Kitschelt, Herbert. 1995. *The Radical Right in Western Europe.* Ann Arbor: University of Michigan Press.

Klausen, Jytte. 2005. *The Islamic Challenge: Politics and Religion in Western Europe.* New York: Oxford University Press.

Kohn, Hans. 1962. *The Age of Nationalism: The First Era of Global History.* New York: Harper & Row.

Koslowski, Rey. 1999. *Migration and Citizenship in World Politics: From Nation–States to European Polity.* Ithaca, NY: Cornell University Press.

Krasner, Stephen D. 1999. *Sovereignty: Organized Hypocrisy.* Princeton, NJ: Princeton University Press.

Krugman, Paul, and Maurice Obstfeld. 1997. *International Economics: Theory and Policy.* Reading, MA: Addison-Wesley.

Kurthen, Hermann, Jürgen Fijalkowski, and Gert G. Wagner, eds., 1998. *Immigration, Citizenship and the Welfare State in Germany and the United States.* Stamford, CT: JAI Press.

Kymlicka, Will. 1995. *Multicultural Citizenship.* Oxford: Clarendon Press.

Lahav, Gallya. 2004. *Immigration and Politics in the New Europe.* Cambridge: Cambridge University Press.

Lamont, Michèle. 1995. "National Identity and National Boundary Patterns in France and the United States," *French Historical Studies* 19/2: 349–65.

———. 1998. *The World in Moral Order: Working Men Define the Boundaries of Race, Class and Citizenship.* Princeton, NJ: Princeton University Press.

———. 2000. *The Dignity of Working Men: Morality and the Boundaries of Race, Class, and Immigration.* Cambridge, MA: Harvard University Press.

Layton-Henry, Zig, ed., 1990. *The Political Rights of Migrant Workers in Western Europe.* London: Sage.

———. 1992. *The Politics of Race: Immigration, "Race" and "Race" Relations in Postwar Britain.* Oxford: Blackwell.

Legomsky, Stephen H. 1987. *Immigration and the Judiciary: Law and Politics in Britain and America.* Oxford: Clarendon.

Lévi-Strauss, Claude. 1952. *Race and History.* Paris: UNESCO.

Levitt, Peggy. 2001. *The Transnational Villagers.* Berkeley and Los Angeles: University of California Press.

Lochak, Danièle. 1985. *Etrangers: de quels droits?* Paris: Presses Universitaires de France.

Lusztig, Michael. 1996. *Risking Free Trade: The Politics of Trade in Britain, Canada, Mexico and the United States.* Pittsburgh, PA: University of Pittsburgh Press.

Markovits, Andrei S., and Simon Reich. 1997. *The German Predicament: Memory and Power in the New Europe.* Ithaca, NY: Cornell University Press.

Marshall, T. H. 1964. *Class, Citizenship and Social Development.* Garden City, NY: Doubleday.

Martin, Philip L. 1993. *Trade and Migration: NAFTA and Agriculture.* Washington, D.C.: Institute for International Economics.

———. 1994a. "The United States: Benign Neglect Toward Immigration," in Wayne A. Cornelius, Philip L. Martin, and James F. Hollifield, eds., *Controlling Immigration: A Global Perspective.* Stanford, CA: Stanford University Press.

_____. 1994b. "Germany: Reluctant Land of Immigration," in Wayne A. Cornelius, Philip L. Martin, and James F. Hollifield, eds., *Controlling Immigration: A Global Perspective*. Stanford, CA: Stanford University Press.

Martin, Philip L., Manolo Abella, and Christiane Kuptsch. 2006. *Managing Labor Migration in the Twenty-first Century*. New Haven, CT: Yale University Press.

Massey, Douglas S. 1987. *Return to Aztlan: The Social Processes of International Migration from Western Mexico*. Berkeley and Los Angeles: University of California Press.

_____. 1998. *Worlds in Motion: Understanding International Migration at the End of the Millennium*. Oxford: Oxford University Press.

_____, ed. 1999a. *Becoming American, American Becoming*. New York: Russell Sage.

_____. 1999b. "International Migration at the Dawn of the Twenty-First Century: The Role of the State," *Population and Development Review* 25/2: 303–22.

Massey, Douglas S., et al. 1993. "Theories of International Migration," *Population and Development Review* 19/3: 431–66.

Mayer, Nonna, and Pascal Perrineau, eds. 1996. *Le Front National à Découvert:* Paris: Presses de la FNSP.

McClain, Paula D., and Albert K. Karnig. 1990. "Black and Hispanic Socioeconomic and Political Competition," *American Political Science Review* 84: 535–45.

Messina, Anthony M. 1989. *Race and Party Competition in Britain*. Oxford: Clarendon Press.

_____. 1996. "The Not So Silent Revolution: Postwar Migration to Western Europe," *World Politics*. 49/1: 130–54.

Meyer, John W., and Michael T. Hannan, eds. 1979. *National Development and the World System: Educational, Economic and Political Change*. Chicago: University of Chicago Press.

Meyers, Eytan. 2004. *International Immigration Policy: A Theoretical and Comparative Analysis*. New York: Palgrave.

Miles, Robert. 1982. *Racism and Migrant Labour: A Critical Text*. London: Routledge.

Miller, Mark J. 1981. *Foreign Workers in Western Europe: An Emerging Political Force*. New York: Praeger.

_____. 1997. "International Migration and Security: Towards Transatlantic Convergence," in Emek M. Uçarer and Donald J. Puchala, eds., *Immigration into Western Societies: Problems and Policies*. London: Pinter.

Miller, Mark J., and Philip L. Martin. 1982. *Administering Foreign Worker Programs*. Lexington, MA: D.C. Heath.

Miller, Warren E., and J. Merrill Shanks. 1996. *The New American Voter*. Cambridge, MA: Harvard University Press.

Milner, Helen V. 1988. *Resisting Protectionism: Global Industries and the Politics of International Trade*. Princeton, NJ: Princeton University Press.

_____. 1997. *Interests, Institutions and Information: Domestic Politics and International Relations*. Princeton, NJ: Princeton University Press.

Minkenberg, Michael. 1992. "The New Right in Germany: The Transformation of Conservatism and the Extreme Right," *European Journal of Political Research* 22: 55–81.

Moch, Leslie Page. 1992. *Moving Europeans: Migration in Western Europe since 1650*. Bloomington: Indiana University Press.

Money, Jeannette. 1998. "Two Dimensional Aliens: Immigration Policy as a Two Dimensional Space," paper prepared for a conference on "Migration and the State," The New School for Social Research, New York.

_____. 1999. *Fences and Neighbors: The Geography of Immigration Control.* Ithaca, NY: Cornell University Press.

Moore, Barrington Jr. 1966. *Social Origins of Dictatorship and Democracy: Lord and Peasant in the Making of the Modern World.* Boston: Beacon Press.

Morris, Lydia. 2002. *Managing Migration: Civic Stratification and Migrants' Rights.* London: Routledge.

Mundell, Robert A. 1957. "International Trade and Factor Mobility," *American Economic Review* 47: 321–35.

Noiriel, Gèrard. 1988. *Le creuset français.* Paris: Seuil.

Norris, Pippa. 2005. *Radical Right: Voters and Parties in the Electoral Market.* Cambridge: Cambridge University Press.

Ohliger, Rainer, Karen Schönwälder, and Triadafilos Triadafilopoulos. 2003. *European Encounters: Migrants, Migration and European Societies since 1945.* Aldershot: Ashgate.

OECD. 2005. *Trends in International Migration.* Paris: Organization for Economic Cooperation and Development.

Park, Robert. 1928. "Human Migration and the Marginal Man," *American Journal of Sociology* 33: 881–893.

Perlmutter, Ted. 1996. "Bringing Parties Back In: Comments on 'Modes of Immigration Politics in Liberal Democratic Societies,'" *International Migration Review* 30: 375–88.

Pickus, Noah M. J., ed. 1998. *Immigration & Citizenship in the 21st Century.* Lanham, MD: Rowman and Littlefield.

_____. 2005. *True Faith and Allegiance: Immigration and American Civic Nationalism.* Princeton, NJ: Princeton University Press.

Piore, Michael J. 1979. *Birds of Passage: Migrant Labor in Industrial Societies.* Cambridge: Cambridge University Press.

Portes, Alejandro. 1996. "Transnational Communities: Their Emergence and Significance in the Contemporary World-System," in R. P. Korzeniewidcz and W. C. Smith, eds., *Latin America in the World Economy.* Westport, CT: Greenwood.

_____. 1997. "Immigration Theory for a New Century," *International Migration Review* 31/4: 799–825.

Portes, Alejandro, and Robert L. Bach. 1985. *Latin Journey: Cuban and Mexican Immigrants to the United States.* Berkeley and Los Angeles: University of California Press.

Portes, Alejandro, and Ruben Rumbaut. 1996. *Immigrant America: A Portrait.* Berkeley and Los Angeles: University of California Press.

Portes, Alejandro, and Min Zhou. 1993. "The New Second Generation: Segmented Assimilation and Its Variants among Post-1965 Immigrant Youth," *Annals of the American Academy of Political and Social Science* 530: 74–96.

Rath, Jan. 1988. "Political Action of Immigrants in the Netherlands: Class or Ethnicity?" *European Journal of Political Research* 16: 623–44.

Rex, John, and R. Moore. 1967. *Race, Community and Conflict.* Oxford: Oxford University Press.

Rogers, Rosemarie, ed. 1985. *Guests Come to Stay: The Effects of European Labor Migration on Sending and Receiving Countries.* Boulder, CO: Westview.

Rosenau, James N. 1990. *Turbulence in World Politics: A Theory of Change and Continuity.* Princeton, NJ: Princeton University Press.

Rosenblum, Marc R. 2004. *The Transnational Politics of U.S. Immigration Policy.* La Jolla: University of California, San Diego Center for Comparative Immigration Studies.

Rudolph, Christopher W. 1998. "Globalization, Sovereignty and Migration: A Conceptual Framework," *UCLA Journal of International Law and Foreign Affairs* 3/2: 325–55.

———. 2006. *National Security and Immigration: Policy Development in the United States and Western Europe since 1945*. Stanford, CA: Stanford University Press.

Ruggie, John Gerard, ed. 1993. *Multilateralism Matters: The Theory and Practice of an Institutional Form*. New York: Columbia University Press.

———. 1998. *Constructing the World Polity: Essays on International Institutionalization*. New York: Routledge.

Russell, Sharon Stanton. 1986. "Remittances from International Migration. A Review in Perspective," *World Development* 41/6: 677–96.

Sadiq, Kamal. 2005. "When States Prefer Non-Citizens Over Citizens: Conflict Over Illegal Immigration into Malaysia," *International Studies Quarterly* 49: 101–22.

Said, Edward W. 1993. *Culture and Imperialism*. New York: Knopf.

Sassen, Saskia. 1988. *The Mobility of Capital and Labor*. Cambridge: Cambridge University Press.

———. 1991. *The Global City: New York, London, Tokyo*. Princeton, NJ: Princeton University Press.

———. 1996. *Losing Control? Sovereignty in an Age of Globalization*. New York: Columbia University Press.

———. 1999. *Guests and Aliens*. New York: The New Press.

———. 2006. *Territory, Authority, Rights: From Medieval to Global Assemblages*. Princeton, NJ: Princeton University Press.

Schain, Martin A. 1988. "Immigration and Change in the French Party System," *European Journal of Political Research* 16: 597–621.

———. 1990. "Immigration and Politics," in Peter A. Hall et al., eds., *Developments in French Politics*. London: Macmillan.

Schlesinger, Arthur Jr. 1992. *The Disuniting of America*. New York: W. W. Norton.

Schmitter, Barbara E. 1979. "Immigration and Citizenship in West Germany and Switzerland," unpublished Ph.D. dissertation, University of Chicago.

Schmitter Heisler, Barbara. 1986. "Immigrant Settlement and the Structure of Emergent Immigrant Communities in Western Europe," *The Annals* 485: 76–86.

———. 1993. "Review of Hollifield, *Immigrants, Markets and States*," in *Work and Occupations* 20/4: 479–80.

Schnapper, Dominique. 1998. *La relation à l'autre*. Paris: Gallimard.

Schuck, Peter H. 1998. *Citizens, Strangers and In-Betweens: Essays on Immigration and Citizenship*. Boulder, CO: Westview.

Schuck, Peter H., and Rogers Smith. 1985. *Citizenship without Consent*. New Haven, CT: Yale University Press.

Shain, Yossi. 1989. *The Frontier of Loyalty: Political Exiles in the Age of the Nation–State*. Middletown, CT: Wesleyan University Press.

Shanks, Cheryl. 2000. *Immigration and the Politics of American Sovereignty, 1890–1990*. Ann Arbor: University of Michigan Press.

Shaw, Malcolm N. 1997. *International Law*. Cambridge: Cambridge University Press.

Simon, Julian. 1989. *The Economic Consequences of Immigration*. Oxford: Blackwell.

Skerry, Peter. 1993. *Mexican Americans: The Ambivalent Minority*. New York: Free Press.

———. 2000. *Counting on the Census: Race, Group Identity, and the Evasion of Politics*. Washington, D.C.: Brookings Institution Press.

Smith, Rogers. 1997. *Civic Ideals: Conflicting Visions of Citizenship in U.S. History*. New Haven, CT: Yale University Press.

Soysal, Yasemin N. 1994. *Limits of Citizenship: Migrants and Postnational Membership in Europe*. Chicago: University of Chicago Press.

Stark, Oded, 1991. *The Migration of Labor*. Cambridge, MA: Basil Blackwell.

Stolper, Wolfgang Friedrich, and Paul A. Samuelson. 1941. "Protection and Real Wages," *Review of Economic Studies* 9: 58–73.

Straubhaar, Thomas. 1988. *On the Economics of International Migration*. Bern and Stuttgart: Verlag Paul Haupt.

Tapinos, Georges. 1974. *L'Economie des migrations internationales*. Paris: Colin.

Teitelbaum, Michael S. 1980. "Right Versus Right: Immigration and Refugee Policy in the United States," *Foreign Affairs* 59/1: 2–59.

———. 1984. "Immigration, Refugees and Foreign Policy," *International Organization* 38/3: 429–50.

Teitelbaum, Michael S., and Myron Weiner. 1995. *Threatened Peoples, Threatened Borders*. New York: W. W. Norton.

Thielemann, Eiko. 2003. "European Burden-Sharing and Forced Migration," *Journal of Refugee Studies* 16/3: 223-35.

Thränhardt, Dietrich. 1993. "Die Ursprünge von Rassismus und Fremdenfeinlichkeit in der Konkurrenzdemokratie," *Leviathan* 21/3: 336–57.

———, ed. 1996. *Europe: A New Immigration Continent*. Münster: Lit Verlag.

Tichenor, Daniel J. 1994. "The Politics of Immigration Reform in the United States," *Polity* 26/3: 333–62.

———. 1996. "Regulating Community: Race, Immigration Policy and American Political Development," unpublished Ph.D. dissertation, Brandeis University.

———. 2002. *The Politics of Immigration Control in America*. Princeton, NJ: Princeton University Press.

Tilly, Charles, ed., 1975. *The Formation of National States in Western Europe*. Princeton, NJ: Princeton University Press.

Todaro, Michael P. 1976. *Internal Migration in Developing Countries: A Review of Theory, Evidence, Methodology and Research Priorities*. Geneva: International Labor Office.

Tolbert, Caroline J., and Rodney E. Hero. 1996. "Race/Ethnicity and Direct Democracy: An Analysis of California's Illegal Immigration Initiative," *Journal of Politics* 58/3: 806–18.

Torpey, John. 1998. "Coming and Going: On the State's Monopolization of the Legitimate 'Means of Movement,'" *Sociological Theory* 16/3: 239–59.

Tribalat, Michèle. 1995. *Faire France*. Paris: La Découverte.

Turner, Bryan S. ed. 1993. *Citizenship and Social Theory*. London: Sage Publications.

Uçarer, Emek M. 1997. "Europe's Search for Policy: The Harmonization of Asylum Policy and European Integration," in Emek M. Uçarer and Donald J. Puchala, eds., *Immigration into Western Societies: Problems and Policies*. London: Pinter.

Uçarer, Emek M., and Sandra Lavenex, eds. 2002. *Migration and the Externalities of European Integration*. Lanham, MD: Lexington Books.

Ueda, Reed, ed. 2006. *A Companion to American Immigration*. Oxford: Blackwell.

Waldinger, Roger, and David Fitzgerald. 2004. "Transnationalism in Question," *American Journal of Sociology* 109/5: 1177–95.

Wallerstein, Immanuel. 1976. *The Modern World System*. New York: Academic Press.

Waltz, Kenneth N. 1979. *Theory of International Politics*. Reading, MA: Addison-Wesley.

Walzer, Michael. 1983. *Spheres of Justice: A Defense of Pluralism and Equality*. New York: Basic Books.

Watts, Julie R. 2002. *Immigration Policy and the Challenge of Globalization: Unions and Employers in Unlikely Alliance*. Ithaca, NY: Cornell University Press.

Weber, Max. 1947. *The Theory of Social and Economic Organization*. New York: Oxford University Press.

Weil, Patrick. 1991. *La France et ses étrangers: L'aventure d'une politique de l'immigration 1938–1991*. Paris: Calmann-Lévy.

———. 1998. "The State Matters: Immigration Control in Developed Countries," New York: United Nations, Department of Social and Economic Affairs, Population Division.

———. 2002. *Qu'est-ce qu'un français? histoire de la nationalité française depuis la Révolution*. Paris: Bernard Grasset.

———. 2005. *La République et sa diversité: immigration, integrations, discriminations*. Paris: Editions du Seuil.

Weiner, Myron, ed. 1993. *International Migration and Security*. Boulder, CO: Westview.

———. 1995. *The Global Migration Crisis: Challenge to States and to Human Rights*. New York: HarperCollins.

Weiner, Myron, and Sharon Stanton Russell, eds. 2001. *Demography and National Security*. New York: Berghahn Books.

Weiner, Myron, and Michael S. Teitelbaum. 2001. *Political Demography, Demographic Engineering*. New York: Berghahn Books.

Wihtol de Wenden, Catherine. 1988. *Les immigrés et la politique*. Paris: Presses de la FNSP.

Wilson, James Q., ed. 1980. *The Politics of Regulation*. New York: Harper.

Zolberg, Aristide R. 1981. "International Migration in Political Perspective," in Mary M. Kritz, Charles B. Keely, and Silvano M. Tomasi, eds., *Global Trends in Migration: Theory and Research in International Population Movements*. New York: Center for Migration Studies.

———. 1999. "Matters of State: Theorizing Immigration Policy," in Douglas Massey, ed., *Becoming American, American Becoming*. New York: Russell Sage.

———. 2006. *A Nation by Design: Immigration Policy in the Fashioning of America*. Cambridge, MA: Harvard University Press and Russell Sage.

Zolberg, Aristide R., Astri Suhrke, and Sergio Aguayo. 1989. *Escape from Violence: Conflict and the Refugee Crisis in the Developing World*. New York: Oxford University Press.

CHAPTER 8

Law and the Study of Migration
Peter H. Schuck

Law has always borne, perhaps vaingloriously, the high prestige of a learned, esteemed profession operating at the center of policy-making, indeed legitimating it. The legal academy also boasts antiquity, having been established in English and Italian universities in medieval times. Yet, despite law's distinguished pedigree, American institutions of higher learning long resisted including it among their academic departments. For this reason, American law schools developed first as independent institutions outside the traditional college or university setting. When the universities did deign to include law schools during the nineteenth century, their welcome was usually a cool one—at least until they realized that legal education could be delivered with large classes, no laboratories, and, often, part-time teachers. Better still, it produced prosperous alumni. Thus it could be a "profit center," cross-subsidizing other, less worldly fields of study (Stevens 1983).

The academy's long disparagement of law reflected a number of considerations, some principled, some not. A principled reason was that law is an intensely practical, cosmopolitan, prescriptive discipline seeking to serve lawyers in practice and to influence the daily behavior of courts, legislators, regulators, and private actors. In this view law, unlike many other academic departments, aspired neither to develop new objective knowledge about the world nor to recover old cultural artifacts and meanings.

This view of law was largely true when it was first advanced in the nineteenth century, but even then it ignored a long, rich, and often fruitful tradition of jurisprudential theory. Jurisprudence was concerned with the nature of law, rules, equity, and justice; with the distinction between legal positivism, natural law, and with other normative legal theories; and other foundational legal ideas that together constitute the philosophy of law. These are theoretical questions, by any standard.

By the late nineteenth century, legal scholarship had grown more ambitious. A scientific approach, associated with Harvard Law School Dean Christopher

Columbus Langdell, sought to infer the corpus of general legal rules from the reasoning used by courts in deciding a mass of specific case decisions. He hoped to use such reasoning, which the judicial methodology often obscured, to predict outcomes in future cases. Langdell's system was derided by many— most famously, by Oliver Wendell Holmes—as an excessively abstract, deductive system ill-suited to a rich understanding of law. Inspired by Holmes's critique of Langdell's case method, the so-called Legal Realists cut another channel of legal scholarship during the 1920s. Many Realist law professors and judges, who foreshadowed many of today's "critical legal studies" scholars, emphasized the irreducibly political and subjective motives for decisions; they doubted that any theoretically valid science of law could or should be developed.

Some other Realists, however, were committed empiricists who held that carefully gathering facts about legal phenomena in the real world would demystify or even discredit many existing legal rules and theories while perhaps justifying others. They and their successors in the legal academy advanced hypotheses about the conduct and decisions of judges and other legal actors and institutions, and then sought to test the hypotheses against these facts. But this empirical tradition has always been exceptional among legal scholars, most of whom devoted themselves instead to analyzing and assessing case law. Almost two decades ago, I lamented (and sought to explain) the relative dearth of legal scholarship concerned with the kind of hypothesis testing and cumulative theory building that is commonplace among social scientists (Schuck 1989). Happily, this situation is changing; empiricism is flourishing in both legal studies and in its closely allied fields, hopefully forging new areas of public policy consensus (Heise 1999; McGinnis 2006).

Theory and theory testing are more prominent in legal scholarship today for an important reason. Although autonomous theories of law have little currency outside of the field of the philosophy of law (jurisprudence), both academic lawyers and practicing lawyers today increasingly appropriate theories drawn from other disciplines. These theoretical borrowings (often called "Law and ...")[1] usually rely on economics and political science but they also include sociology, evolutionary biology, literary theory, game theory, history, and other fields. Skeptics doubt their relevance to many legal phenomena, and also doubt whether lawyers, policymakers, and judges have understood and applied them competently (Posner 1999). In any event, the academic study of law, particularly but not exclusively at the elite institutions, is today a theoretical, eclectic, even parasitic enterprise; it depends on other disciplines for many of its foundational concepts, methodological tools, analytical constructs, and predictive hypotheses.[2]

Whatever the intellectual history and lineaments of legal theory, its most important contribution to the study of migration is to provide insights about how legal rules, institutions, processes, and decisions—their nature, behavior, competence, consequences, and legitimacy—affect the movement of people within and across national borders. Because the law in action and the law in people's minds frequently diverge from the law on the books—a trichotomy discussed in the next section—legal scholars' careful descriptions and analyses of legal phenomena can also help to refine, and in some cases debunk, more general social scientific theories, empirical claims, and applications.

Much of this chapter is devoted to explicating how legal analysis can advance this understanding. I first discuss how law shapes the incentives that drive the decisions of potential migrants. I then turn to the more specific modalities, structures, and institutions through which law attempts to influence decisions and behavior. A third section discusses why contemporary immigration law's enforcement mission has faltered, while also suggesting how this ostensible failure actually serves certain latent social functions. Finally, I consider whether Americans perceive much illegal immigration as a victimless offense and discuss how this perception affects immigration enforcement and politics. In the spirit of this book's comparative and theoretical ambitions, I emphasize throughout the general structures and processes of law that influence migration. I discuss detailed doctrines and operational realities of immigration law only insofar as they help to illuminate the more theoretical claims.

HOW LAW AFFECTS MIGRATION FLOWS

Few migrants know much about law and even fewer would point to law as a major factor in their migration decisions. Nevertheless, law influences those decisions at every turn. Most fundamentally, law defines individuals' rights to property and economic activity, political participation, physical security, religious and cultural identity, and family relationships. The content and configuration of these extra-immigration rights help to structure the set of opportunities that people can exploit in their countries of origin. The greater those opportunities, the less individuals will want to migrate, *ceteris paribus*; the emotional links that hold people in their native land are as powerful as any we know; only deep social convulsions can shatter them. Even when such convulsions occur, the grip of old attachments and the fears of the unknown are powerful reasons to remain; this inertia can only be overcome by the promise of far greater opportunities in possible destination states, opportunities that the law helps to construct. Potential migrants who enjoy the luxury of calculation and choice compare these opportunity sets before deciding whether, when, where, how, and with which others they will migrate.

But law not only shapes individuals' incentives and decisions to migrate; it also constrains them. Some states impose significant restrictions on the right to depart or make it practically difficult for would-be migrants to exercise that right. All states seek to limit immigration and to enforce those limits through legal and extra-legal techniques. Because legal immigrants can naturalize in the United States relatively easily and U.S.-born children of both legal and illegal immigrants enjoy constitutionally protected birthright citizenship (Schuck 1998:185–86), the law defining the categories of legal immigrants, and the law enforcement processes that are used to exclude illegal ones, in effect determine who will constitute the future stock of Americans. In the United States, as in other states, the legal barriers to immigration—and in that sense, to citizenship—have become more restrictive as a matter of both formal law and informal practice (Hailbronner, Martin, and Motomura 1998). In principle, international law protects certain rights of migrants, particularly those of Convention refugees, but these rights are much honored in the breach (Fitzpatrick 1994). Treaties, a species of international law, often regulate important aspects of migration between the subscribing states such as employment, trade, taxation, criminal prosecution, extradition, access to consular assistance, and the like. The international law governing migration, however, is even more difficult to enforce than is domestic immigration law, which is notoriously under-enforced (Schuck and Williams 1999).

Although legal commentators understandably emphasize states' restrictive immigration laws, it is also true that some states use the law to "compete" for immigrants—at least for those who possess valuable skills, investment resources, and attractive political attributes. Industrialized countries like Canada, Australia, and the United States, for example, often target the same groups of potential immigrants—those who possess desired skills in short supply or are willing to invest in job-creating enterprises in the destination country. In a similar spirit, American refugee law traditionally favored those from Communist-bloc countries and the Middle East. Notwithstanding efforts in the Refugee Act of 1980 to eliminate this bias, it still favors those fleeing certain countries for certain reasons (such as China's one-child policy or Russia's treatment of Jews and evangelical Christians).

None of this, of course, is meant to suggest that law is the principal force shaping migration flows—economic and family factors share that distinction—but only that it regulates many (and influences the remainder) of the social conditions that figure so prominently in individual and group migration decisions. Specifically, the kinds of legal systems associated with liberal property, integration, and human rights regimes exhibit powerful tendencies to attract immigration and discourage emigration.[3]

Before discussing how legal rules, institutions, processes, and decisions influence migration, I wish to note an elementary distinction in legal sociology developed by one of the first Legal Realists, Roscoe Pound, between the "law on the books" and the "law in action"—to which I have added a third category, the "law in their minds" (Schuck 1994:904). The importance of distinguishing among these three aspects of legal consciousness in the immigration field can be measured by the immense gaps that separate each of them from the others. This trichotomy reflects the fact that the law as formally enacted ("law on the books") almost always differs from the law as actually implemented ("law in action"). We shall see that this difference, while true to some extent of all legal and social systems, is particularly great in the immigration system. Consequently, many groups of actors in the immigration system see different aspects of the system or see the same aspects differently ("law in their minds").

These perspectival differences affect immigration law and policy in important ways. For example, immigrants view aspects of the immigration experience differently than people in their communities of origin do, despite the close, enduring linkages between the two groups (Levitt 1997). Immigration officials and the (at least nominally) independent immigration judges constantly differ about the bond levels for detainable aliens (Gilboy 1988) and also about the process and standards for immigrant detention and removal decisions (Schuck 1997). A fundamental mismatch of resources, incentives, and perspectives between the federal immigration agency (the Immigration and Naturalization Service [INS] in the Department of Justice until 2003, now the Bureau of Immigration and Customs Enforcement [ICE] in the Department of Homeland Security) and state and local law enforcement agencies seriously compromises the apprehension, processing, and removal of criminal aliens (Kobach 2005; Schuck and Williams 1999). The State Department consular officials who make initial visa decisions often interpret immigration law differently than do Department of Homeland Security and Department of Labor officials; indeed, consular officials differ even with their own bureaucratic superiors (Nafziger 1991). Voluntary agencies on which the ICE heavily relies to help administer refugee, amnesty, and other programs view their roles differently than does the agency; legal immigrants and their undocumented co-ethnics often disagree about how the law should be applied (Schuck 1995). Federal trial judges encounter immigration law in a different context than appellate judges. And so forth.

The most important perspectival difference concerns illegal immigration; the "law on the books," the immigration agency, and American public opinion vigorously condemn it, yet the "law in action" manifestly countenances it: the number of undocumented aliens in the United States in 2006 was estimated at 11 to 12 million and rising. This radical disjunction of views—elsewhere I have called it a "political disconnect" (Schuck 2007a) —helps to render intelligible much about immigration law and policy that might otherwise seem odd or inexplicable. I explore the implications of this disjunction in the final section of the chapter.

THE FORMS, PROCESSES, AND INSTITUTIONS OF IMMIGRATION LAW

In the complex immigration control system constituted by these different groups, law confers authority in many different forms and deploys that authority in diverse ways. The situations of actual and putative migrants vary enormously, and any rational and humane immigration policy will want to take many of these factors into account in determining immigrants' legal status. For this reason, immigration policymakers have chosen to make the law ambiguous and open-ended on many crucial points, leaving considerable room for interpretation and specialized judgment by the officials who administer the law in the first instance, and, in the event of appeal, by appellate administrative tribunals and federal judges. The law thus grants broad discretion to both low-level and high-level decision makers. Even after the enactment of the Illegal Immigration Reform and Immigrant Responsibility Act of 1996 (IIRIRA), a landmark statute that sharply limited immigration officials' authority to grant discretionary relief from removal,[4] the agency continues to enjoy enormous discretion. Indeed, even ranking members of Congress who sponsored IIRIRA's harshest provisions—Lamar Smith, for example—have pressed the agency to exercise more discretion in the interests of a more humanitarian application of the law (Lipton 1999). In August 1999, the INS responded to these pressures by agreeing to release, under administrative criteria, some detainees (including some asylum claimants, as well as some others who cannot as a practical matter be removed) whom the agency previously had insisted could not be released under the rigid provisions of IIRIRA.

Thus, immigration inspectors and enforcement personnel, like police officers, drug enforcement agents, schoolteachers, social workers, and other "street-level bureaucrats" (Lipsky 1980), are the crucial decision makers. As a result, many conventional assumptions about bureaucratic authority, drawn from the Weberian ideal-type, simply do not apply to immigration policy. For example, much of what low-level immigration officials do is invisible, both literally and figuratively, to their bureaucratic superiors, and even visible conduct is often uncontrollable through either the ordinary structure of hierarchical rules or the economy of incentives. In effect, power over day-to-day immigration decisions runs bottom-up instead of top-down.

The unusual operational autonomy enjoyed by low-level immigration officials is further protected by certain legal principles peculiar to the immigration field. The most important of these is the so-called plenary power doctrine, which was announced by the U.S. Supreme Court more than a century ago (*Chinese Exclusion Case* 1889) and has been reaffirmed many times since despite the absence of any clear textual basis in the Constitution and despite repeated criticism by legal scholars. The plenary power doctrine holds that Congress's power over immigration policy is comprehensive, complete, and all but immune to judicial review for unconstitutionality (Legomsky 2005:103–237). Invoking this doctrine or relying on other principles of self-restraint or limited jurisdiction, the federal courts have abjectly deferred to immigration officials' decisions (Schuck 1998:29–31). When one adds to this very broad area of autonomy the fact that the immigrants the agency is supposed to regulate and serve do not vote, as well as the more general principle of federal sovereign immunity that largely protects the agency and its officials against possible monetary liability for illegal conduct (Schuck 1983),[5] one can begin to understand why the agency has been particularly lawless and characterized by chronic administrative failures (Schuck 1998:87; Schuck 1999:88; Schuck and Williams 1999). During the early to mid-1980s, some federal judges issued injunctions in order to bring the agency into compliance with mainstream constitutional and administrative law principles (Schuck 1998:chap. 2). These judicial interventions, however, were spasmodic at best and of doubtful effectiveness, and appellate courts subsequently rejected some of them. Most important, IIRIRA imposed severe, unprecedented, and possibly unconstitutional limitations on the courts' power to review the agency's enforcement or discretionary decisions, as well as on the judicial power to issue injunctions and entertain class actions against it.

Despite these limitations on judicial review, a number of federal courts have sought to rein in the lawlessness of the immigration bureaucracy. The most dramatic example is the Seventh Circuit Court of Appeals, which has repeatedly castigated the Board of Immigration Appeals (BIA), an administrative court that remains within the Department of Justice, for the BIA's habitual lawlessness, and has done so in terms that are perhaps unprecedented in the annals of judicial decisions reviewing agency action. Typical is a 2005 decision written by Judge Richard Posner of that court, who is perhaps the most formidable legal mind in the federal judiciary, if not the entire United States. After noting that his court had reversed the BIA in "a staggering 40 percent" of the cases that year, and quoting from the court's many past rebukes of the BIA, Posner reversed it yet again. He observed, "We are not required to permit [the alien in question] to be ground to bits in the bureaucratic mill against the will of Congress" (Posner 2005).

The sources of the ICE's operational autonomy over immigration enforcement are not merely legal; they are also political. Until the 1980s, when illegal migration first became a prominent policy issue in Washington, the INS was an obscure organization of little interest to anyone other than the chairmen and key members of the Judiciary subcommittees in Congress that exercised legislative and oversight jurisdiction over immigration matters. Except for the special post–World War II and cold-war refugee programs, no major immigration legislation was enacted between 1924 and 1952; the next major reform was enacted in 1965 and another, lesser change in 1978. Administrative initiatives by the INS were also rare and congressional oversight hearings were rarer still. This inactivity reflected an understanding between key Judiciary Committee members and the INS commissioner that the agency would do little but serve as the members' malleable instruments of policy and patronage. Not surprisingly, media coverage of immigration issues during this period was limited (Schuck 1975).

All of this changed in the 1980s, of course, but even in the supercharged immigration politics of recent years, the agency has continued to enjoy freedom of action (or inaction), and bureaucratic growth—in budget, legal authority, and personnel—that most of its federal agency counterparts can only envy.[6] Even the agency's chronically illegal conduct and abject administrative failures, however, have not stemmed its dramatic growth since the early 1990s. Because immigrants are ineligible to vote, immigration politics is conducted through other organized interests—growers, other employers, unions, state and local governments, religious and ethnic groups, immigration lawyers—and the congressional allies of these interests. A remarkably diverse coalition of interest groups concerned with immigration policy exerts substantial influence today, predominantly in a proimmigration direction.[7] Despite the autonomy conferred on the government by the plenary power doctrine, some lower federal courts continue to require the agency to extend additional protections to aliens.

THE "FAILURE" OF IMMIGRATION ENFORCEMENT

The agency's relative institutional autonomy has produced a retarded organizational learning process, an attenuated feedback loop that delays responses to change, which in turn contributes to the agency's chronic incompetence and lack of accountability. In a study, John Williams and I demonstrate this sluggishness in the context of the agency's much belated and still-inadequate program to remove criminal aliens despite the agency's great advantages: a continuing, clear, and emphatic congressional priority for the swift removal of criminal aliens, the issue's high political profile throughout the United States, and the increased legal and fiscal resources provided to the agency. Although Congress deserves most of the blame for this missed (or delayed) opportunity, the agency's many administrative failures also contributed to the inadequate outcome (Schuck and Williams 1999).

The system's inability to remove most criminal aliens, however, is no isolated occurrence; rather, it should be seen as a particularly egregious instance of a much more pervasive failure by Congress and the agency to design, support, and implement a legal and policy framework equal to the immense challenge of contemporary migration. Immigration control, like most other public policy goals, is a far more complex and intractable problem today than in the past. For a variety of technological, geopolitical, military, psychological, economic, and other reasons, the delicate balance of factors influencing potential migrants' behavior has shifted somewhat in favor of a decision to migrate. More people are moving across national borders, and all but a relative handful lack legal permission to reside in their destination states. Often expelled by their own rulers and assisted by others who hope to profit by smuggling them, migrants have grown bolder, more determined, and more resourceful. Short-term ebbs and flows aside, migratory pressures are bound to increase in response to population growth, better information, cheaper communication and transportation, social chaos, and economic mismanagement in many source countries, as well as the greater work opportunities, more stable politics, and strong ethnic communities in the United States and other leading receiving countries.

The control strategies deployed by receiving states, however, have not kept pace with these changes. In recent years, European states have devised new restrictive techniques, including readmission agreements, detention, buffer zones, return policies, agreements to speed (and defeat) the processing of asylum claims, and many others[8] (Hailbronner, Martin, and Motomura 1997, 1998). *Mutatis mutandis,* the United States has done likewise, adopting harsh detention, interdiction, and other control while also dramatically increasing the Border Patrol's physical and technological presence along the long border with Mexico. Despite an increase to 11,000 Border Patrol agents plus approximately 6000 National Guard troops in the summer of 2006, the flow of undocumented migrants to the United States has temporarily declined but certainly not stopped, although the flow may of course have been even greater absent these measures (Swarns 2006). The number of undocumented aliens in Europe has risen sharply in recent years, and the number residing in the United States has reached to a level approximately double that which prevailed in 1986 when Congress, declaring an illegal migration crisis, enacted employer sanctions and other far-reaching enforcement measures.

Today, the obstacles to effective immigration control are even more formidable. Not only are undocumented migrants more numerous and resourceful, the receiving states' ability to respond to the new flows aggressively and effectively is more constrained. The growth of ethnic communities in the receiving states makes enforcement more difficult; these communities are better able to exert domestic political pressure against ICE enforcement or in favor of securing legal status for their co-ethnics. Ethnic communities also facilitate illegal migrants' ability to melt into the community where they can live and work illegally without detection by the authorities. New legal constraints limit what receiving states may do in the name of immigration control, as constitutional courts and international tribunals and instruments affirm rights that even illegal migrants can legitimately assert against the destination states (Jacobson 1996).

Most of these new rights are merely procedural in nature; they prescribe the processes that governments must employ before they may remove aliens but seldom entitle aliens to remain. Similarly, refugee law limits a state's ability to return (*refoule*) asylees to another state in which they may face persecution, but this does not confer a substantive right to remain (although as a practical matter it may enable the asylee to do so). Occasionally, however, the law may go further and grant aliens a new substantive right. One important example is the U.S. Supreme Court's decision holding that Texas could not deny basic public education to undocumented alien children even though this denial was part of an explicit state strategy to discourage illegal migration (*Plyler* v. *Doe* 1982).[9] Other examples are recent amnesty laws granting certain undocumented aliens from some Central American countries the right to seek discretionary relief from removal, which Congress eliminated in 1996 (Schuck 2007a).

But even "merely" procedural rights can drastically alter migrants' incentive structure. Because it is costly for the ICE to undertake effective enforcement proceedings against illegal aliens and even more costly to detain them until their removal can be effectuated, the agency allows many who could be apprehended and removed to remain at large or (which is much the same thing) it apprehends but then releases them pending completion of removal proceedings, whereupon most abscond and disappear into the population. Because their primary objective is to work in the United States, procedural delays and release pending removal enable them to gain most of what they migrated for in the first place (Schuck 1998:chap. 2).

Finally, a growing public acceptance of human rights principles makes it harder for liberal democratic states to remove (or even detain) aliens whose circumstances arouse widespread media attention, public sympathy, or even solidarity expressed through civil disobedience and sanctuary movements. Compared to these compelling political and humanitarian claims, the legalistic arguments advanced by immigration officials often seem petty, hollow, even immoral. Confronted by a courageous, hard-working migrant's well-publicized human drama, liberal societies are strongly tempted to make room for one more. Defense of the larger, inevitably anonymous "system" against such heartrending claims falls largely to the beleaguered, often justly criticized immigration bureaucracy. Even today, of course, most migrants do not arouse this kind of public support, but are unceremoniously detained and removed. Still, the relatively few who do manage to beat the system and elicit criticism of the immigration agency for its heartlessness disproportionately weaken the agency's enforcement incentives in future cases.

These new constraints, of course, hardly leave the receiving states defenseless in the face of the rising migratory pressures. Strong domestic economic and political imperatives impel even liberal, democratic polities committed to free trade policies to tightly control migration, protect national labor markets and resist the more speculative, often more diffuse claims of globalism (Hollifield 1998). Stepped-up border enforcement and crackdowns on undocumented workers in the interior are popular policies in all receiving countries, but state implementation of migration controls has nonetheless become far more costly and problematic. Indeed, it is difficult to imagine a politically viable policy approach to the control of illegal migration that the United States has not already tried or seriously considered.

Confronted by these dynamic external conditions, internal social pressures, and political constraints, immigration enforcers must have nimble and flexible regulatory instruments at their disposal in order to pursue optimal control strategies. Yet, flexibility is precisely what the law denies them. In the United States, constitutionally required separation of powers, fierce competition for influence in the immigration policy domain, mutual suspicion among the various participants, a legal-political culture emphasizing individual rights, and mistrust of public authority all combine to favor rigid criteria and procedures designed to limit official discretion. This rigidity is especially perverse in the important area of immigrant labor certification, where slow bureaucratic processes force employers and workers competing in increasingly dynamic labor markets to devise informal, often illegal, stratagems in order to circumvent legal obstacles and get the job done.

Earlier I observed that immigration law gives agency officials much discretion—and so it does, but it is a matter of degree. Canada and some other parliamentary systems, for example, accord immigration officials even broader discretion, allowing them to apply multifactor point systems for some admission categories and then to adjust admissions criteria as political and economic conditions change. This greater flexibility is possible, of course, because the controlling legislative coalition and the political executives are members of the same ruling group, which under a parliamentary system tends to minimize the conflict and suspicion among them and thus facilitates more trust and greater willingness to delegate discretionary authority to administrators.

But to speak of the failure of immigration enforcement in the United States as I have is a bit too facile and glib. Official behavior that appears on its face to be ineffective may actually serve a deeper, more latent social function (to use Robert Merton's phrase). It may help us to maintain certain cherished myths in the face of contradictory facts we are reluctant to recognize. To put it another way, we may prefer to think that we have certain goals and have failed to achieve them than to acknowledge the possibility that these are not really our goals or, worse still, that the goals were not worth striving for in the first place.

Like the wars on drugs and crime, the battle against illegal immigration and the political rhetoric that it inspires lend themselves to this kind of collective self-delusion. Illegal immigration, after all, confers significant benefits on almost all concerned,[10] while the costs of eliminating it (in terms of enforcement resources, opportunity costs, civil liberties, foreign-policy interests, and so on) would be manifestly prohibitive. This means that the socially optimal level of illegal migration—the policy that balances its social benefits and costs—is far greater than zero. Indeed, in a nation of almost 300 million people, the optimal level of illegal immigration may even exceed today's estimated level of approximately 11 to 12 million undocumented residents, with 250,000 more added each year to the more or less permanent population.[11]

But for the government even to acknowledge that it countenances this amount of illegal immigration, much less that this might be a desirable policy, is politically unthinkable.[12] If so, the "failure" of immigration enforcement serves an important latent function by sustaining the attractive, reassuring, ennobling myth that the rule of law is a paramount, priceless ideal that we relentlessly pursue. At the same time, it obscures the reality that our actual goal is the less exalted one of enriching ourselves by condoning illegality and then concealing this fact beneath a veil of hypocritical high-mindedness.

ILLEGAL IMMIGRATION AS A VICTIMLESS CRIME

I have discussed the limitations on immigration law's effectiveness imposed by legal rules, institutions, processes, and interest group politics. Perhaps the most profound limitation, however, arises out of the tensions created by Americans' complex attitudes toward immigration, their growing attraction to the ideology and imagery of human rights, and the impersonal immigration law on the books.

Americans harbor ambivalent or conflicting attitudes toward immigration and immigrants, attitudes in which they tend to draw subtle but important distinctions. According to survey data, for example, Americans like immigrants more than they like immigration, favor past immigration more than recent immigration, prefer legal immigrants to illegal ones, prefer refugees to other immigrants, support immigrants' access to educational and health benefits but not to welfare or Social Security, and believe that immigrants' distinctive cultures have contributed positively to American life and that diversity continues to strengthen American society. At the same time, they overwhelmingly resist any conception of multiculturalism that discourages immigrants from quickly learning and using the English language. Americans treasure their immigrant roots, yet they are convinced that current immigration levels are either too high or should not be increased (Schuck 2007a). Recent polling evidence indicates that this attitudinal pattern continues (Pew Research Center 2006).

The law exhibits no such ambivalence.[13] It treats illegal entry as a crime justifying the state in imposing tough, far-reaching sanctions, which may include fines, imprisonment, and long-term exile for such aliens and fines or imprisonment for their employers. In December 2005, the House approved a bill that would make mere illegal presence in the United States a felony; even assisting one who is illegally present would be a felony. Many citizens, however, are reluctant to view ordinary illegal border crossing[14] (as distinguished, say, from smuggling illegal migrants, drug trafficking, or other serious criminal activity) as a reprehensible crime warranting harsh penalties. Indeed, the same illegal immigration that the law categorically condemns may reasonably be regarded by citizens as a socially efficient offense (i.e., one whose aggregate social benefits exceed its social costs) or even a Pareto-superior offense (i.e., one that makes at least some people better off and no one worse off). For the sake of simplicity (though somewhat inaccurately), I shall call both socially efficient and Pareto-superior offenses "victimless" ones.[15]

In an intriguing but unpublished analysis, legal sociologist Robert Kagan identifies some characteristic features of victimless offenses and finds that illegal immigration fits the description well.[16] By definition, a victimless offense is one that violates the law but does not directly harm anyone. Because there are no complainants to demand that the agency punish particular offenders and to provide evidence of the offenses to prosecutors, the offenses are hard to detect. Indeed, employers and landlords who know about the illegal conduct are often the ones who benefit most from it.

In order to detect violations in such cases, proactive methods must be devised. Yet, these tend to be costly for the government and intrude on innocent third parties. Kagan cites examples of such methods in immigration enforcement: patrolling borders, establishing mandatory checkpoints, searching cars, interrogating travelers, and trying to distinguish illegal travelers from legal ones. One might add to this list the practice of workplace raids, which are particularly crude and disruptive, affecting American citizens and legal resident aliens along with the agency's undocumented prey. These effects in turn trigger political criticism of the agency. Since these methods impose high social costs and there are no complainants, the agency is less inclined to take aggressive enforcement action against violators, and is subject to less day-to-day pressure from outsiders to do so. The agency grows less zealous, diverts scarce enforcement resources elsewhere, looks for exceptions that can justify nonenforcement, and generally assumes a passive role, which Kagan calls "retreatism." Because violations are not routinely publicized, the agency can more easily trade leniency for something it values, which invites low-level corruption and nurtures deviant subcultures.

Conduct that creates no obvious, well-documented victims but that the law on the books makes illegal is morally ambiguous. After all, if the conduct is voluntary, we can presume that it benefits those who engage in it. If no one else is harmed, then the conduct seems unobjectionable. In such a situation, the rationale for any punishment is so elusive that strict enforcement of the law seems pointless, oppressive, even inhumane.[17] Most undocumented immigrants are otherwise law-abiding, future-oriented individuals who work hard, attend church, raise strong families, surmount daunting obstacles, love their new country, and exemplify many of our cherished social ideals. Their struggles to participate in the American dream resemble the now-mythic struggles of our own ancestors.

Americans unmoved by purely legal arguments, then, may well wonder what justifies the ICE in doggedly pursuing such people. The short answer, good and sufficient for legalistic citizens and agencies, is that the immigration statute demands it. The law demands enforcement not because of a particular alien's conduct, which apart from the illegal entry may well be unimpeachable and have only a *de minimis* effect on others, but because of the supposed aggregate, cumulative burdens that violators wreak on American workers (by taking their jobs, reducing their wages, eroding their labor standards, and weakening their unions), on local communities (by consuming scarce public services), and the national polity (by threatening our sense of sovereignty and control).

But citizens sympathizing and perhaps even identifying with enterprising immigrants whose only offense was to cross the border illegally are unlikely to view the aggregate of such acts with horror or moral indignation. They may be further mollified by empirical studies purporting to show neutral or even positive effects of illegal migration on low-income American workers.[18] Even assuming negative effects, Kagan notes, they would be cumulative and aggregated, not immediate and individual. To punish an individual violator in these circumstances, especially when such violations are ubiquitous, only aggravates the moral dilemma that haunts immigration enforcement. For all of these reasons, then, the agency has strong political, fiscal, and (as we have just seen) moral incentives to avoid investing heavily in the prevention or prosecution of victimless offenses. Scarce resources can almost certainly be deployed elsewhere to greater effect.

Other aspects of the "law in action" make it even more rational for immigration officials to view their enforcement efforts as largely futile, which surely demoralizes them (Harwood 1986:118). These aspects include the often long delays in completing removal proceedings; the agency's limited (though rapidly expanding, with some 27,000 beds planned for 2007) detention capacity and the notorious propensity of non-detained, removable aliens to abscond and go underground before their removal can be adjudicated, much less effectuated; the agency's strong preference for voluntary departure and other swift, low-cost, informal but also low-deterrence sanctions over formal removal proceedings; the "revolving door" resulting from the ease and celerity with which those aliens who are removed or do depart can reenter the country; and the ability of many aliens to delay the proceedings long enough to build up equities, obtain relief from removal, and adjust status. I have already noted the agency's inability to remove most criminal aliens. The agency has also found it difficult or impossible to send home the hundreds of thousands of aliens, most of them undocumented, to whom the agency has granted "temporary" humanitarian refuge on the express, statutorily imposed condition that they return to their countries of origin once the political, environmental, or economic emergency that brought them to (or kept them in) the United States abates. Indeed, most of them end up staying in the United States indefinitely. The immigration law in action—a combination of domestic politics, ethnic solidarity, foreign policy considerations, and an administrative overload that makes the prospect of mass removals impractical and unacceptable—in effect transforms temporary protection into permanent residence (Krikorian 1999). If few illegal aliens are subjected to formal removal proceedings and even fewer are criminally prosecuted (much less convicted), immigration officials' judgments about which few among the many violators will be prosecuted are bound to be arbitrary—and to be regarded as such by the public. As for the courts, their frustration with the agency and low regard for the legal scrupulosity of immigration enforcement is evident from the frequent rebukes by the Seventh Circuit, discussed above.

It is impossible to know how many Americans in fact view ordinary illegal migration as an essentially victimless offense—one to be regretted perhaps or even prosecuted in unusually egregious cases, but not one to be generally reprehended, much less stigmatized. The victimless offense view is quite widespread, judging from the significant number of people who employ workers of whose illegal status they are, or should be, aware; the periodic amnesties that Congress has granted to large numbers of undocumented aliens in the past and is considering again; the refusal of many city governments to cooperate with enforcement actions against undocumented aliens even in defiance of IIRIRA's cooperation mandate; and the manifest unwillingness of schoolteachers, hospital workers, taxi passengers, social service providers, civil servants, and other Americans not covered by employer sanctions to report suspected illegal aliens to the immigration authorities; and immigration scholars, few of whom show any interest in strengthening enforcement against the undocumented (Schuck 2007b).

If this is true, it is bound to undermine the vigor and effectiveness of immigration enforcement and to call into serious question the legitimacy of immigration law—its social acceptance as an authoritative set of social norms supporting widely felt moral duties to obey the law and to punish violators.[19] The agency, Kagan predicts, will respond to this dilemma by adhering to a rigid legalism manifested in strict, ritualistic patterns of enforcement, punctuated by spasms of retreatism. This is a fair description of the agency's behavior over the years.

CONCLUSION

Even today, autonomous theory—that is, hypotheses not largely drawn from theories in other disciplines—does not play a significant role in the law's approach to migration issues. Nevertheless, many of law's characteristic patterns are highly relevant, indeed essential, to any sophisticated understanding of the forces that drive, divert, and blunt migration, and that shape migrants' experiences in destination countries. Legal rules—the law in action, on the books, and in the mind—help to construct the complex array of incentives that individuals and groups take into account in deciding whether, when, how, and where to migrate. Law determines the formal status that migrants may enjoy and the entitlements they may claim, but it also contributes to the normative and cultural settings in which migrants must decide how to behave and find meaning as they seek success in their new homeland. Law must design, discipline, and legitimate the political institutions and legal procedures that regulate the immigration process and the formal statuses through which migrants pass. Law must also join with other social mechanisms to negotiate the terms of their eventual integration into their new society. In all of this, law's inspiring possibilities are yoked to its inherent limitations (Schuck 2000). Both its possibilities and its limitations help to shape the experiences of migrants and their countries of origin and destination.

NOTES

1. The phrase, I believe, was originated by my former colleague Arthur Leff in a meditation on this phenomenon in a characteristically witty, insightful article of the same name (Leff 1978).

2. For a useful discussion of law's methodological relationships to other disciplines, see Rubin 1997.

3. Indeed, some commentators have argued that the economic inequality often found in countries with relatively capitalistic systems tends to attract the more entrepreneurial and highly skilled citizens of more egalitarian countries, while more egalitarian countries tend to attract the less entrepreneurial and skilled citizens of more inegalitarian countries (Borjas 1990).

4. Elsewhere I have characterized this statute as "the most radical reform of immigration law in decades—or perhaps ever. It thoroughly revamps the enforcement process and extends [restrictions adopted earlier in 1996] in ways that even many INS officials find arbitrary, unfair, and unadministrable. For example, it requires the INS to exclude aliens at the border summarily and without judicial review if they seem to lack proper documentation. The IIRIRA makes asylum claiming more difficult and bars the INS from granting discretionary relief from deportation to many aliens even for compelling humanitarian reasons as the previous law permitted. It mandates the detention of many removable aliens—perhaps forever if they come from a country like Vietnam that refuses to take them back. It equates the rights of aliens who entered illegally and live in the United States with those of aliens with no ties in the United States. It limits the rights of illegal aliens to reenter legally. It further expands the category of 'aggravated felon' aliens, who can be deported summarily even if they have been long-term residents of the country. It bars judicial review of INS decisions to deport them. (The definition of 'aggravated felony' is now so broad that it includes almost all drug, weapons, and other nonpetty offenses; it even covers subway fare beating.)" (Schuck 1998:143–44).

5. Rare exceptions do occur. In a possibly unprecedented decision, the federal government agreed to pay $87,500 to a Kenyan who was negligently denied asylum (Murphy 2005). In another unusual case, a federal judge permitted asylum seekers detained by the INS to seek money damages against individual INS officials and contractors based on alleged international human rights violations (*Jama* v. *U.S.I.N.S.* 1998).

6. This is particularly true of the most politically favored, elite unit within the agency, the Border Patrol. Its resources have increased more rapidly since the 1990s than those of almost any other domestic agency in the federal government; they account for most of the growth in the INS and (now) ICE as a whole during this period of budgetary stringency elsewhere in the government.

7. Consider that for a decade, the United States has been admitting approximately one million legal immigrants each year (1.12 in 2005), a level that approaches, if not exceeds, historic highs in terms of absolute totals (not, however, as a percentage of the population), and has also tolerated historically high illegal migration levels. The United States has even accorded legal status to millions of long-resident undocumented aliens, most of whom are low-skilled workers from Latin America, not high-skill workers or the white Europeans who comprised the traditional U.S. migration stream. Even the Republican Party has a powerful pro-immigration element that has succeeded in stifling restrictionist initiatives in Congress, especially in the Senate. Evidently, the fact that migrants to the United States cannot vote and often have insecure immigration statuses (at least in the short-run) does not deprive pro-immigration interests of all political influence (Schuck 2007a).

8. Some of these techniques may violate international human rights law (Fitzpatrick 1994).

9. International human rights law also recognizes limited rights even for undocumented aliens, most notably the right of nonrefoulement if the alien would suffer persecution in his home country based on his race, religion, nationality, membership in a particular social group, or political opinion (Convention Relating to the Status of Refugees 1951: Article 33).

10. The "almost" qualification is added in recognition of the possibility that some individuals and groups are net economic or fiscal losers from illegal migration. The economic literature has not yet clearly established adverse effects on the most plausible group of victims, inner-city black Americans, although economic theory predicts some such effects (Trebilcock and Sudak 2006; *Economist* 2006); but see Borjas 1990 and Borjas 1999. Another plausible group of victims consists of local communities with high concentrations of illegal aliens requiring public services (Trebilcock and Sudak 2006).

11. As a result, certain policy options cannot be fully or candidly explored, such as accepting a certain level of illegal migration but compensating those who suffer economic disadvantage as a result, much as Congress has done for some victims of free trade policies.

12. This was not always the case. Until 1986, the law contained the so-called Texas proviso that made it a crime for aliens to enter the United States illegally but precluded criminal liability for the employers who hired them. Congress repealed the Texas proviso in the Immigration Reform and Control Act of 1986.

13. Americans may be somewhat less sympathetic to those illegal aliens—almost half the total—who originally entered the United States with a legal visa but then violated its terms, but this is purely a matter of conjecture. Needless to say, Americans bear little or no sympathy for those who commit ordinary crimes in the United States (Schuck and Williams 1999:372).

14. Inaccurate because in the case of a socially efficient offense, some may be made worse off (and hence might be considered "victims") even though the offense makes society better off as a whole, as when illegal migration takes away the jobs of a few American workers but creates many more jobs in the aggregate. See supra note 10 and infra note 17.

15. The observations that follow are drawn from Kagan's unpublished notes for a talk at a panel on regulatory enforcement of immigration law at the Law and Society Association's annual meeting in Philadelphia, May 24, 1988.

16. For example, most libertarians, many economists, and the editors of the *Wall Street Journal* take this view.

17. On labor market effects, see the sources cited supra at note 10. The taxpayer-as-victim argument for immigration enforcement was weakened, though not eliminated, in 1996 when the federal welfare reform law made illegal aliens ineligible for almost all federally funded benefits and for some state and local ones (Schuck 1998:199–200).
18. On the question of law's legitimacy, see Schuck 2000, chap. 13.

REFERENCES

Borjas, George J. 1990. *Friends or Strangers: The Impact of Immigrants on the U.S. Economy*. New York: Basic Books.

———. 1999. *Heaven's Door: Immigration Policy and the American Economy*. Princeton, NJ: Princeton University Press.

Chinese Exclusion Case (Chae Chan Ping v. United States), 130 U.S. 581 (1889).

Convention Relating to the Status of Refugees, 189 U.N.T.S. 137 (July 28, 1951).

Economist. 2006. "Economics Focus: Myths and Migration," April 8, p. 76.

Fitzpatrick, Joan. 1994. "Flight from Asylum: Trends toward Temporary 'Refuge' and Local Responses to Forced Migrations," *Virginia Journal of International Law* 35: 13–70.

Gilboy, Janet A. 1988. "Administrative Review in a System of Conflicting Values," *Law & Social Inquiry* 13: 515–79.

Hailbronner, Kai, David A. Martin, and Hiroshi Motomura, eds. 1997. *Immigration Admissions: The Search for Workable Policies in Germany and the United States*. Providence, RI: Berghahn Books.

———. 1998. *Immigration Controls: The Search for Workable Policies in Germany and the United States*. Providence, RI: Berghahn Books.

Harwood, Edwin. 1986. *In Liberty's Shadow: Illegal Aliens and Immigration Law Enforcement*. Stanford, CA: Hoover Institution Press.

Heise, Michael. 1999. "The Importance of Being Empirical," *Pepperdine Law Review* 26: 807–34.

Hollifield, James F. 1998. "Migration, Trade, and the Nation–State: The Myth of Globalization," *UCLA Journal of International Law and Foreign Affairs* 3: 595–636.

Jacobson, David. 1996. *Rights across Borders: Immigration and the Decline of Citizenship*. Baltimore, MD: Johns Hopkins University Press.

Jama v. U.S.I.N.S, 22 F. Supp.2d 353 (D.N.J. 1998).

Kobach, Kris W. 2005. "The Quintessential Force Multiplier: The Inherent Authority of Local Police to Make Immigration Arrests," *Albany Law Review* 69: 179–235.

Krikorian, Mark. 1999. "Here to Stay: There's Nothing as Permanent as a Temporary Refugee." Center for Immigration Studies, Washington, D.C., August.

Leff, Arthur A. 1978. "Law And," *Yale Law Journal* 87: 989–1011.

Legomsky, Stephen H. 2005. *Immigration and Refugee Law and Policy*. New York: Foundation Press.

Levitt, Peggy. 1997. "Transnationalizing Community Development: The Case of Migration between Boston and the Dominican Republic," *Nonprofit and Voluntary Sector Quarterly* 26: 509–26.

Lipsky, Michael. 1980. *Street-Level Bureaucracy: The Dilemmas of the Individual in Public Services*. Cambridge, MA: MIT Press.

Lipton, Eric. 1999. "As More Are Deported: A '96 Law Faces Scrutiny," *New York Times*, December 21, p. 1.

McGinnis, John O. 2006. "Age of the Empirical," *Policy Review* 47–58.

Murphy, Dean E. 2005. "In Rare Accord, Spurned Asylum Seeker to Get $87,500," *New York Times*, April 28, p. A16.

Nafziger, James A. R. 1991. "Review of Visa Denials by Consular Officers," *Washington Law Review* 66: 1–105.

Pew Research Center. 2006. "America's Immigration Quandary."

Plyler v. *Doe,* 457 U.S. 202 (1982).

Posner, Richard A. 1988. *Law and Literature: A Misunderstood Relationship.* Cambridge, MA: Harvard University Press.

———. 1999. *The Problematics of Moral and Legal Theory.* Cambridge, MA: Harvard University Press.

———. 2005. *Benslimane* v. *Gonzales,* 430 F.3d 828 (7th Cir.).

Rubin, Edward L. 1997. "Law and the Methodology of Law," *Wisconsin Law Review* 1997: 521–65.

Schuck, Peter H. 1975. *The Judiciary Committees: A Study of the House and Senate Judiciary Committees.* New York: Viking Press.

———. 1983. *Suing Government: Citizen Remedies for Official Wrongs.* New Haven, CT: Yale University Press.

———. 1989. "Why Don't Law Professors Do More Empirical Research?" *Journal of Legal Studies* 39: 323–36.

———. 1994. "Rethinking Informed Consent," *Yale Law Journal* 103: 899–959.

———. 1995. "The Message of Proposition 187," *The American Prospect* 21: 87–92.

———. 1997. "INS Detention and Removal: A White Paper," *Georgetown Immigration Law Journal* 11: 667–708.

———. 1998. *Citizens, Strangers, and In-Betweens: Essays on Immigration and Citizenship.* Boulder, CO: Westview Press.

———. 1999. "Current Debates About U.S. Citizenship," in *In Defense of the Alien,* L. Tomasi, ed., 21:80–98.

———. 2000. *The Limits of Law: Essays on Democratic Governance.* Boulder, CO: Westview Press.

———. 2007a. "The Disconnect between Public Attitudes and Policy Outcomes in Immigration," in *Debating Immigration: 21st Century Perspectives*, C. Swain, ed., Cambridge University Press.

———. 2007b. "Taking Immigration Federalism Seriously," *University of Chicago Law Forum* (in press).

Schuck, Peter H., and Williams, John. 1999. "Removing Criminal Aliens: The Pitfalls and Promises of Federalism," *Harvard Journal of Law & Public Policy* 22: 367–463.

Stevens, Robert Bocking. 1983. *Legal Education in America from the 1850s to the 1980s.* Chapel Hill: University of North Carolina Press.

Swarns, Rachel L. 2006. "Decline Seen in Illegal Immigrants," *New York Times*, July 26, p. A14.

Trebilcock, Michael J., and Sudak, Matthew. 2006. "The Political Economy of Emigration and Immigration," *New York University Law Review* 81: 234–93.

CHAPTER 9

Rebooting Migration Theory
Interdisciplinarity, Globality, and Postdisciplinarity in Migration Studies
Adrian Favell

It is no small ambition to bring together a comprehensive overview of contemporary migration theory across the social sciences and humanities. Such has been the explosion of interest in international migration in the past decade or so that no scholar nowadays can feel adequate when confronting the avalanche of literature that has followed. The rather heroic enterprise presented here has the virtue of letting disciplinary perspectives speak for themselves in a congenial dialogue, rather than attempting a unified theory, the most prominent of which have typically emerged from a base in economic theory (Massey et al. 1998; Hammar et al. 1997). It is thus highly instructive to read each chapter as a guide to the specific mindset of various disciplines toward the subject. Nonspecialists will learn as much about what political scientists, anthropologists, demographers, economists, or lawyers *do* from reading the respective chapters, as about political science, anthropological, demographic, economic, or legal approaches to migration theory.

The first edition came under fire for its lack of true interdisciplinarity and for a pervasive U.S.-centered bias. Authors were thus asked to engage more with the non-American literature in each discipline, while new chapters on geography and demography fill out a broader range of subjects. To be fair, though, offering a comprehensive overview for the American market—in which international migration (or "immigration," as it is mostly misleadingly titled) is nowadays a central topic on syllabi—is certainly not quite the same thing as it might be in Britain or continental Europe, let alone elsewhere in the world. Immigration is such a central part of the self-narrative of the United States that no one would today question the relevance of studying it in the mainstream social sciences and humanities. Elsewhere in the world, migration is no less a significant subject, but it has taken time for it to be established as a serious academic topic. A major problem in anglophone countries is that it is often lumped together on syllabi and in bookstores with "ethnic and racial studies." It has taken the great effort of some scholars to delineate a research program on migration that is quite distinct from that on race and ethnicity (Castles and Miller 1998; King 2002).

This volume, then, will be useful further ammunition to that end—to the emergence and institutionalization of migration studies as a full-fledged inter-disciplinary field. In this brief bookend to the collection, my goal is to not only explore some other dimensions raised by the question of interdisciplinarity in migration studies, but also to offer some thoughts as to what the core theoretical building blocks of this field might be. In attempting to synthesize our efforts in this volume, I aim to diagnose the weak spots and miscommunications in the research field, as much as to point the way forward to the next decade of (hopefully) increasingly multidisciplinary, multimethods research.

INTERDISCIPLINARITY IN MIGRATION STUDIES

On the face of it, there could hardly be a topic in the contemporary social sciences more naturally ripe for interdisciplinary thinking than migration studies. This should be obvious to anyone sitting down to design a comprehensive course in international migration. In such a course, there is always a need to somehow marry quantitative data sources and basic economic or demographic analysis of migration, with an ethnographic or oral historical sense of the lives and experiences of migrants themselves. Sociology and political science readings are needed to broach the structural background of immigration and incorporation processes; and there is so much interesting work coming out of anthropology and geography—particularly looking at transnational processes—that these approaches clearly must not be overlooked. Migration studies need a simultaneously top-down as well as bottom-up approach, and it needs history to temper the overwhelming topicality of the present. A course such as this should also be comparative and global, although that part is the hardest. Our experiences at the University of California, Los Angeles (UCLA), where I have co-taught an ambitious program with Roger Waldinger, Ivan Light, and Rubén Hernández-León as well organized an interdisciplinary summer school for the Social Science Research Council (SSRC), is that contrary to the constant advice in the United States about the need for specialist technical training, students are well able to appreciate and assimilate readings from across disciplines and methodologies when migration is the singular focus. A course such as this can play a vital role in prising open the disciplinary closing of the American mind, which is often hammered home in departments riven by fruitless quantitative/qualitative divides. In studying migration, multidisciplinarity with a multimethods approach should be a basic premise *even* if the case study focus of the course is exclusively immigration in the United States.

Yet interdisciplinarity, in the social sciences at least, is a struggling ideal. To talk across disciplines in the United States is also to speak against one's disciplinary career interests, which often wholly reflect the business of reproducing disciplinary canons and professional hierarchies that takes up so much of the everyday academic enterprise. There is still quite a bit of this going on in the chapters here, which is a pity. Reading these authors, it is clear how much all of them have been socialized in the *habitus* of their own disciplines, however open-minded their explicit intentions (Bourdieu 1984). None, for example, are writing about disciplines other than their own. In the disciplinary mindset, the canon in each is presented like an accumulation of sanctified knowledge stored in a tall farmyard silo.[1] This is a very American problem. As part of their training, students are taught to prepare for disciplinary "field exams," which teach them to read and retread only familiar literature. Alternative methodologies are sidelined, they are often forced to study the United States (out of practical accessibility), and to pose the questions in a classical mode. The only space for interdisciplinary social studies in the United States has been in international studies units, which often do not have their own faculty, and which are always less prestigious positions than mainstream disciplinary professorships. Woe betide the young graduate student who wanders too far from the disciplinary path. It can be professional suicide in terms of scoring those job-talk, essential first publications in the "top" recognized journals of the given discipline. Young academics in the United States are basically taught that their dream someday should (only) be to become chair of their respective disciplinary association. It is ironic and unfortunate that the willfully diverse, and distinction-obsessed social sciences are behind the times in this sense. Interdisciplinarity is becoming a rule of thumb for natural scientists in scientific fields unifying across old boundaries: for example, in the intersection of biological and physical sciences, or the pathbreaking work in complexity science in which natural sciences are marching boldly into social scientific territories.

In Europe, interdisciplinarity is threatened by the grim progress of bureaucratic research-assessment exercises, spearheaded by the British model, and self-inflicted by a generation of compliant Stakhanovite academics recast by policy makers as standardized organization men (and women). In these, all academic output is reduced to scoring major journal articles, the ranking of which is inevitably defined by disciplinary canons. To put this bluntly, if you are assessed as a geographer, sociologist, or political scientist, publishing an article or two in *International Migration Review* or the *Journal of Ethnic and Migration Studies* (two core migration studies journals) will count for nothing in the disciplinary review. On this basis, it is hard to make a career as a multidisciplinary migration studies scholar. Interdisciplinarity across Europe is now associated with the failure of experiments in university structures in the 1970s and 1980s.[2]

Our idea at UCLA was to run a thoroughly interdisciplinary program with sociology as a base. Sociology students as such were always a minority in classes that drew in students from anthropology, geography, education, health sciences, public policy, and political science. It works very well and is fun to teach. Sociology, at least when it breaks clear of classical questions, has the virtue of being a space in which interdisciplinarity is fairly automatic. The most important areas of sociology are in effect interdisciplinary dialogues— political sociology, economic sociology, comparative historical sociology, ethnography (with anthropology), demography (with economics and statistics), conversation analysis (with linguistics), and so on. This leaves the difficulty of defining who or what a sociologist is—as opposed, say, to economists, political scientists, or anthropologists, who have rather clear conceptions of who they are. But this can be a virtue as well as an identity problem.

Geography, which although rather marginal in the United States, is arguably the most exciting discipline in the social sciences in Europe, has, at its best, a similar quality. Susan Hardwick's chapter here emphasizes the postpositivist, cultural studies wing of population geography. This version of geography is certainly inter- (if not post-) disciplinary, although her presentation does not fully represent the full range of methodologies used by geographers today. To be interdisciplinary does not have to entail the postpositivist stance of endorsing only qualitative work, rejecting explanation, or conceiving of theory as relentless "critique" (as opposed to empirical hypothesis generator). Yet with its central concern about flows, networks, space, place, and transactions across the planet, geography's advantage is that it is much less automatically wedded to methodological nationalism than sociology, whose master concept of "society" is almost impossible to extricate from the historical context of the nation–state (Wimmer and Glick Schiller 2002).

As the volume's introduction makes clear, however, when read in juxtaposition, the chapters can be viewed in an eminently interdisciplinary way, by thinking about where and how the distinct available conceptualizations or objects of study in each discipline overlap and interrelate. There are limits to this binary interdisciplinarity for sure, but learning about a foreign discipline is just like learning a foreign language. One is a start, and it makes it easier to learn more, as well as teaching you to look at the world in a different way. There is in fact, in this sense, any amount of interdisciplinarity out there, in the grey areas that disciplinary approaches find themselves wandering into through unusually imaginative or lateral thinking. For example, despite what Hasia Diner argues, it is hard not to imagine that the best historians, for all their sensitivity to context and the unique complexity of specific migration experiences, never pose themselves theoretical questions about the generalization of their observations. In doing so, they will inevitably reach out to political science theories of the state, sociological theories about immigrant integration processes, or anthropological insights about the interactional workings of ethnicity. Some of the most erudite intellectual heavyweights in the social sciences have come out of the nexus of the Social Science Historical Association; for example, one thinks of the essential work in comparative historical studies of Leslie Page Moch or Ewa Morawska, which has struggled to open the U.S.-centric bias of so much historical production on immigration. There are parallels to this in the intersection of demography, economics, and sociology. Where would migration theory be today without the work of Douglas Massey, Alejandro Portes, or Saskia Sassen, or the very fruitful ethnography and theory dialogue going on in contemporary cultural approaches in anthropology or geography, exemplified in the work of a writer such as Aihwa Ong? There will be no problem with interdisciplinarity in migration studies if these are the inspirations in the future.

GLOBALITY IN MIGRATION STUDIES

That said, certain dimensions of interdisciplinarity are curtailed by the all-enveloping national focus of study in the United States. For sure, navel gazing is a pastime of academics in every major and minor national tradition. It is often at its worse in small, self-regarding nations (as I write this, I am sitting in Denmark, a perfect example) but Americans have a particular propensity for a lack of awareness of how so much of what they take to be "canonical" or "universal" to their respective disciplines is *nothing but* the view from within this particular nation–state, however large and powerful it is in the intellectual landscape. "We are the world," Americans like to think. No you are not.

In her contribution, Barbara Schmitter Heisler in fact offers a very sharp diagnosis of methodological nationalism in (American) sociology that I need not repeat here. I have in the past offered similar diagnoses, critiquing the European (or Europe-focused) literature on integration and citizenship (Favell 2001a, 2005). The biggest problem is that academic studies that reflect most of all the political concerns of national debates always turn discussion of international migration and global mobility into debates about the ethics of im-migration, which inevitably prioritizes the view from the receiving society, and the variable transformation of foreigners into nationalized citizens.

It is particularly tiresome that leaders in the field in the United States make frequent calls for more cross-national comparativism in migration studies to help advance the American debates—one thinks of Portes's very sharp manifesto (1997)—but that the occasional openings and dialogues rarely go anywhere. One looks in vain for evidence of progress, for example, in the update of the absurdly U.S.-centric *Handbook of International Migration* (Hirschman, Kasinitz, and De Wind 1999)—an essential reference in other senses—when it was redone as a conference and published as an *International Migration Review* special issue a couple of years later (Portes and De Wind 2004). A set of familiar European figures were brought in to broaden the scope, but it is painfully apparent that the discussions, which are described repeatedly by the editors as "fruitful," are also admitted to "once again [display] the wide differences in perspective arising from diverse national contexts and intellectual traditions" (843). Most transatlantic dialogue in fact has rarely got any further than "discovering" this. American international conferences suffer from the fact that they often do not get visits from some of the very best European scholars, who are too busy in their local struggles and commitments to take time out for a sabbatical year in the United States, and often do not publish much in English. Americans weaned on the U.S. canon, meanwhile, can pop over to Europe during the summer recess or an occasional international conference, and they might try to build in a comparative agenda, but they rarely stick around long enough to develop a plausible local knowledge. A typical problem they run into is that after a little dialogue in a complex political European setting, they realize that doing comparative work is going to necessitate thoroughly rethinking the theoretical assumptions and data reflexes on which the American canon is based. Faced with this, they often withdraw to familiar territory, and debates that advance theory as if America was the standard to which everything should be measured. One has grown tired of archetypal American observations that compared to the more universal track record of the United States, Germany is a more ethnic nation, or that French republicanism masks cultural particularism (e.g., Alba 2005). What is missing is a realization that U.S. tools and theories have to be completely rethought in the European context. The scale of these societies, the historical nature of nation-building and migration, and the transnational context of the European Union are all factors that ensure European national cases are not directly comparable or amenable to the habits of analysis that work so well in the United States. Comparativism is a wonderful thing, but it also has to be tempered by an awareness of the complete asymmetry in the U.S.–Europe relationship, and the power relations that distort it (Favell 1999). The one area where it might be argued that there has been a fruitful cross-Atlantic comparativism is in studies of the political sociology of citizenship, which is discussed in depth elsewhere in this volume by Hollifield and Schmitter Heisler. Here, the deep methodological nationalism of homegrown European research *was* successfully challenged by a new field of comparative work by American or American-trained scholars.[3] However, the resultant boom in citizenship studies has been highly fertile for new comparative efforts but less helpful in its reproduction of the state- and therefore nation–state-centered optic that talk of citizenship inevitably encourages. Again, I have discussed this in much detail elsewhere (Favell 2001a).[4]

The explosion of political sociology work was a fruitful example of a genuine internationalization of a research field—a case where a far more sophisticated comparative social science was able to cut through the parochial concerns that dominated the debates of national scholars. For example, the *terribly* British postcolonial "race relations" perspective, wholly defined by a generation of famous cultural theory scholars in Britain (the new canon of Stuart Hall, Paul Gilroy, Homi Bhabha, Heidi Mirza, Avtar Brah et al.) looks quite provincial when set against the recent comparative literature on citizenship and immigration (Favell 2001b; Hansen 2000). So many of these debates were defined not by scientific agendas but by the (understandable) activist frustrations of minority scholars in relation to dominant British policy structures. Even then, it can hardly be claimed that it was outsider views of Britain that changed the nature of the debate. Much more influential has been a decade of new immigration on the ground, that has now begun to pry open this set of distinctly British concepts. The "race relations" paradigm simply falls flat in trying to capture the issues involving asylum seekers or new Polish migrants.

Even in such a closely interrelated continent such as Europe, the most basic cross-national awareness is often lacking. European scholars often hold highly stereotypical views of near neighbors—the French see English race relations as "racist," the English see French republicanism as "homogenizing," and so on—which are linked to the usefulness of stereotypes in political debates within the country. This points to a distinctively politicized aspect of migration studies in Europe that in fact has its weaknesses and strengths. With the exception of George Borjas, and some of the scholars circling around the Washington-based think tanks, such as Susan Martin or Phil Martin, American academic production about immigration, as on any other subject, takes place with splendid, Olympian distance from the dirt of everyday politics. Given just how dirty American politics is, this is perhaps a good thing for the academics concerned. It certainly helps academic production establish a credible power of autonomy, by not playing the journalistic game (Bourdieu 1996). At their best, American institutions *are* formidable institutions of independent science, which Europeans could only dream about matching. Now, it is true that it is getting harder to escape the pressures of the Department of State on international studies, which are funded according to shifting U.S. foreign policy criteria, and there is always suspicion that rich U.S. universities headhunt foreign scholars less for their outside knowledge and more as trophies to put on the wall. But social science in the United States is clearly much cleaner and therefore more scientific, in the positivist sense, than in Europe.

European research could hardly be described as politically clean, in continental Europe especially, and even more so in the smaller countries or ones—such as Spain, France, or Denmark, for example—where academics, opinion makers, and policy makers are concentrated on top of each other in the metropolitan centre and capital city. In these contexts, leading academics are almost always also highly politically engaged, and their careers and appointments are themselves often political. When you are constantly running after ministry money or trying to catch the eye of a newspaper editor, the danger again is navel gazing. Work gets framed exclusively in terms of the national political debates of the day, and you certainly do not have time to waste flying to international conferences in the United States. For example, being an internationally recognized studies expert in Denmark does not principally mean doing international work or being part of an international network; it means being an international expert who observes the world outside and translates it to users involved in furiously inward-looking debates about Danish society and national identity. Yet the academic production on a topic such as immigration or international migration can have a political relevance and impact in shaping debates here of which Americans could only dream. Leading academics are routinely invited to appear on TV as experts or write op eds in leading newspapers. They have a status and visibility in the local society that is only ever matched in the United States by academics who have renounced the scientific academic game and become despised "public intellectuals."

One upshot of this is that there might be different criteria for evaluating the value of scientific production in different contexts. Pure research is different than policy situated research: those Danish scholars are not necessarily mistaken in their assessment of what counts most in their research. It might also lead to different theories. The situation means that European research is less naively positivistic. Europeans generally have no problem seeing that the difference between facts and values is very blurred or that political interests lie behind the production of most scientific knowledge. There can be found, then, a more sophisticated *reflexive* consciousness about the way in which power and knowledge-interests shape academic production. Roughly speaking, the Habermasian, Foucauldian, and Bourdieusian approaches in social science are the three main paradigms for understanding this process. The upshot of this is not so much that everyone becomes postmodern. This is actually a bigger problem in the United States, where the rejection of positivism has often led to a naïve (qualitative) postmodernism that mirrors the naive (quantitative) positivism advanced by others. Rather, arguably, there is a more sophisticated awareness, especially in continental Europe, that you do not just throw out good empiricist instincts with the dogmatic positivist bathwater. In other words, that an empirical post-postpositivism is possible (on this, see especially Bourdieu and Wacquant 1992). Even more obviously, the fact/value distinction is routinely crossed in the very large body of normative theorizing in the social science of migration and immigration in Europe. One thinks of quite important figures such as Tariq Modood and Rainer Bauböck, whose academic work, ironically influenced most of all by North American Rawlsian philosophers such as Will Kymlicka or Ronald Dworkin, is very hard to evaluate or place in terms of advancing disciplinary theories.

Beyond Europe, of course, there is an even bigger question about the ethnocentrism of much migration theory in *both* Europe and North America. Decentering America in migration studies in the name of globality would be a process that should also decenter Europe. It would be fair to say that this volume offers very slim pickings in this respect. With the partial exception of Caroline Brettell's chapter, there is remarkably little reflection here about migration studies from the bottom of the heap up, as it were, from the sending side—the "rest" of the world. This is very much the view from the top of the pile. This point ought to be leading us to conceive of migration as a global topic embedded in regional and development studies. We ought to be encouraging the production of far more work about migrations in all the regions of the world, not just those in the West, looking far more at how sending country contexts influence and shape migration trends.[5] It is perhaps surprising that the study of international migration today has lost so much of the world systems or global development perspective that was much more present in the earlier work of Michael Piore (1979), Castles and Kosack (1973), or Portes and Walton (1981), for example, work that stressed relations of power and of economic dependency between the West and the Rest.

Part of the problem, again, is epistemological. We are right to want to foreground the role of power in knowledge construction. But the road to decentering the social sciences can also be a road out of social science entirely. The call to transcend ethnocentrism has often gone hand in hand with a broader philosophical agenda critiquing the whole modernist, developmental paradigm that privileges the view from the West: the old school views that evaluate development in terms of its benefits for the (Western) global economy, and/or the performance of developing economies and political cultures in western terms. The disciplinary mentality of the sciences can certainly be diagnosed as part of this problem: that the notion of knowledge and the techniques for establishing it always rely on and mask the influence of power and dominant ideology. This broadly Foucauldian view of science and modernity, of the disciplining power of bureaucratic systematization and technical specialization—richly illustrated by the technical training components of postgraduate professionalization in the United States—can be a very effective macrohistory of the scientific West and its evaluative relations to "backward" others. Given the relatively uncontroversial acceptance that the developmentalist paradigm and the science it was built on was in part a self-deluding cover for Western self-justification, ethnocentrism, and exploitation, the postcolonial inversion of the Western perspective seems to make good sense. We all want and need a truly global social science that speaks with and for the multitude, not only the global elites, and not one embedded in discredited Western political means of planetary control and dominance. Disciplines such as geography and anthropology have gone through revolutionary change in this sense, when previous paradigms used for mastering and dominating the colonies became discredited. Departments were closed and heads rolled. We might await a similar realization that, say, the highly Americanized and U.S.-centric disciplines of economics and political science, with their often brittle scientific self-presentation, might go through a similar self-critique as their embedded relation to

American political and economic hegemony is revealed. But this call has to be made in the name of better science and truth itself.

Unfortunately, however, the pessimistic currents of postmodernism that raised these doubts, and began to creep across all the social sciences and humanities from the 1980s onward, have also tended to mean that amongst practitioners of "critique" there has developed a thoroughgoing skepticism and deconstructive attitude toward *all* the procedures and goals of the now despised "enlightenment project," not only those that were perverted in the name of Western hegemony. The victim of this revolution, then, has more often not been power, but truth itself (Hollis 1994). Relativism all the way down is not an option for social science—we really might as well give up altogether if that is the conclusion from reading Foucault, Latour, Lyotard, Bourdieu, and company.[6]

The collection does not much reflect these meta-theoretical concerns. Aside from some cautious references in the chapters on geography and anthropology, there is not much here that reflects the enormous and highly creative growth of postcolonial cultural studies in the humanities. In disciplines that begin with novels, theater, or television as windows to the social world, but very soon move to claiming that the whole world is a text to be deconstructed, there is in fact an alternate social analysis of the world being made that often extends far beyond the realm of literary studies per se. The influence of textual and critical discourse analysis techniques can certainly be seen in work to good effect on the representations of migrants in newspapers, public debates and governmental policy documents, and so on. The poststructuralist and postcolonial methodology that cutting-edge literary studies now embrace as a kind of orthodoxy has indeed gone hand in hand with a huge outpouring of work on transnationalism, hybridity, cultural resistance, and the empowerment of subordinate and minority voices through representing the experiential dimension of migrant life. To not reflect more on this kind of postdisciplinary work in this volume is an oversight for sure (good examples are Lionnet and Shih 2005; Papastergiadis 1999).

POSTDISCIPLINARITY IN MIGRATION STUDIES

The postdisciplinary path being blazed by contemporary humanities and literary studies is, however, not the one I want to follow here. A different notion of postdisciplinarity can I think be retrieved for research approaches to migration other than the textual or wholly idealistic in epistemological terms (see also Sayer 1999, 2000). On some level, I would argue, the social scientific enterprise, perhaps in distinction to cultural and literary studies, relies in the end on an underlying possibility of realism in its methods and representations of the world. Realism is often opposed in epistemological terms to constructivism, but this is in fact an unsophisticated view. On some very basic level, *all* social sciences since at least Durkheim have or at least should be constructivist

in their self-understanding (see also Hacking 2000). That is, accept the idea
that the social world is a humanly constructed (i.e., not naturally or essentially given) reality, that our very methods of data gathering, categorization,
and representation themselves construct in a certain way. It accepts that social
scientists are a part of the social world they are constructing knowledge—and
techniques of knowledge gathering—about. But it is no less *real* for that, and
no less *true* when successful, especially if these techniques are embedded in
a socially shared habitus of scientific practice (as opposed to literary, journalistic, political practice, etc.), that sustain the autonomous social power of
recognized academic work (see Bourdieu et al. 1977).[7]

What a constructivist empiricism might enable is a rethinking of migration
theory that helps us rebuild a more politically autonomous and scientific form
of studying the subject, while not letting go of the incontrovertible need for a
less disciplinary and more global approach. The point here is that we do not
want to endorse procedures or methods that remove for us the very material
"fact" that migration is something that happens when a real (physical) person
moves in real (physical) space. While one can accept the point that Susan
Hardwick might make, that all geographies in the end are collective social
representations of space, which are thus socially relative and mental in nature,
it would go too far to suggest that space itself is a wholly subjective or mentally
constructed fiction. People move, and the material physical distance of those
moves matter, as do the physical borders that separate different social units in
space and define what counts as spatial movement. The postmodern cultural
turn in population geography, in rejecting the "objectivist" or "positivist" old
geography, unfortunately has tended to want to collapse all material space into
socially constructed space, thus in a sense negating geography's most interesting and valuable contribution to the social sciences.

The approach to migration studies suggested by the postdisciplinary
approach here is one that begins to question and dismantle some of the fixed
points and conceptualizations provided by our standard definitions of international migration in the international state system. These, clearly, are political
constructions of the modern world, exhaustively carved up as it is into distinct
nation–state units. This world should, in our migration theory, be subject to
political and historical deconstruction. Yet nearly all the chapters assume that
we know what migration is, and that we can accept the units—from which
people move to which they move—given by the political world we live in. But
these are only conventions that happen to be the case here and now. The basic
definition they assume is the standard one. Citizens or (at least) residents of one
nation–state are migrants or have migrated, first when they leave that nation–
state and cross an international border to set foot in another; and second, when
their move has a time dimension—decided by convention (one year in the
statistics)—after which they can be considered to have moved residency. It is
only a short step to fall into the full immigration optic by accepting the third

assumption that the move creates a particular relationship with the receiving society, defined by the new residence: that the migrant is an outside, foreign body that has to be absorbed in some way into the receiving, given "society." Other movers, who are not staying and whose presence is indifferent to the receiving society, cross borders—such as tourists, business people, international lorry drivers—but they remain wholly indifferent and largely invisible forms of movement from the migration/immigration perspective. The literature on transnationalism, it is true, questioned the one-way assumptions of these migration definitions, stressing the interplay or interrelations of the two places, and the migrant networks between. But it did not enlarge or question much the notion of migration itself as a form of mobility. The second generation of this literature, responding to the accusation that it was ignoring the state by stressing only flows and networks has, with the notion of "simultaneity," in fact fallen back into describing the binary interaction of migrants in sending and receiving contexts, and hence retains a focus on essentially the same kind of movers as immigration scholars (Levitt and Glick-Schiller 2004). In all these approaches, no one examines whether migration is in fact something only defined and derived from the state's need to classify and carve up spatial mobility in a certain way, and that it could be defined in another way.

What might happen if we shut down the disciplinary canons for a moment, and reboot our computer? The filing system in the computer has collapsed and we are forced to redescribe our object of study out there in the real world. Nothing appears natural any more: certainly not our definition of what constitutes a migrant or an event/action of migration in the world. We would have to draw new lines and new conventions.

Would sending and receiving "societies" today still automatically appear as units coterminous with the borders of actually existing, politically defined, nation–states? Or would this historical convention now appear a redundant, or certainly a questionable starting point for building a science of spatial movement? We take it for granted, but it wholly defines our idea of who is a citizen and a resident, and who therefore is a foreigner and a migrant, in relation to specific territories and space. But the world is not only one of nation–state units. Some aspects of society are aggregated in very different units, in which social relations, networks, transactions, and events, spanning both physical and virtual spaces, have local, regional, or global patterns that do not correspond in any way to the container that the nation–state view might wish to impose on them. Biologists studying pollination or meteorologists studying the patterns of hurricane formation would never think that the phenomena they describe were in any way defined by the given nation–state borders and definitions of the everyday political world. Should we continue to describe and file human spatial mobility in the same way?

The issue, in a sense, is a reverse of what is argued in the political science and history chapters in this volume. The problem for a rebooted migration theory is not to bring the state back into a scientific field in which the political view was missing. In fact, the political (that is, the conventional) mode of carving up the world into nation–states is utterly pervasive and ever present in *all* the existing disciplines and their debates. A similar thing might be said about history. To be able to theorize freely, we need to *remove* our understanding of migration away from the urge to account for everything in terms of time- and place-specific narratives; that is, the way the world looks to us conventionally because of our history and our inherited political modes of understanding. History and political science almost always end up reproducing the conventional nation–state point of view of spatial mobility, because it is (still) the dominant conventional view of the world. Sociology, as we are told here by Schmitter Heisler, is also deeply embedded in the nation–state view of the world—not least because nearly all the statistics that it and demography uses are generated by nation–states classifying territorially fixed populations in relation to collectivities imagined as national "societies." We might hope or expect economics, which claims to be methodologically individualistic in its approach, to challenge the convention that the world is divided up only into macro units called nation–states, but in fact nearly all economic theories of migration, including the chapter here by Barry Chiswick, take the conventional definition of international migration from nation A to nation B as their starting point for discussing economic differentials between spatial units, or the costs and benefits of migration to societies. Geography and anthropology, it is true, have a less automatic reliance on methodological nationalism in their modes of analyses. But they are prey to a different problem, of reifying a culturalist view of the world, which then often falls in line with the idea of a world divided up into national "ethnic" cultures, languages, institutions, and so forth.

The point here is that in foregrounding the pervasiveness of the nation–state in our conventional understanding of migration, we might in fact reverse the relationship and show how the nation–state gets constructed and reproduced in and through these conventional understandings. Instead of telling a story about how foreign objects (migrants) fit into or challenge the given (nation–state) narrative and institutional structures by which we recognize the world, we might instead look at how the very process by which collectivities manage movers by naming and counting them, and thereby distinguishing them from nonmovers or residents, is the fundamental way in which the territorial nation–state society constitutes itself in the first place. Physical movement across space is the natural, normal given of human social life; what is abnormal, changeable, and historically constructed is the idea that human societies need to construct political borders and institutions that define and constrain spatial mobility in particular, regularized ways, such that immobility becomes the norm.

The step I am advocating here is essentially to expand and redefine migration studies as a subset of (spatial) mobility studies. This is a project that has been advocated by several social theorists in recent times (Castells 2000; Urry

2000). Unlike them, however, my concern is also with preserving the focus, uppermost to migration studies, on real people moving in real space—not virtual and nonhuman forms of mobility. The issue, in fact, is quite simple. What is it that makes the "illegal" migrant crossing a given border different than the "legal" immigrant, the foreigner on a holiday visa, the lorry driver, or the shopper over for the day? The mobility of goods and services, and even sometimes capital, also involves the physical movement of persons across borders. Minus the nation–state, we might very easily see the fruit pickers on the other side of the sea, who pick the bananas we enjoy at breakfast, as part of our society; they are certainly an essential part of our economy, that is, our market for fruit. Similarly, there is a deep truth for the Mexicans in California who complain, when accused of illegality, that they did not cross any borders; the borders crossed them. What makes the "illegal migrant" different is that a nation–state has decided to name the movement that way—as a way of asserting its own sovereign existence.

Just taking the border at Tijuana would make this point very clear. A very small proportion of the cross-border mobility found at this junction of the political world—that is, the starkest political dividing line between the West and the Rest—is actually "migration"—illegal or otherwise. As well as the fun-loving tourists, the commuters, and the shoppers looking for cheap goods, there is a vast number of goods-related crossings that never count, and would never be recognized as migration. These open, mostly economic transactions, in fact dwarf movements counted as migrations. Yet some people have rights to physically move over the border while others do not; an even smaller number have a right to migrate. Some movements are counted as immigration, others illegal migration, still others asylum seeking, and so on. All these distinctions are more or less arbitrary and defined wholly by conventions imposed by the nation–states in question. As citizens we have to recognize the legality of nation–states, but there is no reason why we have to take this power for granted as autonomous scholars, who should be free from such political blinkers. These conventions, we can see, can change or vary over time and space. The border itself only exists because it is the place where all these classifications are made; it is being made and remade every time the state (or one of its representatives) puts into action criteria in its name that classifies a movement as migration or not. In other words, minus the border, there would be no state, or state governance, here. The (American) nation–state in fact constitutes itself in the very act of recognizing, classifying, and then sanctioning or not (that is, governing) the physical movements that are going across its self-declared borders.

Conventional views of governance, sovereignty, and control entirely reproduce the taken-for-granted convention of state power. To think of this power as continually constructed and enacted also brings into sharp focus the absurdity of many of the discussions on incorporation or integration, especially since academic discussions in these subfields so tamely follow political ones. Spatial movements can be highly integrated in social networks and relations—whether familial, communal, political or economic—regardless of whether they are organized or even fall within the receiving society's political perception of incorporation and integration. But again, by recognizing, classifying, and then reshaping the social interactions that follow from movement as "incorporation" or "integration," the receiving society itself is constituted. America is, we know, the sum of all immigrants; that is the very story of the nation. But look again—it might be possible to see there really is no society here other than the controlled, hierarchical system that calls itself a nation because enough "Americans," who were once foreigners and immigrants, at the same time believe it is the primary social and political entity of which they are a part. The historical emergence of the nation–state is one by which collectivities have found ways to cage and penetrate social and economic interactions that would otherwise be unbounded. One of the key historical ways that the state has constituted its powers over society has been to classify movement as migration, and thereby invent a fixed immobile territorial population that can call itself a nation.[8] That, in a globally porous world, this process still works so effectively for nations like America—which feels very little ontological insecurity at a political level—is a remarkable fact.

The effect of understanding how the state works to create itself and society in its own image need not be one that belittles its basic power. We simply see this power for what it is. In a basic social theoretical sense, some collective entity such as a state may well be necessary to the functioning of society. This is the old Hobbesian argument about a leviathan as basic to the nondestructive functioning of social order. But historically, and even in the modern age, there is a range of possible social orders other than the modern nation–state society (see Sassen 2006). Putting it this way in fact underlines just how remarkably dominant and powerful is our taken-for-granted carving up of the world into nation–states. The modern nation–state's sharp ability to designate and recognize which spatial movers are foreigners is a remarkable political achievement—so effective that scholars of migration rarely question who are migrants or not by this definition.

What is of interest in the current global age is the extent to which this conventional patterning and defining of populations, distinguishing citizens, residents, migrants and movers, is or has been changing because of the changing relationship of the global and regional economy to nation–state sovereignty. The subject matter of international political economy, in fact, is principally concerned with the politics of this shifting relationship, and the governance of the mobility on which it turns: of *all* forms of movement—capital, goods, services, and persons. Among these, the global economy is of course challenging the preeminent power of nation–states themselves to define who is and who is not a citizen or a migrant; who is an immobile resident and who is a mover who has crossed some border. The rebooted approach to migration theory I present here may help us recognize the empirical significance of work focusing on these changes, which might otherwise look like fringe questions in migration studies.

Two brief examples will have to suffice here. The GATS Mode 4 (General Agreement on Trade in Services), in which service workers are able move free of typical migrant visa restrictions, is one channel of movement that has been much discussed by migration scholars as a potentially progressive recognition of the manifold new forms of global mobility that escape conventional classifications (Lavenex 2006). This is in effect an interesting example of how a new form of governance, pushed by global economic cooperation, changes the effectiveness with which states delineated some movers as migrants. A posted service worker is no longer a temporary migrant or potential immigrant. Yet move across borders they certainly must—services nearly always require a physical movement—and it is quite possible that they might relocate and work for several years in another society under these regulations, with all the social implications this entails. The space they live in is a space carved out and largely ungoverned within the receiving society. The all-integrating nation–state has many such holes, like a giant Swiss cheese. Nobody sees this issue as migration, and it might not even be clear which social unit, if any, absorbs the externalities generated by the service mover's life and work, other than the multinational corporation that made the move possible in the first place. Enough actions of this kind and we might start seeing multinational corporate social structures, which call themselves incorporated "legal" firms in the national world, but which often function like entire surrogate state authorities, offering their own cultures, welfare structures, and sources of identity for their employees, as alternatives to the nations they once lived in (Bozkurt 2006).

The European Union (EU) is a second example. Uniquely on the planet, the building of a regionally defined internal market, based on the freedom of movement of goods, capital, services, and persons across political borders, creates a space that has dramatically redefined the European nation–state's sovereign need to define and categorize certain movements as migrations. Now when EU citizens move it is a politically unrecognized and invisible act. European nation–states can no longer constitute themselves as they once might have done by legally and politically designating French or German movers as "foreigners." Any EU citizen can "migrate" (move and stay) with none of the usual means by which states recognize the movement as migration applying. They need no visa, no passport; there is no need to commit oneself to becoming a citizen one day, and in many cases they need not even show up as official residents. They do not think of themselves as migrants; they may or may not show up somewhere on state statistics, and they have lives functionally organized across a quite complicated European space that corresponds to no national or cultural lines. For all the talk of unfettered transnationalism elsewhere in the world—at either the high (corporate) or low ("ethnic," diasporic) level—these European free movers are much less constrained and much better endowed to engage in social forms and networks unclassified and unobserved by nation–states, and not in a way captured or contained by national societies. If one was to go looking for a possible new cosmopolitan or transnational society order in our given world of nation–states, the EU is one of the best places to look (Favell 2007).[9]

These thoughts suggest that while the nation–state remains the modern world's great disciplining device, we ought to be able to devise through migration studies a way of seeing how and why it happens. This perhaps ought to be the biggest challenge to a volume with rethinking migration theory as its goal. The nation–state has created the world in its own image, and science for centuries has also been harnessed to these goals. Migration is one of the key anomalies of a world divided up into more or less fixed population containers, which is why the state politically takes its challenge so seriously, and why migration is, by most observers, so conventionally understood. Power is at work here; it is pervasive in our social science of migration. It is perhaps disappointing that social science disciplines today still seem so wedded to these given conventions for understanding migration. Breaking with the disciplinary nature of the social sciences, and developing a postdisciplinary view may well help scholars think, for once, outside of the box. The theory this generates need not be anything other than a straightforwardly empirical, historical, and comparative enterprise, but it will have to recast the subject of migration in a thoroughly decentered, global perspective. We need to renew the conceptual tools with which we think of and recognize migration. The ones we have inherited from scientific disciplines are not sensitive to this need. Disciplines themselves think and see like a (nation) state, to borrow James C. Scott's famous phrase (1999). To really talk across disciplines would also mean finding a way to escape the nation–state-dominated conceptions that conventionally make sense of the world and the migration that takes place within it.

NOTES

1. I owe this lovely agricultural metaphor to Irene Bloemraad, University of California, Berkeley. Thanks are due to her, to the editors, and to Roger Waldinger and Russell King for comments during the development of this chapter.
2. As a member of faculty I have at Sussex and Utrecht experienced the dismantling of two innovative interdisciplinary structures because of outside funding pressures structured by research assessment imperatives, in both cases against the will of those who worked there.
3. See the work of Rogers Brubaker, James Hollifield, Gary Freeman, Yasemin Soysal, and Christian Joppke et al. See Joppke (1998) for the best synthetic collection.

4. A better example of transatlantic cooperation was the Carnegie Endowment's Comparative Citizenship Project, which worked because it strictly focused on formal aspects of citizenship and naturalization rights; see Aleinikoff and Klusmeyer (2000, 2001).

5. Again, we can thank the Castles and Miller volume (1998), which is the leading textbook of the field, for at least very overtly rethinking international migration in a global sense. The work of Massey et al. (1998), although very much driven by the Mexico-U.S. scenario, which is so close to home, can similarly be congratulated.

6. This dominant anglophone reading of French theory has typically been caused by the overenthusiastic *mis*-reading of poor English-language translations. The same scholars are read and understood very differently in France (see Cusset 2003).

7. Bourdieu and Wacquant (1992) speak of this as transcending the false opposition of "social physics" and "social phenomenology." They offer perhaps the most successful and sophisticated paradigm for empirical social science research based on a kind of constructivist realism.

8. Here the story becomes something more familiar to comparative historical sociologists: the rise of classes and nation–states, the invention of the passport, and the containing of otherwise mobile or ambiguously defined populations in the late nineteenth century—a core moment in the formation of the modern nation–state system (Mann 1993; Torpey 2000).

9. *Eurostars and Eurocities* (Favell 2008) takes this as its core subject. In fact, the social closure necessary to preserve European nation–states' sovereign reign over society gets preserved by other informal means, as I show in this book.

REFERENCES

Alba, Richard. 2005. "Bright versus Blurred Boundaries: Second Generation Assimilation and Exclusion in France, Germany and the United States," *Ethnic and Racial Studies* 28(1): 20–49.

Aleinikoff, Alex, and Doug Klusmeyer, eds. 2000. *From Migrants to Citizens: Membership in a Changing World*. Washington, D.C.: Brookings Institute/Carnegie Endowment for International Peace.

———. eds. 2001. *Citizenship Today: Global Perspectives and Practices*. Washington, D.C.: Brookings Institute/Carnegie Endowment for International Peace.

Bourdieu, Pierre. 1984. *Homo academicus*. Paris: Les éditions de minuit.

———. 1996. *Sur la télévision*. Paris: Liber.

Bourdieu, Pierre, J.-C. Chamboredon, and J.-C. Passeron. 1977. *Le métier du sociologue: préalables épistemologiques*. Paris: Mouton.

Bourdieu, Pierre, and Loïc Wacquant. 1992. *An Invitation to Reflexive Sociology*. Cambridge: Polity.

Bozkurt, Ödül. 2006. "Wired for Work: Highly Skilled Employment and Global Mobility in Mobile Telecommunications Multinationals," in Michael Peter Smith and Adrian Favell, eds., *The Human Face of Global Mobility*, pp. 213–48. New Brunswick, NJ: Transaction Press.

Castells, Manuel. 2000. *The Rise of the Network Society*, 2nd ed. Oxford: Blackwell.

Castles, Stephen, and Godula Kosack. 1973. *Immigrant Workers and Class Structure in Western Europe*. Oxford: Oxford University Press.

Castles, Stephen, and Mark Miller. 1998. *The Age of Migration*. London: Macmillan.

Cusset, François. 2003. *French Theory: Foucault, Derrida, Deleuze & Cie et les mutations de la vie intellectuelle aux États-Unis*. Paris: La Découverte.

Favell, Adrian. 1999. "Comments on Glazer, Schain and Fassin: How Can We Be European?" in Christian Joppke and Steven Lukes, eds., *Multicultural Questions*, pp. 242–57. Oxford: Oxford University Press.

_____. 2001a. "Integration Policy and Integration Research in Europe: A Review and Critique," in Alex Aleinikoff and Doug Klusmeyer, eds., *Citizenship Today: Global Perspectives and Practices*, pp. 249–99. Washington, D.C.: Brookings Institute/Carnegie Endowment for International Peace.

_____. 2001b. "Multi-Ethnic Britain: An Exception in Europe?" *Patterns of Prejudice* 35(1): 35–57.

_____. 2005. "Integration Nations: The Nation–State and Research on Immigrants in Western Europe," in Michael Bommes and Ewa Morawska, eds., *International Migration Research: Constructions, Omissions and the Promise of Interdisciplinarity*, pp. 41–67. London: Ashgate.

_____. 2008. *Eurostars and Eurocities: Free Moving Urban Professionals in an Integrating Europe*. Oxford: Blackwell.

Hacking, Ian. 2000. *The Social Construction of What?* Cambridge, MA: Harvard University Press.

Hammar, Tomas, et al. 1997. *International Migration, Immobility and Development*. Oxford: Berg.

Hansen, Randall. 2000. *Citizenship and Immigration in Post-War Britain*. Oxford: Oxford University Press.

Hirschman, Charles, Philip Kasinitz, and Josh De Wind, eds. 1999. *Handbook of International Migration: The American Experience*. New York: Russell Sage.

Hollis, Martin. 1994. *The Philosophy of Social Science: An Introduction*. Oxford: Oxford University Press.

Joppke, Christian. 1998. *Challenge to the Nation State: Immigration in Western Europe and the United States*. Oxford: Oxford University Press.

King, Russell. 2002. "Towards a New Map of European Migration," *International Journal of Population Geography* 8(2): 89–106.

Lavanex, Sandra. 2006. "The Competition State and the Multilateral Liberalization of Highly Skilled Migration," in Michael Peter Smith and Adrian Favell, eds., *The Human Face of Global Mobility*, pp. 29–52. New Brunswick, NJ: Transaction Press.

Levitt, Peggy, and Nina Glick-Schiller. 2004. "Conceptualizing Simultaneity: A Transnational Social Field Perspective on Society," *International Migration Review* 38(3): 885–912.

Lionnet, Françoise, and Shu-Mei Shih, eds., 2005. *Minor Transnationalism*. Durham, NC: Duke University Press.

Mann, Michael. 1993. *The Sources of Social Power. Vol II: The Rise of Classes and Nation–States 1760–1914*. Cambridge: Cambridge University Press.

Massey, Douglas S. et al. 1998. *Worlds in Motion: Understanding International Migration at the End of the Millennium*. Oxford: Clarendon Press.

Papastergiadis, Nikos. 1999. *The Turbulence of Migration: Globalization, Deterritorialization and Hybridity*. Cambridge: Polity Press.

Piore, Michael. 1979. *Birds of Passage: Migrant Labor in Industrial Societies*. Cambridge: Cambridge University Press.

Portes, Alejandro. 1997. "Immigration Theory for a New Century: Some Problems and Opportunities," *International Migration Review* 31(4): 799–825.

Portes, Alejandro, and Josh De Wind. 2004. "A Cross-Atlantic Dialogue: The Progress of Research and Theory in the Study of International Migration," *International Migration Review* 38(3): 828–51.

Portes, Alejandro, and John Walton. 1981. *Labor, Class, and the International System.* New York: Academic Press.

Sassen, Saskia. 2006. *Territory, Authority, Rights: From Medieval to Global Assemblages.* Princeton, NJ: Princeton University Press.

Sayer, Andrew. 1999. "Long Live Postdisciplinary Studies! Sociology and the Curse of Disciplinary Parochialism/Imperialism," paper presented to the British Sociological Association conference, Glasgow, April 1999. Available as a University of Lancaster Sociology Department working paper at: http://www.lancs.ac.uk/fss/sociology/papers/sayer-long-live-postdisciplinary-studies.pdf.

Sayer, Andrew. 2000. *Realism and Social Science.* London: Sage.

Scott, James C. 1999. *Seeing Like a State.* New Haven, CT. Yale University Press.

Torpey, John. 2000. *The Invention of the Passport.* Cambridge: Cambridge University Press.

Urry, John. 2000. *Sociology Beyond Societies: Mobilities for the 21st Century.* London: Routledge.

Wimmer, Andreas, and Nina Glick Schiller. 2002. "Methodological Nationalism and Beyond: Nation–State Building, Migration and the Social Sciences," *Global Networks* 2(4): 301–34.

Contributors

Caroline Brettell is Dedman Family Distinguished Professor of Anthropology at Southern Methodist University and Dean ad Interim of Dedman College. Among her books are *Men Who Migrate, Women Who Wait: Population and History in a Portuguese Parish* (1986), *International Migration: The Female Experience* (1986), *We Have Already Cried Many Tears: The Stories of Three Portuguese Migrant Women* (1982, 1995), and *Anthropology and Migration: Essays on Transnationalism, Ethnicity and Identity* (2003). She has recently been involved in two research projects focused on immigration: Immigrants, Rights and Incorporation in a Suburban Metropolis (funded by the Cultural Anthropology program of the National Science Foundation, 2001–2005) and Practicing Citizenship in a New City of Immigration: An Ethnographic Comparison of Asian Indians and Vietnamese (funded by the Russell Sage Foundation, 2005–2007). She is coeditor (with Audrey Singer and Susan Hardwick) of a forthcoming book to be published by the Brookings Institution on immigration issues in new U.S. gateway cities, and editor of *Crossing Borders/Constructing Boundaries: Race, Ethnicity and Immigration* (2007). Also under contract is another book she is coediting (with Deborah Reed-Danahay), *Immigration and Citizenship in Europe and the United States: Anthropological Perspectives* (Rutgers University Press).

Barry Chiswick is Distinguished Professor and Head of the Department of Economics at the University of Illinois, Chicago, as well as Program Director for Migration Studies at IZA–Institute for the Study of Labor (Bonn). His specialties are in the areas of labor economics, human resources, the economics of immigration, the economics of minorities, and income distribution. His most recent books are *The Economics of Immigration* (Edward Elgar 2005) and his coauthored book *The Economics of Language* (Routledge 2007). Chiswick is recognized for having done the seminal research on the economics of immigration. He is the 2006–2007 President of the European Society for Population Economics.

Hasia R. Diner, the Paul S. and Sylvia Steinberg Professor of American Jewish History at New York University, holds a joint appointment in History and Hebrew and Judaic Studies. She is the author of several books: *In the Almost Promised Land: American Jews and Blacks, 1915–1935*; *Erin's Daughters in America: Irish Immigrant Women in the 19th Century*; and most recently *A Time for Gathering: The Second Migration 1820–1880*. Her comparative study, *Hungering for America: Italian, Irish and Jewish Foodways in the Age* *of Migration* appeared in 2002 and *The Jews of the United States, 1654 to 2000* was published in 2005. She has currently finishing a book, *Fitting Memorials: American Jews Confront the Catastrophe, 1945–1962.*

Adrian Favell is Associate Professor of Sociology at UCLA, and Associate Editor of the *Journal of Ethnic and Migration Studies.* He holds a Ph.D (1995) from the European University Institute, Florence, and has worked in Belgium, France, The Netherlands, Denmark, and Britain. His research lies at the intersection of sociology, human geography, political science, and philosophy. His first book, *Philosophies of Integration* (1998), a comparative study of postwar immigration politics in France and Britain, was followed by other work on the integration of migrants in Europe, notably including a large report for the Carnegie Endowment's "Comparative Citizenship Project" (2001). Migration in the European Union is another focus, with work as an editor of three comprehensive special journal editions of *JEMS* on EU immigration politics and East–West migration. *The European Union: Immigration, Asylum and Citizenship* (1998), *EU Enlargement and East-West Migration* (2001), and *The New Face of East-West Migration in Europe* (fc). Lately, his research has shifted to the study of international skilled migration in Europe and the Asia–Pacific, with the books *The Human Face (2006) and Eurostars and Eurocities* (2008). In a new project, funded with a Japan Foundation Abe Fellowship, is looking at the transnational networks and mobility behind the growing global influence of contemporary Japanese art, music, fashion, and food.

Susan Hardwick is Professor of Geography at the University of Oregon. She has published three scholarly books, three university-level textbooks, and numerous journal articles focusing on immigrants, refugees, and asylees in the American and Canadian West. Among her books are *Mythic Galveston: Reinventing America's Third Coast* (Johns Hopkins 2003), *Valley for Dreams: Life and Landscape in the Sacramento Valley* (Rowman and Littlefield 1996), and *Russian Refuge: Religion, Migration and Settlement on the North American Pacific Rim* (University of Chicago Press 1993). She is also coeditor of a forthcoming book to be published by the Brookings Institution on immigration issues in new U.S. gateway cities.

James F. Hollifield is Arnold Professor of International Political Economy and Director of the Tower Center for Political Studies at Southern Methodist University. He is a member of the Council on Foreign Relations, has worked as a consultant on migration and trade for the United Nations and other international organizations, and has published widely on these issues, including *Immigrants, Markets, and States* (Harvard University Press 1992), *Controlling Immigration* (Stanford University Press 1994, 2004) with Wayne Cornelius and Philip Martin, *L'Immigration et l'Etat Nation* (L'Harmattan 1997),

Herausforderung Migration—Perspektiven der vergleichenden Politikwissenschaft (Lit Verlag 2006) with Sigrid Baringhorst and Uwe Hunger, and *The Emerging Migration State* (forthcoming). His current research looks at the rapidly evolving relationship between trade, migration, and security, and includes a National Science Foundation–funded study of immigrant incorporation in the Dallas-Fort Worth Metroplex.

Barbara Schmitter Heisler is Professor Emerita, Department of Sociology and Anthropology at Gettysburg College. Her long-standing interests in issues of citizenship and the integration of newcomers in advanced industrial societies began with her 1979 University of Chicago dissertation "Immigration and Citizenship in Germany and Switzerland." She has published numerous articles in a range of scholarly journals (including *International Migration Review, Theory and Society*, and the *Journal of Urban Affairs*). She is coeditor of a special issue of the *Annals of the American Academy of Political and Social Science*, titled "From Migrant Workers to Settlers? Transnational Migration and the Emergence of New Minorities" (1986). As a comparative sociologist, she has often drawn comparisons between the post–World War II European and American experiences. Her current research focuses on German prisoners of war in the United States who immigrated after the war.

Peter Schuck joined the faculty of the Yale University Law School in 1979 and has been Simeon E. Baldwin Professor of Law since 1986. Before joining the Yale faculty, he was a public interest lawyer in Washington and Deputy Assistant Secretary for Planning and Evaluation in the Department of Health, Education, and Welfare. His books include *Targeting in Social Programs: Avoiding Bad Bets, Removing Bad Apples* (Brookings Institution Press 2006, with Richard Zeckhauser), *Meditations of a Militant Moderate: Cool Views on Hot Topics* (Rowman & Littlefield 2006), and *Diversity in America: Keeping Government at a Safe Distance* (Harvard University Press 2003). Schuck has written widely on issues of citizenship and immigration, as well as on torts, administrate law, and public policy. He is a graduate of Cornell University and Harvard Law School, and holds advanced degrees from Harvard University and New York University.

Michael Teitelbaum is Vice President of the Alfred P. Sloan Foundation in New York. He was educated at Reed College and at Oxford University. At Oxford, where he was a Rhodes Scholar, he earned the Oxford doctorate in demography. To date his career has spanned academe, government, and the nonprofit sectors, including as a member of the faculties of Princeton University and Oxford University, as Director of the Select Committee on Population of the U.S. House of Representatives, as Vice Chair and Acting Chair of the influential bipartisan U.S. Commission on Immigration Reform, as President and/or board member of a number of scientific societies, and as a foundation executive. He has been elected Fellow of the American Association for the Advancement of Science, First Vice President of the Population Association of America, and a member of the Council on Foreign Relations. In 2006 and 2007 he served as the Edward P. Bass Distinguished Scholar at Yale University. Dr. Teitelbaum's publications include ten books and a large number of articles in scientific and popular journals.

A

academia
  disciplinary focus of, 261–262
  nationalism in, 263–268
Adams, Ruth, 35
adaptation
  cultural, 36, 114, 119, 121, 125,
    130, 136, 173
  economic, 97
admissionist policy, 21, 192
Afghanistan, 58
agency theory, 129
Alamanyali, 117
Alba, Richard, 90
Aleinikoff, Alexander, 212
Alien Nation (Brimelow), 202
American exceptionalism, 38, 45
American Immigration (Jones), 31,
    34
"Americanization," 213
amnesty laws, 248
analysis scale, 10
anthropology
  articulation, 118–123
  data/methodology, 13, 14
  on ethnic enclaves, 129–131
  on ethnicity, 131–135
  feminist theory in, 126–129,
    138n13–15
  focus of migration studies, 4–5, 7
  on identity, 131–135
  sedentarist bias in, 113
  on social organization, 124–131
  transnationalism in, 120–123,
    137n7
  typologies in, 115–118, 137n6
  units of analysis, 10–11

anti-immigrant movements, 15, 21,
    212, 219, 220
Archdeacon, Thomas, 31
Aristotle, 185, 189
articulation
  historical-structuralist approach,
    119–120
  and modernization theory,
    118–119
  and transnationalism, 120–123,
    137n7
assimilation theory, 16–19; *see also*
    segmented assimilation
  Chicago School of Sociology, 83,
    84–86, 163, 167, 183
  invasion-succession model, 164
  new, 90–91
  patterns of assimilation, 216–217
  and second generation, 18
  spatial assimilation theories,
    167–169
  transnationalism and, 97–98
Association of American
    Geographers, 162, 174
asylees, 58, 176, 247
asymmetric information model,
    70
*At America's Gates: Chinese
    Immigration during the
    Exclusion Era* (Lee), 40, 41
Australia, foreign-born population, 1
autonomous theory, 253
Azuma, Eiichiro, 41

B

Baily, Samuel, 15